Electrical Engineering Uncovered

D0731763

SECOND EDITION

Electrical Engineering Uncovered

SECOND EDITION

Dick White
Roger Doering

Prentice Hall
Upper Saddle River, New Jersey 07458

Library of Congress Cataloging-in-Publication Data

White, Richard M., 1930-
   Electrical engineering uncovered / Dick White, Roger Doering.– [2nd ed.].
      p.   cm.
   Includes index.
   ISBN 0-13-091452-5
   1. Electrical engineering. 2. Electronics. I. Doering, Roger (Roger W.), 1951- II. Title.

TK146.W437 2000
621.3—dc21

00-045665

Vice president and editorial director, ECS: Marcia Horton
Publisher: Tom Robbins
Associate editor: Alice Dworkin
Assistant vice-president of production and manufacturing, ESM: David W. Riccardi
Executive managing editor: Vince O'Brien
Managing editor: David A. George
Production editor: Audri Anna Bazlen
Director of creative services: Paul Belfanti
Creative director: Carole Anson
Art editor: Adam Velthaus
Art director: Jayne Conte
Cover design: Bruce Kenselaar
Manufacturing manager: Trudy Pisciotti
Manufacturing buyer: Pat Brown
Marketing manager: Holly Stark

© 2001 by Prentice Hall
Prentice-Hall, Inc.
Upper Saddle River, New Jersey 07458

The authors and publisher of this book have used their best efforts in preparing this book. These efforts include the research, development and testing of the theory, designs and programs in the book to determine their effectiveness. The authors and publisher make no warranty of any kind, expressed of implied, with regard to these designs, programs, or the documentation contained in this book. The authors and publisher shall not be liable in any event for incidental or consequential damages in connection with, or arising out of, the furnishing, performance, or use of these designs or programs.

Printed in the United States of America
10 9 8 7 6 5 4 3

ISBN 0-13-091452-5

Prentice-Hall International (UK) Limited, *London*
Prentice-Hall of Australia Pty. Limited, *Sydney*
Prentice-Hall Canada Inc., *Toronto*
Prentice-Hall Hispanoamericana, S. A., *Mexico*
Prentice-Hall of India Private Limited, *New Delhi*
Prentice-Hall of Japan, Inc., *Tokyo*
Pearson Education Asia Pte. Ltd., *Singapore*
Editora Prentice Hall do Brasil, Ltda., *Rio de Janeiro*

Contents

Part I : On Being an Engineer

Contents

Part II : Electrical Engineering — Survey of the Field

Part III: Appendices

Laboratory Experiments for Electrical Engineering Uncovered

Experiments can be found on the web site for Electrical Engineering Uncovered[1]

0 Custom Lab
1 Oscilloscope
2 Series/Parallel Components
3 Infrared Remote Control
4 Ultrasonic Rangefinder
5 Guitar Tuner & Speaker Response
6 Lissajous 'Scope Patterns
7 Touch-Tone® Telephone
8 Curve Tracer
9 Astable Multivibrator
10 Infrared Door Alarm
11 Television
12 VCR
13 RC Filters
14 Resonant Filters
15 Card Key
16 Loudspeaker Crossover
17 AM Radio Transmitter
18 AM Radio Receiver
19 Operational Amplifiers
20 Multiband Transmitter
21 Radio-Controlled Car
22 CD Player
23 Half Adder
24 Simulink™
25 PSpice™
26 Photoshop™
27 Digital Signal Processing

---

[1] http://www.electronics-uncovered.com

Prefaces to the First Edition

Preface for Students

Electricity is hard to see. We can observe some of its effects, such as the flash from a stroke of lightning, but we cannot sense its fields, charges, or currents — unless the currents pass through our bodies. This inability to perceive electricity makes it difficult to develop an intuitive understanding of its principles. To help, we'll use some models.

All branches of engineering employ models to further understanding. These include actual physical scale models, mathematical models, and computer models. The models we will use are *water models* for electronic concepts and components. Since most of you are familiar with indoor plumbing and have used a garden hose, these water models should help you understand the electronics that we discuss. The models are not perfect, but students before you have found them very helpful.

The course for which this book was developed includes much more than just the beginning elements of electronics. The aim of the course is to give entering students in electrical engineering and computer sciences a warmer welcome and some view of what engineers do professionally. So, you'll find here a bit about student survival techniques and a lot about engineering concepts and skills. There are some short technical articles and even shorter one-page templates for the different kinds of technical writing that you may be called upon to do. Finally, a companion volume, *Laboratory Experiments for Electrical Engineering Uncovered*, contains laboratory experiments with equipment that you've already used, but perhaps not understood — such as a VCR, CD player, remote control for TV, and an ultrasonic rangefinder. (See page xi.)

We hope that you'll enjoy this material while learning from it, and if you find omissions or mistakes or think of topics to add, please get in touch.

Preface for Instructors

A comprehensive description of the development of *Electrical Engineering Uncovered* is contained in the *Instructor's Manual for Electrical Engineering Uncovered*, available to instructors upon request from the publisher. Here, we will only summarize the course in which we've used the text, our assumptions underlying the choice of topics, and suggestions regarding other course organizations.

The challenge was to develop an interesting course for freshmen entering the electrical engineering and computer sciences department at Berkeley, most of whom chose this major while in high school, because of their interest in math, physics, or computers. Our personal goals remain to share our enthusiasm for these subjects and to help students develop a physical understanding of the subject. We believe that hands-on lab work is an important part of the course and that experimenting with consumer electronic equipment that students have used — such as the VCR, CD player, and television — is both interesting and instructive. (See the list of laboratory experiments on page xi.)

The text is divided into two parts. Part I, <u>On Being an Engineer</u>, is concerned with topics that are important to a practicing engineer, but that are not specifically discipline based. It includes short chapters — essays, really — on modeling, design, communication, and the like. Part II, <u>Electronics, with Water Models</u>, introduces electronic principles, as well as topics important in connection with computing — binary numbers, logic gates, computer architecture, and so on. The <u>Appendices</u> contain information about topics, such as grading, significant developments in the field, and terminology, that students should find useful.

Our students had room in their schedules for only a two-unit, one-semester course. Accordingly, we had one class meeting per week at which material was presented by ourselves or by a few outstanding guest lecturers. We did many demonstrations, which are described in detail in the *Instructor's Manual*, and we showed occasional short video segments (e.g., in connection with semiconductor fabrication). Each student was expected to attend a smaller one-hour discussion section. There was a two-hour lab each week in which the students were free to choose which experiments they did, except for three experiments that all were expected to do (oscilloscope, series and parallel components, and ultrasonic rangefinder). Students worked in pairs and were required to hand in answers to simple prelab questions on entering the lab. The students completed each experiment in the two-hour period, turning in a write-up as they left the lab. If possible, we included a field trip to an industrial site, which students found most informative.

We used only part of the material in the text, as there wasn't time to cover nearly all of it. Usually, all of the Part II material was included, and we selected among the topics in Part I. We began with electronics and finished with computers, but the order could be reversed to provide a more gradual entry into the subjects. Homework was assigned weekly, mostly from the electronics and computer problems in Homework II. Some Homework I assignments were included. There was at least one single-page writing assignment, often involving a brainstorming or design element in which having fun with the topic was encouraged. Each student also obtained some writing experience by serving, with a partner, as a classroom scribe. Scribes took notes at one classroom meeting and submitted a typed copy to the instructor for editing, after which the notes were reproduced for distribution to the class.

In a three-unit course, one could treat the topics in Part II a bit more leisurely and include more material from Part I. We have found that students respond well to descriptions of entire systems and to topics related to the profession of engineering. We believe that students should be informed at the start that engineers must spend much of their time in nontechnical activities, such as communicating with others. The central role that cost plays in technical decisions should also be made clear in this course.

A Bit About the Authors

In August 1991, Dick White and Roger Doering first met and began collaborating on a freshman course in the Electrical Engineering and Computer Sciences Department at the University of California, Berkeley. Dick was a professor of EECS who'd spent six years in industry and was then specializing in solid-state devices, especially small sensors that involved ultrasonic elements. Roger was returning to Berkeley for doctoral study, having obtained a Master of Science degree there, left the university, started and sold successful companies, and then briefly tried full-time retirement while not quite 40 years old.

Both authors have enjoyed fatherhood — Dick's sons Rollie and Brendan are professionally involved in environmental issues concerning fish and birds, respectively, while Roger's and his wife Linda's children Heather, Gretchen, and Rick are still discovering their interests. Roger participates in low-impact sports such as bicycling and sailing, but Dick jogs and hikes. All other things being equal, Dick favors analog approaches while Roger leans toward digital. They have a common interest in photography. Another shared interest is music, but Dick's 5-string banjo plays best in the key of G, while Roger's trumpet is pitched in B-flat.

Thanks

Many people have given help and encouragement during the planning of this course for entering EECS students. Engineering Dean David Hodges and EECS Department Chair Paul Gray provided resources and enthusiastic moral support. Professor Ping Ko found lab space. Academic Coordinator Sheila Humphreys gave advice and help to all the students who sought it, and was particularly sensitive to the concerns of women and ethnic minority students in our classes. Advanced students in the department talked to entering students to help them find their way. The teaching assistants helped create new laboratory experiments and improve old ones. There were also many helpful conversations with colleagues in academia and industry, who kept telling us that we were "doing the right thing."

We particularly appreciate an instructional equipment grant provided by the National Science Foundation, which was more than matched by equipment gifts from the Hewlett-Packard Company. We are also grateful to the organizations and individuals who gave us permission to reprint portions of their work here.

Thanks to all of you, and to our students, who helped make this fun.

Special thanks to Linda Doering for all the sacrifices and support rendered during this project and to Rollie and Brendan White for lending their ears.

Dick White and Roger Doering
Electrical Engineering and Computer Sciences Department
University of California, Berkeley
http://www-inst.eecs.berkeley.edu/~ee1

Preface to the Second Edition

In the four years since *Electrical Engineering Uncovered* first appeared, we've all seen our ties to the high-tech world proliferate. There are many more cell phones in use worldwide, we can establish higher speed connections to distant computers, and our computers have become less costly at the same time that their memories have expanded. Internet use has grown further on its exponential path, and the Net has become a force in commerce, where incredible paper fortunes have been made on the promise of "dot com."

This edition includes expanded coverage of fast moving topics such as the Internet and computer architecture. We've more to say about wireless communications now, even though we've replaced the description of university research on the wireless Infopad with that of another exciting interdisciplinary field: MEMS, an acronym for micro-electro-mechanical systems. MEMS practitioners are making tiny devices whose applications range from increasing the storage capacity of disk drives to improving our ability to diagnose and treat disease. We've also added an entirely new chapter on digital signal processing, a crucial field that enables us to find signals in our increasingly noisy world. We list more books that we think you'll find interesting, and our list of favorite programs now includes SETI@home,[1] a program installed by more than two million PC owners around the world to help search for radio signals that might have been sent by intelligent beings in outer space.

The text includes more worked numerical examples, more homework problems, and more references to interesting web sites. One site that you should visit is Prentice Hall,[2] a site on the net server maintained by our publisher. The site now

---

[1] http://setiathome.ssl.berkeley.edu/
This web site has information about downloading software so that when your computer's screen saver is displayed, your computer can help process data received by a radio telescope that is searching for extra-terrestrial intelligence.

[2] http://www.prenhall.com/

holds the *Electrical Engineering Uncovered Laboratory Manual*, which contains more than 25 experiments developed for students exploring our subject matter. (A list of experiments appears on page xi.) The site also contains links to video clips and stills of some of our in-class demonstrations. In addition, on the site, you'll find representations of the electronic and logic circuits that appear in the text. Students can download those circuit files and experiment with the circuits, using either the electronic circuit simulator PSpice™ or the logic simulator LogicWorks™, if you have access to them.

The two real objects on the front cover range from the very large — the generator hall of the Dalles hydroelectric plant — to the very small — a two-millimeter-high MEMS model of the Cal Berkeley bell tower, which is itself patterned after a large campanile in Italy. In addition, there's an abstract object — the schematic of a digital logic circuit. The back cover shows the dozen water models for current, voltage, and many electronic devices that were introduced by Roger as an aid to understanding electrical phenomena.

For help with this edition, we thank teaching assistants Ranjana Sahai and Jason Schamberger for providing the on-line notes for instructors about how to make the experiments work. Special thanks are also due to Professor Ljiljana Trajkovic, who was mostly responsible for developing the digital signal processing laboratory experiment, as well as critiquing the description of DSP and helping design the Photoshop™ experiment. Thanks also to Elliot Hui who designed and fabricated the MEMS model of Cal's campanile, which appears on the front cover and inside the book.

From the start, we've believed that experimenting with electronics can be both instructive and fun. We hope that you agree.

Dick White and Roger Doering
Electrical Engineering and Computer Sciences Department
University of California, Berkeley
http://electronics-uncovered.com/

Read Me First

"On first opening a book I listen for the sound of the human voice. By this device I am absolved from reading much of what is published in a given year. Most writers make use of institutional codes (academic, literary, political, bureaucratic, technical), in which they send messages already deteriorating into the half-life of yesterday's news. Their transmissions remain largely unintelligible, and unless I must decipher them for professional reasons, I am content to let them pass by. I listen instead for a voice in which I can hear the music of the human improvisation as performed through 5,000 years on the stage of recorded time."

Conventions Used in this Book

Student Questions

> "What is meant by the voltage across a circuit component?"

This icon — patterned after the speech bubbles in cartoons — encloses actual questions asked by students in our course. We've included these questions for several reasons. We want to encourage new students to ask questions when they're puzzled, even though they may feel that their questions are not sufficiently important or well formed to ask. We also feel that these examples may be helpful to instructors who have forgotten how puzzling a new topic can be. The questions are collected along with their answers in the Appendix, "Those Student Questions Answered," on page 315.

Optional Math

> **Optional Math**
>
> We can also write the equivalent expression:
>
> $$Q_1 = \int_0^{t_1} i(t)dt.$$

Based on our experience, entering students have limited knowledge of calculus. Typically, they understand differentiation, but not necessarily integration. In the text, we emphasize physical descriptions in preference to analytical developments, but experience shows that the analysis is essential for developing an understanding of these subjects. Thus, we have occasionally relegated some mathematical expressions and justification to these "Optional Math" boxes. You may want to discuss these topics with your instructors.

Homework Placement

We have placed the homework problems at the end of each chapter in this edition.

Extra Data in Homework Problems

As with many real-world problems, many of our homework problems contain information that is not required to obtain the solution. We warn you about this in the first such problem only.

Part I:
On Being an Engineer

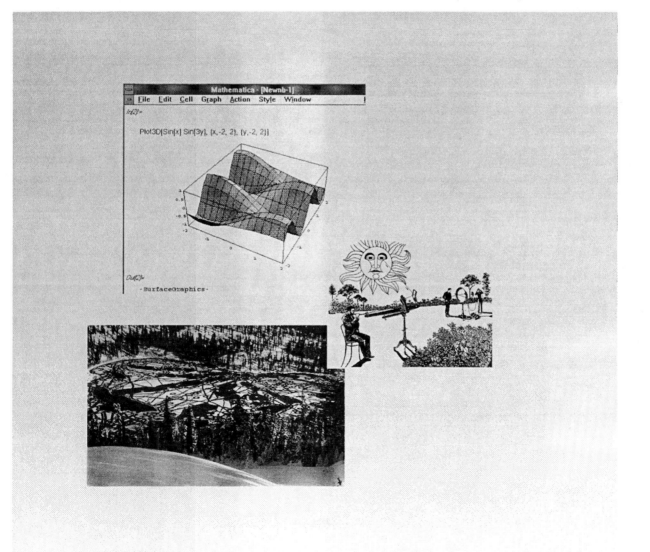

Modeling Processes

1

The very start of your college years may well be one of the most exciting times of your entire life. You've embarked on an adventure that can, and probably should, change you in many ways. By the time you complete college you will likely be more aware of your interests and abilities, better trained academically, better able to understand and deal with social situations, and certainly older. Taking stock of where you are now and where you may be going is both appropriate and somewhat difficult. Let's see if we can represent this in diagrammatic ways that may both help you and also serve as an introduction to an important aspect of analysis and thinking in all fields of engineering: *modeling*.

First, we'll try to model schematically the process of getting a college education. Your college years will transform you — perhaps just a little or perhaps a lot. An engineer might represent such a transformation just like those that take place in a chemical plant, an automobile factory, or a television receiver: All of these have inputs (chemicals, auto engine and body parts, or electrical signals picked up by the antenna). All have outputs — the chemical produced, the cars built, or the TV pictures on your screen. Engineers design the reactors or machines or circuits that transform the inputs into the outputs. The process of transformation is typically indicated by a diagram resembling Figure 1.1. Boxes in a functional diagram, such as the one labelled "PROCESS", are sometimes called "black boxes," since we don't see what's inside. Functional diagrams that contain several such boxes are often referred to by engineers as "block diagrams."

How could such a simple representation be applied to the transformation of you through four years of college? Figure 1.2 is a possible way of doing some justice to the transformation that human students experience. On the left is a collage that represents some of the rich tapestry that is you. The representation doesn't do you justice, because it is two-dimensional, static, silent, concrete, and of limited size. Nevertheless, it represents to some extent cultural, social, physical, mental, emotional, religious, and other aspects that are part of your present makeup — your input state as you start college.

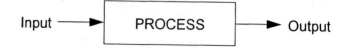

Figure 1.1 Engineer's representation of a process that transforms some input into a certain output

To the right of the symbol of the college is a bigger, more complex, more varied collage that is intended to represent you as you might be at the end of your college career. It represents, as you may find, that certain elements in the input state have been enlarged and enriched. Other elements present at the beginning may have been diminished in importance, or even almost disappeared. Some have persisted, but have become much more complex and deep, and new elements may have appeared.

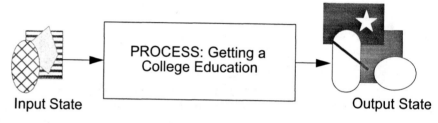

Figure 1.2 One schematic representation of the process of getting a college education. The collages at the left and right are an attempt to suggest the richness of students at the beginning and at the end of the college experience.

You might find it interesting to think about what elements of a collage might best represent you now. It would be a good idea to think a bit about what you'd like to have as important parts of your makeup when you leave college. Try making your own collages, or at least imagining them.

If the faculty at your college discussed education with reference to the diagram in Figure 1.2, they might concentrate attention on course work only, and only consider academic elements of the present and future states. But such a focus would leave out a lot. In college, many nonacademic transformations occur. Many of those take place outside of the classrooms and laboratories, happening in residence halls, in clubs and other organizations, in the sports arenas, and off-campus in any activities you engage in there. Part of your personal transformation will occur simply because of the passage of time during the next four years.

The fundamental task of your teachers is to manage the part of the transformation that involves academic elements. Faculty seldom design their courses with reference to a diagram such as this or the concept of a transformation. Many of their discussions might be more fruitful if carried out with such pictures in mind. For example, when thinking about the initial and final states of students, should this involve descriptions of only the state of knowledge, or should it also involve emotional and other states? How similar are the initial states of the entire entering class in a given academic field? Is it possible for faculty, or for those in industry who hire the students that the faculty "output," to agree on a desired final state of knowledge even in that one discipline? For two students who enter in roughly the same initial state, will a single transformation (set of courses) produce nearly identical outcomes (for example, what about differences in learning styles)?

When you choose courses and when you choose nonacademic activities in college, you might try to think of the transformations that you would like for yourself. One part that is important to most students is to emerge from college employable. An alternative goal is to emerge admissible to graduate school, should you desire to go that route. Since the process of education shouldn't end when you emerge from college, a worthwhile goal that many students have is to be able to learn on their own, even after they've finished with their formal schooling. It might be wise to choose courses along the way with several criteria in mind: Choose some courses that make you employable when you emerge, choose some that will be of value to you for your entire life, and choose some that are fun or that stimulate you into new areas.

Having taken care of the process of education (!), we now move on to the university itself. Here we can diagram its inputs and outputs as shown in Figure 1.3. Note that the processes modeled here, in most cases, are dynamic — the inputs and outputs vary with time. In other words, they are functions of time.

The money that supports the university may come in the form of student fees, gifts and endowments, grants or contracts from industry and government agencies, foundation grants, internally generated income from licenses and royalties, and direct government support in the case of public universities. The institution itself is a nonprofit entity whose continued financial support depends upon trust and the belief of its public that it is performing well. Primary criteria of a university's success are acceptance by the outside world of its products — hiring of its emerging students, acclaim for published accounts of its research, and demand for its public services. High quality of applicants for admission is another important indicator of its continued success.

Industry can be represented in this highly simplified approach by the diagram of Figure 1.4. The profit made by selling the product generates at least some of the money that fuels the enterprise. Not shown explicitly is the flow of entering staff members who may bring with them new information for use in the transformation process that leads to the emergent product. The criterion of success is return on investment (ROI); if the ROI is not high enough, funds may be sent elsewhere for a greater return.

Finally, Figure 1.5 represents government in similar schematic terms. Money from citizens and corporations fuels the enterprise and also flows through, with somewhat less emerging in the form of support to specific groups of citizens. The individual bits of information that enter — from the census and from information

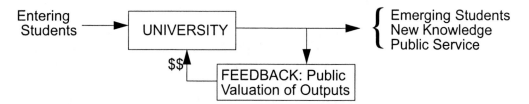

Figure 1.3 System representation of the university. The "energy" that powers the operation is represented by the dollars supplied at the bottom, which depends on the existence of public trust in the university. The primary outputs of the university are educated students and the new knowledge developed as a result of the research done there. "Public service" includes activities such as renting to outside users unique facilities that the university may have, offering the community athletic contests and concerts, and providing expert advice on agricultural or other questions.

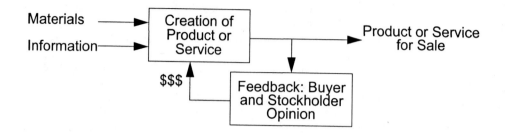

Figure 1.4 System representation of manufacturing or service industry. Money provides the energy for operation, a portion of which may come from sale of the product or service. Information used may be input from the outside or may be generated internally.

provided on tax forms and in other ways by individual citizens and by companies — are combined and interpreted; aggregated information is one of government's outputs. Public services include protection from military attack and from threats to human health. The evidence of success for a democratic government is its continuance in office.

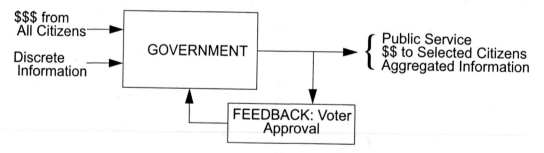

Figure 1.5 Model of a democratic government

We could go further with this discussion to consider how universities, industry, and the government interact. Our primary goal here has been to stimulate you to think about yourself and what you expect from the educational process. We hope that you find this brief introduction to showing transformations in terms of inputs and outputs from the perspective of an engineer interesting.

This approach isn't limited to engineers, incidentally. A famous economist, Vassily Leontieff, introduced "input-output matrices" to represent how a change in one factor, such as the cost of sheet steel, affected the price of some product, such as television sets. The inputs and the outputs were the prices of hundreds of items. The influences between them were represented in terms of a huge matrix — an ordered array of numbers — with specific values drawn from the aggregated data supplied by the government. In spite of this well-known example from economics, it might be wise if you were to keep the simple representations put forth in this essay just between us. Your political science and business administration professors might not really be sympathetic with these engineers' representations of their turf.

1.1 Problems

1.1 Draw a model for an organization in which you might participate, such as a student club or a volunteer service organization. Indicate the inputs and outputs, as well as any feedback loops. Describe what the organization does and how the model pertains to it.

1.2 Draw up a model, in the form of a block diagram, of a household device such as a microwave oven or a telephone answering machine. Don't concern yourself with details of the circuitry that may be involved, but rather focus on the functions carried out when the controls are activated.

Engineering Design:

Why? What? How?

The engineer's primary goal is to solve practical problems. This contrasts with the scientist — the chemist, biologist or physicist — who attempts to understand how the natural world functions. What the engineer produces will ultimately be used by people; therefore, the engineer must consider the user's needs as he or she works. Inevitably, an engineering project involves constraints within which one must work, one of the most important being the cost of the resultant product.

The term **engineering design** denotes the process of **fashioning a product made for a practical goal in the presence of constraints.** The goal of the earliest Roman aqueducts was to bring water to ancient cities in structures that were constrained to be made of stones that were held together only by gravity. The modern auto is designed to provide reliable service subject to the constraint that the owner will probably pay scant attention to its maintenance. The automotive engineer has access to a vast array of structural materials and fabrication techniques, but must also meet legally imposed constraints on fuel economy, permissible exhaust system emission levels, and passenger protection in case of accident.

Until recently, engineering students seldom encountered design in their studies. Today, the importance of being able to carry out engineering designs is well recognized, and accredited engineering schools must show that their students obtain sufficient design experience. This requirement may be met through lab projects, homework assignments, examination problems, and class-time instruction. Outside of courses, engineering students sometimes obtain design experience in competitions whose rules express both the goal and the constraints. Examples are: "build a functioning canoe made of concrete," "build and race a radio-controlled robot that navigates through a maze and that is built from parts whose total cost is less than $50," and the ever-popular challenge to "build a structure using only certain approved low-cost materials that will cushion an egg dropped from a tall building."

Powerful computer tools now exist that enable designers to simulate and "test" the characteristics of their proposed devices in advance, whether they be dams, automobile transmissions, or electronic circuits. Such computer-aided design

(CAD) programs are available in virtually all fields of engineering. These CAD tools exist in part because of the rapid progress made — by integrated circuit designers! — in reducing the cost per calculation. A next step is the marriage of the CAD tools to systems for controlling the manufacture of designed parts: The combined tool is called CAD/CAM, where CAM means computer-aided manufacture.

2.1 A Design Problem

To illustrate the importance of clearly defining both the design goal and the constraints, consider the following design assignment:

Design a system that counts the number of people who go through a door.

Sounds easy, no? You could use a beam of light, shining across the doorway onto a photocell, that is interrupted by a person walking through the door. Or, if you wanted a less obvious people detector, you could embed a pressure sensor in the floor that would be stepped on by someone going through the door. Another solution to the assignment as stated would be to hire a security guard (or guards, for 24-hour coverage) to count people passing through. But possibly this last solution would be undesirably expensive.

In this situation, you should resist jumping into the technical part of the design and first ask the client questions that really define the design problem. See if you can think of the questions you'd ask the client in this case.

2.2 Examining the Design Problem

The engineering design problem just stated is obviously incomplete: It doesn't clearly indicate the real goal of the design and gives no constraints on the solution. The following questions might bring out possible goals and constraints:

Goals:

- Should this system total all people, regardless of size or weight? (What about counting babies carried through the doorway?)
- Should it only count people going one way through the door?
- Should it count passages through, or is counting the number of times the door is opened an acceptable goal?
- Should it operate reliably 24 hours a day under any conditions?

Constraints:

- What are the cost constraints for the finished system? Of the project to design the system?
- What is the time allotted for doing the design?
- What is the time allotted for building this system?
- Again, what cost constraints are there?
- How many systems are to be built?

- How fast must the system respond?
- How well hidden must the detector be?
- How far from the doorway is the total to be indicated?
- What are the cost constraints?
- How should the total be represented (for example, by a big lighted sign, a bell that rings each time a person goes through, or a radio signal sent to a distant security office)?
- What disturbing influences might be present (such as floor vibration due to machinery operating near a factory door)?
- What about the ambient temperature and relative humidity?
- Cost constraints?
- How long should the counter operate?
- How accurate must the counter be?
- How reliable must the counter be?
- How large a count should the system be capable of registering?
- Are there any constraints on the technologies that can be used to solve this problem?
- Costs?

After you get the answers to such questions, you'll have a much better understanding of the problem. Then you can start considering actual technical approaches to a solution. As with most design problems, and unlike most homework problems, this one won't have a *unique* solution. It may, however, have an *optimum* solution — one that accomplishes the goals within the constraints, while optimizing an identified characteristic. An example of an optimum solution would be the design having the lowest unit system cost.

2.3 Reflections

Successful engineering design is a challenging activity that demands imagination and command of many different skills. As this simple example shows, it is necessary to identify concretely the design goals and constraints before proposing solutions. The questions posed here obviously suggest that cost constraints may be primary. Also, as the technology in a field advances, even the optimal solution to a particular design problem will change. The successful engineer must therefore maintain a flexible viewpoint and continually learn about relevant technical advances in his or her field. Just as with inventing, neatly solving a difficult design problem can be tremendous fun.

Postscript

On one of his recruiting visits to the Berkeley campus, Dr. Jerry Tieman, of General Electric, was asked what he looked for when recruiting students for employment. He thought a moment, and then said that he didn't look for the students who "remembered all the answers." He wanted to find the student who "remembered all the questions" — that is, who recalled all the things one could do if only one missing piece of technology were available. When that piece appeared, this employee was ready to move rapidly ahead by using it.

2.4 Problems

2.1 Consider the design problems involved in providing security for a student laboratory room such as the one used in your course. Discuss briefly or list concisely the situations to be detected and dealt with, such as entry of an unauthorized person or removal of equipment from the room. Questions to be considered include detecting that a person *is* unauthorized, detecting that equipment is being *removed*, actions to be taken, false alarms, and the effect of a limited budget on the design. Where could you find information about such systems?

2.2 Assume that you are going to design the ultimate music system for a five-room dwelling. Outline briefly how a superb system would function, and outline a less fancy — and costly — system. Estimate the costs of each system.

2.3 Most of you have probably seen the television ad in which a toy bunny powered by an Energizer-brand battery keeps on going … and going …, long after a similar toy powered by the Duracell "coppertop" battery has stopped working. The problem here is to design a sensible experiment (or several different experiments, if you get motivated) to determine whether the Energizer battery really delivers better performance than the Duracell. Feel free to ask anybody associated with your course for further information. If you already work with a partner in the lab you might consider this problem jointly with your partner — this is the kind of problem for which it is good to be able to discuss your ideas with others. Output: Please write up your proposal for the testing to establish whether the TV ad tells the truth about these batteries. You can use the "proposal" template in this text. DO NOT WRITE MORE THAN ONE PAGE ON THIS. Use your computer's word-processor. Be imaginative. Here are some questions to consider (answer):

(a) What does "better performance" really mean to you as a potential battery customer? Longest functioning? How would you factor purchase prices of the two different batteries into the evaluation?

(b) Since you probably don't have a battery-powered bunny toy, what electrical "load" will you use in the evaluation?

(c) How long would your actual testing take in order to produce meaningful results? If the duration is longer than you'd like to spend sitting in the testing lab, how would you be able to get results and still do other things with your life?

(d) Cost (always important!): How much would your proposed evaluation method cost?

Engineering Ethics

Computer Firm Shuts Down Revlon
Giant cosmetics company sues small software maker over incident

By Ken Siegmann
Chronicle Staff Writer

It was a confrontation that could happen only in the computer age. A tiny Silicon Valley software company shut down cosmetic giant Revlon, Inc. last week with a simple telephone call plus a little late night computer hacking.

Logisticon, Inc., a $20 million Santa Clara company that makes software for inventory and distribution control, said its midnight mission was prompted by a contract dispute. In essence, Revlon refused to pay for software, so Logisticon electronically repossessed the program.

Revlon responded this week by suing Logisticon, claiming in its lawsuit that it was unable to ship its products for three days after it lost use of the software.

Logisticon had been working with Revlon since January 1989 to install a system to track the company's $3 billion worth of sales and shipments from various distribution sites around the country.

After complaining on October 9 that the software never worked properly, Revlon told Logisticon that it would make no more payments on the $1.2 million contract until the bugs were fixed. Revlon has paid $420,000 for the first phase of installation.

Logisticon responded by using a phone link and Revlon's computer access codes to shut down its software in Revlon's computer systems early in the morning of October 16.

Logisticon engineers dialed Revlon's computers and gave the software commands to stop its operations and temporarily scramble Revlon's computerized information about its shipments and inventories.

With the computer system frozen, Revlon was forced to shut down its two largest distribution centers in Phoenix and Edison, N.J., and send about 400 workers home for three days. Revlon spokesman James Conroy said Revlon continued to distribute products from distributions centers in Jacksonville, Fla., and Oxford, N.C., but Curry said the company was unable to ship products in the Northeast and West.

Logisticon President Donald Gallagher called his company's actions a "repossession."

Conroy called it "commercial terrorism."

© SAN FRANCISCO CHRONICLE, June 25, 1990 Reprinted by permission.

You can see from this newspaper article about an actual event that as a working engineer you may have to make ethical choices. Would you, as a professional engineer whose bill for service had not been paid, have put pressure on your client by taking this technologically easy step — deactivating the client's computer system?

Chances are that this decision was made in a high-level meeting with the top managers of the company. Perhaps they were tired of getting the runaround from this giant corporation, which was violating its contract. If Revlon needed this software to operate the company, then they were obviously relying on it operating on a day-to-day basis. The implication is that the bugs they were complaining of weren't all that critical.

If you say you'd never have done such a thing, consider a slightly different question: If you'd known that your fellow engineer was going to disable the program, would you have reported this? Should you have done so? To whom would you have reported? Would you be acting in a disloyal fashion toward your employer, or just doing the right thing?

Often, the costs of taking the easy course and remaining silent can be very high. In the Challenger spacecraft disaster, seven astronauts died because of a decision to launch in cold weather in spite of evidence that O-ring seals on the rocket would not function well when cold. Reporting unethical behavior is known as "blowing the whistle" on the guilty person; "whistle-blowers" are often subjected to discrimination, transfer to a meaningless job at a distant and unpleasant location, or outright dismissal. So, taking the ethical course of action may entail personal sacrifice.

The rules or standards governing the members of a profession are called ethics. As with the medical ethics governing the actions of physicians and nurses, engineering ethics have been codified. The following statements are from the "Canons of Conduct" of the Association for Computing Machinery (ACM).

> Recognition of professional status by the public depends not only on skill and dedication, but also on adherence to a recognized Code of Professional Conduct. The following Code sets forth the general principles (Canons) ... applicable to each member ... An ACM member shall:
>
> **1.** Act at all times with integrity.
> **2.** Strive to increase competence and prestige of profession.
> **3.** Accept responsibility for own work.
> **4.** Act with professional responsibility.
> **5.** Use special knowledge and skills for advancement of human welfare.

Under each canon in the complete document are ethical considerations ("ECs") giving specific examples of the conduct called for. For example, these are excerpts from the ethical considerations under the fifth canon:

> EC5.1. ... consider health, privacy, and general welfare of public in performance of work.
> EC5.2. ... whenever dealing with data concerning individuals, always consider principle of the individual's privacy and seek the following:
> —to minimize the data collected.
> —to limit authorized access to the data.
> —to provide proper security for the data.
> —to determine the required retention period of the data.
> —to ensure proper disposal of the data.

You may have read a statement of student ethics for your school that denounces copying and other forms of cheating on exams. <u>The usual motivation to cheat is simply the urge for survival</u>. This same basic urge also leads to lapses with respect to engineering ethics. Behavior that you as an engineer would shun in good economic times might be quite tempting if your job or your company's survival were "on the line." As you read through the factual descriptions that follow, ask yourself, "What would I have done in this situation?"

Also, try to imagine other ethical problems that you might face in your intended career.

3.1 Case Studies

Ford's Pinto

As an example of an ethical case study, we reprint next the article, "Ford's Pinto" [from *BUSINESS ETHICS*, *1st edition*, by Shaw © 1991. Reprinted with permission of Wadsworth, a division of Thomson Learning. Fax 800 730-2215.]

There was a time when the "made in Japan" label brought a predictable smirk of superiority to the face of most Americans. The quality of most Japanese products usually was as low as their price. In fact, few imports could match their domestic counterparts, the proud products of 'Yankee know-how.' But by the late 1960s, an invasion of foreign made goods chiseled a few worry-lines into the countenance of American industry. And in Detroit, worry was fast fading to panic as the Japanese, not to mention the Germans, began to gobble up more and more of the subcompact auto market.

Never one to take a back seat to the competition, Ford Motor Company decided to meet the threat from abroad head-on. In 1968, Ford executives decided to produce the Pinto. Known inside the company as "Lee's car," after Ford president Lee Iacocca, the Pinto was to weigh no more than 2,000 pounds and cost no more than $2,000.

Eager to have its own sub-compact ready for the 1971 model year, Ford decided to compress the normal drafting-board-to-show-room time of about three-and-a-half years into two. The compressed schedule meant that any design changes typically made before production-line tooling would have to be made during it.

Prior to producing the Pinto, Ford crash-tested eleven of them, in part to learn if they met the National Highway Traffic Safety Administration (NHTSA) proposed safety standard that all autos be able to withstand a fixed-barrier impact of 30 m.p.h. without fuel loss. Eight standard-design Pintos failed the tests. The three cars that passed the test all had some kind of gas-tank modification. One had a plastic baffle between the front of the tank and the differential housing; the second had a piece of steel between the tank and the rear bumper; and the third had a rubber-lined gas tank.

Ford officials faced a tough decision. Should they go ahead with the standard design, thereby meeting the production timetable but possibly jeopardizing consumer safety? Or should they delay production of the Pinto by redesigning the tank to make it safer and thus concede another year of subcompact dominance to foreign companies?

To determine whether to proceed with the original design of the Pinto fuel tank, Ford decided to do a cost-benefit study, which is an analysis of the expected costs and the social benefits of doing something. Would the social benefits of a new tank design outweigh design costs, or would they not?

To find the answer, Ford had to assign specific values to the variables involved. For some factors in the equation, this posed no problem. The costs of design improvement, for example, could be estimated at eleven dollars per vehicle. But what about human life? Could a dollar-and-cents figure be assigned to a human being?

Do you think Ford's cost–benefit analysis was legitimate or complete? What responsibilities to its customers do you think Ford had? What would you have done if you had been a Ford employee working on this problem?

Inside Intel:
The Pentium Glitch

The following scenario is becoming increasingly common in the commercial world of computers and computer chips: A product is released for sale that has a few known "bugs." (See 1947 "Grace Hopper" on page 337 for the origin of this term.) The manufacturer faces a difficult dilemma: Do you hold up the release of a product until you can find and fix its bugs, or do you release the product for sale, hoping that the bugs won't cause many people trouble? The pace of innovation in these fields is so rapid that product lifetimes are no more than a few years, so holding a product back may cause the company to lose much of its share of the market. On the other hand, releasing the product with a bug may anger important customers. So what do you do?

A famous example of a bug in a microprocessor chip is the Intel Pentium incident. Intel, a leading maker of microprocessor chips, developed a new, fast microprocessor chip that it dubbed the "Pentium." In 1994, at just about the time it was running newspaper and television ads built around the theme "Intel Inside" to show which computers contained Intel chips, a research mathematician in Virginia reported that the Pentium could produce wrong answers in complex division problems. The reason was that some numbers had been left out of a table on the chip that contained certain division results. The question was, what was ethical and prudent to do about it?

Apparently hoping that the problem would just go away, the company at first asserted that the glitch would affect very, very few users. The company initially refused to simply replace old flawed chips with new corrected chips. Customers who sought replacements were queried about what kinds of computations they did routinely in order to weed out replacements for those unlikely to trigger wrong results.

After much critical airing in the press, Intel eventually agreed to exchange all flawed Pentium chips. The company also agreed to expand on its previous policy of confidentially informing computer manufacturers about known flaws in its chips; now, after the computer-makers have had the information about flaws for 30 days, the information is released to the general public. Threatened lawsuits were dropped, information about chip and circuit board flaws were posted on the Internet, and the price of Intel stock rose.

To make complex devices that work perfectly is extremely difficult, even though manufacturers use programs that "exercise" their products to ensure that they perform correctly. What was learned from the Pentium incident was that it's important to deal responsibly with flaws as soon as they're found. Was Intel alone in this situation? Not at all. In just the next year, a popular income tax preparation program was found to have a serious flaw, and security on a widely used network access system was shown by outsiders to be easily breached. In this last case, the company took quick action, admitting the problem, generating corrective software quickly, and finally enlisting the aid of its customers by offering a cash payment to anyone who found new bugs in its product.

3.2 Problems

3.1   You are a civil engineer working for your city, and have been asked to spend some of your time on the design of a rapid-transit system. Most of the money for the rapid-transit work comes from state and federal government funds. Your boss asks you to charge all your rapid-transit time on overtime "since it's being paid for by the government and they can afford it." What do you say?

3.2   Suppose you had been a mechanical engineer working for the Morton-Thiokol Company and had learned that the O-ring seals on the space shuttle Challenger's propulsion tanks might fail if a launch occurred when the rings were cold and therefore stiff. How would you have used this information to persuade NASA managers not to launch the Challenger?

3.3   You are asked by your boss to "reverse engineer" a new laptop computer that your main competitor has just featured at a trade show. Do you agree to carry out this unethical task? Explain. (Reverse engineering means finding how to duplicate a product made by someone else, so that your company can avoid the costs of research, development, and preproduction engineering that are borne by the first manufacturer.)

Meaningless Precision:

22.6 Grams of Fat per Serving

"I seldom read the food section of newspapers. The reviews of restaurants frequently seem pretentious or overly cute, and I'm not interested in the recipes. I do have one mathematical observation regarding the latter, however. I will sometimes read a recipe that calls for about a cup of this, a few tablespoons of that, a smidgen of something, four or five slices of something else, a couple of medium-sized other things, and seasoning to taste. This vagueness is not objectionable, but the arithmetic that comes from it is. In italic print at the end, it's affirmed that the recipe yields, say, four servings with 761 calories, 428 milligrams of sodium, and 22.6 grams of fat per serving. These numbers are much too precise, given what went into computing them. The 1 in the 761 is completely meaningless, and the 6 is almost so. The 7 is the only significant number. Saying that each serving is 700 to 800 calories would make more sense, and an estimate of 600 to 900 calories would be even better. An added benefit to having a reasonable range of numbers rather than a figure of unwarranted precision is that one isn't as tempted to swell the recipe and pretend that one is consuming only 761 calories."[1]

In your engineering work, you should use in your answers to numerical questions <u>only</u> as many figures as are justified by the data you're given. For example, if you're asked what current flows when a 10-volt battery is connected to a 300-ohm resistor, your calculator display may show 3.333333×10^{-2}, but the data you started with don't warrant that much precision in your answer for the current. As with the calories in the recipe example, any 3s beyond the second one are completely meaningless, and even the second 3 is suspect.

A practical issue that arises in electronics is the degree to which the actual values of resistors and other components correspond to the values indicated by the

---

[1] From J. A. Paulos, *A Mathematician Reads the Newspaper* (New York, NY: Basic Books, 1995).

color bands or the values printed on the cases of the components. The least expensive "47-ohm" resistor is only guaranteed to be between -10% and +10% of that value — in other words, the actual resistance could range from about 42 to 52 ohms. In fact, you may be unlikely to find that the values of 10%, 47-ohm resistors fall in the middle of that range, because the ones nearest the indicated value may be selected out for sale at higher prices as 5% or 1% resistors!

About Those Other

Fields of Engineering

They all have the word "engineering" attached to them, but what really goes on in those other branches of engineering? For example, what do mechanical engineers do, and how does it differ from what electrical, chemical, and civil engineers do?

We tackle these questions for the benefit of students who are required to select a college major when they have very little knowledge about these fields. It's worthwhile to learn a bit about the different branches, which do differ in some ways, as you might find your interests better served by one rather than the other. So, we're going to compare the branches of engineering briefly, pointing out what they have in common and in what ways they differ.

What follows resulted in part from asking practicing engineers in various fields, "What are the two or three most important concepts in your field?" This question initially surprised the engineers who'd engaged in formal academic study for anywhere from four to nine years, and then worked as a professional for many years more. But all the people we asked were willing to help, once they understood why we were asking.

Informal Answers

A somewhat formal summary of the answers appears next, but the informal responses were more fun. One was:

> "If you can't see it, it's electrical; if it smells, it's chemical; if it hums, it's mechanical; and if it doesn't move, it's civil."

Another interesting response came from a retired civil engineer who commented thus about his field:

> "Civil engineering is what's left of what used to be just engineering. The other branches, like mechanical and electrical, moved out as they became specialties in their own right. Three things distinguish what civil engineers do: They make only one exact copy of a thing, such as a bridge or a dam; they manufacture it on site; and they must always deal with the earth, which is a very difficult material to work with."

What the Fields Have in Common

1. All branches of engineering are <u>quantitative</u>. Computations yielding numerical results are essential in all engineering design. Engineers rely increasingly on computer programs written by commercial programming teams instead of writing their own programs.

2. <u>Modeling</u> of components and systems is done in all branches of engineering. Electrical engineers represent devices such as transistors in terms of electric circuit components such as voltage and current sources, resistors, and capacitors. Mechanical engineers often work with electrical analogs of mechanical elements, such as masses and springs, and then analyze the behavior of the model to determine how far things will move and find the frequencies at which their motion is largest.

3. The properties of <u>materials</u> are important to all engineers. Civil and mechanical engineers must know how their materials respond to force, chemical engineers must know how their components will react chemically with the substances they contact, and electrical engineers must take account of the electric and magnetic properties of insulators, conductors, and semiconductors.

4. All branches of engineering relate back to particular <u>sciences</u>. Chemical engineers relate most closely to chemistry, materials engineers to chemistry and somewhat to physics, mechanical engineers to thermal physics and elasticity, and electrical engineers particularly to physics.

5. All practical engineers allow for a <u>safety factor</u> in their designs. The bridge builder must allow for the unusually large weight due to bunches of vehicles or people, or to the once-in-a-hundred-year windstorm. The aeronautical engineer must build in enough strength to keep the craft functioning even when engaging in extreme maneuvers under emergency conditions.

6. All engineers are concerned about the <u>cost</u> of what they design, build, or operate.

7. All engineers are concerned about the <u>useful operating lifetimes</u> of their products.

8. Increasingly, engineers are taking a <u>systems approach</u> in their work, in which the concepts of <u>control</u> and <u>stability</u> are fundamental. Here the engineer is concerned about the large collection of individual components that must function well together to produce a product, such as fuel for vehicles, or provide a service, such as telephone communications. Often these components, such as valves, in addition to performing their function, will also produce an electrical output signal that provides feedback for use in controlling the entire system.

9. All engineers must work with other humans, which involves <u>communication</u>.

5.1 Key Concepts in Different Branches of Engineering

We have just discussed a number of elements that are common to all branches of engineering. Next we characterize each branch and list separately some of its key concepts. Where a common element mentioned previously is particularly important in a given branch, it is listed again. An example is control and stability in aeronautical and aerospace engineering.

Aeronautical and Aerospace Engineering

This branch involves the design, analysis, and evaluation of structures for flight in the Earth's atmosphere and in space.
Key topics include

- Fluid flow, heat flow, and thermal processes
- Turbulent and laminar (smooth) flow of gases
- Lift and drag
- Plus: Properties of materials, control, and stability

Chemical Engineering

Chemical engineering involves the development, design, and operation of chemical processes and process equipment.
Key topics include

- Activation energy
- Heat transfer, thermally activated processes
- Approach to equilibrium
- Plus: Control, system stability

Civil Engineering

Civil engineering can be subdivided into the following engineering specialties:

- Construction: management and engineering to plan and execute construction projects
- Environmental: applying scientific and engineering principles of water quality; waste and hazardous materials management; air pollution control; and ecological engineering
- Geotechnical: planning, design, and construction on, in, and with soil and rock (examples: foundations, highways, and earthquake-resistant structures)
- Structural: analysis and design of structures (examples: bridges, dams, office buildings, and harbors)
- Structural materials: understanding and applying properties such as mechanical and thermal response, and durability of materials (examples: steel, concrete, and composites)
- Transportation: planning, design, construction, operation, evaluation, and rehabilitation of systems and facilities (examples: highways, railroads, and urban transit systems)

Key topics include

- Force and moment analysis
- Elasticity and strength of materials
- Subsurface geology
- Plus: Properties of materials, structure stability

Computer Engineering

Computer engineering involves the analysis, design, and evaluation of both the hardware (devices) and the software (programs) for computing systems, along with those for computer networks, memory devices, and input/output devices.

Key topics include

- Computer architecture
- Algorithms
- Correctness and robustness
- Security
- Plus: Cost of computation

Electrical Engineering

Electrical engineering encompasses solid-state devices, integrated circuits, and micro-electromechanical devices; microwave, quantum, and optical electronics, bio-electronics; electromagnetic wave radiation and propagation; plasmas; power systems; control systems; circuit, communications, and information theory; large-scale networks and systems, ecological systems; and pattern recognition.

Key topics include

- Determination of currents and voltages in a circuit, network, or system
- Energy and power transfer and dissipation

- Quantifying information and performance of information-handling systems
- Plus: Control, system stability

Materials Engineering

Materials engineering deals with natural and man-made materials — their extraction, development, and characterization for uses, particularly in advanced applications such as solid-state electronics and transportation.

Figure 5.1 suggests the interrelation of four key aspects of materials engineering: the synthesis techniques (processing) by which the materials are made; their microstructures, often as revealed by sophisticated microscopic and surface characterization methods; their physical properties; and their performance in intended applications.

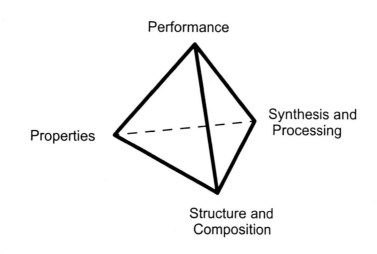

Figure 5.1   Materials engineering pyramid

Key topics include

- Thermal processes
- Material phases and phase transitions
- Activation energy
- Surface and volume forces

Mechanical Engineering

Mechanical engineering includes the science and art of the formulation, design, development, and control of systems and components involving thermodynamics, mechanics of solid bodies, fluid mechanics, mechanisms, and the conversion of energy into useful work.

Key topics include

- Flow of heat, flow of fluids

- Analysis of static and dynamic forces and moments
- Thermal processes
- Plus: Properties of materials, system stability

Nuclear Engineering

Nuclear engineering is concerned with the applications of nuclear reactions, including the design, analysis, and operation of nuclear reactors and their nuclear fuel cycles.

Key topics include

- Flow of heat
- Nuclear chemistry
- Plus: Properties of materials, control, system stability

Logarithmic Unit for a Person's Pay:

The Salarybel

6

Engineers use curious units called *"decibels"* to measure all sorts of things, such as electric power, voltages, currents, and the amplitudes of sounds. The decibel (dB) is a logarithmic unit that was introduced to express meaningfully physical quantities that may differ from each other by orders of magnitude. We'll show how this works with the use of an outrageous analogy where we suppose that people's salaries are quoted in a similar kind of logarithmic unit. We'll call the logarithmic salary unit the "salarybel."

6.1 Logarithmic Measure for Salaries: The Salarybel

The idea is to relate a person's salary in dollars, S, to some reference number of dollars, $S_{reference}$. The definition of the salarybel is then

$$\text{Salary in salarybels} = 10\log_{10}|S/S_{reference}|.$$

The vertical bars mean that we take the absolute value of the ratio, which may be important when dealing with voltages and currents but shouldn't be needed when dealing with salaries! The logical choice for $S_{reference}$ is one dollar, so we'll set

$$S_{reference} = \$1.$$

Let's try some examples. Suppose that the annual salary of your friendly teaching assistant (TA) is $7,200. The TA's salary in salarybels would be

$$\text{TA's salarybels} = 10\log_{10}|\$7200/\$1| = 10\,(3.857) = 39.$$

Colloquially, you could say that this TA's salary was "39 salarybels above a buck." For comparison, let's calculate the salarybels received by the head of General Motors, whose annual salary was reduced a few years ago to only (!) about one million dollars, because the company had a bad year:

$$\text{GM Head's salarybels} = 10\log_{10}|\$1,000,000/\$1| = 60.$$

You see that using this logarithmic measure to express salaries makes your TA's salary look much closer to that of the head of GM. In other words, **using such a logarithmic measure compresses numbers that differ by a lot into a much smaller range of values, making them more convenient to write and compare.**

6.2 Logarithmic Measure for Power: The Decibel (dB)

Now let's look at how an engineer actually uses the logarithmic measure, the decibel, to express electric power. To express the power, P, in terms of decibels, one starts by choosing a reference power, $P_{reference}$, and writing

$$\text{Power in decibels} = 10 \log_{10} |P/P_{reference}|.$$

To understand how this works with power, consider the following examples.

Exercise 6.1

  (a) Express 50 milliwatts in decibels referred to 1 watt (dB_W).
  (b) Express 50 milliwatts in dB_{mW}.
  (c) Given that $\log_{10} 2 = 0.30103$, express (to one significant figure) a power that is twice $P_{reference}$.
  (d) Similarly, for a power that is one-half $P_{reference}$.

Solution: (a) $-13\,dB_W$. (b) $17\,dB_{mW}$. (c) $3\,dB$. (d) $-3\,dB$.

6.3 Decibel Measures for Voltage and Current

From the expression for power ratios in decibels, we can readily derive the corresponding expressions for voltage or current ratios. Suppose that the voltage V (or current I) appears across (or flows in) a resistor having value R. The corresponding power, P, is V^2/R (or $I^2 R$). We can similarly relate the reference voltage or current to the reference power, as

$$P_{reference} = (V_{reference})^2/R \text{ or } P_{reference} = (I_{reference})^2 R.$$

Hence,

$$\text{Voltage, } V, \text{ in decibels} = 20\log_{10}|V/V_{reference}|,$$
$$\text{Current, } I, \text{ in decibels} = 20\log_{10}|I/I_{reference}|.$$

The voltage and current expressions are just like the power expression except that they have 20 as the multiplicative factor because power is proportional to the square of the voltage or the current.

Exercise 6.2

  (a) How many decibels larger is the voltage of a 9-volt transistor battery than that of a 1.5-volt AA battery (let $V_{reference} = 1.5$)?
  (b) Express in decibels [to one significant figure] a current that exactly equals $I_{reference}$.
  (c) Given that $\log_{10} 2 = 0.30103$, express (to one significant figure) a voltage that is twice $V_{reference}$.
  (d) Similarly, for a voltage that is one-half $V_{reference}$.

Solution: (a) $15.6\,dB$. (b) $0\,dB$ (c) $6\,dB$ (d) $-6\,dB$.

6.4 Decibel Measure for Sound Pressure

Audio engineers use a decibel measure for the amplitude of sound pressure. The definition of sound pressure level (SPL) in decibels for a sound whose pressure is p is

$$\text{Sound pressure level in dB}_{\text{SPL}} = 20\log_{10}|p/p_{\text{reference}}|,$$

where $p_{\text{reference}}$ is the pressure level corresponding to the average threshold of hearing for humans, which is $0.0002\,\mu\text{bar}$ (0.0002 millionths of an atmosphere). For example, a one-microbar sound pressure is about 74 dB $_{\text{SPL}}$. This sound pressure corresponds approximately to the sound produced by loud conversation.

6.5 Gain or Loss Expressed in Decibels

Often the gain produced by an amplifier is specified by giving the ratio of the amplifier output voltage (or current) to the input voltage (or current). When the gain is expressed in decibels, the input voltage (current) is taken as the reference value of voltage (current) in the decibel defining expression:

$$\text{Voltage gain in dB} = 20 \log_{10} |V_{\text{output}}/V_{\text{input}}|,$$
$$\text{Current gain in dB} = 20 \log_{10} |I_{\text{output}}/I_{\text{input}}|.$$

For example, if a certain amplifier produces a one-volt output when the input is two millivolts, it has a voltage gain of about 54 dB. Similar relations are used to express the ratio of the output to the input of circuits whose output is smaller than the input, such as filters.

6.6 Summary

The decibel is a logarithmic measure that is often used to express the ratio of two quantities that have the same units — voltage, current, power, etc.
The defining expression for power ratios is

$$\text{Power, } P, \text{ in decibels} = 10 \log_{10} |P/P_{\text{reference}}|.$$

The defining expression for voltage is

$$\text{Voltage, } V, \text{ in decibels} = 20 \log_{10} |V/V_{\text{reference}}|.$$

The defining expression for current is

$$\text{Current, } I, \text{ in decibels} = 20\log_{10}|I/I_{\text{reference}}|.$$

When expressing the gain of an amplifier, the reference quantity is taken as the input quantity, and the quantity in the numerator of the above expressions is the output quantity. For example, the gain of a voltage amplifier in decibels is

$$\text{Voltage gain} = 20 \log_{10} |V_{\text{output}}/V_{\text{input}}|.$$

6.7 Problems

6.1 Express the power dissipation of a 100-watt light bulb in decibels referred to 1 watt, and referred to one microwatt.

6.2 The most sensitive human hearing occurs at about 1000 Hz and corresponds to a sound pressure of 0.0002 microbar (0.0002 millionths of an atmosphere). The sound of a nearby jet engine is typically 130 decibels referred to that sound pressure. What is the engine's sound pressure in bars (atmospheres)?

6.3 Suppose that the audio amplifier in your sound system can deliver 50 watts to the 8-ohm load that represents your loudspeakers. If the input voltage to the amplifier that produced this output is 5 millivolts, what is the voltage gain of your amplifier in decibels?

How Many Words Is a Picture

Really Worth?

You've always heard that a picture is worth a thousand words. Let's check that out. We'll compare the number of bits it takes to specify 1000 words with the number it takes to specify all the dots that make up a picture. Let's start with the picture.

7.1 Picture on a Computer Screen

A picture on the screen is composed of spots of light created wherever the electron beam in the picture tube strikes the phosphor or where an electric potential is present locally on a liquid crystal display.

To calculate the number of bits it takes to display a single arbitrary picture (or pattern) on the screen, we need to know how many discrete "spots" the screen has and how many bits it takes to specify whether a spot is light or dark. Here are the assumptions about the pictures on which we'll base our calculations:

- P1: The screen has 480 lines in one direction and 640 in the other, or 307,200 discrete picture elements (called "pixels"). This number is typical of an ordinary PC or Macintosh screen.

- P2: The picture is black and white, and any pixel is either bright or dark. In other words, there are no "gray" spots, only black or white.

By assumption P2, we have a choice of only two intensities at each pixel, which we could represent by a **1** for bright or a **0** for dark. Thus, it takes just one bit to specify the intensity setting for any pixel. As there are (by Assumption P1) 480 × 640 = 307,200 pixels, specifying an arbitrary picture requires 307,200 bits. If we were to use colors or shades of gray, we would require 8, 16, or even 24 bits per pixel!

7.2 Words

Now let's calculate how many bits are required to specify 1000 arbitrary English words. We'll make these assumptions about the words:

- W1: A "word" contains on average five characters plus one space — six characters altogether.

- W2: A word can be formed from a combination of any of the 26 English letters, 10 numerals, and the 13 punctuation marks — ,./?!;:'-() and space.

- W3: Any letter may be either uppercase or lowercase.

The question is now how many bits must be used to indicate which of the possible characters listed in Assumption W2 is to appear next in any given word. Putting it differently, how many elements do we have to choose from, and, therefore, how many bits would it take to indicate our choice? From W2 we see that we have 49 characters, and another 26 when we allow lower and upper case, giving a total of 75 characters to choose from. Since this is more than 64 characters ($64 = 2^6$), which would require 6 bits, we'll need at least 7 bits ($2^7 = 128$) to represent our character set. (Western languages typically use all eight bits of computer bytes to represent characters.)

The answer, then, is that each character requires 7 bits, and since there are 6 characters per word, each word requires 42 bits. Hence, 1,000 words require 42,000 bits to represent them.

Result

The calculations show that a simple black-and-white picture is "worth" much more than 1,000 words. In fact,

A PICTURE IS WORTH 7,315 WORDS!

This size equivalence applies to the storage of (uncompressed) pictures and the storage of words, and to the lengths of time required to transmit each over a network.

The very high-performance digital cameras being produced by Kodak now generate images that are 3,000 by 2,000 pixels, with each pixel using 8 or 10 bits for each primary color (red, green, and blue). The resulting digital image will require 180,000,000 bits for storage or transmission. Such a picture would be worth over four million words.

7.3 Bit Rate

It is interesting to calculate how many bits per second must be transmitted in certain real-world situations — forming a screen of a computer display, representing speech, representing music, and so on.

A computer <u>display</u> that involves a cathode-ray tube like those used for television will be refreshed 30 times per second. Our eyes integrate the rapidly presented images so we don't see them as individual images. The bit rate for displaying the arbitrary picture on the screen just described is therefore 30 per second times 307,200 bits, or 9,216,000 bits/s (bits per second).

If we want to represent <u>speech</u> or <u>music</u> digitally, we can sample the speech or music waveform at fixed intervals, determine the amplitude of the waveform at each sampling time, and convert those amplitudes into bits for transmission. Suppose we consider digitally encoding music and make the following "music" assumptions:

- M1: We are interested in musical tones whose frequencies may be as high as 10,000 Hz.

- M2: We will determine the amplitude of the waveform at the sampling times to the nearest of 65,536 values ($65,536 = 2^{16}$).

A theoretical result relating to sampling states that we must "sample a waveform at least twice per cycle in order to be able to represent it adequately." Hence, by Assumption M1, we see that the period of the highest musical frequency is 1/10,000 seconds, and we must sample the waveform twice every 0.0001 seconds. In other words, our sampling rate is 20,000 samples per second. Assumption M2 indicates that we require 16 bits to represent the amplitude of each sample of the waveform. Hence, the bit rate for the digitized music is 3.2×10^5 bits/s.

These quantities are relevant to determining what memory capacities are required to store particular samples of speech, music, or graphics. The common 3½-inch floppy diskette can hold approximately 1.4 megabytes, and the CD-ROM can hold 680 megabytes. Computer hard disks with capacities of gigabytes are available for use with personal computer systems.

7.4 Problems

7.1   How many words would be equivalent to an arbitrary black-and-white picture displayed on an Apple II screen? Such a screen contains 24 lines, with 40 characters per line, where each character is made up of selected dots from a 5×7 dot matrix.

7.2   How many bits can be displayed on a conventional $8\frac{1}{2} \times 11$ inch page by a black-and-white ThinkJet printer that prints 300 dots per inch? Since these printers can't print all the way to the edge of the paper, assume that they have a 0.25 inch margin. One would say of such a printer that it had a resolution of 300 dpi (dots per inch).

7.3   What is the bit rate of a system that transmits a picture 30 times per second with a resolution of 640×480 and any of 256 different colors?

7.4   This question concerns the information content of a DNA molecule. The DNA molecules in a human cell have the well-known double-helix structure and contain three billion "base pairs." These are pairs of particular molecules known as organic bases that connect between the two helices at regular intervals along the helices. (The bases are represented by the letters A, C, G and T, which stand for adenine, cytosine, guanine and thymine, respectively. A and T always occur together, as do C and G.) The development of a human being is guided by the order in which these bases occur along the DNA molecule.

(a) How many bits are required to specify a particular human DNA molecule?

(b) How many bytes is this?

(c) Would this amount of information fit on a typical personal computer hard disk?

(d) How many personal computer diskettes would be required to hold this much information?

(e) How many CD-ROMs would be required to hold this much information?

Favorite Programs

We all have favorites — favorite games, favorite music, comics, movies, people, books, and *even* favorite computer programs. Some of our favorite programs are highlighted next to enable you to check them out for use in your academic and professional work. Sorry, computer games aren't included — you don't need our help to find them!

We can divide computers roughly into central machines and personal machines. Examples of the former are networks of time-shared computers using the UNIX operating system; these networks are accessed with a keyboard that's part of a terminal that can display only alphanumeric characters on its screen. The personal computers have consisted chiefly of IBM PC (or IBM-clone) machines and Apple Macintosh computers. You control these with a keyboard and a graphical input device, called a "mouse," with which you can select portions of the screen and even draw on it. (With the introduction of Microsoft Windows software, the differences between the Macintosh and the IBM personal computers have lessened.) A scale-up from the personal computers in speed and capability are "workstations," made by companies such as Sun, Digital Equipment Corp., and Hewlett-Packard. On these, one may run UNIX programs and some of the applications programs described next.

In what follows, we'll describe several types of programs that can really act as "wheels for the mind" — they really extend your ability to solve problems and express yourself. (This term was coined by computer visionary Alan Kay in the 1970s while developing user-friendly ways of interacting with computers.) The programs will be described generically as paint program, word processor, desktop publishing program, hypermedia, database, spreadsheet, symbolic mathematics program, and finite-element analysis programs. For much more detailed information about engineering software, you can find articles in many technical periodicals; an example is *IEEE Spectrum*, 28:11, November 1991.

8.1 Painting Programs

With a paint program (such as **MacPaint™**, **Superpaint™**, **Paintbrush™** — see Figure 8.1 — or **Canvas™**), you use the mouse to select and manipulate painting tools (brush, pencil, spray can) and drawing tools (drawing straight or curved lines, boxes, circles, ellipses). With the keyboard, you can enter alphanumeric text. You can select textures (such as crosshatching or fields of dots) and fill closed figures with them. If your computer, monitor, and printer support color, you can color selected portions of each page. It is also possible to scan images into a computer with a device known as a "scanner." Once the image is in digital form, you can manipulate it readily. For example, with the **Adobe Photoshop™** program you can alter images that originated as photographs, using tools such as the "airbrush" that professionals use to retouch photos.

Errors that you recognize before further typing can be removed with the "Undo" command; other changes can be made with the eraser provided in the menu. Programs offer rulers and grid lines that are useful for engineering work. You can

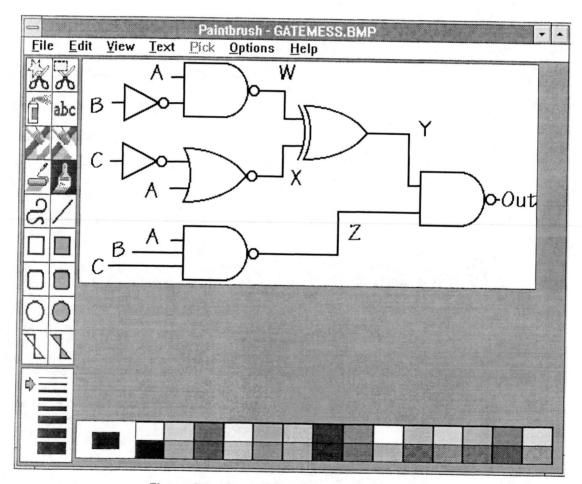

Figure 8.1 Windows Paintbrush screen image

move selected sections of drawings around, and can "Copy," "Cut," and "Paste" selected parts of drawings. You can adjust the orientation and size of a document before printing it.

8.2 Word Processors

These programs enable you to create documents such as term papers, resumés and reports. You can include footnotes, tables, and equations in the text. The word processors that are easiest to use have the WYSIWYG feature — meaning "what you see is what you get." (This contrasts with character editors, which require you to embed formatting commands in the text. You must then wait to see the printed output to be sure you asked for what you really wanted. Examples are many of the editors in computers using the UNIX operating system.)

Microsoft **Word** and **WordPerfect**™, popular WYSIWYG word-processing programs, allow you to put into your document graphics that might be generated with a paint program or a scanner that reads in photographs and sketches. Some programs include features to ease the task of writing — outlining features, spelling checkers, style analyses, and so on. As you write, you can see on the screen how your work will appear when printed; thus, you can experiment with different type faces and font sizes before actually printing your document.

Here are some examples of text written with FrameMaker:

Small font (7 point)..... "Symbol" written in Symbol font, 12 point is

$\forall \Sigma \psi \mu \beta o \lambda \forall$

Here in 18-point type are these fonts:

Script, `Courier`, **Helvetica**, and Times.

These are some of the special effects available:

$x^2 + y_0 =$ not much   Bold + *Italic* + <u>*Underline*</u> + ~~*Strikethrough*~~

8.3 Desktop Publishing

These systems are essentially expanded word processors. They allow you to produce work whose design is nearly as professional as that produced by a good publishing house. These programs give you more control than word processors over the placement and printing of graphical and textual material.

The approach taken by the highly regarded program **FrameMaker**™ (which was used to produce this book) is to offer you templates for standard forms you might want to write — memos, letters, reports, periodic newsletters, and books. Graphics designers have done the layout, and you can simply replace their text with yours.

8.4 Hypermedia

In 1947, computers were in their infancy, having only performed numerical calculations during World War II. Even so, at that time the scientist Vannevar Bush envisioned the use of computers to give human beings access to a vast array of information. He fantasized that, someday, if you wanted to know about a topic, you would enter the topic into a computer and receive increasingly detailed material about it. Bush felt that retrieving information this way would be more satisfactory than conventional library retrieval, since most of the detail would be hidden from you unless you requested it. When Apple Computer introduced the language Hypertalk, and the related program **Hypercard™**, Bush's vision approached reality.

Hypercard enables you to store individual computer screen images (text, graphics, and even sounds) that are linked so that you can move from one to another in a personally meaningful way. Each computer screen can contain *"buttons"* (sensitive regions that you can choose with the cursor) with which you make your way through the collection ("stack") of cards.

Now standard with Mac computers, Hypercard has many uses. For instance, it can be used to create and access lists, such as addresses or phone numbers; it can be used to provide dictionary meanings for unfamiliar words that appear in some text; and it can produce information about geographical features as you click on particular regions.

World Wide Web browsers such as **Netscape Navigator™** carry the hypertext concept to extremes, allowing links to any document, picture, e-mail, or news group on the Internet.

8.5 Database

Frequently one wants to store and retrieve lists of information about entire classes of items. Examples include all the undergraduates in a particular college department, the replacement parts for all the Fords built between 1989 and today, and the names and addresses of all the clients of a small business. Some of the major database programs for doing this are **dBase™**, **Paradox™**, and **Ingres™** (for UNIX-based computers). Spreadsheets such as **Excel™** and **Quattro Pro™** also have some database capabilities.

In a database, you enter individual records (for example, a particular student) in terms of fields (such as the student's year in school, city of origin, and major field of study). The program provides utilities for entering and changing records (for example, entering new students and deleting names of graduates), finding records that meet certain criteria (such as students majoring in engineering), sorting records (for example, putting them in alphabetical or numerical order), and using the records in various ways (for example, preparing mailing lists).

A particularly useful but specialized database program for academic and engineering professionals is the bibliographic program **refer™**, which can be used on UNIX, IBM (DOS), and Mac systems. The database is for storing and retrieving references to articles and books. The program prompts you for information about an entry — name of the author, title, name of the journal or publisher, and so on. It stores the information in a readable form.

The following article is shown in conventional reference format:

Young, AM, J.E. Goldsberry, J.H. Haritonidis, R. L. Smith, and S. D. Senturia, "A twin-interferometer fiber-optic readout for diaphragm pressure transducers," *Technical Digest, IEEE Solid-State Sensor and Actuator Workshop,* pp 19-22, Hilton Head, S.C. 6-9 June 1988

It is stored in **refer**™ in the following form (%A stands for author, %T for title, and so on.):

> %A A. M. Young
> %A J. E. Goldsberry
> %A J. H. Haritonidis
> %A R. L. Smith
> %A S. D. Senturia
> %T A twin-interferometer fiber-optic
>   readout for diaphragm pressure
>   transducers
> %J Technical Digest IEEE Solid-State
>   Sensor and Actuator Workshop
> %C Hilton Head, S.C.
> %P 19-22
> %D 6-9 June 1988

You can sort the entries (by author name, title, date of publication, etc.). You can have **refer**™ print out full references for the items you request. You can also have the program put references in a manuscript simply by typing into your manuscript at least two strings that uniquely define the reference you want to cite (such as author's name and the year of publication). For more information about **refer**™, see P. M. Birns, P. Brown, J. C. C. Muster, *UNIX For People* (Englewood Cliffs, NJ: Prentice Hall, 1985).

8.6 Spreadsheet

The first spreadsheet, **Visicalc**™, and successors, such as **Lotus l-2-3**™, **Quattro Pro**™, and **Excel**™, revolutionized the keeping and manipulation of financial records. But the utility of spreadsheets extends far beyond the financial domain. In fact, they can be very useful to students of engineering and the sciences, as we'll show.

The spreadsheet is simply an array of rectangular boxes arranged in columns (vertically) and rows (horizontally). Each box is identified with a number and letter (such as C8 or F301). Into any box you can enter text, values, or formulas.

You can link boxes together by referring to their labels. For example, in **Excel**™ (available for both IBM and Mac personal computers) if you type into box D12 the formula =sum(C1:C9) the computer will write into box D12 the sum of all the values contained in boxes C1, C2, C3,... C9. And if you change the number in box C5, for instance, the total appearing in box D12 will change as well. This feature permits you to explore "what if" design questions. For example, you could enter formulas that express the weight of a vehicle in terms of its dimensions and the materials employed in its manufacture. You could then explore how dimensional or material changes affect the total weight and look for an optimum low-weight design.

Spreadsheet programs such as **Quattro Pro**™ and **Excel**™ enable you to produce sophisticated plots or charts based on the values in the sheet. You can produce histograms, pie charts, ordinary rectangular plots of many dependent variables, and so on.

In addition to these features, it is possible to write macros that cause sequences of calculations to be performed. You can also easily generate series of input numerical values (such as piston settings in a mechanical problem) or dates (each Monday for a year starting in 1994). It is also possible to force spreadsheets such as **Excel** to do recursive calculations, continuing through either a specified number of iterations or until the final value changes less than a specified amount between successive iterations. Because of these features, many engineering students have used spreadsheets extensively in doing homework assignments, preferring them to the use of certain engineering programming languages such as **Fortran**™. An example spreadsheet appears in Figure 8.2.

8.7 Symbolic Mathematics Programs

Amazingly, there are programs that will do your algebraic and trigonometric manipulations for you and will do differentiation and integration, even though you are using symbolic expressions containing unknowns such as x and y.

The first such program, written for a central computing system at MIT, was called **Macsyma**™; a version was then written for VAX computers and called, of course, **Vaxima**™. (**Vaxima** can be accessed on some networked UNIX machines.) There is now a superb program available for personal computers called **Mathematica**™. The program, written by a team headed by Stephen Wolfram, is described in detail in the book by Stephen Wolfram, *Mathematica: A System for Doing Mathematics by Computer* (Redwood City, CA: Addison-Wesley Publishing Co., 1988).

Mathematica™ can be run on IBM and Mac personal computers, on Sun workstations, and so on. The heart (kernel) of each program is the same, but the input and output details are tailored for the specific computer system.

One use of **Mathematica**™ was made by a Berkeley graduate research student. We had discovered that we could pump water with ultrasonic waves traveling in a thin sheet made as part of a silicon chip. We had developed about five pages of analysis — algebra, trigonometry, and calculus — that should give us an approximate expression for the speed at which the water should flow. Unfortunately, we got a different answer each time we went by hand through the analysis! So we put the expressions into files that we input to **Mathematica**, so that the program would do the algebra, the trigonometric simplifications, the differentiation, and the integrations. As a result of doing this, we got a consistent answer each time — which also was within 10% of what we found experimentally.

Mathematica™ contains useful and simple plotting capabilities to help you visualize its results. For example, the single command expression

In[2]:=Plot3D[Sin[x] Sin[3y], {x,-2, 2}, {y,-2, 2}]

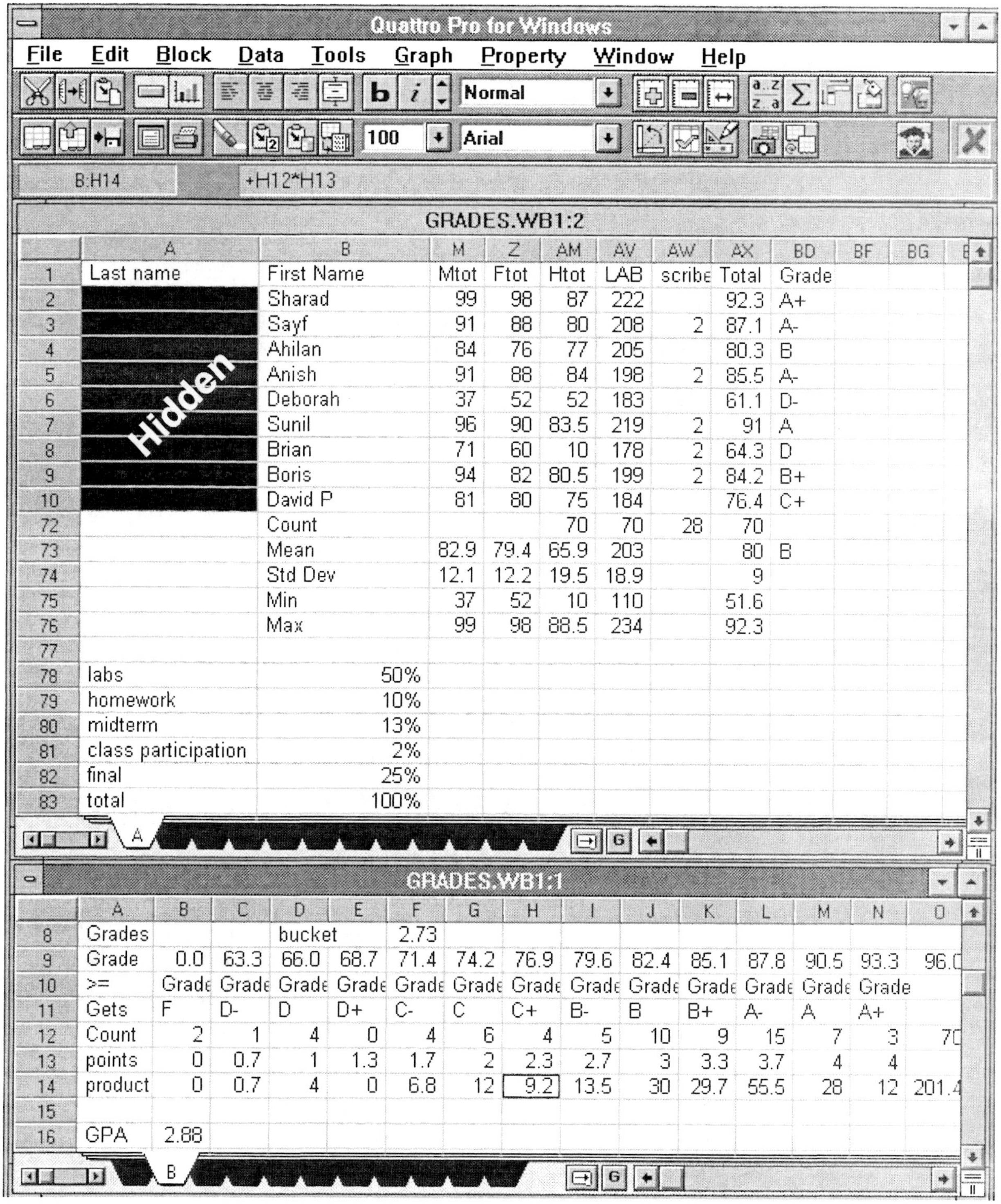

Quattro Pro for Windows

File   Edit   Block   Data   Tools   Graph   Property   Window   Help

Normal | Arial

B:H14 | +H12*H13

GRADES.WB1:2

	A	B	M	Z	AM	AV	AW	AX	BD	BF	BG
1	Last name	First Name	Mtot	Ftot	Htot	LAB	scribe	Total	Grade		
2		Sharad	99	98	87	222		92.3	A+		
3		Sayf	91	88	80	208	2	87.1	A-		
4		Ahilan	84	76	77	205		80.3	B		
5		Anish	91	88	84	198	2	85.5	A-		
6		Deborah	37	52	52	183		61.1	D-		
7		Sunil	96	90	83.5	219	2	91	A		
8		Brian	71	60	10	178	2	64.3	D		
9		Boris	94	82	80.5	199	2	84.2	B+		
10		David P	81	80	75	184		76.4	C+		
72		Count		70	70	28	70				
73		Mean	82.9	79.4	65.9	203		80	B		
74		Std Dev	12.1	12.2	19.5	18.9		9			
75		Min	37	52	10	110		51.6			
76		Max	99	98	88.5	234		92.3			
77											
78	labs	50%									
79	homework	10%									
80	midterm	13%									
81	class participation	2%									
82	final	25%									
83	total	100%									

(Column A cells for rows 2–10 are marked "Hidden")

GRADES.WB1:1

	A	B	C	D	E	F	G	H	I	J	K	L	M	N	O
8	Grades			bucket		2.73									
9	Grade	0.0	63.3	66.0	68.7	71.4	74.2	76.9	79.6	82.4	85.1	87.8	90.5	93.3	96.0
10	>=	Grade	Grade	Grade	Grade	Grade	Grade	Grade	Grade	Grade	Grade	Grade	Grade	Grade	
11	Gets	F	D-	D	D+	C-	C	C+	B-	B	B+	A-	A	A+	
12	Count	2	1	4	0	4	6	4	5	10	9	15	7	3	70
13	points	0	0.7	1	1.3	1.7	2	2.3	2.7	3	3.3	3.7	4	4	
14	product	0	0.7	4	0	6.8	12	9.2	13.5	30	29.7	55.5	28	12	201.4
15															
16	GPA	2.88													

Figure 8.2 Quattro Pro screen image showing course grading spreadsheet

produces a 3-D contour plot of sin(x) times sin($3y$) for x and y between -2 and +2. The resulting screen image is shown in Figure 8.3.

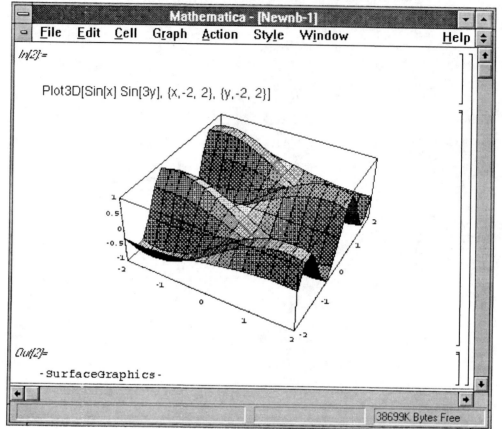

Figure 8.3 Mathematica screen image

In the preceding expression, the term In[2] identifies the particular function that follows the equals sign. Experienced **Mathematica**™ users suggest writing all the expressions you intend to use in files before running the analytical part of **Mathematica**™, so you can be sure that you get the terms exactly right. In addition to graphical output, **Mathematica**™ can produce output equations that can be input directly — and hence correctly — into a UNIX file for printing or even typesetting.

Another very useful mathematics program is **Mathcad**™, which is available on all popular computing platforms. It features a user interface that is much more friendly than other such programs. Formulas and text may be placed wherever the user desires on the page image. It is great for preparing homework! Figure 8.4 shows an example of **Mathcad™** in action.

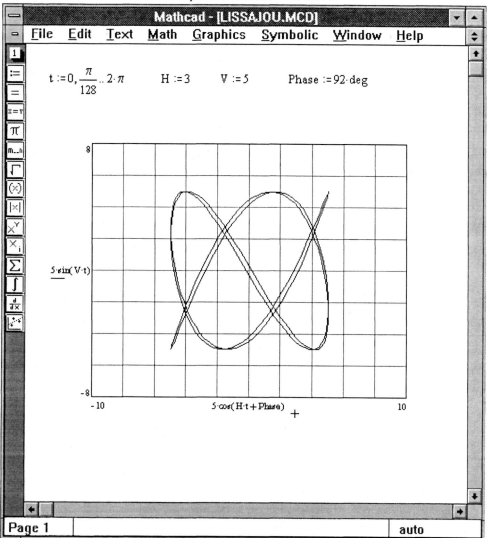

Figure 8.4 Mathcad screen showing generation of Lissajou figures

MATLAB™ is another mathematics program that is in wide use. "**MATLAB** is an interactive, matrix-based system for scientific and engineering numeric computation and visualization. You can solve complex numerical problems in a fraction of the time required with a programming language such as **Fortran** or **C**. The name **MATLAB** is derived from MATrix LABoratory."[1]

---

[1] From Kermit Sigmon, *MATLAB Primer*, 4th Ed. (Boca Raton, FL: CRC Press, 1994).

8.8 Computer-Aided Design (CAD) Tools

As the warrior of old relied on his sword, so an engineer today relies on CAD tools. Many design tasks today are extremely complex, and these tools can simplify the tasks of specification, design, verification, testing, manufacture, and maintenance. These tools enable engineers to create their designs on a computer screen, where they can be easily manipulated, and hierarchy can be exploited, instead of on paper. The design can be checked for rule violations either in a checking phase or in some programs continuously as it is created. The great strength of computers comes into play when these programs simulate the design, without ever having to build it.

Our two example programs are both circuit design programs. **LogicWorks™** (Figure 8.5) is for digital designs, and **PSpice™** (Figures 8.6-8.7) is for analog designs. **SPICE** stands for Simulation Program with Integrated Circuit Emphasis.

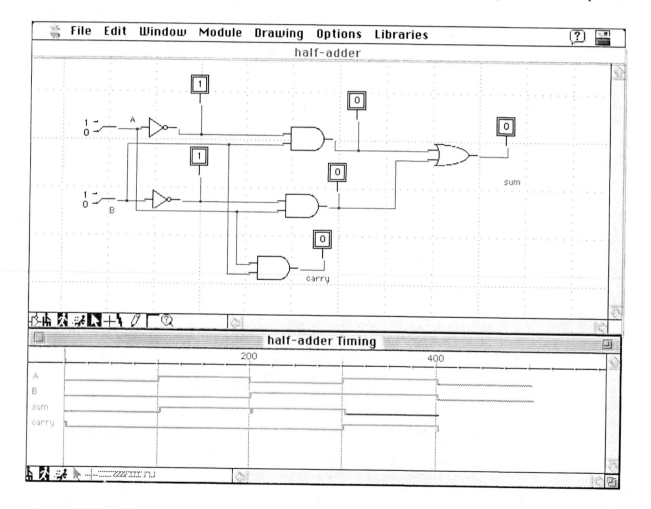

Figure 8.5 LogicWorks™ screen images. The top window is the schematic, and the bottom window is the timing diagram.

Both programs allow the user to create a schematic drawing of their circuit using symbols from their libraries. They can then simulate the behavior of the circuit, generating graphs of circuit behavior.

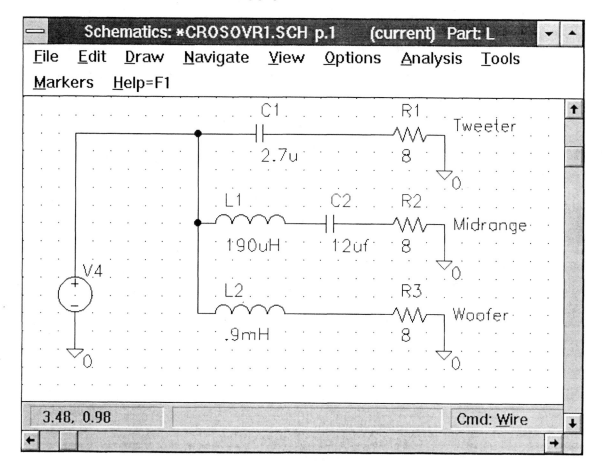

Figure 8.6 PSpice™ schematic drawing of a loudspeaker crossover circuit

8.9 Finite-Element Method (FEM) Analysis

To solve engineering problems that involve objects having complex shapes, you may need to resort to purely numerical solutions, instead of using familiar analytic functions such as sines and cosines, exponentials, and polynomials. The boundaries of most real objects — such as a football helmet or a shovel — don't consist just of planes, cylinders, or spheres, so a numerical approach may be needed. A way of doing the numerical analysis is called the finite-element method (abbreviated as

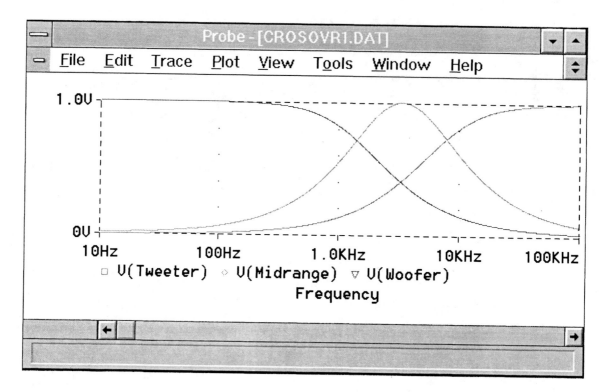

Figure 8.7 PSpice probe window graphing the crossover circuit's frequency response

"FEM"). **Abaqus**™ and **Maxwell**™ are two well-known commercial FEM programs; they are used to analyze mechanical stress-strain problems and electric field problems, respectively.

To get a feeling for how these numerical analysis programs work, consider the problem of finding the electric field near a set of conductors to which voltages are applied. The specific example shown in Figure 8.8 arose in connection with research on micromachined devices. Onto a silicon wafer, the researcher deposited a conducting "ground" plane, an insulating layer, and on upper conducting electrode. Then, a trench was etched in the upper electrode and the insulating layer, exposing the ground plane. Finally, a voltage difference was established with a power supply between each portion of the upper electrode and the ground plane.

Before describing how the program solved the problem and discussing the result, let's think about what we'd expect to happen. First, we'd expect that there would be an electric field everywhere in the narrow insulating region between the ground plane and each upper electrode. (That region is just like a capacitor, since it is an insulator bounded by two conductors that have a potential difference between them.) We'd also expect that near the edges of each upper electrode, there would be an electric field, as a result of the positive and negative charges located there. Far above the electrodes, we'd expect that the electric field would be very small, since the positive and negative charges are far away and have opposite signs anyway.

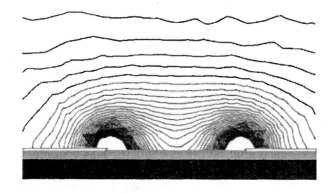

Figure 8.8 Finite-element analysis of electric fields near a pair of micromachined electrodes

What the Program Does

To determine the electric field distribution in this space, the finite-element analysis program called **Maxwell**™ first divided the space with a mesh into small regions, filling the space with little polygons. The program has built into it a rule that causes it to divide the region more finely, with smaller polygons wherever the conductor shapes change most rapidly with distance.

After the mesh has been created, the program makes use of a fundamental fact of electricity — that the electric field inside a region is completely determined once the electric potentials on the boundary of the region have been specified. Using a formal analytical expression of that principle, the program then proceeds to guess the potentials in each polygon, starting with approximate values of the potentials on the boundaries of each polygon. (The values are known for the polygons that touch the electrodes and ground plane, but the program must start by guessing for the other polygons.) The program works its way through the entire space, until it arrives at a potential distribution that "fits" with the applied potentials on the electrodes and the ground plane.

The Final Result

The magnitude of the electric field at each point in the figure is indicated by the degree of shading. As we had guessed, the electric field is highest between the electrodes and the ground plane, and near the gaps in the electrodes. The contours on the plot represent electric equipotential lines. In other words, along any one of those lines, the electric potential is the same everywhere. Notice that equipotential lines are slightly jagged, an indication of the approximate nature of the solution; we'd expect the actual equipotential lines to vary smoothly with distance, as nature is generally continuous. Incidentally, the original output of this FEM program was presented in false color (the fields don't have color, but we use color to take advantage of our eyes' ability to distinguish colors to portray fine gradations in the generated image), where red represents the highest field and blue the lowest.

8.10 Extraterrestrials Instead of Flying Toasters?

How would you like to join more than two million other people worldwide, without effort at home or at work, in the search for extraterrestrial intelligence (SETI)? You can do this with a free downloaded computer program known as SETI@home that runs in place of a screen saver on your networked PC.

The search is being conducted by radio astronomers using the world's largest radio telescope, which is built into bowl-shaped depression in a mountain at Arecibo, Puerto Rico. Scientists believe that using radio is the best, and perhaps the only, chance we have of contacting intelligent civilizations located in interstellar space. Consider that the one-way travel time for a radio wave traveling at the speed of light, 3×10^8 m/s, from earth to the nearest star, Proxima Centauri, is about four years. In contrast, the travel time for a rocket traveling at an impressive 25,000 miles per hour is 300,000 years! So radio waves received on earth are being studied to see whether particularly strong radio emissions seem to be coming from particular directions in space, and whether there is a pattern to those emissions that might indicate an attempt to communicate with us. The frequencies presently studied are near 1.42 GHz, because that is a frequency characteristic of energy emission from the hydrogen atom. The rationale is that a distant civilization might monitor that frequency for incoming messages because of the importance and abundance of hydrogen.

The SETI program, which is supported by both private and corporate funds, requires huge numbers of computer cycles to search thoroughly for possible communications in the radio emissions being received. It was realized that personal computers were wasting millions of CPU cycles running their screen savers — flying toasters, mazes of pipes, a virtual aquarium — when they were otherwise idle. Why not apply those cycles to analyzing SETI data?

You can take part in this search if you have a Macintosh, Windows, or UNIX computer that is hooked at times to the Internet. To get involved, contact SETI@home[2] at the University of California's Space Sciences Laboratory in Berkeley. You can download the appropriate program, and when you would otherwise have a screen saver running you will see instead a screen image like that in Figure 8.9. The part at the bottom of the image that looks like a card file is actually in color, just to make it look pleasing when it takes over from your regular screen saver.

It is claimed that you will receive credit — perhaps a share of a Nobel Prize! — if the first firm evidence for the existence of an extraterrestrial civilization comes from data that your computer processed.

Data from the radio antenna near 1.42 GHz are shifted downward in frequency to a 2.5 MHz band. The data are recorded on 35 Gbyte digital tapes and shipped to Berkeley. The antenna is fixed in location on the earth, but it sweeps the sky as the earth moves. Data from one complete sky sweep fills 1100 tapes! Small blocks of the raw data are shipped electronically from Berkeley via the Internet to each participating personal computer, where they are analyzed for energy distribution as a function of frequency and other characteristics. The analysis program tests for short- and long-duration signals, as well as doppler-shifted signals that could indicate that the emission came from a moving extraterrestrial source. The results are then automatically sent back to Berkeley for further examination. Strong

---

[2] http://setiathome.ssl.berkeley.edu

received peaks are naturally of great interest, but so far they have all been found to result from radio interference produced by terrestrial sources.

As of February, 2000, SETI@home has grown to encompass 1.6 million participants in 224 countries. The amount of computing time contributed since May, 1999 is equal to 165,000 years, averaging 10 Teraflops (about 10 times more than the largest supercomputer on the planet). It is the largest computation ever done and has attracted the participation of 20,000 groups such as schools and private companies.

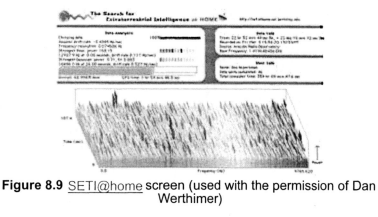

Figure 8.9 SETI@home screen (used with the permission of Dan Werthimer)

8.11 Problem

8.1   Send an e-mail message to your instructor, containing at least two questions about the material covered in a recent class meeting.

Some Really Interesting Technical and Semi-Technical Books

How Things Work

David Macaulay, *The Way Things Work* (Boston, MA: Houghton Mifflin, 1988). Vividly and humorously illustrated book that explains, with the aid of elephants and angels, to kids of all ages how the familiar devices of our modern world actually work.

Creativity and Problem Solving

James L. Adams, *Conceptual Blockbusting: A Pleasurable Guide to Better Problem Solving* (New York, NY: W. Norton & Co., 1976). When he wrote this book, Adams was an engineer, teacher of design at Stanford, and a collector of tractors.

Pepper White, *The Idea Factory: Learning to Think at MIT* (New York, NY: Penguin Books/Dutton, 1991). Pepper describes life as a mechanical engineering graduate student at MIT, and admires the lucid explanations in *The Way Things Work* of the operation of the spark plug and the internal combustion engine.

Robert Weisberg, *Creativity: Beyond the Myth of Genius* (San Francisco, CA: W. H. Freeman, 1993). With case studies ranging from Picasso to Watson and Crick, Weisberg shows how creative leaps come from building on fairly simple elements.

Ed N. Sickafus, *Unified Structured Inventive Thinking: How to Invent,* (Grosse Ile, MI: Ntelleck, 1997). This book describes a disciplined process for creative thinking about design problems that require an invention, or an existing system that needs improvement.

Written and Graphical Presentation of informatiOn

William Strunk, Jr., and E. B. White, *The Elements of Style*, 2nd Ed. (New York, NY: Macmillan Publishing Co., 1972). Very short, no-nonsense guide to writing well.

Edward R. Tufte, *The Visual Display of Quantitative Information* (Cheshire, CT: Graphics Press, 1983). "ET," as he refers to himself, discusses and displays beautiful examples of graphical work from 1700 to today, showing successful ways of conveying quantitative information.

Edward R. Tufte, *Envisioning Information* (Cheshire, CT: Graphics Press, 1990). Tufte's second handsome and informative book about presenting information well.

Edward R. Tufte, *Visual Explanations* (Cheshire, CT: Graphics Press, 1997). Tufte's final book in his series shows kinetic presentations of information from simulations of weather to useful ways of displaying the records of hospital patients.

Engineering Tools

Theodore Wildi, *Units and Conversion Charts: A Handbook for Engineers and Scientists,* (Piscataway, NJ: IEEE Press, 1991). The author simplifies the thorny issue of units conversions with cleanly designed charts that cover quantities from acceleration to volume.

P. Horowitz and W. Hill, *The Art of Electronics*, 2nd ed. (Cambridge, England: Cambridge University Press, 1989). Textbooks present the science, but this hefty volume presents the art of getting electronics to work for you. Over three hundred thousand copies have been sold.

J. L. Jones and A. M. Flynn, *Mobile Robots: Inspiration to Implementation* (Wellesley, MA: A. K. Peters, 1993). Practical guide to designing and building inexpensive robots able to perform simple tasks such as exploring mazes, collecting soft-drink cans, and hiding.

Pencils, Bridges, Buildings and More

John McPhee, *The Control of Nature* (New York, NY: Farrar, Straus, Giroux, 1990). Lively account of human attempts to keep the Mississippi River in its banks, stop the San Gabriel Mountains of California from rolling down, and halt an Icelandic lava flow by squirting cold water on it. McPhee has written many other books that you might want to sample.

M. Levy and M. Salvadori, *Why Buildings Fall Down* (New York, NY: W. Norton & Co., 1994). Guided tour of architectural and structural disasters from ancient times to the present. The second author also has a companion book titled, naturally, *Why Buildings Stand Up*.

Henry Petroski, *The Pencil* (New York, NY: Alfred A. Knopf, 1990). Petroski is an engineering storyteller who provides a fascinating account of the long development of this important tool from the days when it contained real lead.

Henry Petroski, *Engineers of Dreams: Building Great Bridge*s (New York, NY: Alfred A. Knopf, 1995). Petroski sees a bridge as "a poem stretched across a river" and "an index to civilization." He says, "…in the stories of bridges…we also see more clearly the inextricable interrelationships between technology and humanity."

Ray Kurzweil, *The Age of Spiritual Machines: When Computers Exceed Human Intelligence* (New York, NY: Viking, 1999). This entrepreneur and inventor of a reading machine for the visually impaired, traces the exponential growth of computing speeds from before the electronics revolution and speculates about future computer capabilities and their challenges to our human self-image.

Advice to Freshmen

10

10.1 Advice to Freshmen from Some Graduates

It is natural for students starting the study of engineering to have apprehensions and anxieties, along with positive aspirations. The comments that follow are from Berkeley graduates Andy Yang and Tom Parker, who were willing to "tell it like it is" — or at least as they observed it. Their comments probably apply to most U.S. engineering colleges, but some references to your specific school may be available from your instructor.

"Most of you are probably now taking your math and physics classes. Although it may sound obvious, you should strive for a clear conceptual understanding of the course material, not just an ability to solve the specific problems assigned in class. Many of the concepts introduced now will show up again. For example, I found that differential equations and parts of electromagnetic theory were essential later to solving electrical circuit problems. And I thought I'd never need a Fourier transform, but sure enough, I had to re-learn and use them in a more advanced undergraduate course on an applied topic.

"Many or most of you probably ranked near the top of your high school or preparatory school class. Because your professors in college likely grade 'on a curve', the letter grades you receive will not be determined solely by your performance, but also by those of your classmates. Consequently, you may experience a lot of competitiveness in your courses. It is critical that you develop the proper perspective about this. You will find that if you help your fellow students, they will reciprocate when you need assistance. Often group efforts are more effective for learning than 'going it alone'. Most professors encourage this, but you should find out whether your profs do. Working with a group facilitates examining different perspectives and discussing the pros and cons of different approaches. Also, you may be required to work with other students in your lab courses, and you'll find later in industry that working in teams is very common.

"Some of your course work will be extremely difficult, so you may want some help with it. Don't be intimidated by your professors or teaching assistants:

Ask them for help during their office hours. Not only will you get your questions answered, but you may see a different side of your teachers there.

"People's learning styles vary: Try to understand how you best learn, and use the method that is most effective for you. This may involve discussing problems with your prof, teaching assistant, or even outside tutors. Also, someday you'll need recommendations from your teachers for employment or graduate school admission, so try to get acquainted with them now. Performing well in a student tutoring job is a great way to get to know a professor. Student research positions are also an excellent way of working with a professor while pursuing fields that interest you.

"You should keep in mind that your learning depends not only on how your teachers present the course material, but also on how you receive it. It always helps to skim the material before class so that the lectures are more meaningful. Starting on the homework when it's first handed out — rather than the night before it's due — is another very wise technique that can pay off in terms of understanding and good grades.

"It's never too early to start thinking about your future, especially when your efforts now could make things much easier for you down the road. Locate and visit your campus center for career planning and job placement where you can sign up to interview on campus for summer jobs, internships, or full-time employment. Your campus may have a co-op program in which you are paid to spend six months or so away from campus working in a company getting practical engineering experience. Interviewing for a job is not most people's favorite activity, but it is one in which practice helps enormously. Campus student organizations sometimes sponsor job fairs at which prospective employers describe what their companies do and indicate what sort of employees they seek.

"Your school may have a useful 'peer advising' program in which experienced students describe their views of particular courses and teachers. Peer advisors can be helpful, but remember that your tastes and learning styles may be different from theirs. Note that 'extra credit' is often a myth: If your course is graded on a curve, you may end up being penalized for NOT doing the extra credit work. Finally, in case your haven't figured it out yet, your books will cost an arm and a leg, and the introductory texts may weigh a ton. But think twice before trying to sell them at the end of the term, since you may want to refer to them in the years to come."

10.2 Those Non-Technical Electives

Why should a busy and promising engineering student have to take those five-unit humanistic and social-studies (Hum/Soc) electives? The modes of thinking in them are often so unscientific. Most of the other students in them are really different, and those classes are held clear across campus in a large, crowded lecture hall. Your engineering advisor probably doesn't even talk to you about which non-technical courses you should take, just about how many you must have. And it's rumored that they only look at your technical grade-point average when you apply for a job or graduate school. So what gives?

You can probably guess much of what we'll say next: Part of the value of those courses is exactly the diversity of their subject matter, viewpoint, and student composition. In the late 1980s the business press commented widely on how industry in the United States was looking more for graduates with good preparation in, or exposure to, the humanities, because those graduates were able to reason and weigh different hypotheses well. Another feature of those courses that technical students often complain about — the large amount of reading they require — has its flip side, too. Technical texts usually require you to read very slowly, word by word, perhaps only a few pages a day, one book per term. Believe it or not, continued exposure to this may get you in the habit of reading v-e-r-y—s-l-o-w-l-y. In the Hum/Soc courses, the book-a-week pace is different, but you might find it has survival value in your later professional life. There you have to skim over or be buried by the mounds of technical reports, journals, memos, and professional junk mail that you'll receive.

The "concept count" is an illuminating indication of another difference between technical and Hum/Soc courses. Someone actually tallied the number of new "concepts" introduced in typical college courses, looking at an introductory philosophy course, a modern European history course, an introductory chemical engineering course, and so on. The finding was that the technical courses introduced many more concepts per term, but those introduced in the Hum/Soc courses were more global. For example, the chemical engineers got the concept of "valence," but the philosophers got "Good" and "Evil." The count in Hum/Soc courses was around fifty per term, while the technical courses averaged about three times that.

Everyone agrees that the Hum/Soc courses are very different from technical courses, but many engineers who've completed college consider their well-chosen Hum/Soc courses to have been worthwhile, and, in some cases, the sources of life-long interests.

10.3 On Language

If the only language you know is English, start learning another language. Computer languages don't count. An Asian language would be best, and if English is not your first language, you should aim to be relatively comfortable speaking and writing English fairly soon.

Why should you do these things? Aren't people who go into engineering often "bad" at languages? And aren't Asian languages very different from English and so almost impossible to learn when you're an adult?

It's true that years ago, an engineer in the United States could get along purely in English. There was some important scientific literature in German, but the feeling was that if any of it was really important someone would translate it into English. Contrast that earlier time with conditions today, when we find that the cars and electronic equipment we buy come to the United States from Japan or Korea, when travel to other countries often does not require a visa, and when the countries of Western Europe have agreed on a common currency. It is also difficult today to identify the nationality of many companies, since so many international buy-outs and mergers have taken place.

These changes mean that you, as a working engineer, will be learning from, working with, competing with, and selling to citizens of countries other than the United States. So, as a practical matter, it would be advisable to broaden your view so that it extends comfortably outside the United States. The study of language can be an important component of such a broadening.

Here are some reasons that we have found learning another language to be worthwhile:

- Most languages have characteristic ways of expressing ideas. To the extent that those are different from our customary ways, observing them is broadening.

- Through studying a foreign language, you may get some insight into the people who use that language. You'll need to pick a good teacher to get both the language and the cultural view of the people, but such teachers do exist.

- If you have even a rudimentary ability to use some foreign language, you may find that your employer may ask you to use that skill professionally and get paid for doing it — in money or with an assignment to that country for awhile. Whether you travel for fun or professionally, you'll find that the experience of living in another country will be much more memorable if you know and can use at least some of the local language. In other words, when choosing a language course, be sure that it involves conversation.

- Hard to measure, but certainly real to many people, is the pleasure of meeting the challenge of learning something new, such as a very different language.

10.4 Learning Styles, Mental Models, Creativity, and Brainstorming

Any parent who's tried it has found that you can't really teach a child to ride a bicycle. What you can do, however, is to set up the conditions under which the child can learn. We believe that the same is true of teaching and learning engineering. This book, and the lab and instructor's manuals that accompany it, are attempts to provide the setting in which you can learn.

Learning Styles

To learn most effectively, you should reflect on your personal <u>learning styles</u>. How have you learned most quickly or well in the past? Perhaps it was through reading. If so, did you learn most from the text, the graphics, or the mathematical analyses? Perhaps the combination of all of those was important to your learning. Have you learned well by listening to someone describe how things worked? Maybe your best learning experiences involved experimenting — or playing around on your own or under direction — with equipment. Likely, asking questions of your peers and mentors contributed to your learning. Reflect on what worked best for you in the past; that indicates your own learning style, so you should seek out those opportunities again in this course.

Mental Models

Psychologists and biochemists are still trying to find the mechanisms by which people learn. While we all wait for their definitive answers, it does seem to us that we, Dick and Roger, learn best by deliberately associating new information with things we already know. By hanging new concepts on the same mental hooks as related familiar concepts, we can make sense of the new, remember it, and work with it.

An example is the subject of waves. It seems like we associate a new fact about a light wave, for example, with what we know about audible sound waves, and that in turn with what we learned experimentally and visually about water waves at the beach. In this way, we have built up <u>mental models</u> of waves of all kinds. We encourage you to do the same, constructing your own mental models of current, voltage, and even entire computers.

What you develop are your mental models, but you might profitably ask your instructors about what mental models they have developed while studying this subject. You'll probably find that by attending to your mental models, you can find your way more surely than if you merely memorize or start calculating immediately as you start to work on a new problem.

Creativity and Brainstorming

It's been reported that students in college math courses often report feeling that they could never be professional mathematicians — they don't think they'd ever be as creative as the professional mathematicians whose theorems they're studying. This negative assessment could result in part from the way college math is usually taught, where it seems as if all the progress was made by wizards and not by flesh-and-blood human beings. The truth is, when you look carefully into almost any great discovery, such as deciphering the structure of DNA, you find that a series of small steps led incrementally up to the final act. What the successful scientists — Watson and Crick, in this case — did is something that you can do: Learn thoroughly about the subject, become familiar with what has been established to date, and work hard in a dedicated fashion on the problem at hand. For more on this topic, see the book by Robert Weisberg, *Creativity: Beyond the Myth of Genius*, referenced in Chapter 9.

We personally don't think that one teaches people to be creative: One encourages and allows it. A setting where being creative is cultivated is the <u>brainstorming session</u>. In it, a number of people gather to seek solutions to some problem. Experience shows that the most successful brainstorming session has no set ending time and involves three elements:

1. **Formulating the problem precisely.** Often, this can be done most efficiently by one participant before the session begins.

2. **Suggesting possible solutions with little regard for supposed constraints.** Someone should record, on a chalk or white board, or on a large pad on an easel, quickly and concisely the suggestions as they're made for all to view as this phase proceeds. The crucial ground rule for this phase is that <u>no one criticizes any solution proposed</u>. Censorship is out, for the time being. Another way of putting it is that this is the time for all participants to attempt the "willful suspension of disbelief."

   In a productive brainstorming session, you may find some very outlandish (and humorous!) solutions being suggested. When the flow of suggestions has subsided, you're ready for return to rationality in the final phase.

3. **Critically examining the solutions proposed.** Identify the ones that singly, in combination, or with modification really solve the problem at hand.

Here's an example of a real brainstorming session. In a seminar for college seniors, we asked students to make lists of what had "bugged" them about their college experience. From these lists, we found a promising theme that we took as the problem to solve:

"The routine here is squelching student creativity."

Phase Two began with students calling out partial solutions, such as no homework assignments, the college should support more social events for students, and so on. Suggestions became wilder and funnier, reaching a peak with "Join the Army." As things began to subside, Phase Three began with an examination of all the suggestions that had been written on the board, to see what might actually work. Some apparently feasible remedies were identified, and students left with a plan to seek implementation of those.

10.5 Specialties Within Electrical and Computer Engineering

Each college has its own way of organizing the specialties within electrical and computer engineering. The three intersecting circles in Figure 10.1 represent one way of looking at the specialties that make up electrical engineering and computer science.

The lower circles contain the foundations for topics in the topmost circle. On the right is "Computer Science," which consists of relatively theoretical topics such as complexity theory, artificial intelligence, computability, programming languages, compiler theory, real-time operating systems, and so on. The leftmost circle represents the "Electrical Engineering" fundamentals, topics such as solid-state electronics, optics, electronic circuit design, and electronic network theory. Topics in the upper circle, labelled "Information Engineering", include digital signal processing (DSP), computer networks, control theory, and so on. The regions where these circles overlap represent topics on which people primarily in one circle or another cooperate. An example is the cooperation of optical device specialists in the "Electrical Engineering" circle with information network specialists in the "Information Engineering" circle to tackle optical communication problems. You could expand this sort of diagram to indicate interactions with disciplines other than electrical engineering and computer science. For example, you could represent in this way the strong involvement of materials scientists and engineers with those working in solid-state and optical devices, or mathematicians working with theoretical computer scientists.

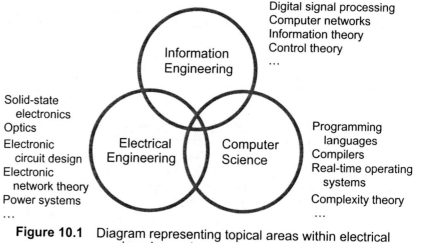

Figure 10.1　Diagram representing topical areas within electrical engineering and computer sciences

10.6 Courses, Industry, and Graduate School

In addition to deciding what technical area you will focus on in your undergraduate years, you must choose specific courses from the wide assortment that your school offers. You may also need to make decisions regarding working in industry during your undergraduate years. Finally, what about graduate school? Here are some of our thoughts.

Courses

To what extent should you specialize while in an undergraduate engineering program? You will have to decide what's best for you, and you should bring up this question with your faculty and peer advisors, advanced students, and anyone in industry that you can question. Our advice is to be sure that your program includes two kinds of courses: subjects that might be useful at any time in an engineering career and subjects that are current enough to help you get a job as soon as you obtain your desired degree.

What subjects might these both be? The first kind are useful subjects that don't change very rapidly, such as mathematics or electromagnetic theory. When some new engineering device is invented or useful new phenomena are discovered, the person who has some background in such fundamental subjects will be better able than others to tool up for productive work in the new field. Revolutionary innovations from the past that required people to leap into new areas rapidly include the transistor, the laser, and the integrated circuit. When these radically different devices appear, there is a major change in technical thinking — what has been termed a "paradigm shift" — that requires flexibility in one's thinking.

The second category of subjects includes topics from current technology that you know will change at some time, but for which there appear to be job openings in the near future. Examples are currently popular programming systems, and current technologies for fabricating integrated circuits. Certainly 10 years from now, there will be almost entirely new techniques in these fields, but, in the meantime, you will have been earning a salary!

Industrial Experience

We strongly recommend getting industrial engineering experience while you are an undergraduate, whether through a summer job or a cooperative-study program. For most engineers, industry is the "real world" and the sooner you learn about it the better. Students who return to academia after a three- or six-month job in industry tend to be better focused than their peers and better able to get on with the job at hand. You may also identify from such experience certain topics within engineering that don't interest you, and this can save you from wasting your time on those.

Graduate Study

Let's start with a short quiz about graduate study. Which of the following possible reasons for going to graduate school are valid:

1. You haven't been able to decide what else to do after college.
2. Your Mother has a Ph. D. degree.
3. You'll get a higher salary than you will with just a Bachelor's degree.
4. You want to continue learning.
5. The world outside academia scares you.
6. You've never worked in industry.

7. There's an economic downturn, so it's a good time to stay in school.

Depending on your own life experience so far, any of the reasons above may be valid — for you. We suggest, however, that the best reason for going on for graduate study is the additional freedom those degrees bring in choosing your work.

Here's what we mean. If you enter industry with a Bachelor's degree in engineering, the tasks that you work on will be chosen for the most part by someone else — your boss. If you choose to do some graduate study, in one additional year, you can usually earn a Master's degree. This will enable you to delve further into several technical topics; if you then enter industry, you will probably be given somewhat more freedom to choose what part of a project you work on and what approaches you'll take in the engineering choices you make. Finally, if you continue on for the Doctor of Philosophy (Ph. D.) degree, you will likely spend four or five more years at the university, taking courses in a major field of specialization and likely two minor fields; you must also complete a body of research that contributes new knowledge to the field. The Ph.D. (or its design-oriented counterpart, the Doctor of Engineering degree) is a formal certification — some liken it to a union card — for teaching in a university. Alternatively, if you enter industrial employment, with either doctoral degree you would have considerably more freedom than Bachelor's and Master's degree holders to select the problems you tackle.

On Communicating

Many of your engineering classmates will say that they hate writing. Many professional engineers will say the same thing. When surveys have been made about what is most feared by the population at large, the top fear is public speaking! Many people even rank it above dying as something they fear.

Unfortunately for engineers, these two forms of communicating — writing and speaking — typically occupy about one-third of a professional engineer's time. The message is that if you plan on being an engineer, you'd better learn how to communicate.

That term includes several activities: writing letters, memos, and reports; talking in person or over the phone with other engineers, with customers, and with vendors, and communicating via electronic mail, faxes, and the like. Since you'll be spending a lot of time communicating, it makes sense to do what you can to become proficient at the activity, if only to minimize the difficulties it causes you.

Fortunately, all these forms of communicating can be approached from the same starting point: **Identify your audience.** After that's been done, **determine what you want to achieve** with this communication to this audience. In other words, approach the task of communicating professionally just as you do your technical work — **identify the problem before looking for solutions.** If you really determine what you want to achieve with a given communication — such as a letter or an oral report — then you've gone 90% of the way toward solving the problem.

Read the following examples of problems you might face and think about their solutions:

Case 1: You are to write a 10-page report on a topic of your choice, instead of taking a final exam this term, and your instructor has asked that you prepare an outline for approval before you start writing the paper. Describe what you think your audience (the instructor) wants and what you should provide.

Case 2: You are applying for a summer job and have been asked to provide a resumé. What should the resumé contain?

Case 3: It is the end of your summer job, and your boss has asked for a report on what you did. Why does the boss ask for this, and what level of detail should your report contain? How should the report be organized?

Case 4: You've been told that an important customer is considering placing an order with your company, is sending three representatives to the company next Tuesday, and you (as chief of the X-Widget development team) are to give them a 15-minute presentation. What do you want to accomplish, and how might you do it?

Case 5: You've finally decided to go out on your own and start a small company to develop and manufacture a new machine for medical diagnosis. You're going to talk to the partners of a venture capital firm, hoping to interest them in investing in your company. What should your presentation contain?

In the pages that follow, we present some tips about writing and offer templates that show the forms that many types of written professional communications take.

11.1 Avis Contraire

Each line below, from William Safire, *Fumblerules: A Lighthearted Guide to Grammar and Good Usage* (Garden City, NY: Doubleday Press, 1975), provides a suggestion about writing — while contradicting its own suggestion in the process of stating it. Probably, there's an ancient name for this rhetorical technique, but we've been unable to discover what it is, so we made up a French term that feels right: "avis contraire,"[1] meaning "contrary advice".

1. Avoid run-on sentences they are hard to read.
2. No sentence fragments.
3. It behooves us to avoid archaisms.
4. Also, avoid awkward or affected alliteration.
5. Don't use no double negatives.
6. If I've told you once, I've told you a thousand times: Resist hyperbole.
7. Avoid commas, that are not necessary.
8. Verbs has to agree with their subjects.
9. Avoid trendy locutions that sound flaky.
10. Writing carefully, dangling participles should not be used.
11. Kill all exclamation points!!!
12. Never use a long word when a diminutive one will do.
13. Proofread carefully to see if you any words out.
14. Take the bull by the hand, and don't mix metaphors.
15. Don't verb nouns.
16. Never, ever use repetitive redundancies.

---

[1] (pronounced 'ah-vee kon-trair')

17. Last but not least, avoid cliches like the plague.

11.2 On Brevity

Brevity is often effective. Here are several real examples of extreme brevity. You should decide for yourself about their effectiveness.

1. The entire text of an actual recommendation "letter" written about a student by a teacher:

   "Naaahh!"

2. A famous single-sentence book review by literary curmudgeon Ambrose Bierce:

   "The covers of this book are too far apart."

3. This one takes a little more explanation. It is the entire (approximate) text of a so-called "correspondence item" (relatively short technical article) that appeared in the technical journal, the *Proceedings of the IEEE*. The item's author, R. H. Barker, had earlier found particular sequences of bits — 1s and 0s — that had a very special kind of internal order. These sequences, which became known as "Barker codes," could be embedded in a stream of digital data from a spacecraft, for example, to indicate where the first bit of an eight-bit character appeared. You'd need this information in order to decode a message by converting the bit stream into a set of numbers and letters.

   Barker had found special sequences of bits that had internal order that enabled them to be found easily in a stream of seemingly random bits. The sequences that he'd found and published earlier had 3, 5, 7 or 13 bits. People wondered whether any longer Barker codes might exist. Barker found one such code and made the information known with a single line of text:

   "The Barker code for n = 26 is **11111110000111100110101010**."

11.3 The Secret of Vigorous Writing

In their famous 78-page book, *"The Elements of Style,"* William Strunk and E. B. White summarized the secret of vigorous writing. What they wrote appears on the next page.

VIGOROUS WRITING IS CONCISE.

11.4 It Doesn't Have to be Dull

The following two excerpts show that writing about technical topics can be made very interesting:

"Two computer programs in their native habitat — the memory chips of a digital computer — stalk each other from address to address. Sometimes they go scouting for the enemy, sometimes they lay down a barrage of numeric bombs; sometimes they copy themselves out of danger or stop to repair damage. This is the game I call Core War."

From "Computer Recreations," *Scientific American*, May 1984.

"In the early 1800s a French army captain named Mingaud took up the game of billiards at the prison where he was doing time. Sticking a bit of leather on the tip of his all-wood cue stick, he discovered that when he hit the ball off-center — something his predecessors sought to avoid — the extra friction at the tip gave the ball spin and made it do wondrous things. He promptly asked for an extension of his sentence so he could practice."

From "Pool: Isaac Newton meets Minnesota Fats," *Science 84*, 1984.

Templates for Technical Writing

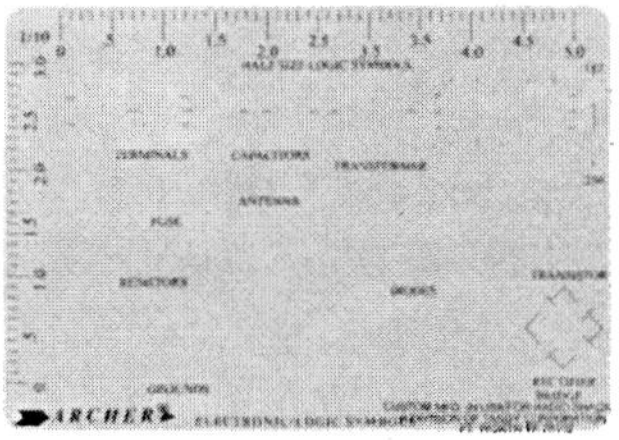

Figure 12.1
Template for drawing
electronic components
(Courtesy of RadioShack)

Before computer graphics programs existed, engineers used plastic drawing aids called templates to draw everything from piping layouts to electrical circuits. Long before that, woodworkers and weavers used templates made from thin metal sheets for reproducing patterns in wood or cloth. On the pages following this discussion are templates for some of the types of technical writing that engineers may do.

The dictionary defines a template as "a pattern or gauge … used as a guide in making something accurately." Templates, such as the drawing template shown in Figure 12.1, save a worker time by providing the forms needed for a given product. It is possible — though unconventional — to think of templates for much of engineering writing because of the frequent re-use of patterns in such writing. For example, if you work for an engineering firm, the periodic progress reports you'll be required to write will have a regular form or pattern. The same can be said for personal resumés, patents, and for most articles in technical journals. The use of conventional forms saves the reader time (it's easy to find the elements quickly) and ensures that all the important elements are included.

You'll see some of these templates in this chapter, but first a word of assurance: The fact that much of the professional writing you'll do in the "real world" must follow a pattern needn't force you to write colorless prose. Your writing can still have a personal style and be interesting, instructive, and even memorable. It's up to you to make it outstanding.

Consider the parallel between technical writing and musical composition. Both jazz and Baroque classical music had patterns within which composers worked. While much of the music written in these forms was not remarkable, that of the outstanding jazz and Baroque musicians was superb.

On the pages that follow, you'll find commented mock-ups or excerpted one-page samples of typical engineering writing. (As you can tell, in some cases, the material is entirely fictional.) To the right of each example are "flags" that point out particular features or conventions (except in the case of the resumes, where two examples are given that are fairly self-explanatory). While some of these forms may not concern you early in your engineering education, you'll probably use or encounter them all at some point in your career.

12.1 Why Just One Page?

The writing examples that follow each occupy just one page (when printed with normal-sized 12-point font). This makes it easier to summarize these forms for you, but there's a more important reason for using a single page where possible. Communications written for high-level managers must be concise, or they won't be read. You can write a long report for a manager, but it had better begin with a very brief "Executive Summary" that hits the high points on no more than a single page. Many managers also like such summaries to use bullets (•) in order to

- identify main points
- enumerate options concisely
- enhance readability

You'll find templates for the following:

1. Student laboratory report
2. Student term paper
3. Resumé
4. Technical journal article
5. Proposal for research and development (R&D) funding
6. U.S. patent
7. Business plan for a startup company

These are arranged in roughly the chronological order in which you might encounter them in your own career.

A final note: Computerized writing aids exist! Some computer applications provide help with your writing. For example, the Microsoft Word word-processing program is one of several that has an *outlining* feature. You can outline your writing with a number of headings and subheadings, and then write the text that belongs under each. A toggle permits you to hide all but initial lines of the text so as to focus (again) on the outline. You can change the order of presentation of topics by moving the outline headings, and the associated text follows automatically.

12.2 A Writing Tip from TV

Your writing may have surprising impact if you use a technique supposedly employed when editing TV commentaries: Throw away the first two paragraphs and start with the third one. You'll find that often, the initial paragraphs of your writing serve mostly to get you rolling. That may help you, but it may bore the reader. Try it!

12.3 Student Laboratory Report

Topic, authors, course, and date clearly listed; check with instructor for exact report format desired.

Note the use of headings throughout for organizing report.

References to original literature, textbook, etc., facilitate looking up details.

(We use ... in these notes to indicate text left out.)

Perhaps also list exact serial numbers, so you could check later on calibrations in case of strange results.

Note listing of probable error throughout.

In a formal report or article, each table would have a caption.

Units and probable errors listed.

Always summarize conclusions reached, discuss error, and suggest improvements if you think of any.

Use standard accepted reference format.

Laboratory Report: Cold Fusion
T. Swift and M. Thatcher
Nuclear Engineering 122: Alternative Energy Approaches
13 August 1991

Objectives:

1. Assemble cold fusion apparatus.
2. Run test and determine whether output energy exceeds input.

Background:

In 1989 chemists Pons and Fleischman[1], U. of Utah, made a controversial report of the production of excess energy in an electrolytic cell consisting of a glass (Mason) jar containing heavy water and palladium electrodes to which a power supply was connected. ... Controlled nuclear fusion was believed achieved.

Equipment:

Mason jar (Del Monte Co., Salinas, CA) No. 6 size. Palladium electrodes (Electrodes 'R Us, Palm Beach, FL) 15 x 2 x 0.1 cm3. Heavy water electrolyte (Calistoga Geyser Co., Santa Rosa, CA) 1 liter. Thermocouples (Omega, Stamford, CT) Type K. Geiger counter (Edmund Scientific, Barrington, NJ) Model N. Power supply ...

Test Procedures, Data, Sources of Error and Analysis:

We measured radioactive count before and after power supply was turned on, temperature of apparatus, supply voltage and current, all to ±3%. We converted temperature readings to thermal energies using handbook values of the thermal properties of electrolyte, electrodes and the Mason jar. Computer analysis of all energy inputs and outputs was attempted (unfortunately we had a PC head crash, so some data were lost). Data and computed energies are in Table I:

Table I.

Emissions (no./min)	Voltage (volts)	Current (mA)	Temp. ($^{\circ}$C)	Net energy (mJ)
306±12	0	0	24.1±0.1	0
307±12	-12±0.1	27±0.2	26.3±0.1	0.0006±0.07
...				

Conclusions:

Like the original investigators, we were unable to prove convincingly that the cold fusion process results in net energy production. Possible sources of error are ... An improved experiment would be ...

[1] See .... (References should be made to original articles that are relevant.)

12.4 Student Term Paper

Note the reference to the source from which this was adapted.

Title is indicative of contents, while being interesting.

Complete identification is appreciated by instructor.

Date is helpful in deciding where to file or when to toss out.

Introductory section to set the stage and to interest reader; this first part need not have a heading if it is short.

Note how headings organize paper for reader.

Starting with a human being is often interesting, but not always possible in technical writing.

References permit checking original sources.

(We use … in these notes to indicate text left out.)

Table has explanatory caption; we would refer to it in text as Table II (with capital T), as it is a specific table (proper noun).

Both summarize what has been covered, and comment on it.

Use standard accepted reference format.

Illustrative adaptation of the article "Of Mice and Windows," by David Patterson, *IEEE Electro-Technology Review*, 1984.

Of Mice and Windows
Olga Petersen
CS 122: Computer History
13 August 1991

The Apple Macintosh computer is a revolutionary product in the microcomputer marketplace. Computer store customers must marvel at how Apple could invent such a radically different microcomputer. As is usually the case, this revolutionary invention is really an evolutionary by-product of decades of work by dozens of people at several institutions. Key inventions used are the mouse, overlapped windows and pop-up menus. This report examines some of these inventions and their creators.

Beginnings

The story begins with Doug Engelbart in 1950. As a graduate student in the earliest days of computing, Engelbart dreamed of humans interacting with computers. This dream was a radical notion, since this was before programming languages were invented and the "user interface" was a bank of toggle switches. [1] Doug's advisor told him to keep his ideas to himself so others would not question his sanity. He kept quiet, but he also dedicated his career to making his dream come true.

One problem was the way humans pointed to information on the computer's screen. A solution came to Doug while attending a boring lecture at a computer conference: a box that could be held in a hand resting on a table next to the screen, with a marker on the screen tracking the movements of the box. The size of the box and the wire connecting the box to the computer led Engelbart's group at the Stanford Research Institute to nickname this pointing device a mouse. …

Other Contributions

Five years later … a group of computer scientists at Xerox still harbored Engelbart's dream. Alan Kay became the resident visionary, conceiving the dynabook, a book-sized computer so useful that you'd never leave home without it. …

Table II. Selected computer inventions and their inventor.

INVENTION	DESCRIPTION	INVENTOR
Overlapped windows	User can overlap work areas	Dan Ingalls
Pop-up menus	User selects from boxed options that pop up on screen	Dan Ingalls
…		

Summary and Comments

In 1984 Apple announced the Macintosh. A tasteful combination of low-cost hardware, high-volume manufacturing technology, careful tuning of the software, and polishing of the user interface — and two decades of ideas and hard work by dozens of people — made this microcomputer an "overnight" commercial and artistic success.

[1] See … (References would be located in footnotes at bottom of page or end of paper.)

12.5 Resumés

Janice Knight

3317 Bellevue
Oakland, CA 94610

Home Phone: (510)555-5831
Work Phone: (510)555-1725

Objective
A position using laboratory, data management and research skills in biomedical research.

Skills Summary

Laboratory
Performed analytical determinations

Data Management
Executed data management and interactive programs to create large computer files in preparation for computer simulations of insect/plant fecundity. Reproduced and interpreted graphs of transformed data.

Research
Assist with curation of zoological specimens. Consulted with investigators on specific research topics. Wrote periodic reports to summarize progress.

Education
University of California, Berkeley
BA Biology May 1995   Specialization: Cellular Biology
Relevant Coursework:

Cell Physiology	Genetics
Chemistry	Mammalian Physiology/Anatomy
Entomology	Vertebrate Embryology

Special Projects
Coordinated two-day seminar on genetic research.
Volunteer instructor for independent biology course, Berkeley Public Schools.
Senior Research: Isolation and Characterization of Plasmid DNA.

Experience

Spring 1995
Laboratory Assistant, U.S. Department of Agriculture, Division of Biological Control, Albany CA.

Summer 1994
Hostess/Waitress, Highlands Inn, Carmel, CA.

Spring 1994
Laboratory Assistant, University of California, Biology Department, Berkeley, CA.

Fall 1992
Hospital Aide, Children's Hospital, Oakland, CA.

Interests
Cross country skiing, swimming, quilting.

JASON LEE
65 Hearst Avenue
Berkeley, CA 94708
(510) 555-6543

OBJECTIVE: Physics-related summer employment

EDUCATION: University of California, Berkeley
BA Physics, May 1996
Campus Activities: Sigma Pi Sigma, Physics Honor Society
University Symphony Orchestra (clarinet)

TECHNICAL COURSES:

Physics of Scientists	Properties of Materials
Quantum Mechanics	Calculus
Electromagnetism & Optics	Differential Equations
Advanced Electrical	Linear Algebra
Laboratory	Abstract Algebra
Introduction to Electrical Engineering	

EXPERIENCE:

Summer 1994
Lawrence Berkeley Laboratory, Berkeley, CA
Research Assistant: Performed sulfur solubility experiments; prepared samples and analyzed them with a gas chromatograph. Created a computer database to track sabbaticals.

Summer 1993
University of California, Berkeley,
University Art Museum, Berkeley, CA
Gallery Attendant: Provided security for the art displays.

AREAS OF SPECIAL KNOWLEDGE: FORTRAN, BASIC computer languages; UNIX operating system; electrical circuits design; oscilloscopes and gas chromatograph.

COMMUNITY ACTIVITIES: Boy Scouts of America - Troop Leader
YMCA - Basketball Coach

12.6 Technical Journal Article

Note the reference to the source from which this was adapted.

Title succinctly describes the subject. (Choose the words carefully for sensible retrieval.)

Arrange names of multiple authors in descending order of contribution to the work, or alphabetically if all contributed equally.

Abstract cites some real results of the work.

Numbers used in subject classification for retrieval.

Headings used for organizing to benefit reader. Introduction refers to background literature, sets the stage for this work, defines the problem considered by this investigator.

Figure refers to specific illustration, so it is a proper noun (capital f).

Note that this author actually used the personal pronoun "I" and active voice, rather than "A heliox gas was used".

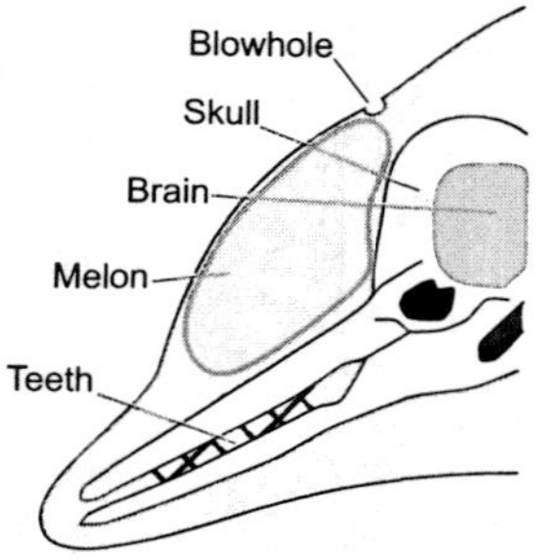

Figure has explanatory concise caption.

Equation is punctuated as if it were being read aloud.

Note the punctuation of i.e., (which stands for "id est." Latin for "that is").

Discussion of results is an essential part of such a paper.

Standard reference format; details given in this society's "Style Manual."

Illustrative adaptation of a journal article by Mats Amundin, *J. Acoust. Soc. Am.*, 90 [1] , 53-59 (July 91).

Helium effects on the sounds made by the Harbor porpoise

Mats Amundin
University of Stockholm, Department of Functional Morphology, S-10691 Stockholm and Kolmårdens Djurpark, S-61800 Kolmården, Sweden.

In order to determine in which medium, air or tissue, harbor porpoise (*Phocoena phocoena*) sounds are produced, the air in the nasal cavities was substituted with heliox (80% helium and 20% oxygen), and the effect on click frequency spectrum was studied. ... The results show that the stronger high-frequency component was not at all affected by the heliox, suggesting that it was produced and shaped in some tissue structure(s), and not in gas.

PACS numbers: 43.80.Lb, 43.80.Jz, 43.80.Nd

INTRODUCTION

Recent hypotheses on sound production in dolphins suggest a sound source at or near the nasal plugs. Giro and Dubrovskii (1975) suggest that the low-frequency component of the delphiniid sonar clicks is shaped by resonance .... of the diverticula situated above the bony nares. ... This paper deals with the possible air cavity resonance shaping/filtering of the ... click emissions of the harbor porpoise, (*Phocoena phocoena*). Details of the anatomy of the upper airways in the harbor porpoise ... are shown in Fig. 1.

I. MATERIALS AND METHODS

The experimental subjects were one female and three male harbor porpoises. ... During each recording session ... they were held 30-40 cm below the surface of the water in a stretcher.

I used a heliox gas mixture of 80% helium and 20% oxygen, ±0.1%. Replacing air in a fixed cavity with this mixture ... would shift the normal high-frequency peak frequency of 130-242 kHz. ...

... where the velocity of sound, v_s, is

$$v_s = (K/p)^{1/2},$$

K being the bulk modulus and p the density of the liquid (i.e., the water)....

Blowhole
Skull
Brain
Melon
Teeth

Figure 1. Section of porpoise head. Blowhole, skull....

III. DISCUSSION

... Although the exact process behind the shaping of the high-frequency click remains unclear, it is obviously not a gas bound phenomenon, as its spectrum was unaffected by the heliox gas mixture.

---

[1] Giro, L. R., and Dubrovskii, N. A. (1975): "Possible role of pericranial diverticula in the production of the dolphin echo-location signals," *Sov. Phys. Acoust.* 20(5), 428-430.

12.7 Proposal for R&D Funding

Note the attractive, but meaningful, title.
This is the hypothetical agency from which funding is sought.
Make it easy for the customer (or agency) to contact you.
Make a clear summary of what you are proposing, and use a positive tone.
State the problem to be solved.

Outline your solution.

Divide the work clearly into parts having measurable milestones, time lines, and costs.

Tabular or graphical presentation conveys information quickly.

Shows fund flow by year and category of use.

Overhead is a percentage of costs other than equipment; may be around 50-60% for universities, >100% in companies.
Full proposal would contain info about company and people who will direct and work on project.

"Abundant Electric Power"

Proposal to the Exploratory Branch, National Funding Agency, Washington, DC
Submitted 14 August 1991 by: Macro Thoughts, Inc.
Milpitis, CA 94555
Contact: Dr. Henrietta Able, (510)555-1776

Summary: We propose a novel solution to California and the World's electric supply problem. We request funds for a twelve-stage project that will demonstrate our approach to electric generation via inexpensive modular wind-powered generators.

Background: It is well known that humans, whose average thermal energy output equals about 100 watts each, in highly developed countries consume electric power at a kilowatt rate. Fossil fuels are being exhausted, and other sources such as fish oil have proven inadequate. Renewable energy sources such as solar and wind must be utilized.

The Macro Thoughts Solution: Extensive analysis and proprietary computer studies have shown that we could meet foreseeable electric power needs with the power developed by a large bank of engines from old Lionel model electric trains that are outfitted with propellers and set up along seacoasts facing into the wind.

Project Phases, Timing, Milestones and Funding:

Phase 1: Feasibility Demonstration: Utilize one (1) Lionel toy train locomotive; measure its power output on windy and still days; analyze results.
Phase 2: Acquire 2999 more locomotives and test response; address networking problem;   analyze results.
Phase 3: Perform economic analysis for 3000-element system; extrapolate to worldwide expansion.
...

PHASE/TASK	YEAR 1	YEAR 2	YEAR 3	YEAR 4	YEAR 5
1/purchase	x				
1/attach propeller	xx				
2/purchase	.	xxx			
...					

FUNDS REQD	YEAR 1	YEAR 2	YEAR 3	YEAR 4	YEAR 5
Salaries	$500,000	$1,500,000	$2,000,000	$3,000,000	$1,500,000
Equipment*	$57,000	$30,000	...		
Supplies	$37	$92,500	...		
Travel	$5000	$12,000	...		
Overhead	$247,468	$786,205	...		
TOTALS	$809,505	$2,420,705	...		

* Macro Thoughts, Inc. does not charge overhead on equipment purchases

About Macro Thoughts, Inc.: In business continuously since 1989, Macro Thoughts, Inc. is a full-spectrum interdisciplinary research, development and manufacturing firm located in the heart of California's famed Silicone Valley. Our staff includes electrical and mechanical engineers, computer scientists, and support technicians. C.V.s of key staff members who will carry out this vital project appear in Appendix A. Appendix B contains a floor plan of our building and a photo of our facilities. ...

12.8 Patent

Note dates of issue and date filed (item [22]).

Can you figure out how it works from the ABSTRACT?

Inventor has assigned invention to employer (U. of California) according to a signed agreement about how any proceeds would be shared.

Classes indicate other patents searched to see if invented previously by others; even in 1991, this is hand searching.

These are related references to U.S. and foreign patents, and journals.

The claims are what you really have protected.

Descriptive material, written by patent attorney, describes invention fully.

An invention must meet some need and be useful.

Drawings for patents have fixed, distinctive style; structures are what are protected.

The claims are the most important part of a patent.

United States Patent [19]
White

[11] Patent Number: 4,668,861

[45] Date of Patent: May 26, 1987

[54] TACTILE SENSOR EMPLOYING A LIGHT CONDUCTING ELEMENT AND A RESILIENTLY DEFORMABLE SHEET

[75] Inventor: Richard M. White, Berkeley, Calif.

[73] Assignee: The Regents of the University of California, Berkeley, Calif.

[21] Appl. No.: 680,759

[22] Filed: Dec. 12, 1984

[51] Int. Cl. H01J 5/16

[52] U.S.Cl. 250/227; 340/407; 901/33

[58] Field of Search .... 250/227; 340/347 P, 340/780, 365 P, 407, 825.19; 901/46, 47, 33; 350/96.23

[56] References Cited

U.S. PATENT DOCUMENTS

3,624,619 11/1971 Ambrosio .... 340/347 P
4,484,179 11/1984 Kasday 250/227

FOREIGN PATENT DOCUMENTS

2058394 4/1981 United Kingdom 350/96.23

OTHER PUBLICATIONS

J.D. Chodera and M. Lord. "Retraining of Standing Balance Using a Pedobarograph," Proceedings of the Sixth International Symposium on External Control of Human

Extremities Aug. 28-Sep. 1, 1978, Dubrovnik, pp. 333-341.

[57] ABSTRACT

A tactile sensing device for use in robotics and medical prosthetics includes. transparent sheet-like element and a second resilient sheet-like element positioned adjacent the first transparent element. A light detection and imaging means is positioned to observe the interface between the two elements. A light source is provided to illuminate the interior of one of the two elements. Any object pressing against the resilient element deforms the same into contact with the transparent element. Areas of contact caused by the pressing object produce a lighted area that can be detected by the light detecting means. The output from the light detecting means may be processed by a computer and an image of the contact area produced by the pressing object can he displayed on a monitor or processed to operate an electromechanical control.

8 Claims, 14 Drawing Figures

BACKGROUND OF THE INVENTION

With the advent of sophisticated electronic circuitry, ... the problem of ... producing high quality, high volume industrial parts has begun to be solved. ... From the standpoint of robotics and medical prostheses, a "human hand-like" apparatus would be an extremely important and vital apparatus essential to the advancement of the art.

BRIEF DESCRIPTION OF THE INVENTION

The present invention relates to tactile sensors for use both in industry and in medicine ... The sensor comprises an element that has the property of conducting visible light through its interior volume, ... and a second element comprising a resilient or rubber-like material ...

It is an object of the invention to provide tactile sensing devices. ...

BRIEF DESCRIPTION OF THE DRAWINGS

In the accompanying drawings, Fig. 1 is a schematic view of a tactile sensor illustrating the principles upon which the invention operates. ...

DETAILED DESCRIPTION OF THE INVENTION

The invention comprises tactile sensing devices wherein an object ...

I claim:

1. A tactile sensor device comprising:
a first sheet-like element of light conducting material having opposed surfaces and an edge,
a second sheet-like element ...

12.9 Business Plan

Make it easy to contact you.

Executive Summary lays it out, with very positive tone; in a real case, it might summarize financial matters also.

Venture capitalists worry about three risks: technical, management, and market. Here the technical is being addressed. Note use of additional material (Exhibit 1) so flow of main text isn't disturbed.

Previous success mentioned.

Here the market is described.

Actually, approval of medical devices may take years.

ChemChip is proud of its great management team.

Timing and amounts of venture capital infusions and payments from corporate clients for whom ChemChip will develop products are crucial. Are their figures believable? What happens if the schedules slip or Client 2 doesn't decide to buy their services? Can they weather the storm?

Income (inc.) on Product 1 ramps up very rapidly. Believable?

Business Plan: ChemChip, Inc.
1 Opportunity Road, Berkeley, CA 94555
Phone: (510)555-2000   FAX: (510)555-1984

Executive Summary

The future of the chemical industry lies not in plastics but in the localized production of products in miniature chemical factories. We term this the chemical plant on-a-chip. Our unique micro-flow technology, seasoned management team and able marketing staff ensure our dominance of this exploding field. We invite venture capitalists and corporate clients to join us in this exciting and profitable enterprise.

The Technology

Working with University of California scientists, ChemChip has pioneered the microplant-on-a-chip. As shown in technical articles, conference presentations and trade journal offprints (Exhibit 1), this approach employs IC microfabrication processes to make miniature versions of the pumps, valves, mixers and other components found in the typical sprawling chemical plant. Following on our successful introduction of the ChemChip battery-powered HemoRefractoDialyzer, we are now able to engineer miniature chemical production facilities for making a wide variety of organic products for the home and office. The technology can be summarized as …

The Business Opportunity

Analysis shows that a multi-billion-dollar market exists for chemicals that can be made in miniature plants small enough to fit under the dining table. Such a plant could be powered with a single AAA battery and would convert annually up to three tons of suitable reactants into products ranging from snake anti-venom to salad dressing. Because of the chip's small size and ChemChip's excellent rapport with the regulatory agencies, rapid approval for either *in vitro* or *in vivo* use is virtually assured. A marketing study commissioned by ChemChip (Exhibit 3) shows that ….

The ChemChip Team

ChemChip is run by founders Celia Collins, CEO, and Marshall Bracken, President, both of whom have distinguished themselves managing hundreds of employees dismissed from other firms. Dr. V. Fussy leads ChemChip's research department, while Arthur Wristlock manages the production line and shipping department. Tom Friendly heads Sales. See Exhibit 5 for a corporate profile and C.V.s of team members.

Financial Schedule — Timeline and Cash Flow

Table I summarizes ChemChip's anticipated annual expenses, sales, income, and profit for its chemical plant on-a-chip. Suggested dollar amounts for Round 1 venture capital investment and corporate client contracts are indicated.

CATEGORY	YEAR 1	YEAR 2	YEAR 3	YEAR 4
Venture Cap. 1	$2,000,000			
Client 1	$500,000	$600,000	$700,000	
Client 2	$750,000	$900,000	$1,500,000	
Expenses	$900,000	$1,200,000	$1,300,000	$1,500,000
Product 1 inc.		$10,000	$500,000	$10,000,000
Product 2 inc.		$500	$250,000	$3,000,000
Profit on sales	($900,000)	($1,189,500)	($550,000)	$11,500,000

12.10 Problems

12.1 Brainstorm about and write up in a one-page report inexpensive ways of mounting solar-cell-powered flashing red lights on the 21-kilovolt distribution power lines inside your city. A constraint is that the power may not be turned off, which would anger the customers. Another constraint is cost: Tasks like this are done now at high cost by using "cherry picker" trucks that raise a worker up to the line in an insulated bucket. Think about alternatives, which could involve slingshots or catapults or... Be imaginative — humor is certainly encouraged — and use sketches to explain your suggestions.

12.2 Write, using your word processor, a one-page article about the positive and the negative aspects of the widespread use of computer networks, such as the Internet. Use the template for an article. Your article should have a title, your name as author, an introductory section, subheadings to help the reader, and at least one of each of the following: an equation (for example, expressing the growth of the net), a reference to a book or a newspaper article, and, if possible, a captioned illustration.

12.3 Prepare, using a word processor, a one-page resume for yourself that you might use when seeking a summer job at the end of this school year.

12.4 To help you look ahead a bit, prepare (using a word processor) an imaginary one-page resumé for yourself that might be used to seek a job upon graduation from college.

12.5 Using the proper template, write with your word processor a one-page proposal to a funding agency or a foundation to support an imaginary project, such as an engineering study (for example, to install an automatic pizza delivery system in your dorm) or the creation of a work of art (such as a video on the native dances of the Bronx). The proposal should contain all the elements of a real proposal — your name and hypothetical organization, contact information, a title, background of the project, your approach, a list of what will result (called deliverables), a timeline and a budget. Have fun with the content, while learning about the art of proposal writing.

The Internet

In the 1960s, decades before the Internet had been conceived, the RAND Corporation, America's foremost Cold War think tank, faced a strange strategic problem: How could the U.S. authorities successfully communicate after a nuclear war?[1]

Postnuclear America would need a command-and-control network, linked from city to city, state to state, and base to base. But no matter how thoroughly that network was armored or protected, its switches and wiring would always be vulnerable to the impact of atomic bombs. A nuclear attack would reduce any conceivable network to tatters. And how would the network itself be commanded and controlled? Any central authority, any network central citadel, would be an obvious and immediate target for an enemy missile. The center of the network would be the very first place to go.

RAND mulled over this grim puzzle in deep military secrecy, and arrived at a daring solution that was made public in 1964. In the first place, the network would "have no central authority." Furthermore, it would be "designed from the beginning to operate while in tatters." The network that was begun then, years later became the Internet.

13.1 Packets and Nodes

The principles were simple. The network itself would be assumed to be unreliable at all times. It would be designed from the get-go to transcend its own unreliability. All the nodes in the network would be equal in status to all other nodes, each node having its own authority to originate, pass, and

---

[1] Much of this is excerpted by permission from an article by Bruce Sterling titled, "A Short History of the Internet."
http://w3.aces.uiuc.edu/AIM/scale/nethistory.html

receive messages. The messages themselves would be divided into packets, each separately addressed. Each packet would begin at some specified source node, and end at some other specified destination node. Each packet would wind its way through the network on an individual basis.

The particular route that the packet took would be unimportant. Only final results would count. Basically, the packet would be tossed like a hot potato from node to node to node, more or less in the direction of its destination, until it ended up in the proper place. If big pieces of the network had been blown away, that simply wouldn't matter; the packets would still stay airborne, lateralled wildly across the field by whatever nodes happened to survive. This rather haphazard delivery system might be "inefficient" in the usual sense (especially compared to, say, the telephone system), but it would be extremely rugged.

During the 1960s, this intriguing concept of a decentralized, blastproof, packet-switching network was kicked around by RAND, MIT, and UCLA. Late in the decade, the Pentagon's Advanced Research Projects Agency (ARPA) decided to fund the ARPANET, a network of high-speed supercomputers for the sake of national research and development projects. In Fall 1969, the first network node was installed at UCLA. By December 1969, there were four nodes on the infant network.

The supercomputers — four of them at first — could transfer data on dedicated high-speed transmission lines and could even be programmed remotely from the other nodes. Scientists and researchers could share one another's computer facilities by long-distance. But by the second year of operation, an odd fact became clear: ARPANET's users had warped the computer-sharing network into a dedicated, high-speed, federally subsidized electronic post-office! The main traffic on ARPANET was not long-distance computing — instead, it was news and personal messages. Researchers were using the network to collaborate on projects, to trade notes on work and, eventually, to downright gossip and schmooze. People had their own personal user accounts on the ARPANET computers and their own personal addresses for electronic mail.

It wasn't long before the invention of the mailing-list, a broadcasting technique in which an identical message could be sent automatically to large numbers of network subscribers. Interestingly, one of the first really big mailing-lists was "SF-LOVERS," for science fiction fans. Discussing science fiction on the network was not work-related and was frowned upon by many ARPANET computer administrators, but this didn't stop it from happening.

13.2 The Network Grows

Throughout the '70s, ARPA's network grew. Its decentralized structure made expansion easy. Unlike standard corporate computer networks, the ARPA network could accommodate many different kinds of machines. As long as individual machines could speak the packet-switching *lingua franca* of the new, anarchic network, their brand-names, their content, and even their ownership were irrelevant.

As the '70s and '80s advanced, many different social groups found themselves in possession of powerful computers. It was fairly easy to link these computers to the growing network of networks. With the use of a common network protocol (Transmission Control Protocol/Internet Protocol, or TCP/IP), other entire networks fell into the digital embrace of the network, and messily adhered. The branching complex of networks came to be known as the "Internet."

Connecting to the Internet cost the taxpayer little or nothing, since each node was independent, and had to handle its own financing and its own technical requirements. The attitude was, the more, the merrier. Like the telephone network, the computer network became steadily more valuable as it embraced larger and larger territories of people and resources.

The nodes in this growing network of networks were divvied up into basic varieties. Foreign computers, and a few American ones, chose to be denoted by their geographical locations. The others were grouped by the six basic Internet "domains": gov, mil, edu, com, org, and net. Gov, mil, and edu denoted governmental, military, and educational institutions, respectively, which were, of course, the pioneers, since ARPANET had begun as a high-tech research exercise in national security. Com, however, stood for "commercial" institutions, which were soon bursting into the network like rodeo bulls, surrounded by a dust-cloud of eager non-profit "orgs." The "net" computers served as gateways between networks.

ARPANET itself formally expired in 1989, but its functions continued and steadily improved, being taken over by follow-on networks. Now, in the 2000s, there are millions of nodes in the Internet, with more coming on-line every day. Millions of people use this gigantic mother of all computer networks.

The Internet is especially popular among scientists and is probably the most important scientific instrument of the late 20th century. The powerful, sophisticated access that it provides to specialized data and personal communication has sped up the pace of scientific research enormously. The Internet's pace of growth in the early 1990s is spectacular, almost ferocious. It spread faster than cellular phones and faster than fax machines. In 1994, the growth rate was 20% a month. The number of directly connected "host" machines has been doubling every year since 1988. The Internet is moving out of its original base in military and research institutions into elementary and high schools, as well as into public libraries and the commercial sector.

Why do people want to be "on the Internet?" One of the main reasons is simple freedom. The Internet is a rare example of a true, modern, functional anarchy. There is no "Internet, Inc." There are no official censors, no bosses, no board of directors, and no stockholders. In principle, any node can speak as a peer to any other node, as long as it obeys the rules of the network protocols, which are strictly technical, not social or political.

The Internet is also a bargain. The Internet as a whole, unlike the phone system, doesn't charge for long-distance service. And unlike most commercial computer networks, it doesn't charge for access time, either. In fact the "Internet" itself, which doesn't even officially exist as an entity, never "charges" for anything. Each group of people accessing the Internet is responsible for its own machine and its own section of line. The Internet belongs to everyone and no one.

Still, its various interest groups all have a claim. Business people want the Internet put on a sounder financial footing. Government people want the Internet more fully regulated. Academics want it dedicated exclusively to scholarly research. Military people want it spyproof and secure. All these sources of conflict remain in a stumbling balance today, and the Internet, so far, remains in a thrivingly anarchical condition.

13.3 What Does One Do with the Internet?

The answer is, many different things, including mail, discussion groups, chat, telephone, video conference, streaming media, long-distance computing, file transfers, and Web browsing.

Internet mail is "e-mail," electronic mail, faster by several orders of magnitude than the U. S. Mail, which is scornfully known by Internet regulars as "snail mail," abbreviated "s-mail." Internet mail is somewhat like fax: It's electronic text. But you don't have to pay for it (at least not directly), and it's global in scope; E-mail can also send software and digital imagery. New forms of mail are in the works.

The discussion groups, or "newsgroups," are a world of their own. This world of news, debate, and argument is generally known as "USENET." USENET is quite an active part of the Internet. USENET is rather like an enormous billowing crowd of gossipy, news-hungry people, wandering in and through the Internet on their way to various private backyard barbecues. USENET is not so much a physical network as a set of social conventions. Naturally there is a vast amount of talk about computers on USENET, but the variety of subjects discussed is enormous, and it's growing larger all the time. USENET also distributes various free electronic journals and publications.

Long-distance computing was an original inspiration for ARPANET and is still a very useful service, at least for some. Programmers can maintain accounts on distant, powerful computers, and run programs there or write their own. Scientists can make use of powerful supercomputers a continent away. Libraries offer their electronic card catalogs for free search. Enormous catalogs are increasingly available through this service, and there are fantastic amounts of free software available.

File transfers allow Internet users to access remote machines and retrieve programs or data. Many Internet computers allow any person to access them anonymously and to simply copy their public files free of charge. This is no small deal, since entire books can be transferred through direct Internet access in a matter of minutes. Million of such public files are available to anyone who asked for them (and many more millions of files were available to people with accounts). Internet file transfers are becoming a new form of publishing, in which the reader simply electronically copies the work on demand, in any quantity he or she wants, for free.

Much of the material available on the Internet is now in hypertext text form in a subset known as the World Wide Web (www). Browser programs such as Netscape Navigator allow users to click on hypertext links that can take them to anywhere in the world. To help you locate web pages that you might be interested in, there are enormous search engines running on the Web, such as Google.[1] Pages are written in Hypertext Markup Language (html), and located using universal resource locators (URLs), which can include mail, news, File Transfer Protocol (ftp), gopher, and Hypertext Transfer Protocol (http).

The headless, million-limbed Internet is spreading like bread mold. Any computer of sufficient power is a potential spore for the Internet, and in 2000, such computers sold for less than $500 and were in the hands of people all over the world. ARPA's network, designed to assure control of a ravaged society after a nuclear holocaust, has been superseded by its mutant child the Internet, which is thoroughly out of control and spreading exponentially through the post-Cold War electronic

---

[1] http://www.google.com/

global village. The spread of the Internet in the 1990s resembled the spread of personal computing in the 1970s, although it was even faster. It is perhaps more important as well, because it gives those personal computers a means of cheap, easy storage and access that is truly planetary in scale.

13.4 What Has the Internet Brought Us?

First, the positives:

Actuation at a distance:
Tele-surgery; operating equipment such as an electron microscope at a distance

Business:
Instant, but perhaps temporary, fortunes; E-commerce, such as "shopping in your underwear" with secure servers to accept credit cards; auctions; investing; banking; new business models (virtual inventory as result of just-in-time delivery)

Communications:
E-mail without national borders; scholarly and business collaborations at a distance; on-line buddies and chat rooms; voting from home; high-bandwidth, low-cost telephone; picturephone; video conferencing

Entertainment:
Downloaded music and pictures; high-bandwidth, high-definition interactive television; games and gaming simulations

Information:
About commercial products, medical terms, travel sites, etc., with ubiquitous access (Internet cafes); instant news; unlimited information search capability, distributed database access

Learning:
True distance learning, participatory programming as people create their own web sites

We've also seen some negative effects of the Internet:

- International hacker or terrorist attacks, such as denial-of-service assault on web sites such as Amazon.com and CNN.com; viruses; breaches of security
- New forms of fraud
- New threats to privacy
- New threats of censorship
- New sources for terrorist handbooks and recipes for making bombs
- On-line predation

13.5 Some Internet Terminology

Here, in Table 13.1, are some terms related to the Internet. You will find additional terms in the "Glossary" on page 323.

Table 13.1 Internet Glossary

Term	Definition
attach-ment	Formatted file, such as a picture, that can be included in an e-mail message
browser	Software that facilitates accessing materials stored on the Internet. Examples are Netscape Navigator and Internet Explorer
cookie	One line of text stored in a file on a user's computer created and accessed by certain Internet web sites
Directory site	A web site that categorizes and organizes pointers to other information on the Web
DNS	Domain Name Server — translates domain names to IP addresses
domain	Like "berkeley" in "eecs.berkeley.edu"
e-mail	Electronic mail, which can be sent electronically between users having network access and addresses
ftp	File Transfer Protocol — a type of URL protocol for transferring formatted files between network sites
Gopher	A type of URL used for text-based information retrieval before the creation of the World Wide Web
html	HyperText Markup Language — the primary language in which web pages are authored, used for writing text containing click-on links to other locations
http	HyperText Transfer Protocol — a type of URL used to transfer files that contain hypertext links
Internet café	Café offering patrons Internet access in a comfortable setting
IP address	Unique identification number of a network address expressed as four 8-bit numbers presented in decimal notation separated by periods.
ISP	Internet Service Provider — organization providing connection to the Internet and other services. Examples are America Online and Earthlink
mailto	A type of URL used to send e-mail
Mosaic	The first web browser
MP3	music compression standard that is part of MPEG
news	A type of URL
pdf	Portable Document Format generated and displayed by Adobe Acrobat™
search engine	Application that locates network sites containing desired information. Examples are Google, Snap, and AskJeeves

Table 13.1   Internet Glossary (continued)

snail mail	Derisive term for communications on paper delivered by a postal employee on foot and carrying a bag made from animal skin
telnet	A type of URL that provides remote access to console functionality
TCP/IP	Transmission Control Protocol/Internet Protocol — a layer of standards that provide for reliable communications on the Internet
URL	Uniform Resource Locator — the full address specification of any Internet resource
USENET	A collection of bulletin board or news servers
web site, web page	Term for a virtual location containing accessible items such as text and pictures, maintained by an individual, company, or organization
www	World Wide Web — used as a prefix to host names to allow mapping to a separate IP address

13.6 Future Prospects for Internet

We can expect the Internet to continue expanding, with more users, web sites, and computers connected. Higher speeds will permit video on demand. Commercialization of the Internet is a very hot topic, with every manner of wild new commercial information service promised. A huge electronic shopping mall is forming. The federal government, pleased with an unsought success, is also still very much in the act. Computer networks worldwide will feature 3-D animated graphics, radio and cellular phone-links to portable computers, as well as fax, voice, and high-definition television. A multimedia global circus, or so it's hoped and planned.

Serious issues of security remain to be solved, and there is a need for better means for finding what is available. The real Internet of the future may bear very little resemblance to today's plans. Planning has never seemed to have much to do with the seething, fungal development of the Internet. After all, today's Internet bears little resemblance to those original grim plans for RAND's post-holocaust command grid. It's a fine and happy irony.

In the near term,

- The Internet will deliver real-time television images. (At the end of 1999, delivery of high-definition television — HDTV — images over an Internet link was demonstrated. The key invention was an effective compression algorithm.)

- Widely dispersed sensors and actuators will be operated via their connection to the Internet. (Tele-surgery has been demonstrated, with the surgeon in one location and the patient in another, as has distant diagnosis, permitting expert medical care to be made available anywhere.)

- The preceding will permit the delivery and collection of geographically dispersed data on weather, disease, and environmental conditions.

- Access to very high-bandwidth networks. (One application is to the making of small experimental parts, in which fabrication, inspection, and testing are accomplished at a centralized facility that is far from the engineer or scientist controlling the operation. Remotely operated microscopes for inspecting parts have been implemented already. High bandwidths are needed to accommodate the high-resolution video images produced.)

In a slightly longer view, experts[2] predict that by the year 2002,

- The Internet will "disappear" in the sense that access will be so easy and fast that the net becomes a facility that is simply taken for granted.

- We will have "smart" information retrieval that will be fast and accurately focussed.

- Our connections to the Internet will be persistent and fast, instead of intermittent and slow as in the past.

- As we use tinier, portable, and even wearable computers for Internet access, control via buttons will be replaced with control by voice and the widespread use of speech recognition software.

- Forceful attempts will be made to tax internet commercial transactions.

- The paying of bills will occur largely via the Internet .

- A wireless technology chip will become ubiquitous, enabling you to control all sorts of devices near you from a computer without needing wires to connect them.

- Inexpensive "e-tags" will be incorporated in all sorts of manufactured items that will call up the associated informative web sites when they get near a computer equipped with an e-tag reader. This will eliminate learning so many web site addresses.

13.7 For Further Reading

Tracy LaQuey with Jeanne C. Ryer, *"The Internet Companion"* (Redding, MA: Addison Wesley, 1992). Evangelical etiquette guide to the Internet featuring anecdotal tales of life-changing Internet experiences. Foreword by then-Senator Al Gore.

Paul Gilster, *"The Internet Navigator"*, 2nd Ed. (New York: John Wiley & Sons, 1994). Compendium that tells you all you need to know to get onto and find your way around the Internet.

John Quarterman, *"The Matrix: Computer Networks and Conferencing Systems Worldwide"* (Bedford, MA: Digital Press, 1990). Massive and highly technical compendium detailing the mind-boggling scope and complexity of our newly networked planet.

Brendan P. Kehoe, *"Zen and the Art of the Internet: A Beginner's Guide"* (Englewood Cliffs, NJ: Prentice Hall, 1992). Brief but useful Internet guide with plenty of good advice on useful machines to paw over for data. Mr. Kehoe's guide bears the singularly wonderful distinction of being available in electronic form free of charge.

---

[2] From "Visions: The Internet in 2002", *Worth*, November 1999, pp. 152-163.

Angus J. Kennedy, *"The Internet — The Rough Guide"* (London, UK: Rough Guides, Ltd., 1999). Up-to-date, comprehensive, pocket-sized treatment of the Internet with overviews, details, and an actual guide to many web sites.

For an excellent ongoing history of the Internet, see Robert H. Zakon.[3]

13.8 Problems

13.1   The number of web sites doubled in the first 6 months of the year 2000, to 17 million (with over one billion indexable pages). Assuming that this rate continues, calculate how many web sites there would be at the end of the year 2005? Is your upper estimate reasonable?

---

[3]   http://www.isoc.org/zakon/Internet/History/HIT.html

Optical Communications

Alexander Graham Bell not only contributed to the development of the telephone, but also experimented with optical communications. In experiments conducted in 1880, Bell showed that he could use human speech to modulate a ray of sunlight that was directed to a receiver some distance away. At the receiving end, the speech signal was extracted and could be heard by a human listener. While Bell used a sunbeam propagating freely in the open air, today's communication networks use light from a laser traveling in a threadlike fiber made of special low-loss glass to carry information over long distances. Here's the story.

Bell's Photophone experiment is shown in Figure 14.1. Sunlight is directed by a small mirror onto a thin reflective diaphragm that distorts when the seated gentleman on the left speaks into a tube leading to the diaphragm. The entire reflected light beam reaches a detector at the right when the speaker is silent, but when the speaker talks the diaphragm moves and that causes the sunbeam to be deflected partially to one side of its initial path. The louder the sound, the greater the deflection of the sunbeam is, producing a form of what is called amplitude modulation. At the receiving end, the undeflected portion of the sunbeam falls on an early type of solar cell; it is a photoconductive device made of elemental selenium, whose electrical resistance depends upon the amount of light incident upon it. Changes in the resistance of this cell cause a changing current to flow through the earphones. (The current was produced by the set of batteries at the listener's feet.)

The experiment worked, as explained in an amusing article in the *New York Times* of August 30, 1880 (the full article is reprinted as Appendix G starting on page 341):

"The Professor's explanation is, however, all that a truly scientific mind could desire... When he wishes to communicate with any given place he takes a mirror and flashes a beam of light to the place in question. It is along this beam of light that he sends an audible message. The person at the other end hears it as plainly as he would hear a telephonic message, and answers it in the best telephonic style. Thus the two continue

Figure 14.1 Sketch of Bell's Photophone experiment in which a beam of sunlight carried spoken messages to the listener on the right (see text for details). (Illustration reprinted with permission of AT&T.)

to say, 'Hullo,' 'What's that?' 'Don't hear,' and 'Speak louder,' until they are tired, just exactly as they would do if they were connected by the best pattern of telephone. When the conversation is over, the mirror is moved and the sunbeam disappears. As experiments have shown that a mirror can flash a sunbeam thirty miles, unless, of course, there are hills, houses, or fat men in the way, ...it follows that the photophone can be used as a means of communication between places at least thirty miles apart when the sun is sufficiently bright."

14.1 The Fiber-Optic Approach

While Bell's system worked, its range was limited by the spreading of the beam (dispersion) and by losses in the atmosphere. And, of course, the system didn't work at night. The advances that have made truly long-distance optical communications possible are using optical fibers that trap the light, so that it doesn't spread, and using electrically powered laser light sources. (The laser is discussed near the end of this section.)

The structure and operating principle of the optical fiber are shown in Figure 14.2. The fibers now in use have two or three parts. In the center is a cylindrical <u>core</u> of glass which has a high index of refraction (meaning that light travels rather slowly in it). Surrounding this is the so-called <u>cladding</u>, which is made of a glass in which light moves faster than in the core material. As a result, light beams introduced into the core at a small angle to the central axis will reflect at the core-cladding boundary, in accordance with Snell's Law, which you probably learned

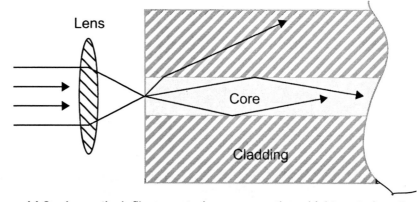

Figure 14.2 An optical fiber seen in cross-section. Light entering the central core of the fiber at the left from a lens or laser moves through the fiber to the right, being reflected repeatedly at the cylindrical core-cladding boundary.

about in a physics course. The third component is usually a protective polymer jacket that covers the composite fiber, whose diameter is typically only tens of micrometers.

Manufacturing an optical fiber involves drawing glass from the bottom of a heated double crucible, as shown in Figure 14.3. The chemical compositions of the materials that make up the core and cladding are carefully controlled, as it has been found that unwanted impurities can greatly increase the loss of optical energy as the

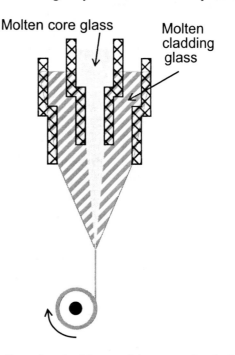

Figure 14.3 Cross-section of a double crucible apparatus holding molten core and molten cladding glasses. The finished fiber is pulled at a steady rate from the bottom of the apparatus and wound onto a reel for installation.

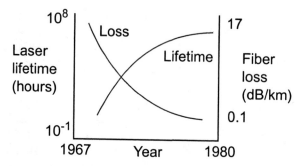

Figure 14.4 Optical fiber loss and semiconductor laser lifetime vs. year. The lowest loss occurs in rather narrow ranges of optical wavelength, so fibers and laser sources were developed concurrently.

beam travels. (See Figure 14.4.) Also plotted in Figure 14.4 is the lifetime of the lasers designed for use in optical communications. It was the work of electrical and materials engineers that made possible fibers and lasers that had low enough losses and long enough lifetimes to make optical communications commercially viable.

14.2 Semiconductor Light Sources

Certain semiconductors can be made to emit light when an electric current flows through them. This property is exploited in the commonly used light-emitting diode (LED). LEDs that emit visible light are used as indicator lamps in electronic equipment. LEDs that emit longer wavelength infrared energy — which cannot be seen by the unaided human eye — are used in handheld remote tuners for television sets and VCRs, and in intrusion detectors.

A light source for use with an optical fiber must be more directive than LEDs in order to get most of the light into the tiny core. Therefore, semiconductor <u>lasers</u> are used. Lasers produce light that is highly collimated: The width of a typical laser beam increases very little as the beam travels from the source. In addition, the optical energy produced by a laser is monochromatic, as you may have noticed while waiting in line at the supermarket where laser scanners utilizing red light read the bar codes on the packages. Why do lasers behave in these unusual and interesting ways? You could truthfully say that it's done with mirrors! All the atoms capable of emitting light in a typical laser are located between two highly parallel mirrors. The light emitted by one atom bounces back from a mirror and can cause other atoms to emit their light in synchronism. The ultimate result is laser light with its unusual, but very useful, properties. For a more complete story, ask your instructor.

To encode information on a laser beam is quite simple: just turn the laser current on and off in accordance with the signal you want to transmit. Thus, you can easily use a laser diode coupled to an optical fiber to generate and transmit a string of digital 1s and 0s, as suggested in the front cover illustration on this book. Another way of encoding information on a light beam is to change the wavelength (color) of the light beam in accordance with the information to be transmitted. This is a form of frequency modulation, as the wavelength is determined by the frequency. Because the frequency of infrared radiation can be so high — 10^{14} Hz or so — it is possible to transmit information optically at a very high rate. If each user of a communication system is given a well-defined portion of the spectrum to use, a single fiber can carry a large number of different messages at once. And, of course, one can put a number of fibers together in a single thin cable that can transmit information at an enormous rate.

14.3 Practical Problems, and Some Solutions

The *New York Times* article joked about a coil of sunbeams carried on the shoulder, but it might seem that handling tiny optical fibers would be nearly as difficult. Part of the solution is to put a soft polymeric sheath around each fiber to give it mechanical protection. Ten or twenty fibers can be assembled around a sturdy inner cylinder and covered with a still larger sheath to form a multifiber cable that is strong enough to pull through underground conduits.

Another practical problem results from the finite length of the fiber. What do you do when you come to the end of the roll? Since you can't just solder the fibers together, as you do copper wires, engineers developed fiber splicing kits in which the ends of adjoining fibers were aligned and butted up against each other. Then, the ends were heated to the melting point with a finely controlled flame, splicing the lengths of fiber together. A temporary joint can be made by just butting the fiber ends together, with a little liquid between them to facilitate transmission between fibers. Inexpensive snap-together connectors for doing this easily are available.

Another problem for which a really high-tech solution has been proposed is that of aligning semiconductor laser chips accurately with respect to the ends of optical fibers. Misalignment of only a few micrometers will cause much of the laser light to miss the core and degrade performance. A promising solution is to use a tiny micromotor to move the end of the fiber incrementally until maximum transmission from laser to fiber is obtained.

Industry–University Cooperation in MEMS

The general public imagines that most advances in science or engineering occur as the result of the hard work of a single individual in a cluttered laboratory. In fact, engineers in either industry or a university usually work together in groups, attacking different aspects of a problem. Each engineer brings his or her own specialized knowledge to the task, but all members of the team need to understand the overarching goals of the project in order to be most effective. The members of the project team also need to communicate well with each other. These communications may be in written form — reports and memos — or may be more personal, ranging from talks delivered at project meetings to very informal interactions at staff lunches and around the copy machine.

In this chapter, we'll look at an industry–university research cooperation in a very new field that has an extremely promising future — *micro-electro-mechanical systems* (MEMS). We focus on engineering research at the University of California at Berkeley in this subject area for three reasons. First, MEMS devices are new and utterly fascinating; second, from this example, we can learn how industry and academia can work together on research in a field; and, finally, because it is an example familiar to your authors.

15.1 Differences Between Industrial and University Research

In simplest terms, industries exist to make money, and universities exist to educate students. Product innovation is important to industry, and many large companies maintained research laboratories that carried out the research that might lead to the next generation of technology. What is research? A good dictionary definition of research (see the glossary that starts on page 323) is "a careful, systematic, patient study and investigation in some field of knowledge, undertaken to discover or establish facts or principles." Today, industry is looking increasingly to universities to do research, which is certainly consistent with the university goal of educating students. Let's examine one way in which industry and the universities cooperate on MEMS research.

15.2 A Short History of MEMS

As electrical, chemical, and materials engineers developed smaller, faster, and more complex electronic integrated circuits, they became convinced that computers would be able to process almost any amount of data. A few visionaries focused attention on the missing element — the devices that would *collect the data* to be processed. They asked whether one could apply some integrated circuit processing techniques to fabricate small *microsensors* whose outputs would be electrical representations of real-world quantities such as vehicle accelerations or chemical vapor concentrations. Computers could then process the data in order to initiate corrective actions — deploy a vehicle's airbag or sound a toxic hazard alarm. Soon after silicon's superior mechanical properties had been realized, means for making tiny movable mechanical parts on a silicon chip were developed, and *microactuators* were born.

The initial work was done at several universities and first published in the late 1980s. After that, industry became interested and involved, as did governmental agencies in the U.S. and abroad. Extensive work in MEMS is now underway worldwide, and an economic study by *Electronic Business*[1] predicts that MEMS sales will amount to $9 billion annually by the year 2003.

MEMS devices contain mechanical parts, such as cantilever beams, membranes, possibly gears, and other parts, whose dimensions are measured in microns. (One micron is 10^{-6} meters, about 1/100th the diameter of a human hair. To appreciate this and other dimensions in human terms, see Figure 29.8.) MEMS devices also contain electrical elements, such as resistors, capacitors, and transistors.

Two early MEMS devices are shown in Figure 15.1 — both are electrically driven micromechanical actuators. With proper electrical drive, the toothed wheel in the center of the scanning electron microscope photo on the left can be made to rotate, and the horizontal beam on the right can be made to oscillate up and down, under the watchful eye of the mite sitting on the underlying silicon chip.

Both of these devices were made in a university lab by graduate students who were exploring the possibilities of micromachining in order to earn their doctoral degrees (Ph.D.). Since then, a host of exciting and more complex MEMS devices have been conceived, designed and built, as described in Section 29.4 on page 256. Here are some of the MEMS devices whose feasibility has been demonstrated:

- Tiny sensors for physical quantities such as acceleration, rotation rate, pressure, and rate of fluid flow

- Miniature sensors for biological and chemical quantities such as antigens and toxic vapors in the atmosphere

---

[1] http://www.eb-mag.com/eb-mag/issues/1999/9905/0599mems.asp

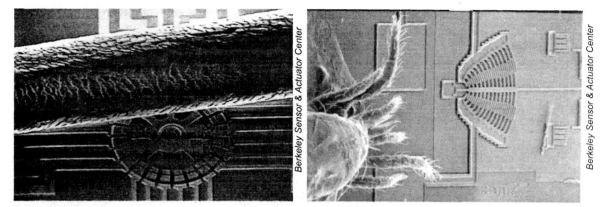

Figure 15.1 Early MEMS devices. Left: electrostatic micromotor with human hair. Right: Surface micromachined resonator and a mite.

- Microscopic motors that move mirrors or tune a radio circuit

- Pumps that move liquids for chemical analysis, medical diagnosis and therapeutic drug delivery

- Miniature chemically powered turbines to cool IC chips or replace batteries in small portable electronic devices

More information about MEMS appears later in this book. (See Chapter 29.) You might guess correctly from the examples just listed that research in this field involves people having many different backgrounds and technical specialties, such as electrical, mechanical, and chemical engineering, as well as biology and medicine. It should also be clear that many different types of companies might be interested in developing MEMS products, including automobile manufacturers, instrumentation suppliers, and medical equipment suppliers.

As the MEMS field began to grow, how could companies obtain the necessary knowledge to enter it? One answer that has been quite successful is the industry/university cooperative research project.

One Model for Industry–University Cooperative Research

When MEMS began, a so-called Industry–University Cooperative Research Center was established at the University of California at Berkeley, with the help of the U.S. National Science Foundation. Companies could join the Center (later named the Berkeley Sensor & Actuator Center, or BSAC) upon paying a yearly fee that funded lab costs and researchers' salaries. Representatives from the member companies visited the Center at least twice a year, where research goals and results were presented and evaluated. The focus remained on research, rather than short-term industrial questions; companies that did want to have attention devoted to a particular problem could fund a focussed research project. To obtain rights to the intellectual property (patents) that resulted, the company could pay a roughly 50% overhead on such a project (see the section entitled "Where Does the Money Go?" on page 107). The Federal government could also sponsor projects.

One of the benefits of this type of cooperation is the generation of new knowledge. Another is the educational benefit of having students in different fields working together, and the frequent contact of students with the industrial members.

Often, a student may be hired by a member company after graduation, by which time both parties know each other well.

This kind of industry–university collaborative research is fairly widespread today. Industry is funding far less research in-house than it was when dramatic advances were made at excellent industrial research laboratories, such as Lucent's Bell Laboratories or the IBM Watson Research Laboratory. The present collaborations appear to benefit amply both the companies and the university researchers. In the case of Berkeley's BSAC, in the year 2000, MEMS research occupied nearly 100 graduate students from the departments of electrical, mechanical, and chemical engineering, materials science and engineering, and bioengineering, as well as others from multi-disciplinary academic units. Approximately 20 faculty members conducted all or part of their research in this field, and the total annual budget amounted to approximately $8 million. The research involves extensive use of computers for simulation, design and the control of experiments to test devices that are made either in the Berkeley microfabrication facility or in a commercial "foundry" elsewhere. The students involved obtain valuable experience both in conducting research and in publishing their results, orally in talks before the industrial supporters and at technical conferences, and in print in journal articles. Half a dozen startup companies making MEMS products have been started by graduates from the program.

Next we will consider a bit about the backgrounds that are required for working on such a project. We will start by looking at the traditional specialities around which the relevant college courses are organized.

Brief Technical Articles

The brief articles that follow are from a magazine that Dick White edited for the Institute of Electrical and Electronics Engineers (IEEE), the primary professional organization for engineers in these fields. The objective of the magazine, *IEEE ElectroTechnology Review*, was to describe new technical developments in a very readable way. The articles were written by experts working in industry, universities, or government labs.

Article 1: "If the Machine is So Smart, Why Do I Feel So Dumb?" This article is about the need to consider human factors in the design of microprocessor-based gadgets. Is a high-tech solution necessarily best?

Article 2: "The ThinkJet Printer — From Concept to Product." Hewlett-Packard engineers developed a computer printer with manufacturability firmly in mind — but who invented it first?

16.1 "If the Machine Is So Smart, Why Do I Feel So Dumb?"

Lloyd H. Nakatani,
AT&T Bell Laboratories,
Murray Hill, NJ

Fulminations against "user hostile" machines became widespread when personal computers (PCs) hit the masses. Adventurers lured by the promises of the Information Age were frustrated by early PCs that responded only to the arcane incantations of the computer priesthood. Much progress has been made since [1], witness the Apple Macintosh.

But overt PCs are only part of the problem. Beware the covert PCs! Even die-hards who shy away from anything recognizable as a PC are being subverted by an insidious and pervasive trend to "smarten" commonplace machines such as kitchen appliances, watches and stereos with microprocessor implants. Confronted with these newfangled smart machines replete with push-button controls and data entry keypad, we are often rendered dumb.

Surely the increased complexity of smart machines, especially of the programmable variety, accounts for some of our tribulations. But there must be more. Even nominally simple machines often seem inordinately difficult to operate.

Two Ovens

Take a simple microwave oven in Dumb and Smart versions. To operate a Dumb oven, turn the TIMER knob to set the timer, turn the POWER knob to set the power level, and push the START button. Check the current state of the oven with a quick glance at the knobs and push-button. Adjust either time or power — even in mid-operation — by simply turning the knobs.

Contrast this with a Smart oven sporting push-button controls and digital display. To set the timer, push the TIMER button and key in the time on the numeric keypad. Is the time specified in seconds, minutes or both? Guess. To set the power level, push the POWER button and key in the power level on the numeric keypad. What is the unit and range of power level? Guess. Wrong power level? Push POWER, push the CLEAR button, and key in the correct power level. Want to check the settings? Push TIMER to display the timer setting. Why is time set to zero? Unbeknownst to us, CLEAR used earlier to correct the power level also cleared time. Reset the time and push START to start the oven. Want to add a minute to the cooking time? Push STOP to stop oven operation, push TIMER (but don't do the obvious and push CLEAR else the power level will be reset to the default maximum setting!), mentally add a minute more to the displayed time and key it in, and finally push START to resume. Want to check the power level in mid-operation? Push STOP and POWER, read the displayed value, and push START to resume.

Dumb and Smart have the same functionality, but Smart is much more difficult to operate. Some of this difficulty stems from the following factors:

- **More Controls:** Dumb has only three controls, but Smart has 15 (counting the numeric keypad), which make it look more complex.

- **Syntax:** The controls on Dumb are operable in any sequence, but the controls on Smart must be pushed in the correct sequence and combination in accordance with a hidden syntax.

- **Modes:** Each control on Dumb is independent of the prior operation of any other control and whether the oven is running or not. But not so on Smart: a numeric entry is either time or power level depending on the prior operation of TIMER or POWER, and most controls do not work when the oven is running.

- **Changes:** Merely adjust a knob to change a setting on Dumb, but a procedure akin to text editing is necessary to change a setting on Smart.

- **Persnicketiness:** Less than exact operation results in imprecise but acceptable settings on Dumb. Comparable inexactness on Smart (say, pushing the wrong key or an extra digit) may result in a charred dinner.

- **Invisible States:** The state of Dumb is visible in the control settings, but a sequence of operations is needed to make visible the state of Smart. This is especially problematic if Smart reverts surreptitiously to some default state.

There is nothing intrinsic to microprocessors that entails these factors. Instead, they are a result of economics and poor design. To save cost and space, only the bare minimum of controls and displays are provided. Hence both time and power level are entered with the same keypad, and all values appear in a single display. Costs saved here ultimately penalize users who have to cope daily with the consequent modes. To avoid relatively costly analog-to-digital converters, uninformative digital push-buttons replace informative analog knobs. This requires that continuous values be entered as numbers wherein a small slip can become a big mistake, and changing a value involves an editing procedure as opposed to a simple knob adjustment. All too often, simple machines become computer-like in appearance and operation when they acquire microprocessor brains. Perhaps the hi-tech look sells. More likely, such poor designs reflect force of habit and insensitivity to user interface issues on the part of designers.

The future looks brighter. Progress on cheap displays and touch screens — touch-sensitive position sensors superimposed over computer-controlled displays — promises better interfaces to smart machines [2,3].

Take again the microwave oven in a future version. On the control panel, comprised of a display with touch screen, appear a clock-like TIMER dial, a dim POWER bar, and a dim START button. Touch a point on the perimeter of the dial to set the time, and a pie-shaped wedge brightens to indicate the setting. Touch the bar to set the power level, and a portion of the bar brightens to indicate the setting. Touch START to start the oven, and the button brightens to indicate that the oven is running. As the oven runs, the wedge on the dial shrinks to indicate the remaining time. Time and power level are easily reset whether the oven is running or not.

Why use hi-tech to mimic old-fashioned controls? To conquer complexity through simplification and modularization. Simplification comes from good design as we just saw with the future oven. The now simple must be kept simple because the future holds enough necessary complexity. Modularization enables us to cope with the razzle-dazzle of new "features" by designing complex machines as a composite of many simple machines. With computer-controlled displays and touch screens, a smart machine can have many control panels, each designed to simplify some aspect of machine operation. Push a button and — *voila!* — the display changes to a control panel for setting a built-in clock easily on the oven. Push

another button and — *voila!* — a control panel for programming the oven easily to cook dinner in our absence.

Adventurers and diehards alike benefit from hi-tech complexity to achieve old-fashioned simplicity.

REFERENCES

[1] B. Shneiderman, "Direct Manipulation: A Step Beyond Programming Languages," *Computer,* vol. 16, no. 8, pp. 57-69, Aug. 1983.

[2] K.C. Knowlton, "Computer Displays Optically Superimposed on Input Devices," *Bell System Technical Journal,* vol. 56, no. 3, pp. 367-383, Mar. 1977.

[3] L.H. Nakatani and J.A. Rohrlich, "Soft Machines: A Philosophy of User-Computer Interface Design," *Proc. CH1 '83 Human Factors in Computing Systems,* Boston, pp. 19-23. NY: ACM, 1983.

(Reprinted by permission of the author.)

16.2 Problem

16.1 This article described the difficulty of operating a high-tech microwave oven. Describe some piece of equipment or software whose lack of user friendliness has frustrated you, and outline a better user interface for it.

16.3 The ThinkJet Printer — from Concept to Product

R. P. Dolan,
Hewlett-Packard Company

Editor's Note: Rarely does one obtain a view of a complete engineering development, from initial conception to large-volume manufacture. The Hewlett-Packard Journal issue of May 1985,[1] from which this article is excerpted, provides that view for a remarkably rapid development — the thermal ink-jet printer whose printhead projects individual ink drops at the paper by vaporizing tiny volumes of ink in just microseconds. This printer offers substantial advantages over impact and conventional thermal printers in many applications.

Ink-jet printing is inherently quiet, since nothing strikes the paper except the ink. Conventional thermal printing technology — in which a thinfilm resistor array is dragged across heat-sensitive paper that darkens in response to minute bursts of heat from the resistors — is just as quiet, but its application to high-speed, high quality printing is limited by several factors. The thermal mass of the printhead makes high print speed and high dot density difficult to achieve simultaneously. Vertical dot density is limited by the size of the resistor required to transfer heat to the paper. The exotic chemistry of thermal paper limits the print color, causes premature printhead failure if an unapproved grade of paper is used, ruins the printed output if it is exposed to strong light, heat, or chemical vapors, and drives up the manufacturing cost of the paper. Ink-jet technology, while not without its own drawbacks, is not affected by these limitations to the extent that conventional thermal printing is.

To put one mark on a piece of paper, a typical full-sized impact printer consumes 6 millijoules of energy. One portable thermal printer does only slightly better at 3.4 mJ per dot. But thermal ink-jet technology requires only about 0.04 mJ to print one dot. This enormous improvement in energy efficiency means that a portable, 80-column page printer capable of several hundred pages of output per battery charge becomes feasible for the first time.

Initial Development

Thermal ink-jet printing — boiling ink to make it spit out of a hole and make dots on paper — was, so far as anyone at HP knew at the time, the original idea of John Vaught of Hewlett-Packard Laboratories. The great potential of this new idea infused the project with an excitement that carried through the many months of research and development that were needed to take the idea from primitive prototypes to a commercially successful product. There was a midcourse shock in the sudden discovery that Canon, Inc. had conceived of the thermal ink-jet earlier, a dilemma resolved by the signing of a technology exchange agreement between the two companies.

The first embodiment of this simple concept featured an orifice plate made from a piece of thin brass shim stock in which a single orifice was punched by hand, using a sewing machine needle borrowed from an engineer's wife. This plate was aligned by hand over a conventional thermal printhead substrate. This simple printhead shot fountain pen ink several inches through the air, much to the delight of all concerned, and proved itself capable of eventually delivering enough ink to black out the objective lens of the microscope used to observe it in action.

Later a switch was made to laser-punched stainless-steel shim stock which could be chemically polished after punching to yield a smoother bore. Ultimately,

---

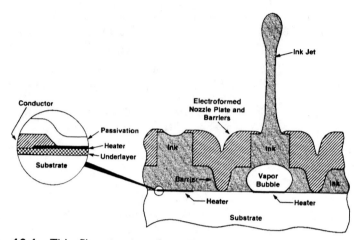

Figure 16.1 Thin-film structure for a ThinkJet printhead. Close-up view on the left shows the conductor-heater interface.

one of the engineers had an idea for electroforming the orifice plates to get smooth and accurately positioned bores more easily. In electroforming, an object is electroplated with a metal, but the plating is then separated from the object. The removed plating is the finished product, and retains the basic shape of the mandrel. Examples of electroformed items are electric razor screens and stamping dies for records.

Next Stages

One of the most fundamental initial design criteria for the proposed printhead was that it provide better print quality than that provided by the dot-matrix impact printer it was intended to replace. This was achieved by increasing the number of vertical dots in the font beyond nine, thereby making the characters more fully formed, and by exploiting the ink droplets' tendency to bleed together once on the paper, thereby masking the normally jagged appearance of dot-matrix text. By this time, the printhead development team was fabricating heads with 12 orifices on 0.25-mm centers using orifice plates electroformed out of nickel and featuring built-in separator walls to prevent hydraulic crosstalk — ink ejection from orifices other than those desired. Experimentation found that a six-microsecond firing pulse offered the best compromise between minimal power consumption and voltage sensitivity.

Thin Films, the Bubble and Ink

A cross-sectional view of a ThinkJet printhead's thinfilm structures is shown in Figure 16.1. It consists of a substrate of silicon, an underlayer beneath the heater, a thin-film resistor heater, metallic electrical conductors, and a passivation layer.

Control of bubble nucleation requires precise thermal design of the substrate and thin films, but experimental temperature measurement is complicated by the short times and small dimensions of the heating process. A typical thermal ink-jet heater is 50 to 100 microns square and 100 nanometers thick, and can reach 400°C within five microseconds. Much of the experimental evaluation of drop ejection was done by microscopic observation of droplets under flashtube illumination. Measurements of drop velocity and shape were made with calibrated optics and photographic or video recording. But, even with these experimental tools, it was difficult to correlate observed effects with underlying physical processes. So a computer simulation of the thermal ink jet was developed to gain a fundamental understanding of the physics of drop ejection (see Figure 16.2).

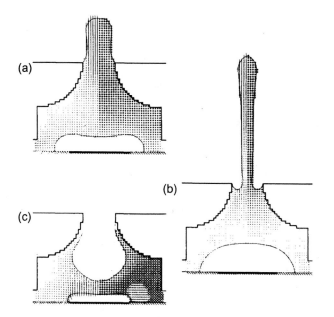

Figure 16.2 Simulation of ink droplet ejection through converging nozzle. (a) Five microseconds after bubble formation. (b) Fifteen microseconds. The bubble is beginning to collapse. (c) Twenty-four microseconds. The droplet has been ejected upward and the bubble is in the final stage of collapse.

Why Disposable?

Early ink-jet printers used permanent printhead assemblies with ink plumbed out to the printhead carnage through a system of flexible hoses leading from a remote ink bottle. These plumbing systems were generally quite complex and delicate. To be cost-competitive with existing low-end thermal and impact printers, an ink-jet technology was required in which the cost of the printhead's droplet generating mechanism was roughly the same order as the cost of its expendable ink supply. This in turn presented the possibility of manufacturing the printhead assembly as a disposable unit, thrown away when its self-contained ink supply has run dry — no hoses, plumbing, nor valves to add complexity and drive up cost or size.

Size and Ink Constraints

The printhead had to be able to print at least 500,000 characters. Since the font under development averaged about 17 dots per character, this implied that the printhead contain between 8,500,000 and 12,750,000 droplets in a reservoir within the one cubic-inch volume available for the printhead, only part of which would actually be available for ink storage. It was also assumed likely that the printer's output would be handled almost immediately after printing, making ink absorption and drying times of less than one second essential. The conflicting requirements of quick absorption and freedom from nozzle clogging could both be met only if a paper specially designed for ink-jet printing was used with a water/glycol ink solvent system. Hence, an ink-jet paper was chosen for use in the new printer, since at this time no ink system existed that was capable of producing 0.025-mm diameter dots from droplets weighing less than 3×10^{-7} gram without asymmetrical spreading or long absorption times on plain papers.

101

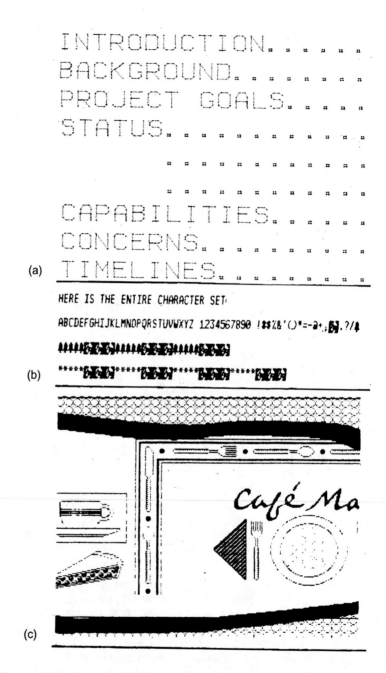

Figure 16.3 Print quality improvement, (a) First text produced by a ThinkJet printhead, mounted on an X-Y plotter and fired on the fly as the plotter moved the printhead to write letters. (b) Later text produced with 12-nozzle orifice plate. Nozzles are spaced on 0.25-mm centers in a single column. (c) Graphics output, 192 x 96 dots/inch.

Later Stumbling Blocks

The plastic parts initially used had nothing to prevent the ink from spurting out when a printhead cartridge was dropped. One of the engineers had the idea of using a rubber thimble of some sort to hold the ink. A team of engineers that hit the road to visit major glue manufacturers eventually settled on a UV-curable adhesive for attaching the substrate to the reservoir cartridge. Then a major stumbling block was discovered — the ink dye tended to bake on the substrate resisters in layers thick enough to affect printhead performance. This problem was addressed by changing the composition of the ink. The team began buying and installing production tooling and machinery and several months later started shakedown runs through the new facility. However, two months away from the printer's introduction date, one stumbling block remained that stubbornly resisted all attempts at a solution — hydraulic crosstalk! One of the engineers finally saved the day by proposing a change to the orifice plate design that dampened the fluid surges in the ink supply caused by the resister firings.

With this last-minute fix in place, the printhead and the ThinkJet Printer were announced to the world in April of 1984.

A Backward Glance

Some may attribute the successful completion of such a project in only a few years to luck and persistence, but there were other important reasons for this success. First, the various design teams were able to adjust to each other's requirements and negotiate what could and could not be done as the printhead and process technologies were being invented. Second, the performance goals for the printhead were not altered after the engineers demonstrated breadboard feasibility. They still had a massive amount of engineering work to do to turn the breadboard head into a real, live product (see Figure 16.3), but did not have to redefine the product after the breadboard stage.

Finally, the design teams did not make nontechnology-driven redefinitions of the product in midstream. The designers felt that they were fortunate to have demonstrated a breadboard device that stood the test of time and represented a technological contribution when it was introduced, but still considered that the best way to succeed at turning a technology into a product is to drive the process with engineering alone. This way, the designers burn midnight oil, not blueprints.

FURTHER READING

R.P. Dolan, Ed., *Hewlett-Packard Journal*, vol. 36, no. 5, May 1985.

16.4 Problem

16.2 The traditional tasks involved in taking a new idea from its conception as an invention to a commercial product may be described as research to establish feasibility, development of a product design, preproduction engineering, and manufacturing. Identify the specific steps in this process in the case of the ThinkJet printer.

Entrepreneurship:

It's Your Business

The rewards of a career in engineering or science include tackling challenging problems, conversing and working with smart people, being in an ever-changing environment, and, sometimes, being able to make a positive contribution to the world. But what about that other reward — making money?

17.1 Three Ways of Making Money

As an engineer, you have three very different ways of making money. Let's look at them and see what monetary rewards each might offer:

1. Providing service. The most common way engineers make money is by selling their services — working for a firm or possibly as an independent consultant. You are paid at an hourly rate, or at a monthly or annual salary rate.

2. Selling. You might earn a living by selling retail customers devices, systems or software made by others. To make a profit, you must buy low and sell high. Your monetary rewards might come from a combination of regular pay (hourly, monthly, or annual rate), a commission (percentage of the money received on each sale transacted), and the difference between your costs and your selling price.

3. Manufacturing. You design, build, and distribute a product. As we'll see, this is the only one of the three ways to make lots of money.

To compare the potential gains from each of these three ways, consider that there are roughly 50 work weeks, 250 work days, or 2,000 working hours in a year; we might assume that an individual's working lifetime is about 35 years. Consultants may receive on average perhaps $1,000 per day, so a full-time consultant might receive a maximum of $250,000 per year. Such full-time consultancies are very rare, and salaried engineers are generally paid at a much lower rate. It is hard to estimate upper bounds on selling, but experience suggests that it is generally much less than the annual figure for full-time consulting.

What about Option 3? This is the entrepreneurial option, where an individual starts his or her own business and ultimately realizes financial gain by selling the business in whole — to another company, for example — or in part, by selling shares of the business to investors. We'll examine the details of this activity in a moment, but first let's take an actual example of how this might proceed. Incidentally, this is properly a topic for the Business School, but we've found that so many engineering students are interested that we'll just proceed. After all, one of your authors (Roger) has had firsthand experience and notable success at this.

17.2 Your Startup Company

Suppose that you have an idea for a product that might be very desirable to customers. It might be an electrical or mechanical device, an entire system that performs some needed function, or a wonderful software program that performs a needed function in an especially efficient fashion. You decide not to go to work for a large company and hope to convince them to pursue the development and production of this product, but rather to form a company yourself so as to reap the profit from your idea. (There are other ways to make money from your idea, such as selling rights to the thing outright, but let's assume that you decide on a company of your own.) How do you fund a startup company, what sorts of people do you need in the company, what are the costs, and how much money might you make?

Funding the Startup Company

The most profitable way to fund a new company may be to fund it yourself or with the help of your associates. This can be better than going to a venture capitalist for funds, since this way you and your associates will own the company. While venture capitalists may be willing to provide funds for a promising venture, they will insist on having a majority share in the ownership of the company, and a deciding voice in what the company does. This isn't necessarily all bad, as they have valuable experience to draw on. Also, it's a lot better to own a small piece of a big success than to own a large piece of a small struggling firm.

The people who start the company designate themselves as Founders. They incorporate the company and declare that the company has some number of shares of stock that it can issue; let's assume that this number is five million shares. The Founders might set aside some shares for later employees, to act as incentives, or for public sale, and then split the remaining shares (say, 2.5 million) among themselves. If the company started with, say, $50,000 collected in equal $10,000 amounts from the five Founders, then each Founder would receive 500,000 shares for $0.02 each. After a few years and lots of hard work, the company might appear to have such bright prospects that outsiders would be willing to buy shares at a much higher price, say, $4 per share. The shares already issued to Founders would then in principle be worth a total of $10 million, and each Founder's shares would then in principle be worth $2 million, or 200 times what the Founder paid for them!

There's a lot more to be said about this, but you can see from this simplified example that there can be an opportunity for making lots of money by starting a company.

Whom Do You Need As You Start the Company?

A common, and usually fatal, error is to start with only people like yourself: engineers. What you really need are specialists in the following areas doing the following things:

1. Engineering — designing the product
2. Manufacturing — producing the product
3. Marketing and sales — developing "ads" and selling the product
4. Finance and accounting — keeping the financial issues on track
5. Managing — making the company's decisions

Where Does the Money Go?

Once the company is selling its product, how is the money spent? A typical breakdown for a company that manufactures a product is shown in Figure 17.1.

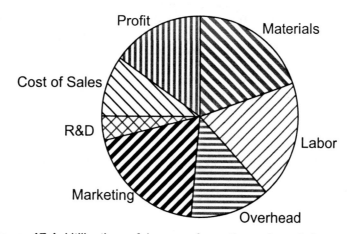

Figure 17.1 Utilization of income from the sales of the product. "R&D" stands for research and development. See text for other definitions and comments.

Clearly, the price of the product must cover the cost of the raw materials used and the cost of the labor required to make the product. Incidentally, the cost of raw materials is very low if the product is software. The sales must produce a profit if this business is to be viable. The research and development budget is used to generate product improvements or new products that will keep the company in operation after the demand for the initial products has decreased. The item labelled "overhead" covers such items as rent, utilities (such as water and electricity), computers, and the salaries of everybody not directly associated with hands-on work on the product, such as the secretarial and custodial staff members. An often overlooked or undervalued item is that labelled "marketing." This includes all the costs incurred in letting customers know of the existence of your product. An old adage says that "if you invent a better mousetrap, the world will beat a path to your door," but this is almost never true: You must advertise and seek out customers for even the best of products. Advertising may be very expensive: A full-page color ad might cost $10,000 or more for a single appearance in a monthly trade magazine. One such appearance is usually not enough, as some time may pass between the time your would-be customer first glances at your ad and when she decides to look you up to make an inquiry. In the Internet age, it is mandatory that your company have a presence on the Web, whether you are selling to the end-user or simply to other businesses. Simply having a web site isn't a guarantee that your potential customers will find it — advertising is still required. Whether you chose to use print or the Internet will depend on how well you can target your intended audience. Finally, "cost of sales" covers getting the product into their hands. When the company is young, it may rely on sales representatives (reps), firms that represent a number of different manufacturers in a local geographical area in return for a hefty commission. Once the area covered by a rep firm generates enough sales volume, the company may hire its own local sales force to work on a salary plus a nominal commission.

17.3 Is This for You?

The good parts of starting your own company are the possibility of making lots of money, having a feeling of accomplishment, and having control over your own destiny. There are lots of pitfalls, and the success rate for new companies is dismal — only about one in four survives more than a year or two. You will almost certainly put in longer hours than you would if you were working for someone else. There may be huge financial hardships and risk involved. You may end up bankrupt. Figuring out what your company should really be making and selling is difficult, and entrepreneurs often write up a business plan based on one concept and ultimately find their company doing something quite different. The goal can be elusive, but the chase exhilarating.

Unsolved Problems and

Unanswered Questions

Engineering students in college are required to complete hundreds of sets of homework problems. From their regularity and finite size — "handed out in Tuesday's lecture and due next Tuesday" — you might be led to conclude that all problems you'll be called upon to solve as a professional will be of similar size and duration.

In fact, real-world engineering problems may be very different. They may take years to solve, require the coordinated effort of large teams of professionals, and may remain unsolved until a crucial new process or device is invented or discovered. Often, the essential invention may have been conceived for an entirely different purpose.

Typical homework problems usually involve the topics most recently introduced in the course — which is a great help in finding their solutions. With real-world problems, it is less clear where to find the right tools to use in the solution process. The homework problems you're assigned have usually been solved by your instructor beforehand, but you can't count on it. Once an unworked problem on a final exam had such unexpected subtleties that it took the instructor eight hours to solve the problem fully!

There are some good books about general methods for solving problems. Two of these are the following:

G. Polya, *How To Solve It* (Garden City, NY: Doubleday & Co., 1957). [Concentrates on mathematical problems]

M. F. Rubinstein, *Patterns of Problem Solving* (Englewood Cliffs, NJ: Prentice Hall, Inc., 1975). [Written for an interdisciplinary problem-solving course given at UCLA]

Another book that you might enjoy deals with getting over — or around(!) — mental blocks when problem solving:

J. L. Adams, *Conceptual Blockbusting: A Pleasurable Guide to Better Problem Solving* (New York, NY: W. W. Norton & Co., 1976). [Adams was an engineer, teacher of design in an engineering school, and a collector of tractors.]

One of the things that such books agree on is that you need to attack a difficult problem repeatedly, as you can't always expect to solve a really hard problem the first time.

The next few pages contain two problems or puzzling questions. They concern a frozen lake and the origin of paper. These have intrigued me (Dick White) for some time, as they might you. I don't know the answers to either of them. If you want some questions to think about in your odd moments, try these.

18.1 Frozen Lake

The photograph of Figure 18.1 shows the amazing sight that greeted Dick White and three friends in November 1976 when they skied to the top of a ridge in the Sierra Nevada in California. We had visited this 1/4-mile × 1/2-mile lake many times in summer — when it was cool but unfrozen — and several times in winter, when it was covered uniformly with ice topped with many feet of snow. But we had never seen anything like this! The problem is to figure out what caused the perfectly circular and donut-shaped patterns this particular time.

Figure 18.1 Strangely frozen lake in the Sierra Nevada, California

Some additional facts might help. The freshwater lake is approximately 7300 feet above sea level. It was not frozen two weeks before this picture was taken, but a very cold blizzard was starting about then. The darkest regions appeared to be patches of open (unfrozen) water. The somewhat lighter regions appeared to be very thin ice, and the white regions were snow-covered. The snow we skied on was very light and fluffy, and so the air temperature must have been very low when the snow fell.

A few other facts may help lead to the answer or help rule out prospective solutions. By scaling the dimensions, we found that the circles were about 30 feet across and the outer edges of the donuts were about 60 feet in diameter. There are more than 140 circular regions. We don't think the lake contained hot springs (judging from our summertime swims in it), and the ice would have been too thin to support snowmobiles (or flying saucers). The long curved lines are likely cracks that broke open because of wind or circulation of water; the water in them froze again from the two edges and met in the center leaving the barely visible central lines. Finally, notice that the photo contains a few "negative" circles, where there's a black circle in a white area.

Over 200 people have seen this photograph, and many have speculated on the mechanisms involved. You're invited to join in figuring out this amazing natural phenomenon.

18.2 Was Paper Discovered or Invented?

Did you ever wonder about the origin of paper? Real paper, that is — not papyrus, which is formed from split reeds laid side by side, but paper formed from a slurry of separated fibers put in a sieve and then dried in the form of a sheet.

The conventional wisdom about paper says that it was invented by Tsai Lun in 105 A.D. in China. Mr. Lun is said to have thought of taking fibers obtained by rubbing cloth on a rough surface, forming a slurry by mixing these with water, allowing the water to drain out and then drying the resulting sheets. Incidentally, after achieving prominence because of his papermaking, Mr. Lun became active in politics and was eventually killed by opposition forces.

Curiously, a traditional account of the invention of paper mentions that Mr. Lun had on his property a small pond. This detail attracted my attention because of another mountain experience I (Dick White) had — less dramatic than finding the frozen lake, but nevertheless intriguing. You've probably noticed the thing I'm about to describe yourself.

I hiked into a mountain meadow in late August and found a number of small ponds that contained varying amounts of water. The stream that fed them had run dry and the water was evaporating and seeping into the ground. Some ponds contained standing water and grasses that were decomposing in the warm, bacteria-filled liquid. On the bottoms of ponds where the decomposition had proceeded quite far, you could see a mushy layer of fibers that had built up. And the bottoms of the ponds that had dried up entirely were covered with a white mat of cellulose fibers — natural paper!

The natural paper could be peeled off the bottom in large sheets. Charcoal from an old fire pit made marks on it, as expected, and when viewed by transmitted light, this material looked like some of the fine handmade papers exhibited at handcraft fairs and markets.

Tsai Lun developed a practical process for making paper. But isn't it possible that the inspiration for this invention was the natural substance he saw on the bottom of his pond late one August?

18.3 What's Coming Next?

Predicting the future is a very risky business. A glance at some notable wrong guesses made in the past by highly qualified observers illustrates this:

- "We don't like their sound, and guitar music is on the way out." [Decca Recording Company rejecting the Beatles, 1962]
- "I think there is a world market for maybe five computers." [Thomas J. Watson, Chairman of IBM, 1943]
- "640K ought to be enough for anybody." [Bill Gates, Chairman of Microsoft, 1981]
- "Heavier-than-air machines are impossible." [Lord Kelvin, President, British Royal Society, 1895]
- "Drill for oil? You mean drill into the ground to try and find oil? You're crazy." [Drillers whom Edwin L. Drake tried to enlist in his project to drill for oil in 1859]
- "Professor Goddard does not know the relation between action and reaction and the need to have something better than a vacuum against which to react. He seems to lack the basic knowledge ladled out daily in high schools." [New York Times editorial about Robert Goddard's revolutionary rocket work, 1921]

These were all negative judgments — what couldn't be done or wasn't going to work or be useful. We'll play it a bit safer and list a few things we do expect to see in the future:

- Faster and more accurate medical diagnosis based in part on improved instrumentation and on the growing understanding of human DNA.
- Much faster broadband electronic communications.
- Compact display devices (goodbye cathode-ray tubes).
- Much better software for searching for information on the Internet.

Now, add your own entries — it's going to be your world.

Part II: Electrical Engineering — Survey of the Field

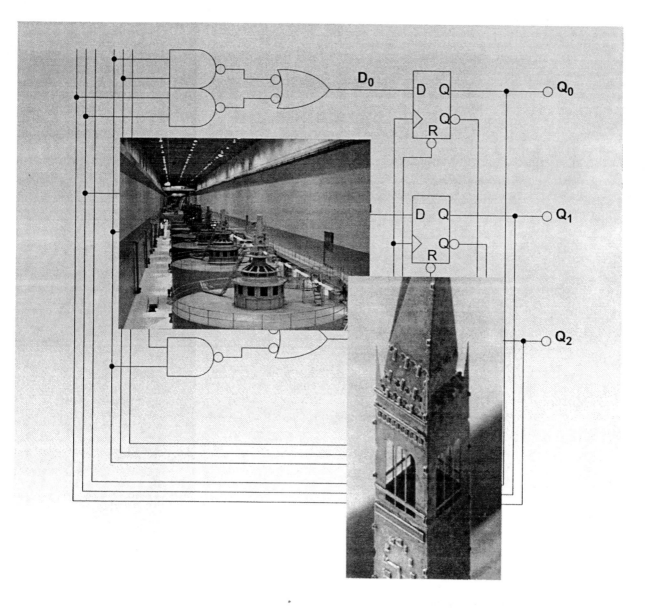

On the preceding page, the photograph of the generator hall at the Dalles, a hydroelectric generating facility on the Columbia River, was made by Roger Doering. The MEMS model of the campanile at U. C. Berkeley was both made and photographed by Elliot Hui. The authors are grateful to Elliot for permission to use his photograph. We chose these photographs to represent the breadth of the field — something huge and something vanishingly small set against the background of a digital schematic drawing to represent the abstract.

Direct Current Fundamentals

19.1 Current and Charge

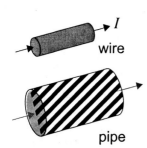

Figure 19.1 Wire carrying current I (top) and its water model (bottom)

You can't see electric current flowing in a wire. Since that makes it hard to get a feeling for what is happening, as we discuss electricity, we'll use some simple models to help you visualize what is happening. We call them *water models*, since they are based on the analogy between the flow of electrical charge and the flow of ordinary water. An electric current simply consists of electric charges moving in a wire. The water model for the current-carrying wire is just a pipe with water flowing in it. (See Figure 19.1.) A certain number of water molecules flow past a point in the pipe in a given amount of time, just as in the electrical case a certain number of charges (typically electrons) move in a given amount of time past a point in the wire.

We could measure the flow of water through a pipe in molecules per second, but this would produce extremely large values for the flow rate. Instead, we commonly express the flow rate for water in gallons per minute or per second. Similarly, we could express the rate of flow of electric current through a wire in charged particles per second, but this would also produce a large, cumbersome number. Therefore, we speak instead of the flow of units of charge known as the coulomb. Since the charge on an electron is -1.602×10^{-19} coulombs, a charge of 1 coulomb, denoted by the letter C, would be equal to the magnitude of the charge of 6.242×10^{18} electrons. Table 20.2 at the end of Chapter 20 summarizes the electrical quantities, units, circuit laws, and defining relations for circuit components discussed in this book.

A Student's Question: "Do we ignore the kinetic energy carried by a current in a wire?"

Optional Math

We can also write the equivalent expression:

$$Q_1 = \int_0^{t_1} i(t)\,dt$$

meaning the charge Q_1 that flows in time t_1 is the integral of the current from time zero to time t_1.

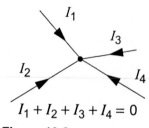

$$I_1 + I_2 + I_3 + I_4 = 0$$

Figure 19.2
A circuit node

A flow rate of one coulomb per second constitutes, by definition, a current of one ampere. The symbol for the ampere is the letter A. (For definitions of all the electrical units, see the "Glossary" starting on page 323.) We might thus say that "the current through the green light bulb is 0.8 A." We could also say that the current is 800 mA, where the small "m" represents the prefix "milli-", meaning one thousandth. (See the box entitled "Engineering Unit Prefixes" on page 119.)

The symbol for electric charge is Q, and the symbol for electric current is I. When we deal with circuits where we need to identify more than one current, we will use subscripts, so the currents might be represented by symbols such as I_3 and I_{be}.

The formal relationship of current to the flow of charge is:

$$I = \frac{dQ}{dt},$$

where $\frac{d}{dt}$ means "the derivative with respect to time t."

Incidentally, with all the water models, we consider the pipes to be entirely full of incompressible water. In addition, gravity plays no role in the water flow in our models (except in connection with Figure 19.4). It should not be surprising to learn that, just as the same amount of water leaves one end of a single pipe as enters it at the other end, the same amount of electric current leaves a single wire as enters it. Current doesn't get "used up" in a wire. If a pipe has a junction, then the rate at which water flows into the junction must equal the rate at which it flows out of the junction. By analogy, the electrical current(s) entering a junction between wires must leave the junction at an equal rate.

In our home plumbing system, we take it for granted that water comes out of a faucet, not into it. In our hydraulic analogies for electrical devices, water is allowed to flow in the reverse direction, which we can think of as representing a negative current. It is always important to specify the directions assumed for positive current flow when analyzing electric circuits. If a particular current actually flows in the opposite direction, then that current will turn out to have a negative value when we complete our analysis.

The indestructibility of electrical currents is expressed quite nicely by Kirchhoff's Current Law (KCL), which states that the sum of all the currents into a node is zero. (See Figure 19.2.) This implies, by the word "into," that all of the currents have the same direction pointing into the node. If a current is flowing into the node, then one or more of the currents must be negative, that is, coming out of the node. A "node" may be a simple junction between wires, any component, or even a large system. Kirchhoff's Current Law is written as

$$\textbf{Kirchhoff's Current Law:} \quad \sum_{n=1}^{N} I_n = 0.$$

"Doesn't the current always flow the same way in a wire?"

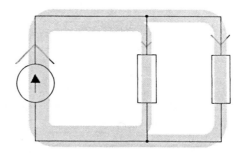
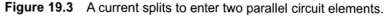

Figure 19.3   A current splits to enter two parallel circuit elements.

The light-colored bands in Figure 19.3 indicates how a current might split up, pass through different parts of a circuit, and then rejoin.

19.2 Conductors, Insulators, Semiconductors, and Superconductors

Conductors are materials through which electric currents flow relatively easily. Metals such as silver, copper, gold, and aluminum are among the best conductors. Silver, while being the best conductor, tarnishes and thus has very limited practical use. Copper and aluminum are used to form most electrical wires. Aluminum is tricky to use, because the surface oxidizes rapidly, but it is much less expensive and lighter than copper. Gold is used as a coating to protect other metals in connectors. An amalgam of tin and lead, called solder, is used to connect electrical components, because it has a relatively low melting temperature.

The charged particles that move easily in these metals are called electrons. Electrons are a fundamental part of every atom, but in metals the outer electrons can easily be moved to adjacent atoms. By now, you might have guessed that an electric current moving in a wire is like a river of electrons flowing through the material. There is, unfortunately, a small problem with this picture. Because the charge of the electron is labeled as negative (a perhaps unfortunate historical choice), a current of these charge carriers ends up being a negative current. The confusing result is that the direction of positive current flow is actually opposite that of the electron motion!

Two wires may be electrically connected by touching or being soldered. Of course, two pipes in a water model must be joined together with a fitting that doesn't leak.

Insulators are materials that do not conduct electricity. Ceramics, glass, plastic, rubber, dry paper, air, and vacuum are all good insulators. Most wires are coated with a layer of insulation to prevent current from finding unintended paths. The walls of the pipes in our water models are insulators. A wire that is cut can not carry current, because the air is an insulator — but it could still be dangerous to touch, since it is still "ready" to conduct current. In order to cut a pipe in the water models and have it behave the same way, we must cap the pipe when we cut it.

Semiconductors are materials such as silicon and germanium, which are relatively poor conductors until they are "doped" with trace quantities of other materials such as arsenic, phosphorous, or boron. Semiconductors are used to form electronic devices such as diodes and transistors. These are covered in "Semiconductors: From Ns and Ps to CMOS."

Superconductors are very special materials that, when cooled below their critical temperature (anywhere from a few degrees Kelvin up to more than one hundred degrees Kelvin for the so-called high-temperature superconductors), become perfect conductors. Superconductors are used to generate the enormous magnetic fields required for nuclear magnetic resonance imaging and may eventually be used in motors and for levitating trains. Since their present use in electronics is extremely limited, we will not discuss them further.

19.3 Voltage

> Complete Text of a Student's Question in Office Hour: "Now, about voltage …"

You may have heard the term "voltage" applied to flashlight cells (1.5 volts), radio batteries (9 volts), car batteries (12 volts), and household electrical outlets (120 volts). Just what is this quantity? In the case of a battery, the voltage is determined experimentally by connecting the two leads of a voltmeter to the two battery terminals. A physicist would say that the battery voltage equals the electrostatic potential at the positive terminal minus the electrostatic potential at the negative terminal. For now, we don't want to go into the meaning of electrostatic potential, so let's turn to the water model for voltage, or potential difference.

In our water model, voltage becomes water pressure. When we try to operate a drinking fountain with a low water pressure, only a trickle comes out. On the other hand, if the pressure is too high, the water will shoot past the fountain's edge. We can see that the higher the pressure, the more water will be forced through a given size pipe. In contrast, if we hook up a full hose between two faucets with the same water pressure, no water will flow. You might guess that the flow through a pipe is related to the pressure *difference* from one end to the other. Similarly, the current that flows through a wire will be proportional to the potential difference between the two ends of the wire.

> "Since both batteries are 1.5 volts, what's the difference between the big D one and the little AAA one?"

A voltage source, such as a battery, always has two terminals. The rated voltage is measured between these two terminals. In order for a current to flow, a complete path (called a circuit), made with wires and other electrical components, must be connected between the two terminals.

Our first model for a simple voltage source is the water tower shown in Figure 19.4. A pump is used to keep the tower full, so that the pressure delivered at the base of the tower is constant. The higher the tower, the higher the pressure is. Higher pressure models higher voltage. The second terminal on this voltage source is a drain pipe flowing into a reservoir. The water pressure in this return pipe is always zero. The voltage modeled by this pair of pipes is just the pressure produced by the force of gravity in the tower. (We did say that in most of our models, we didn't want any gravity effects. This is the exception.)

A second model for a voltage source is a turbine driven by a constant torque motor (Figure 19.5). The constant torque drive produces a constant pressure difference between the input and output of the voltage source. This model is more flexible than the water tower, as we can easily imagine hooking several of these in series to model voltage cells in a battery.

When a numeric quantity is expressed in engineering units, rather than in scientific notation with its exponent form, we move the decimal point so that the exponent of 10 becomes the nearest multiple of 3, and then replace the 10 and its exponent with the appropriate prefix to the unit of measurement. The prefix is written as a one letter symbol preceding the unit.

For example, 12,000 Hertz would be written as 1.20×10^4 Hz in scientific notation, but as 12.0kHz in engineering notation.

Many calculators include a button for adjusting exponents to engineering form.

Prefix	Symbol	Value
yotta	Y	10^{24}
zetta	Z	10^{21}
exa	E	10^{18}
peta	P	10^{15}
tera	T	10^{12}
giga	G	10^{9}
mega	M	10^{6}
kilo	k	10^{3}
(no prefix)		10^{0}
milli	m	10^{-3}
micro	μ	10^{-6}
nano	n	10^{-9}
pico	p	10^{-12}
femto	f	10^{-15}
atto	a	10^{-18}
zepto	z	10^{-21}
yocto	y	10^{-24}

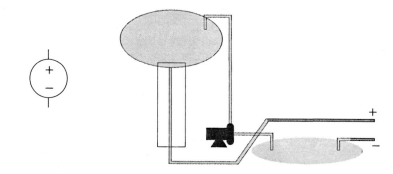

Figure 19.4 Water model for a steady voltage source, with schematic symbol at left. (See text for details.)

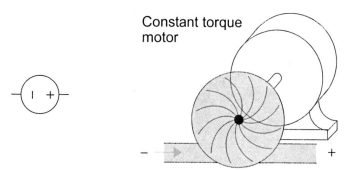

Constant torque motor

Figure 19.5 Another water model for a steady voltage source (schematic symbol at left)

The unit of voltage is the volt, represented by the letter V. Since the letter V is also used to represent the actual voltage (just as I is used to represent current), you must be careful to distinguish what each "V" means. (The variable is italicized, but the unit is not.) Often, the letter that represents a given voltage in a circuit has a subscript, so we might speak of an output voltage, V_{out}.

The voltages of components connected in series add up. This fact is formalized by Kirchhoff's Voltage Law (KVL), which states that the sum of the voltages around any closed circuit is zero.

$$\textbf{Kirchhoff's Voltage Law:} \quad \sum_{n=1}^{N} V_n = 0$$

This means that as we follow around any loop in a circuit in a specific direction, some of the voltages across components will be negative, and some will be positive, but when we've traveled all the way around the loop, the sum of all the voltages will be zero.

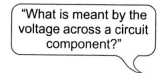

"What is meant by the voltage across a circuit component?"

Exercise 19.1   Sum the voltages around each of the three loops shown in Figure 19.6.

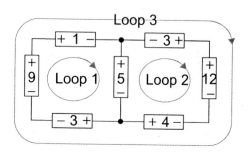

Figure 19.6   Example illustrating Kirchhoff's Voltage Law (KVL)

Solution: Start at any arbitrary point on each loop. We will choose the component nearest the arrowhead on each loop. Move around the loop summing the voltage drops. Pay close attention to the signs. When the minus sign is encountered first while moving in the direction of travel around the loop, then the voltage drop is negative. For loop 1, the voltages we sum are $+ 5 + 3 - 9 + 1 = 0$. For loop 2, we get $+ 12 - 4 - 5 - 3 = 0$. For loop 3, we get $+ 12 - 4 + 3 - 9 + 1 - 3 = 0$.

A famous illustration by M. C. Escher that might help you picture Kirchhoff's Voltage Law is shown in Figure 19.7. The waterfall is like a resistive voltage drop. The channel through which the water flows up to the top of the fall again acts like a battery, which raises the potential energy of charges through chemical action.

19.4 Power

The rate at which energy changes — being produced or dissipated — is called power. We are most familiar with power from horsepower ratings on engines and wattage ratings on lights and appliances. The unit of measure for electrical power is the watt, and the customary variable is P. When water flows over a water wheel to power a mill, both the amount of water flowing (the current) and the height of the drop (the voltage) determine the power that can be delivered. The product of the two quantities gives the amount of power. The formula that expresses this is

$$P = IV,$$

where P is the power in watts, I is the current in amperes, and V is the voltage in volts. A current that flows in a circuit will cause some work to be done, and the amount of power that will be delivered by a given current is proportional to the voltage drop in the circuit. If we are trying to clean a sidewalk with a water hose, we would like to have high water pressure, because the higher pressure causes faster currents, which can do more work moving debris. We can also see that more work would be done by a larger current.

"Doesn't power depend on <u>both</u> voltage and current? Like, if you had 50,000 volts and no current, would you have any power?"

Looking back at the equation for power we can see that it is just the derivative of this equation with respect to time (assuming a constant voltage):

$$P = \frac{dU}{dt},$$

$$P = \frac{d}{dt}(QV) = IV,$$

where we have substituted I for

$$\frac{dQ}{dt}.$$

Figure 19.7 M. C. Escher's Waterfall

19.5 Energy

"Why do we have to do work to move a charge? Isn't the charge on an electron really small?"

When a charge moves through an electric field, it converts energy from one form to another. A charge moving through a battery converts chemical energy to electrical energy. A charge moving through an electric field in a vacuum converts the potential energy to kinetic energy in its motion. The quantity of energy can be expressed by the formula

$$U = QV,$$

where U is the energy in joules, Q is the charge in coulombs, and V is the voltage in volts.

Energy from your local electric utility is measured (and billed) in kilowatt-hours, a unit that equals 3.6 million joules. A joule equals one watt-second, a kilowatt is 1,000 watts, and an hour is 3,600 seconds, so that one kilowatt-hour equals 3,600,000 watt-seconds.

Energy usage is becoming a larger concern for engineers. There was a time when it was thought that energy would be so cheap and plentiful that there would be no need to worry about using too much. This notion seems quite funny to us these days. With battery-powered portable equipment, like laptop computers, the goal must be to lower the energy utilization, so that the batteries will serve for a very long time.

19.6 Resistance

"What, exactly, does a resistor resist?"

A lot of water can flow through a large-diameter pipe. (See Figure 19.8 which shows where a truck backed into a fire hydrant.) A small pipe hooked up to the same source of water pressure will deliver a much smaller current of water. The smaller pipe is said to have more *resistance* to the flow of water than the large pipe. Similarly, a small-diameter wire will have more resistance to the flow of electric current than a large-diameter wire. In fact, a wire with twice the cross-sectional area of an otherwise identical wire will have one half the resistance. Less obvious is the fact that if a wire is twice as long, it will have twice the resistance. The resistance of short lengths of conventional metallic wires is very low.

"What is the broken fire hydrant of Figure 19.8 analogous to in electrical terms?"

Dick White

Figure 19.8 Speaking of water models, this impromptu fountain was produced when a truck backed into and broke off a fire hydrant. Workers under a tarpaulin just to the right of the water pipe are attempting to close the hydrant valve located in the street.

"The two resistors have the same resistance value, but different sizes; what's the difference?"

Other materials, such as carbon, are not such good conductors. We can build components, called resistors, which have high values of resistance out of these materials or by making very thin films of metals. The *ohm* is the unit of measure for resistance. This is abbreviated by the Greek letter Omega (Ω). Resistors are readily available in values ranging from 1Ω to $10\text{M}\Omega$.

Some practical examples of uses of resistors include: incandescent light bulbs; electric heaters, ovens, ranges, blankets, car window defrosters; fuses; voltage-to-current converters; current-to-voltage converters; and current-limiting devices.

Resistors can have their value marked with colored bands, according to the scheme listed in Table 19.1. The first two bands are significant digits, the third is a multiplier, and an optional fourth is the tolerance.

Table 19.1 Color Code for Resistors.

Band Color	Significant Digit	Multiplier	Tolerance
Black	0	1	-
Brown	1	10	1%
Red	2	100	2%
Orange	3	1000	3%
Yellow	4	10000	4%
Green	5	100000	-
Blue	6	1000000	flame proof
Violet	7	10000000	-
Gray	8	-	-
White	9	-	-
Gold	-	0.1	5%
Silver	-	0.01	10%
No Band	-	-	20%

There are two useful water models for resistors. (See Figure 19.9.) The first is a pipe with a sponge wedged into it, and the second is a pipe with a very tiny cross section. The sponge with all of its tortuous passages generates a large resistance to water flow. To make a resistor that has a higher resistance, we can make the sponge denser, longer, or narrower. To make a resistor with a lower value we can reduce the sponge density, make it shorter, or make it wider.

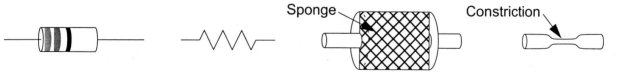

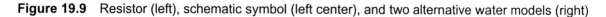

Figure 19.9 Resistor (left), schematic symbol (left center), and two alternative water models (right)

Ohm's Law

A simple way to remember Ohm's Law: Cover the variable you want to solve for (such as R), and it will be equal to the formula that is left uncovered (V/I). Just remember that the voltage goes on top.

The relationship between voltage and current in a resistance is expressed by

Ohm's Law: $V = IR$,

where V is the variable for voltage in volts, I is the variable for current in amps, and R is the variable for resistance in ohms.

From this formula, we see that if we double the voltage across a given resistor the current flowing through it will double. If we change resistors to one that is 100 times larger, we can expect one hundredth of the current. If we force a current of two amps through a two-ohm resistor, we will need to supply a voltage of four volts.

In our water model of a resistor, if we double the water pressure across it, the current passing through it will double (approximately, since water flow in real pipes is fairly complicated). If we increase the resistance by making the pipe much narrower, the water flow will be reduced, as one expects intuitively.

Resistors Connected in Series

We can use Ohm's Law to derive the formula for the value of two resistors that are connected in series, as shown in Figure 19.10. Being connected "in series" simply means that a current flowing in these devices must go serially through them: first through one and then through the other. Since the two resistors are connected in series, the current that flows through R_1 also must flow through R_2. Remember that no leaks are allowed. Assume that a current I is flowing through the resistors. Then, apply Ohm's Law to each resistor. We get $V_1 = IR_1$ and $V_2 = IR_2$. Using KVL, we can add the two voltages: $V_{tot} = V_1 + V_2 = IR_1 + IR_2$. Now, we can reapply Ohm's Law to see what resistance we must have. Since we know V_{tot} and I, we can find R_{tot}:

$$R_{tot} = \frac{V_{tot}}{I} = \frac{IR_1 + IR_2}{I} = R_1 + R_2$$

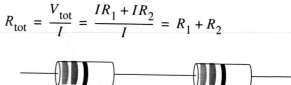

Figure 19.10 Series-connected resistors

Exercise 19.2 Calculate the resistance obtained by combining the following pairs of resistors, and formulate in words what this indicates: 100Ω resistor connected in series with: (a) another 100Ω resistor; (b) a 1000Ω resistor; (c) a 1 MΩ resistor; and (d) a 1Ω resistor.

Solution: Results are (a) 200Ω; (b) 1100Ω; (c) 1 MΩ (1,000,100Ω); and (d) 100Ω (101Ω). In words, the resistance of two resistors connected in series is dominated by the value of the larger resistor. [Note: The non-parenthesized numbers have been rounded to the appropriate number of significant figures, while the numbers in parentheses are "straight from the calculator" before rounding. (See Chapter 4.)]

Resistors Connected in Parallel

We can also connect two resistors in parallel. (See Figure 19.11.) Being connected "in parallel" means that a current must split, like a river flowing around an island. The two currents are not necessarily equal, but the voltage difference between the point where the currents diverge and the point where they rejoin must be the same for all paths. The formulas for parallel components are to be derived as homework or lab problems.

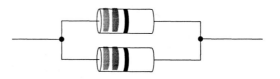

Figure 19.11   Resistors connected in parallel

Exercise 19.3   What is the effective resistance of a $100\,\Omega$ resistor when connected in parallel across (a) another $100\,\Omega$ resistor; (b) a $1000\,\Omega$ resistor; (c) a $1\,M\Omega$ resistor; or (d) a $1\,\Omega$ resistor? Try to verbalize the message behind these particular answers.

Solution: The formula, which you're asked to derive in Problem 19.29 and Problem 19.30, is $R_{\text{parallel}} = 1/(1/R_1 + 1/R_2 + 1/R_3 \ldots)$, which reduces for just two resistors to $R_{\text{parallel}} = R_1 R_2/(R_1 + R_2)$. The answers then become (a) $50\,\Omega$; (b) $91\,\Omega$ ($90.90\ldots\Omega$); (c) $100\,\Omega$ ($99.990001\ldots\Omega$); (d) $1\,\Omega$ ($0.990099009\ldots\Omega$). In words, the resistance of two very different resistors is roughly equal to the value of the smaller resistor. The resistance of two equal resistors paralleled is just half the resistance of one resistor alone.

The power dissipated in a resistor is the product of the current I_R and the voltage V_R, as defined in Figure 19.12a. Since the value of the resistance is assumed to be constant, we can combine Ohm's Law and the power formula to get

> "What happens when power is dissipated in a resistor? Does it heat up like an incandescent lamp?"

$$P = I_R^2 R = \frac{V_R^2}{R}.$$

If we have a circuit element as shown in Figure 19.12b in which the current I_E is negative and V_E is positive, the power dissipated in the element, $P = I_E V_E$, is a negative quantity. This means that the element supplies power to the rest of the circuit, as a battery would.

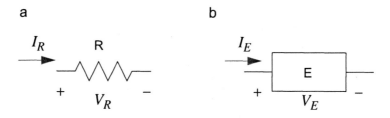

Figure 19.12   (a) Resistor R; (b) unknown element E

Exercise 19.4 A human being engaging in normal activity converts the chemical energy contained in food into heat at a rate corresponding to about 100 watts. What resistance values would you need to produce the same power dissipation from a 120 V DC power supply?

Solution: Since $R = V^2/P$, $R = 140\,\Omega$ $(144\,\Omega)$.

Exercise 19.5 If the maximum current that you can draw from a particular DC power supply is 15 A, what resistance would you need to dissipate energy at the same rate as a 1500-watt hairdrier?

Solution: Here $R = P/I^2$, so $R = 6.7\,\Omega$ $(6.66666...\,\Omega)$.

Exercise 19.6 (For electric car buffs) What current must a 120 V DC power source provide if the rate of power delivery equals that of a 200-horsepower engine? (Assume that 1 horsepower is equivalent to 746 electrical watts.)

Solution: Since $P = I\,V$ and the power required is $200 \times 746 = 149{,}200$ watts, $I = 1.24\,\text{kA}$ $(1{,}243.33...\,\text{A})$.

19.7 Schematics

We use drawings of circuits to express our circuit designs. These drawings are in a symbolic or schematic form, rather than a pictorial form. These schematic drawings are organized to best convey the intended functions of the circuit without regard to the physical construction details. Generally, input signals are on the left, and output signals are on the right, with signals progressing across the page from left to right. Similarly, power supply connections are arranged so that higher voltages are placed near the top of the page and lower voltages near the bottom.

We use the standardized symbols shown in Figure 19.13 to represent electrical components. We will introduce other schematic symbols as we encounter each component.

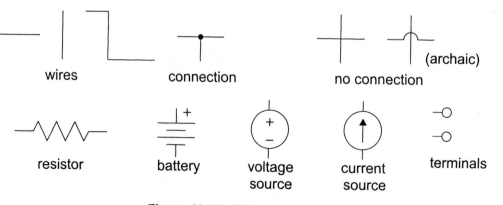

Figure 19.13 Schematic symbols

19.8 Potential Variations in Resistive Circuits

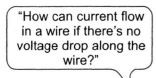

Figure 19.14 shows schematically the variation of electric potential around four different circuits that contain only batteries and resistors. Electric potential is plotted vertically upwards. Hence, one sees that the potential drops when one passes through a resistor in the direction of current flow. This is the so-called resistor voltage drop. The potential also rises as one goes from the negative to the positive terminal of a battery. Upon traversing entirely around any loop in one of these circuits, one finds the potential returns to its initial value, a consequence of Kirchhoff's Voltage Law.

Considering first the upper row of circuits, we see that in Figure 19.14a, there

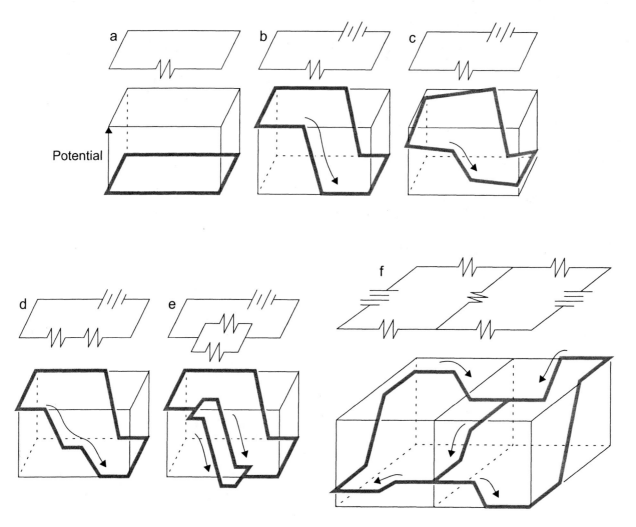

Figure 19.14   Resistor/battery circuits
(These illustrations were kindly given to one of the authors by Jim Hauser of San Luis Obispo, CA.)

127

is no voltage source, so the potential is zero everywhere. In **b**, a circuit assumed to have perfectly conducting wires, the voltage drop across the resistor equals the voltage increase produced by the battery. In **c**, the resistor has a very small value, so that the resistance of the wires becomes significant and one sees voltage drops along each wire, as well as along the resistor. In the lower row of circuits, **d** shows that the sum of the voltage drops across the resistors that are connected in series equals the voltage rise produced by the battery. In **d**, each of the resistors connected in parallel has a voltage drop that is the negative of the voltage rise produced by the battery. In **f**, two batteries provide energy to the circuit.

19.9 Voltage Dividers

If we connect two resistors in series with each other and a battery or other voltage source, as shown in Figure 19.15, a current will flow through the resistors. We can calculate the value of that current using Ohm's Law. We can then find the voltage across each individual resistor by reapplying Ohm's Law. These two voltages add up to the voltage produced by the voltage source. They divide the voltage in the sense that you might divide a pile of sand into smaller piles: You don't change the total amount of sand.

Exercise 19.7   Solve for V_{out} in terms of V_1 and R_1 and R_2.

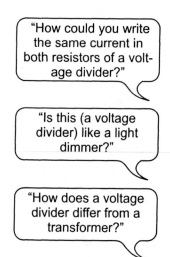

"How could you write the same current in both resistors of a voltage divider?"

"Is this (a voltage divider) like a light dimmer?"

"How does a voltage divider differ from a transformer?"

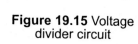

Figure 19.15 Voltage divider circuit

Solution: The series resistance of R_1 and R_2 is the sum $R_1 + R_2$. Use Ohm's Law to find $I = \dfrac{V_1}{R_1 + R_2}$. Then, use Ohm's Law again to find $V_{out} = IR_2$. Substituting the expression for I into the expression for V_{out}, we get $V_{out} = V_1\dfrac{R_2}{R_1 + R_2}$.

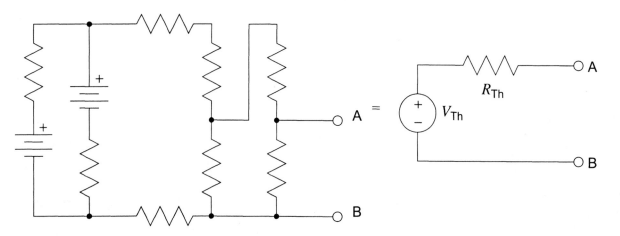

Figure 19.16 The simple, two-component Thévenin equivalent circuit on the right can model the behavior of the more complex circuit at left if V_{Th} and R_{Th} are chosen properly.

19.10 Thévenin Equivalent Circuits

In the voltage divider shown in the previous section, if we add another resistor across the output, it will change the voltage that appears at the output. We can see that the voltage divider is not suitable for producing a steady voltage if the load is going to vary. We can represent the voltage divider by a simpler circuit that makes it easier to calculate what happens when we connect a different load. The Thévenin equivalent circuit can represent any collection of DC voltage sources and resistors as a single voltage and a single resistor. It makes no difference in which order the two components are placed in series. Figure 19.16 shows a multi-component circuit and its simple Thévenin equivalent circuit.

We can find the equivalent circuit one of two ways. The measurement approach is to first connect a voltmeter across the output to find the open-circuit voltage, V_{oc}, and then to connect an ammeter to find the short-circuit current, I_{sc}. The voltmeter looks like an open circuit, because it shouldn't allow current to flow, and the ammeter looks like a short circuit, because it shouldn't have a voltage drop across its terminals. Once we have these two measurements, we can find the Thévenin voltage, V_{Th}, and the Thévenin resistance, R_{Th}. V_{Th} is simply equal to the open-circuit voltage, $V_{th} = V_{oc}$. R_{Th} is simply the open-circuit voltage divided by the short-circuit current, $R_{th} = V_{oc}/I_{sc}$. This method is easy to apply if you have a physical circuit to measure or if these quantities can be easily calculated from the schematic.

Here's an example of how to derive the Thévenin equivalent for a circuit (in this case, two Thévenin equivalent circuits connected in series). The circuit and its equivalent are shown in Figure 19.17.

The open-circuit voltage, V_{oc}, is just equal to the sum of the two voltages V_1 and V_2, and this is V_{Th}:

$$V_{Th} = V_1 + V_2.$$

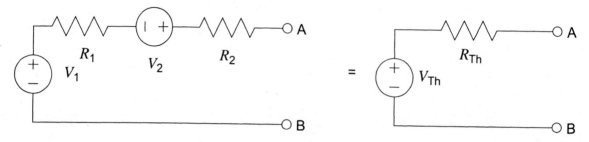

Figure 19.17   Finding the Thévenin equivalent for a circuit containing two voltage sources

To find R_{Th}, we divide V_{Th} by I_{sc}, which flows when we connect a resistance-less wire from A to B. Applying KVL and Ohm's Law gives use the needed equation:

$$-V_1 + I_{sc}R_1 - V_2 + I_{sc}R_2 = 0$$

$$I_{sc} = \frac{V_1 + V_2}{R_1 + R_2}.$$

Thus,

$$R_{Th} = \frac{V_{Th}}{I_{sc}} = R_1 + R_2.$$

You will find other problems on this topic in Section 19.12.

19.11 Ground

In the early days of the telegraph only a single wire was used to carry the current to the receiver. The return path for the current was provided by making a connection to the earth. The moisture and the ion content allow the soil to conduct electricity. The term *ground* has come to mean any common connection point to which other points in a circuit are referenced. The symbols for grounds are shown in Figure 19.18. In a circuit schematic drawing, all the nodes that are drawn using the same type of ground symbol are connected to a common conductor. This saves having to draw all of these wires, which might clutter the schematic without adding meaning. If more than one type of symbol is used, these grounds are usually separated at all but one point. Voltages marked on the schematic are usually referred to ground, and oscilloscopes measure voltage with respect to a ground connection.

In circuit boards with more than two layers, it is customary to have one or more ground planes. These are layers of copper that provide low-resistance connection wherever required on the board.

Some electronic devices housed in metal enclosures or on metal chassis make use of what is known as a chassis ground.

a. Digital ground   b. Analog ground   c. Chassis or earth ground

Figure 19.18   Schematic symbols for ground

19.12 Problems

19.1 Give the abbreviation and corresponding variable for the following units of measure:
  (a) Coulomb
  (b) Ampere
  (c) Volt
  (d) Watt
  (e) Joule

19.2 Why is a water model (with the rules we have established) useful for representing common electronic components?

19.3 What is the water model for current flowing in a wire?

19.4 What in the water model is analogous to voltage?

19.5 Few newspaper reporters are electrical engineers, so bloopers like the following can appear in print. An Associated Press article headlined "Suit Accuses Teacher of Using Electric Shocks" reported that a shop teacher disciplined a student named Justin by forcing him to hold a spark plug in one hand "and a piece of metal connected to an electric current in the other." The lawsuit claims that this "caused three volts of electricity to course through Justin's body." Comment on the mistakes you find in this story.

19.6 These questions, aimed at ensuring that you understand the fundamental sign conventions we use, relate to the circuit shown in Figure P19.6.

(a) If the voltage V_{AB} is 3 volts, what is the voltage V_{BA}?

(b) If the current $I_1 = -2$ mA and is due to the flow of electrons in the metallic wire, do the electrons move through circuit element 1 toward or away from terminal A?

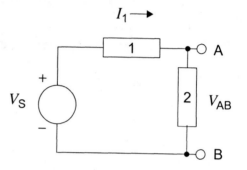

Figure P19.6

19.7 In the battery-powered warning light of Figure P19.7a, what is the electric potential with respect to ground at terminal A at the positive terminal of the 3.0-volt battery? How about at terminal B? In Figure P19.7b, the warning light has been mounted on (and connected to) a high-voltage source. Now what are the electric potentials with respect to ground at terminals A and B? Same question for Figure P19.7c, where the magnitude of the battery voltage is the same as in (a) and (b).

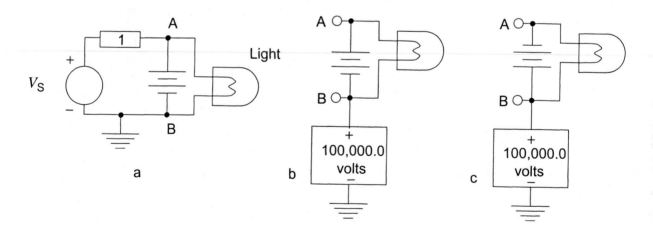

Figure P19.7

19.8 If a 100-watt light bulb is operated for one hour, how many joules of electrical energy are dissipated in the filament?

19.9   In a battery, electrical energy is produced by means of a reaction among the chemicals contained inside. Until near the end of its life, a battery's output voltage is nearly constant, and so a battery's capacity is typically denoted in ampere-hours, the product of the current it can deliver at the rated voltage times the hours of life. How much electrical energy could be delivered by a 1.4-ampere-hour, 1.25-volt rechargeable, size-C nickel-cadmium battery?

19.10 Find the unknown current I in the fragment of a circuit shown in Figure P19.10, assuming that $I_1 = -2$ mA, $I_2 = 9$ mA, $I_3 = -3$ mA, and $R = 18$ kilohm. WARNING: Real-world problems often appear to contain more or less data than is needed for their solution. In such a case, the extra data must be ignored, or assumptions must be made about the missing data. This particular problem, as well as some others that follow, contains more data than you need for its solution. (Hint: The value of R does not affect the answer.)

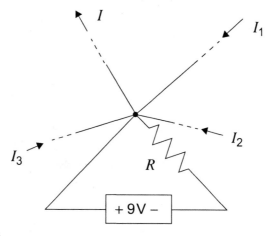

Figure P19.10

19.11 Find the unknown voltage V_{AB} in the circuit of Figure P19.11. Assume the following values: $V_S = 9$ V, $V_1 = -3$ V, $V_2 = 5$ V, $V_3 = 1$ V, $R_1 = 1$ kΩ, and $R_2 = 3$ kΩ. (Hint: You can obtain the answer from a single Kirchhoff's 's voltage law equation.)

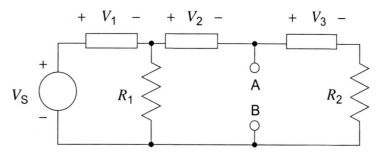

Figure P19.11

19.12 Figure P19.12 shows a fragment of a DC circuit that contains circuit elements indicated by rectangular boxes. Determine the power dissipated within the box labelled **1**, assuming that $I_1 = 2$ mA, $V_S = 9$ V, and $V_{AB} = 3$ V.

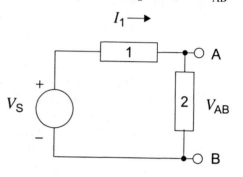

Figure P19.12

19.13 What is the power dissipated in the source V_S in Figure P19.12, assuming that $V_S = 9$ V and $I_1 = 2$ mA? What does your result mean physically?

19.14 What does it mean if you find that the calculated power dissipated in a circuit element is a negative quantity?

19.15 Sketch and describe the water model for a resistor.

19.16 How does the amount of current change when it flows through a resistor (compare with the water flow analogy)?

19.17 What happens to the potential along a resistor when a current flows through the resistor?

19.18 In the water model, what happens to the pressure difference as the water flows through the obstruction (sponge) in a water resistor"?

19.19 Find the current I that will flow when a potential difference of 3.3 volts is established across a 16.5 kΩ resistor.

19.20 What voltage V would cause a 5 mA current to flow through a resistance of 5 kΩ?

19.21 Using Ohm's Law and the circuit of Figure P19.21, answer the following questions, assuming that $R_2 = 3$ kΩ:

(a) What resistance R_1 would cause a current $I = 3$ mA to flow when the source voltage V_S is 12V?

(b) What resistance R_1 would cause V_2 to be two-thirds of V_1?

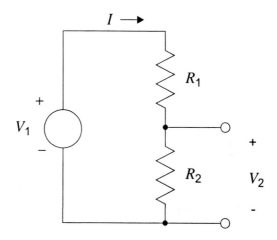

Figure P19.21

19.22 Find the short-circuit current I_{sc} that flows when a wire is connected across terminals A and B in the circuit of Figure P19.22, assuming that $V_1 = 3$ V, $R_1 = 1$ kΩ, and $R_2 = 3$ kΩ.

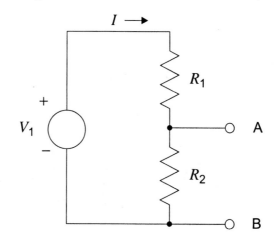

Figure P19.22

19.23 Find the voltage drop V_{AB} across the 1.5 kΩ resistor R shown as part of a larger circuit in Figure P19.23, assuming that $V_S = 9$ V, $I_1 = -7$ mA, $I_2 = 5$ mA, and $I_3 = 2$ mA.

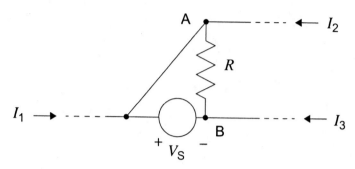

Figure P19.23

19.24 Assuming that $V_{AB} = 9$ volts in Figure P19.24, find the current I that flows into the upper lead connected to the paralleled 1 kΩ (R_1), 2 kΩ (R_2), and 4 kΩ (R_3) resistors.

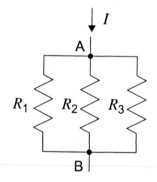

Figure P19.24

19.25 Working with high voltages can be dangerous, so experimenters often connect a current-limiting resistor in series with their high-voltage supply to protect themselves in case of accidental contact with the wires. What value resistor would you use to limit the current that could flow from a 500-volt supply to 100 µA?

19.26 Using Figure P19.21 find
   (a) A general formula for V_2 in terms of R_1, R_2, and V_1.
   (b) The current I that flows, assuming that $V_1 = 10$ V, $R_1 = 3$ kΩ, and $R_2 = 6$ kΩ.
   (c) The voltage V_2 across R_2 that results from the current flow.

19.27 Derive the formula for the equivalent resistance of resistors R_1 and R_2 connected in series. (<u>Hint</u>: Start by assuming that a current I flows through the resistors, and sum the voltage drops across each resistor.)

19.28 Evaluate the formula for the effective resistance R_{eff} of two resistors connected in series for the following special cases. Obtain approximate expressions and summarize with rules of thumb for the result. Describe the water model for each case.
(a)   Two resistors of equal value (say, 10 kΩ).
(b)   Two very unequal resistors (say, a 10 Ω and a 10 MΩ resistor).

19.29 Derive the formula for the equivalent resistance of resistors R_1 and R_2 connected in parallel. (<u>Hint</u>: Start by assuming that a voltage V connected across the two resistors produces two currents whose sum is the current that flows in the common lead.)

19.30 Generalize the case of the effective resistance of resistors in parallel to more than two resistors, as shown in Figure P19.30.

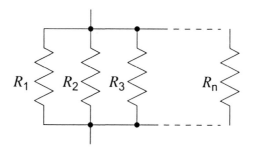

Figure P19.30

19.31 Evaluate the formula for the effective resistance R_{eff} of two resistors connected in parallel for the following special cases. Obtain approximate expressions and summarize with rules of thumb for the result. Describe the water model for each case.
(a)   Two resistors of equal value (say, 5 kΩ).
(b)   Two very unequal resistors (say, a 5 Ω and a 10 MΩ resistor).

19.32 For the case where a three-volt supply is connected across two parallel-connected resistors of quite unequal value, 5Ω and 10MΩ, find the approximate total current and the current flowing in each resistor. State a qualitative rule of thumb regarding how the current flow divides between the resistors in this case. Note that this type of circuit is sometimes known as a current divider, because of its similarity to the voltage divider.

19.33 Draw the Thévenin equivalent circuit with its correct element values for the circuit of Figure P19.22, assuming that $V_1 = 9$ V, $R_1 = 5$ kΩ, and $R_2 = 8$ kΩ.

19.34 Find the values for V_{Th} and R_{Th} for the Thévenin equivalent circuit for the circuit to the left of terminals A and B in Figure P19.34. Find both an algebraic answer and a numerical answer, assuming that $V_S = 3\,V$, and $R_1 = R_2 = R_3 = 5\,k\Omega$.

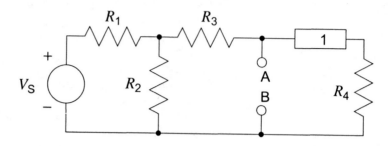

Figure P19.34

19.35 If you were given a voltmeter and a 1000-ohm, 10-watt resistor, what measurements could you make to determine the values of V_{Th} and R_{Th} for a Thévenin circuit that was equivalent to the circuit of Figure P19.22?

19.36 If you were to use a voltmeter and a resistive load to determine experimentally the Thévenin circuit equivalent to a given circuit, you'd want to be sure that you didn't apply too large a voltage to the resistor. If you have only one-eighth-watt resistors available whose values range from 10 ohms to 100 kilohms, what is the maximum permissible Thévenin voltage?

19.37 Without doing any algebra, how can you tell by inspection that the circuit of Figure P19.37 cannot be the Thévenin equivalent circuit for the circuit and element values of Figure P19.34?

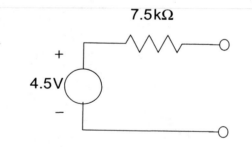

Figure P19.37

19.38 When a resistor is connected in parallel with a Thévenin equivalent circuit, as shown in Figure P19.38, the resulting circuit may be replaced with a new Thévenin equivalent circuit. Obtain an expression for the new Thévenin voltage and the new Thévenin resistance. (<u>Hint</u>: Recall the voltage divider when starting this problem.)

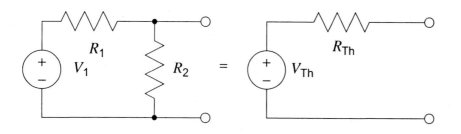

Figure P19.38

19.39 Suppose you want to find the Thévenin equivalent circuit for the wall power outlet in your lab. You can't measure the short-circuit current. You do, however, have at your disposal a collection of different values of 10-watt resistors. Select the proper value of resistance (R) to avoid smoke. Measure the open-circuit voltage (V_{oc}), and the voltage with the resistor connected (V_R) across the line. (Please don't actually try this: we don't want you to electrocute yourself.) Using these two measurements, calculate the Thévenin equivalent circuit.

19.40 Find the Thévenin equivalent circuit for the circuit in Figure P19.40, where a voltage source V_2 has been connected across a series-connected voltage source and resistor. Use the method from Problem 19.39 to avoid shorting out the voltage source.

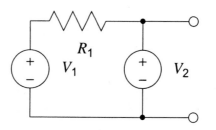

Figure P19.40

19.41 Find the Thévenin equivalent circuit that is equivalent to two Thévenin equivalent circuits connected in parallel as shown in Figure P19.41

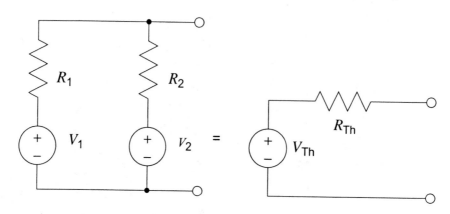

Figure P19.41

19.42 Norton equivalent circuits are similar to Thévenin equivalent circuits in function, but instead of using a voltage source in series with a resistor, Norton equivalents employ a <u>current</u> source I_N in <u>parallel</u> with a resistor R_N. (See Figure P19.42.) Determine the components in the Norton circuit that is equivalent to the Thévenin circuit shown on the left.

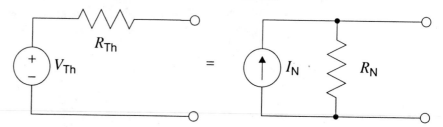

Figure P19.42

19.43 Plot together on one graph the I-V characteristics of a 50 Ω and a 1 kΩ resistor.)

19.44 Plot the I-V characteristic of the Thévenin equivalent circuit shown in Figure P19.37.

19.45 Use plots of the I-V characteristic of a resistor and of a Thévenin equivalent circuit to find graphically the current that will flow in the circuit formed by connecting a 1 kΩ resistor R_1 across the terminals of a Thévenin circuit for which $V_{Th} = 1.5$ V and $R_{Th} = 100$ Ω. Verify your answer analytically.

19.46 Considered most simply as a circuit element, a flashlight bulb behaves as a resistor, but because the filament in the bulb heats up when current passes through it, the resistance depends upon the amount of current flowing though the bulb, as indicated in Table P19.46.

(a)   From the data given, plot the *I-V* characteristic of this light bulb.

(b)   Find the current that would flow if the bulb were connected to the Thévenin circuit of Figure P19.37, assuming that $R_{Th} = 500$ Ω.

Table P19.46   Resistance of flashlight bulb at various currents

Current (mA)	Resistance (Ω)
2	20
4	45
6	100
8	160
10	300

Alternating Currents and Components

20.1 Alternating Currents

In the previous chapter we dealt with DC, or direct current. Direct current is easily visualized, since it flows in only one direction like a river or the water in a garden hose. Alternating current (AC), in contrast, flows back and forth, much like the tides that flood in and out under the Golden Gate Bridge or the air when you breathe. Alternating current is preferred over direct current for the distribution of electrical energy, and alternating current is well suited for representing signals such as speech and music, generating radio waves, and encoding information.

A water model for an alternating current generator is shown in Figure 20.1. A piston in a cylinder full of water is driven by a connecting rod. The rod is pushed back and forth by the rotation of a pin on the driving wheel. When the wheel is driven at a constant speed, the motion of the piston is sinusoidal, as only the horizontal component of the pin's motion is coupled to the rod.

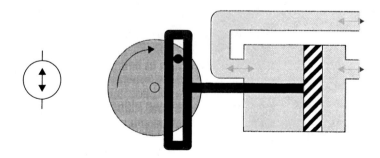

Figure 20.1   Water model (right) and hypothetical schematic symbol (left) for an alternating current generator

It is possible to combine a direct and an alternating current. The two components are just added together. Similarly it is possible to combine any number of AC currents at different frequencies.

20.2 AC Voltages

If we pass an alternating current through a resistor, we can observe across the resistor an AC voltage whose instantaneous value obeys Ohm's Law. This voltage will alternate its polarity as the current reverses directions. The frequency f of the alternations is expressed as the number of complete cycles that the voltage goes through each second. The unit of frequency is the hertz, abbreviated Hz. An alternating voltage $v(t)$ can be expressed as a sinusoidal function of time,

$$v(t) = V_p \sin(\omega t) ,$$

where V_p is the peak value of the voltage, ω is the angular frequency in radians per second, and t represents time. This voltage is sketched in Figure 20.2. The angular frequency is related to the frequency in Hz by the expression $\omega = 2\pi f$. (Note: we will use the lowercase symbols v and i to represent time-varying voltages or currents, respectively.)

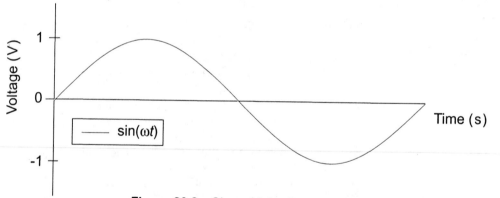

Figure 20.2 Sinusoidal voltage

Figure 20.3 Schematic symbol for an AC voltage source.

The schematic symbol for an AC voltage source is shown in Figure 20.3.

Since the voltage and the current have positive and negative peak values and pass through zero as the direction reverses, the instantaneous power dissipated in a resistor is not constant. The power varies with the square of the voltage: $P = V^2/R$. When we substitute in the formula for an alternating voltage, we get a moderately complicated expression that gives us the instantaneous power. Usually, though, we are concerned with the average power.

Wouldn't it be nice if we could represent an alternating voltage in such a way that the formula for average power dissipation in a resistor was similar to the foregoing one of $P = V^2/R$? The trick is to define a voltage amplitude V_{rms}, known as the *root mean square voltage*, which is related to the peak voltage by the formula

$$V_{rms} = V_p \frac{1}{\sqrt{2}}.$$

Here's the reasoning. If we square $v(t)$, we have $[v(t)]^2 = V_p^2[\sin(\omega t)]^2$. But what does this mean? We can use the trigonometric identity

$$[\sin(\omega t)]^2 = \frac{1}{2}[1-\cos(2\omega t)]$$

to obtain a function that we can understand:

$$P = \frac{V_p^2}{2R}[1-\cos(2\omega t)].$$

This is still a periodically changing function, at twice the angular frequency of the voltage, but there is a term that does not change with time, namely $V_p^2/(2R)$. (See Figure 20.4.) If we want to determine the average effect of this wave, over time, we can just ignore the cosine part, since its average is zero, and we're left with the constant term.

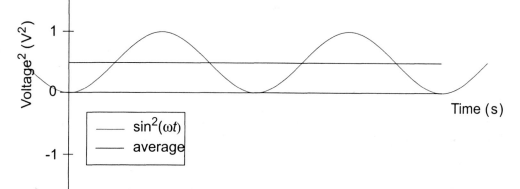

Figure 20.4 Terms related to the root-mean-square (rms) calculation. Plotted are the functions $\sin^2(\omega t)$ and the mean of $\sin^2(\omega t)$.

This gives us

$$P = \frac{V_{rms}^2}{R} = \frac{V_p^2}{(2R)},$$

which we can solve for V_{rms}:

$$V_{rms} = V_p \frac{1}{\sqrt{2}}.$$

We choose to label AC voltages with this rms value, as indicated in Figure 20.5. To calculate the rms value, we first square the instantaneous value of the voltage; then, we average the value over time (find its mean). Finally, we take the square root of the average. For a sinusoidal voltage, then, the rms value is given by

$$V_{rms} = \sqrt{\overline{\left[(V_p \sin(\omega t))^2 \right]}} = \sqrt{\overline{\left[V_p^2 \frac{1}{2} [1 - \cos(2\omega t)] \right]}} = V_p \sqrt{\frac{1}{2}} = 0.707 V_p.$$

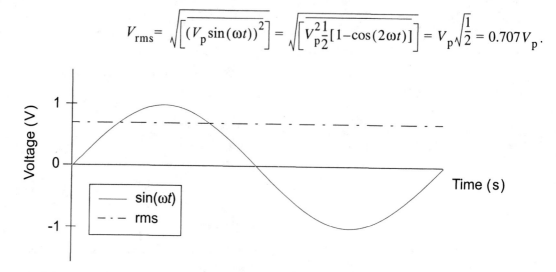

Figure 20.5 Sinusoidal voltage (solid curve); rms voltage (broken line)

Exercise 20.1 The voltage at household electrical outlets in the U.S. is 120 volts rms at a 60 Hz frequency. Calculate the peak-to-peak voltage.

"Do the lights flicker (when driven with an alternating current)?"

Solution: The peak-to-peak voltage is difference between the highest voltage and the lowest voltage. In the case of a sinusoid, this difference is twice the peak voltage. We can find the peak voltage from the rms voltage by reversing the operation just given.

$$V_{pp} = 2 \cdot V_p = 2 \cdot \sqrt{2} \cdot V_{rms}; \quad V_{pp} = 2 \cdot 1.414 \cdot 120V = 340V.$$

Notice that we retained in the final answer no more significant digits than those in the numbers with which we started.

Sinusoidally varying voltages are particularly important, because of their universal use in the distribution of electric power. Another periodically varying voltage waveform of importance is the rectangular wave (also known as the square wave) sketched in Figure 20.6. The amplitude of the waveform shown is 2 volts peak-to-peak, and the period of this waveform — the time interval between successive equivalent points on the waveform — is 6 ms. In the laboratory, one may find a function generator that produces sinusoidal, rectangular, and triangular (sawtooth) waveforms having selectable amplitudes and periods. The amplitude of a sinusoidal wave may be denoted as the rms value, the peak value, or the peak-to-peak value; for a given waveform, these amplitudes are in the ratio of $1/(2)^{1/2}:1:2$, respectively. For rectangular and triangular waveforms, one usually speaks of the peak-to-peak amplitude. The minimum voltage of these last two waveforms may be zero volts, or, with a so-called "floating" power supply, the waveform may have both negative and positive portions.

20.3 Capacitance

A student's exclamation (upon seeing a charged capacitor discharged by a screwdriver): "So, capacitors store energy!"

"Is the charge on each capacitor plate Q, or is it Q/2?"

If we align two conductive plates parallel to each other, separate them with an insulating material, and then connect a wire to each plate, we will have formed a component called a *capacitor*. Capacitor symbols for capacitors appear in Figure 20.7, and the physical structure of a capacitor is shown in Figure 20.8. While we cannot continuously pass a direct current through this device, we can pass a current through it for a short time or pass an alternating current. Inside the device, the charge that moves into the device covers the surface of one plate. To maintain local charge balance, an equal and opposite charge covers the other plate, freeing up the carriers to leave on the other wire. While a current "passes" through in this manner, no single charge actually goes all the way through the device. The quantity of balanced charges Q "stored" in the device is directly proportional to the voltage measured between the two wires (or leads) and to the capacitance measured in farads. The variable that we use to represent the capacitance is C:

$$Q = CV.$$

This formula can be differentiated to arrive at an expression for the current:

$$I = \frac{dQ}{dt} = C\frac{dV}{dt}.$$

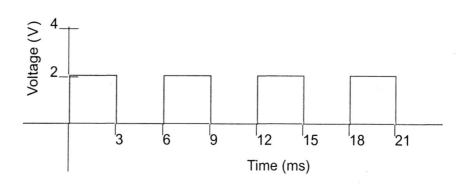

Figure 20.6 Rectangular voltage waveform

Most capacitors have a value far less than a farad, so capacitances are frequently expressed in microfarads (μF) or picofarads (pF).

Figure 20.7 Schematic symbols for (a) polarized, (b) non-polarized and (c) variable capacitors

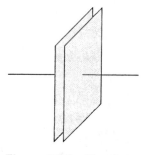

Figure 20.8 Parallel-plate capacitor

The capacity of a parallel-plate capacitor depends on its dimensions and the insulating material that separates the plates, called the dielectric. The larger the area of the plates, the larger the capacity is. The closer together the plates are placed, the higher the capacity is. For a parallel-plate capacitor, we can calculate the capacity from the formula

$$C = \frac{\kappa \varepsilon_0 A}{d},$$

where κ is the relative dielectric constant of the dielectric material, ε_0 is the permittivity constant, 8.85 pF/m, A is the area of the plates (in square meters), and d is the distance (in meters) that separates them.

Practical capacitors are rarely as simple as those sketched here. They may involve wound films, stacked layers, and possibly even a liquid that substitutes for one of the plates.

Table 20.1 Dielectric properties of selected materials[a]

Material	Relative Dielectric Constant	Dielectric Strength (kV/cm)
Vacuum	1.00000	∞
Air	1.00054	8
Paper	3.5	140
Polystyrene	2.6	250
Teflon	2.1	600
Titanium Dioxide	100	60

[a] David Halliday and Robert Resnick, *Physics* (John Wiley & Sons, Inc.,1962), p. 750.

As you can see in Table 20.1, dielectric materials also have a strength that, when multiplied by the thickness of the dielectric material, is an indication of how much voltage you can place across the capacitor. This gives rise to a maximum volt-

Figure 20.9 Schematic symbol and water model for a capacitor

age rating for any practical capacitor. It is good engineering practice to avoid exceeding the maximum voltage rating.

The water model for a capacitor is a water-filled cylinder with a movable piston. (See Figure 20.9.) The piston is attached to one end of the cylinder by a spring. In operation, no water passes around the piston. As water (charge) moves into the device through one pipe, an equal amount must leave through the other. As water flows, it displaces the piston, and compresses or stretches the spring. The spring responds by exerting a force on the piston, which will be translated into a difference in water pressure between the two sides (corresponding to a potential difference, or a voltage across the capacitor). Externally applied changes of water pressure on one side are instantly passed through to the other side.

When the piston reaches one end or the other, the situation is analogous to reaching the maximum voltage for the capacitor. Some capacitors are polarized, meaning that a voltage of only one polarity should be applied to them. Such capacitors are marked with a plus sign to indicate which side is to have the higher potential. When a voltage of the wrong polarity is applied, the capacitor may "break down" and exhibit a low resistance, or it might even explode. Incidentally, the water model can be modified to be polarized by offsetting the rest position of the piston to the far left hand end.

Capacitors do not dissipate power; instead, they store energy when charging and return it to the circuit when discharging. The energy U stored in a capacitor can be found from the formula:

$$U = \frac{1}{2}CV^2.$$

> So, how could a distant nuclear blast burn out the electronics in my car?"

20.4 RC Circuits

Circuits that combine a resistor and a capacitor (RC circuits) are frequently used in electronic systems. With those two elements, one can make circuits that separate signals on the basis of their frequencies, circuits that differentiate or integrate signals, and much more. In considering RC circuits we'll start with a water model to develop our intuition, and then examine a graphical depiction of what happens in electronic circuits containing a resistor, a capacitor, and a battery. Finally, we'll introduce mathematical expressions for the currents and voltages in RC circuits.

Figure 20.10 shows a complete water-model circuit. The voltage source is powered by a constant torque motor, as described earlier. The resistor is a pipe containing a constriction, and the capacitor is the chamber fitted with a piston and a spring. Consider the "charging" of this capacitor by the voltage source. Let us suppose that the piston of the capacitor is initially in its equilibrium position in the middle of the chamber. In other words, when we start, there is no pressure difference (no voltage) across the capacitor. Now we turn on the constant torque motor and start to fill the capacitor, pushing the piston to the right and establishing a pressure difference between the two ends of the capacitor. Let's think about how the time to drive the piston to a given position, say, halfway beyond middle to the right, would depend on the values of the resistor and the capacitor.

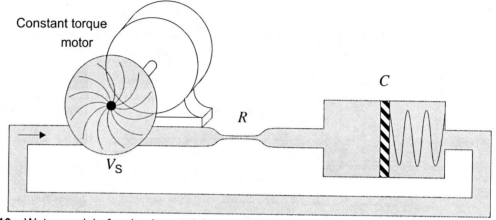

Figure 20.10 Water model of a circuit containing a steady voltage source, a resistor, and a capacitor

First, if the resistance is high (i.e., if the pipe is severely constricted), it will take a long time to get a given amount of water through it and into the capacitor. Thus, we'd expect that the time required for charging the capacitor would rise as the value of the resistance rises. If instead the capacitance were to increase, it would take more water to push the piston to the three-quarter position; since getting more water in would require more time, the time required for charging should increase as the capacitance increases. We'll soon find analytically that the time constant does behave as our intuition suggests. In fact, we'll show that the time constant — the time for the capacitor to charge to about 63% of its maximum value — is simply equal to the product RC.

The behavior of electrical circuits that contain a capacitor is shown graphically in Figure 20.11. Electric potential is plotted vertically upwards. Figure 20.11a, b, and c show, for reference, how the potential changes in circuits containing, respectively, only an uncharged capacitor, a battery that has charged a capacitor to the full battery potential, and only a battery and a resistor.

The circuits in Figure 20.11d, e, and f form a sequence showing the charging of a capacitor through a resistor. In d, initially, the capacitor is uncharged, and the battery has just been connected. As the capacitor is initially not charged, it has no potential across it, and a current flows through the resistor, so that the resistor's voltage drop exactly equals the negative of the battery potential. This current flow starts to charge the capacitor, as shown in e, where the capacitor voltage has risen to a bit more than one-half of the battery potential. Finally, some time later, as shown in f, the capacitor is charged to the battery potential, no more current flows in the circuit, and there is no longer any voltage drop across the resistor.

The discharge of an initially charged capacitor through a resistor is shown in the remaining sketches. In Figure 20.11g, the charged capacitor has just been connected to the resistor, causing a current to flow and producing a resistive voltage Po-

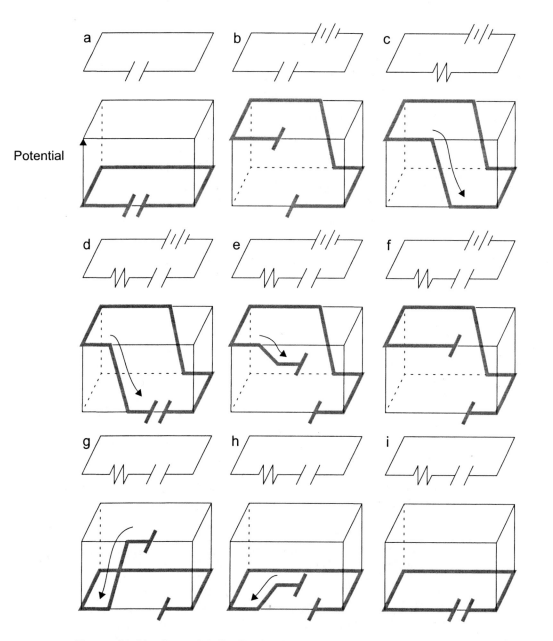

Potential

Figure 20.11 Potential distribution in capacitive circuits. (See text for details.) (Illustration kindly given to one of the authors by Jim Hauser of San Luis Obispo, CA.)

tential drop that equals the capacitor's initial potential. In Figure 20.11h, much of the capacitor's charge has drained off. (That is, electrons have moved through the resistor and wire, neutralizing some of the initial positive charge on the left-hand capacitor plate). Finally, in Figure 20.11i, the capacitor has discharged completely.

Analytic Expressions for Charging and Discharging

Consider the charging and discharging in circuits that contain resistors and only one capacitor. We can obtain analytic expressions for the currents and voltages by using KVL, the current-voltage relations for resistors and capacitors, and a bit of mathematics that you've probably already seen.

As an example, take the circuit of Figure 20.11d, redrawn slightly modified by the addition of a switch in Figure 20.12. We will suppose that the capacitor is initially uncharged and that the switch is closed at time t = 0. At any time thereafter, KVL applies to the circuit, and we have the relation

$$-V_S + v_R + v_C = 0.$$

The voltage across the resistor and that across the capacitor are functions of time. Solving for them involves details we'll leave to be discussed by your mathematics instructor. We'll simply state the final results:

Result 1. In circuits involving only one capacitor and some resistors, the time-varying voltages have the form

$$v(t) = V_A + V_B e^{\left(\frac{-t}{\tau}\right)}.$$

Result 2. Likewise, in circuits containing only one capacitor and some resistors, the time-varying currents that flow have the form

$$i(t) = I_A + I_B e^{\left(\frac{-t}{\tau}\right)}.$$

There are three as-yet undetermined coefficients in each expression: V_A, V_B, and τ in the expression for voltage, and I_A, I_B and τ in the expression for current. The value of τ is the same in both expressions. The term τ is known as the *time constant*; you can see from the way it appears in these two equations, τ must have the dimensions of time, since the exponent of e must be dimensionless. We will see shortly how to determine the value of τ from the circuit elements

First, let us determine I_A and I_B by applying physical reasoning to the problem of charging a capacitor through a resistor (see Figure 20.12) for two extreme times — immediately after its closure and a long time after the switch has been closed. At very long times after $t = 0$, no current flows as the capacitor is fully charged. As t approaches infinity, the exponential term approaches zero, and we have the limiting condition

$$i(t) \rightarrow 0 = I_A.$$

We can find the value of the unknown coefficient I_B for this problem by finding the value of I_B that gives the known current at the instant the switch is closed, at time $t = 0$. At that time, the capacitor is uncharged, so the current is just the current through resistor R when the voltage V_S is connected across it:

$$i(0) = I_A + I_B = \frac{V_S}{R}.$$

Thus, since $I_A = 0$, we have $I_B = V_S/R$.

Math Review

The base of the natural logarithm function is the irrational number e, which is approximately equal to 2.718. When e is raised to the power of x it graphs as follows:

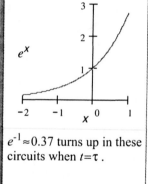

$e^{-1} \approx 0.37$ turns up in these circuits when $t = \tau$.

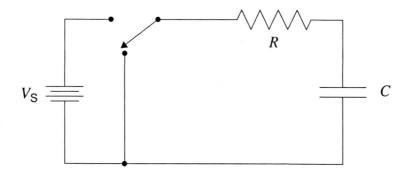

Figure 20.12 An RC circuit with a switch

We can finally obtain the third of our unknown terms, the time constant τ, by returning to the formal expression of KVL:

$$-V_S + v_R + v_C = -V_S + iR + \frac{1}{C}q_C = 0.$$

The math is a little simpler if we differentiate the equation first with respect to time. This yields the expression

$$R\frac{di}{dt} + \frac{1}{C}i = 0.$$

Differentiating our generic expression for the current with respect to time, we see that

$$i(t) = \frac{V_S}{R}e^{\frac{-t}{\tau}} \text{ gives } \frac{di}{dt} = -\frac{V_S}{\tau R}e^{\frac{-t}{\tau}} = -\frac{1}{\tau}i.$$

Substituting this into the previous equation gives

$$-R\frac{1}{\tau}i + \frac{1}{C}i = 0.$$

Thus,

$$\tau = RC,$$

> "Why does the product RC have dimensions of seconds?"

so the time constant for the RC circuit is just the product of R and C. If R is in ohms and C is in farads, RC has the dimensions of seconds.

Figure 20.13 shows a plot of the current $i(t)$ versus the normalized ratio t/RC for any V_S and any R. The initial current just after the switch is closed is V_S/R. You can see that the current in the circuit has fallen to $1/e$, or about 37%, of its initial high value after a time equal to one time constant. You can use your calculator to find that after roughly five time constants have passed, the current is down to below

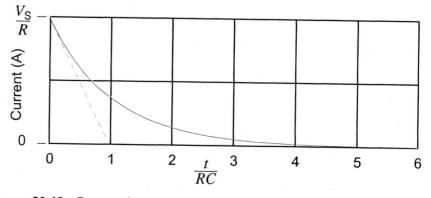

Figure 20.13 Decay of current versus time in the circuit of Figure 20.12. Initial current value is V_S/R. The initial slope intersects the time axis at one time constant, as shown by the dotted line.

1% of its initial value. If $V_S = 9\,V$, $R = 3\,k\Omega$, and $C = 10\,\mu F$, then the initial current is 3 mA, and the time constant, RC, is 30 milliseconds,

Applications of RC Circuits

We have shown that by including one capacitor together with a resistor, we have a circuit whose rate of response to a changing voltage depends on the product of the resistance and the capacitance used. If we want a circuit that responds rapidly, we need to use one whose RC product is small. For slow response, a large RC product is needed; we'll see an example of this application later when we discuss a circuit that converts an alternating voltage to a steady voltage. We'll also see that we can use RC circuits to separate different signals on the basis of their frequencies; this capability is used in the so-called crossover network in a home music system that gets the low-frequency power to the woofer and the high-frequency power to the tweeter. While we have not actually derived expressions for the currents and voltages in these circuits, we have given you a generic solution that you can specialize to the actual RC circuits that you use.

20.5 Inductance

When an electric current passes through a wire, it creates a magnetic field around the wire. For ordinary wires, we can usually ignore this effect. However, when we wind many turns of wire in the same direction, the effect becomes significant. Such a coil of wire is known as an *inductor*, denoted by the letter L. The unit of inductance is the henry, abbreviated H. Typical inductor values range from nanohenries to millihenries.

Energy is stored in the space around an inductor as the magnetic field builds up due to increased current flow. A voltage V across the terminals of an inductor produces a change in the current i flowing through it that is given by the relation

$$V = L\frac{di}{dt}.$$

"Does a coil work the other way too, producing a voltage or current in a magnetic field?"

Conversely, if some external circuit causes the current to increase, the voltage across the inductor will respond accordingly. The equation holds if the current is decreasing as well. When the current decreases, the magnetic field collapses, and the energy that was stored in the field is returned to the circuit. This generates a voltage whose polarity is opposite to the polarity for increasing current.

The water model for an inductor is a turbine driving a flywheel. (See Figure 20.14.) This is assumed to be a perfect frictionless, bidirectional turbine with no leaks. A pressure difference (voltage) will be needed to cause the current to flow. Once the current is flowing, no pressure difference is present. When the current is reduced, the momentum of the flywheel will generate a pressure that tends to keep the current flowing.

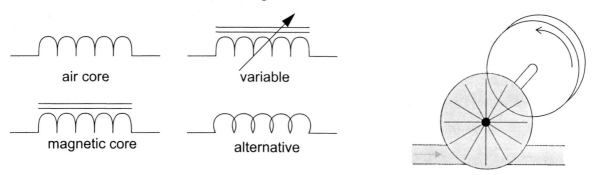

air core

variable

magnetic core

alternative

Figure 20.14   Schematics for various types of inductors and water model of an inductor

The magnetic fields are better coupled to each loop of the inductor if the loops are wound around a core of magnetic material such as iron or ferrite. This results in an increase in the value of inductance L. If the core is built in a manner that allows the magnetic material to move in and out, the resulting circuit component is a variable inductor. Variable inductors are commonly used in radios to allow tuning of resonant filters.

20.6 Transformers

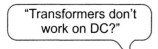

"Transformers don't work on DC?"

When two or more inductors share a common magnetic core, the resulting device is called a transformer. (See Figure 20.14.) When an AC voltage is applied to one of the windings of a transformer, the resulting alternating current produces an alternating magnetic field in the magnetic core material. Because all the coils of wire sharing the core are subject to the same changes in the magnetic field, the voltage on each winding will be proportional to the number of turns of wire in it.

The voltages across the windings of a transformer are related by the *turns ratio* $N_1{:}N_2 = V_1{:}V_2$, where N is the number of turns, V is the voltage on the winding, and 1 and 2 refer to the primary and secondary windings, respectively.

For example, if a transformer has 500 turns of wire on its primary (or input) winding and 50 turns of wire on its secondary (or output) winding, then the input voltage will be stepped down by a factor of 10. If such a transformer has $120\,\text{V}_{\text{rms}}$ on the primary, then the voltage that appears on the secondary will be $12\,\text{V}_{\text{rms}}$. If the secondary has the larger number of turns, then the transformer would be called a step-up transformer, instead of a step-down transformer.

The power that is output from a transformer is ideally equal to the power that is input. For now, let's assume that transformers are perfectly efficient and, therefore, that "power in equals power out" for a transformer, which means

$$P = V_1 I_1 = V_2 I_2.$$

The water model for a transformer is shown in Figure 20.15. The input circuit is connected to the two pipes on the left side of the device, and the output circuit is connected to the two pipes on the right side. There are four pistons that slide in four cylinders. In the center of the model is a pivot point, around which the four pistons revolve. The pistons must alternate back and forth, driven by an alternating current, in order for it to operate. The model is drawn for a transformer whose turns ratio is 1:1. Let's suppose that we want a transformer with a 2:1 turns ratio. We can make this transformer by doubling the areas of the *output* pistons (and the cylinders, of course). We will get a doubling of the output current, but the force (the voltage) will be halved, as we would expect from a 2:1 transformer.

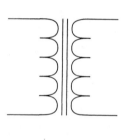 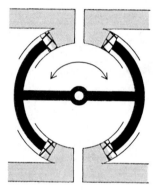

Figure 20.15 Schematic symbol and water model of a transformer

20.7 Summary Table of Electrical Quantities

Table 20.2 brings together salient information about electrical quantities (charge, current, and voltage), electric energy, power, and time, and fundamental circuit components (resistor, capacitor, and inductor). Symbols, units, defining relations, typical values and important equations are also included in the table. Statements of Kirchhoff's Current Law, Kirchhoff's Voltage Law, and Ohm's Law appear in the columns headed "Important Equations".

Table 20.2   Summary of Electrical Quantities

Quantity	Variable	Unit	Unit Symbol	Typical Values	Defining Relations	Important Equations	Schematic Symbol
Charge	Q	coulomb	C	1 aC to 1 C	magnitude of 6.242×10^{18} electron charges	$i = dq/dt$	
Current	I	ampere	A	1 μA to 1 kA	1 A = 1 C/s	$\displaystyle\sum_{n=1}^{N_{node}} I_n = 0$	
Voltage	V	volt	V	1 μV to 500 kV	1 V = 1 N-m/C	$\displaystyle\sum_{n=1}^{N_{loop}} V_n = 0$	
Power	P	watt	W	1 μW to 100 MW	1 W = 1 J/s	$P = dU/dt$; $P = IV$	
Energy	U	joule	J	1 fJ to 1 TJ	1 J = 1 N-m	$U = QV$	
Force	F	newton	N		$1\,N = 1\,kg\text{-}m/s^2$		
Time	t	second	s				
Resistance	R	ohm	Ω	1 Ω to 10 MΩ		$V = IR$; $P = V^2/R = I^2R$	
Capacitance	C	farad	F	1 fF to 5 F		$Q = CV$; $U = (1/2)CV^2$	
Inductance	L	henry	H	1 μH to 1 H		$V = L\,di/dt$; $U = (1/2)LI^2$	

20.8 Problems

20.1   In actual electronic work, capacitances range from 30 picofarads (the capacitance of a foot of coaxial cable), to 60 microfarads (the capacitance of a typical power supply filter capacitor), to 5 farads (for a "supercap" capacitor). Assuming that each of these capacitances is charged to five volts, find for each (a) the stored charge in coulombs, (b) the number of electrons stored on one plate, and (c) the energy in joules that is stored.

20.2   Suppose a voltage V_{AB} is applied between terminals A and B, to which capacitors C_1 and C_2 are connected in parallel. Find the effective capacitance of this pair. (Hint: With this connection, the voltage of each capacitor is V_{AB}.)

20.3   Suppose a voltage V_S is applied between terminals A and B, to which two capacitors C_1 and C_2 are connected in series. Find the equivalent capacitance of the pair. (<u>Hint</u>: With this connection, each capacitor must have the same amount of stored charge.)

20.4 Consider the RL circuit shown in Figure P20.4. As was done for the RC circuit, write KVL in terms of the current, $i(t)$. Assume that $i(t)$ has the form shown on page 152 from RC, substitute into the KVL expression and show that the time constant τ is equal to the ratio L/R. Assume that the switch is first down and that at time $t = 0$, it moves to the upper position. Find the values of A and B for this particular situation.

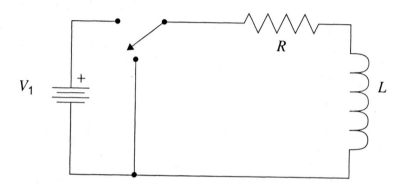

Figure P20.4

20.5 The light from a camera's electronic flash is produced when a high voltage, obtained by charging a capacitor, is applied to electrodes in a xenon-filled flash bulb.
   (a) To what voltage would a 60-microfarad capacitor be charged by a 6 mA current lasting 10 seconds?
   (b) If the bulb, when conducting current and emitting light, acts as an 0.1-ohm resistor, what is the time constant for discharging this capacitor?

20.6 At the <u>instant</u> that a power supply is connected to an initially uncharged capacitor, the capacitor voltage is zero, and a high charging current can flow. Find this current when an ideal 3-volt battery having a 1-ohm internal resistance ($R_{\text{Thévenin}} = 1$ ohm) is connected to:
   (a) a 30 picofarad capacitor;
   (b) a 60 microfarad capacitor; and
   (c) a 5 farad supercapacitor having a 2-ohm resistor in series with it.

20.7 Capacitor charging and discharging is frequently used in electronics, so it is handy to have mental "rules of thumb" with which to gauge these effects.
   (a) What is the analytical expression for the voltage of a capacitor, having capacitance C, that was charged to voltage V_0, that is discharged

through a resistor having resistance R connected across the capacitor terminals?

(b)   To what fraction of its initial value has the capacitor voltage dropped after a time equal to the time constant for discharge?

(c)   How long, in terms of time constants, does it take after the resistor is connected for the capacitor voltage to drop to 1% of its initial value?

(d)   Write the analytical expression for the charging by a voltage source V_0 of an initially uncharged capacitor C through resistance R.

(e)   Make both linear and semi-logarithmic plots of the discharging event as a function of time.

20.8   Using the expression relating the rate at which current changes in an inductor to the voltage produced across it, find the inductor voltage V_{AB} in Figure P20.8 when a switch supplying 10 A to a 5 mH inductor L is suddenly opened. (Assume that the current drops linearly to zero in 10 μs.)

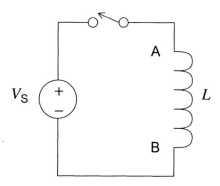

Figure P20.8

20.9   When dealing with alternating voltages, it is convenient to introduce the concept of an rms voltage. Explain why.

20.10   Suppose that you heated two identically shaped resistors, R_1 and R_2, supplied with a steady 10 mA current and a sinusoidal current, respectively. What is the peak amplitude of the sinusoidal current required so that both resistors reach the same temperature (that is, so that the same amount of time-average power is dissipated in them) if (a) $R_1 = R_2$, and (b) $R_1 = 2R_2$?

20.11   To show that capacitors store energy, in class Dick and Roger charge a large 30,000 μF capacitor to 60V by connecting it to a DC power supply. (See the demonstration on the book's web site.[1]) They then disconnect the capacitor, measure its voltage, and then put a metal can opener across its terminals, pro-

---

[1]   http://www.electronics_uncovered.com/

ducing a bright flash, a loud snapping sound, and enough heat to weld the can opener to the terminals of the capacitor. Surprised by the welding, they measured the discharge time with an oscilloscope and found it was about one millisecond.

(a) Calculate the current in amperes that flows just after the can opener shorts the capacitor.

(b) Calculate the rate of power dissipation in watts just after the can opener is placed across the terminals.

(c) What is the average power dissipated during the discharge?

What Can You Do with These Components?

You might be wondering, "How can I use these electronic components?" and "What are they good for?" There are many ways that the components can be used (examples are shown in square brackets.)

Resistors:

- Dissipate electrical energy, producing heat [electric stove element; light bulb]
- Turn a current into a voltage, as current flow in resistor produces a voltage drop [ammeter]
- Reduce voltage from source to desired value with voltage divider [transistor bias circuit]
- Terminate signal cable to prevent reflections [computer phone-net cable]
- Model conductive path in an electrical device [imperfect conductor, lamp filament]
- Model energy dissipation in mechanical systems [friction, viscosity]

Capacitors:

- Store electrical energy by storing charge [photoflash bulb circuit]
- Pass high-frequency currents easily [coupling capacitor in an amplifier]
- Prevent steady currents from passing [coupling capacitor in an amplifier]
- With resistor, make RC lowpass or highpass filter [loudspeaker crossover network]
- With an inductor, make an LCR resonator or filter [radio tuner, card key]
- Model devices where charges appear across an insulator [coaxial cable, gate of FET]
- Model storage of potential energy in mechanical component [spring]

Inductors:

- Store energy in a magnetic field produced by current [DC-to-DC power supply]
- Generate magnetic fields [electromagnets]
- With a capacitor, make an LC resonator or filter [radio tuner, card key]
- Couple noninvasively to time-varying current [clip-on ammeter]
- Coupled to another inductor, change level of time-varying voltage [transformer]
- Inhibit flow of high-frequency current [RF choke in powerline communications]
- Model storage of kinetic energy in mechanical component [flywheel]

Transformers:

- Raise or lower time-varying voltages or currents [electric power delivery, automobile ignition coil, public address system speakers, switching power converters]
- Isolate AC circuits having different grounds [geographically spread-out measuring system]
- Interface between two circuits for optimum power transfer [coupling between TV antenna and coaxial cable]
- Model mechanical transmissions and electromechanical transducers

Diodes:

- Pass current preferentially in one direction [rectifier in AC-DC converter]
- Limit voltage to a certain range of values [clamp, regulator]
- Convert current flow to light [light-emitting diode]
- Convert light to flowing electric charge [solar cell, photodiode receiver for remote tuner]

Transistors:

- Amplify current or voltage [bipolar junction transistor, op-amp]
- Match an electrical source to an electrical load [microphone/speaker hookup]
- Convert a control voltage to a corresponding current flow [field-effect transistor]
- Convert light to flowing electric charge and amplify the current [phototransistor]
- Perform logic operations such as AND, OR, NOT, and NAND [NAND chip]
- Act as electrically controlled switch [infrared door alarm]

Op-amps:

- Amplify current or voltage [stereo preamplifier]
- Isolate circuits having different grounds [distributed measuring system]
- Process differential signals [reducing noise in communications gear]
- Analog computation [summing circuit]
- Active filter [hearing aid]
- Analog function inversion [logarithmic amplifier]

Other Components Whose Use is Obvious:

- Switch, lamp, microphone, speaker, socket, plug, and meter

Digital Logic Devices

Your digital wristwatch uses them to count seconds and display the time correctly. The telephone company uses them to route your call to the phone you dialed. Computers are full of them. What are they? *Digital logic devices* — electronic circuits that handle information encoded in binary form.

In the digital realm, the signals that are transmitted over wires consist of voltages or currents having only high or low values that represent a logical "**1**" or a logical "**0**". Special circuits have been developed for handling binary valued signals quickly and reliably.

22.1 Binary Number System

This information may already be familiar to many readers. It is included to be sure that everyone is clear about the binary number system, which is the foundation upon which digital logic systems rest.

Our goal is to represent any number in terms of a sequence of just two symbols. We could use as the two symbols the words "true" and "false," a choice that relates what we're doing to human logic. Since we're going to deal with electronic circuits, we could choose two voltage levels — "high" and "low." But the conventional choice, which we adopt here, is to use the symbols for one and zero — **1** and **0**. We use boldface type to indicate that these are different from the ordinary numbers one and zero.

> A student's question about multimeters: "What's better — analog or digital?"

Before talking about binary numbers, let's consider what is really meant when we write a number in the familiar decimal system. A number such as 340, for example, really means that the value represented is the sum of "three one-hundreds" and "four tens." We can generalize this to say that when we write a decimal number JKLM it stands for the following expression written using successive powers of ten:

$$JKLM = J \times 10^3 + K \times 10^2 + L \times 10^1 + M \times 10^0 = J \times 1000 + K \times 100 + L \times 10 + M$$

× 1. In the decimal number system, the multipliers such as J, K, and M can have any one of 10 values, from 0 to 9.

Let's now consider the binary number system where the binary digits — the binary multipliers **J**, **K**, and so on, represented in boldface type — can only have one of two possible values, binary one (**1**) or binary zero (**0**). (Incidentally, binary digits are usually referred to by the contraction "bit,") The value of a binary number **JKLM** is the sum of successive powers of two: $\textbf{JKLM} = \textbf{J} \times 2^3 + \textbf{K} \times 2^2 + \textbf{L} \times 2^1 + \textbf{M} \times 2^0 = \textbf{J} \times 8 + \textbf{K} \times 4 + \textbf{L} \times 2 + \textbf{M} \times 1$. Thus the binary number **101** can be written out more explicitly as $\textbf{1} \times 2^2 + \textbf{0} \times 2^1 + \textbf{1} \times 2^0 = 4 + 0 + 1 = 5$. Similarly, the binary number **11100** is equivalent to decimal 28, and the binary number **11101** is equivalent to decimal 29.

To represent in the binary system numbers that have a fractional part, we can put in a period (called a binary point) and continue the sequence of **1**s and **0**s to represent negative powers of two. For example, the decimal number 3.5 would be **11.1** in binary, and the decimal number 5.25 would be **101.01** in binary.

22.2 Converting a Decimal Number to its Binary Equivalent

Table 22.1 Example of a decimal-to-binary conversion

Digits	Bits
340	0
170	0
85	1
42	0
21	1
10	0
5	1
2	0
1	1

A surefire procedure for converting a number from decimal to binary form is to divide the decimal number by the number 2 repeatedly, each time writing down the remainder (either a **0** or a **1**) in the next most significant position.

Exercise 22.1   Find the binary equivalent of the decimal number 340.

Solution: See Table 22.1. Divide 340 by two to get 170 with remainder **0**. Divide 170 by two to get 85 with remainder **0**. Divide 85 by two to get 42 with remainder 1. Continuing the process, we finally obtain the result that 340 = **101010100**.

It is also possible to generate the bits in the opposite order by subtracting successive powers of two, as presented in Exercise 22.2, starting with the largest power of two less than or equal to the number. For each power of two that can be subtracted, a binary one is placed in the answer at the corresponding bit position.

Exercise 22.2   Find the binary equivalent of the decimal number 522 using the subtractive method. The powers of two are presented in Table 22.2.

Solution: Locate the largest power of two that is less than or equal to 522, that is, 512. Since $512 = 2^9$, or **100000000**, write down the binary result as **1** ☐☐☐☐☐☐☐☐ (a one followed by 8 placeholders), since we don't yet know the values of the other bits. Subtract the 512 from the 522, leaving 10. Continue by finding a power of two that is less than or equal to 10, that is, 8. The binary result becomes **1 0 0 0 0 1** ☐☐☐ . Notice that we fill in the intervening placeholders with **0**s. When we subtract, we are left with 2. This being a power of two, we can add the appropriate bit and fill in the remaining position(s) with **0**(s). The binary result becomes **1 0 0 0 0 1 0 1 0** .

> "How long have people been using binary?"

Table 22.2   Powers of 2

N	2^N	Comments
0	1	
1	2	
2	4	
3	8	
4	16	
5	32	
6	64	
7	128	
8	256	
9	512	
10	1,024	$2^{10} = 1024$ is the closest power of 2 to the decimal number
11	2,048	1000, so the prefix kilo has been used when labeling
12	4,096	binary quantities such as 64 kilobytes (64 kB) $\approx 64 \times$
13	8,192	10^{24} B $= 65,536$ B. A new (1998) standard attempts to correct the inaccuracy of this by creating the prefix Kibi (Ki)
14	16,384	(from kilo binary) For more on this standard see NIST.[a]
15	32,768	$2^{15} = 32768$ is often used as the frequency in Hz of a digital
16	65,536	wristwatch's clock crystal — the master timing source for
17	131,072	the watch. If you successively half the frequency of the electrical output from the clock crystal 15 times, you get
18	262,144	an electrical pulse exactly once per second.
19	524,288	
20	1,048,576	$2^{20} = 1,048,576$ is close to one million, so this number is similarly denoted as Mebi (Mi), when describing the size of a computer file or memory.
.		
.		
30	1,073,741,824	Similarly, denoted Gibi (Gi)
32	4,294,967,296	Size of the address space of most 32-bit computers = 4 GiB

[a]   http://physics.nist.gov/cuu/Units/binary.html

22.3 Logic Operations and Truth Tables

We can design circuits for doing arithmetic operations with binary digits by combining elementary elements called *logic gates*. Each gate performs a single logic operation, and each gate can be realized by combining electronic components such as transistors, resistors, and voltage sources. The operations required to perform a computation in a digital computer are carried out by circuits containing the logic gates that we will now describe. For example, a binary adder may be used in doing addition that is called for in arithmetic manipulations of data input to a computer. A different application of a binary adder is to increment a counter by one unit each time a programmed sequence of operations is carried out.

The seven basic logic gates are identified and characterized in Table 22.3. In each row, the truth table (which is a list of the output that the gate produces for every possible combination of its inputs) that characterizes the gate is on the left-hand side. The name of the logical operation appears in the leftmost column. Two schematic symbols for the gate are shown along with boolean algebra formulas for the gate function. In each figure, the schematic symbol on the left is the standard representation, and the one on the right is the so-called DeMorgan equivalent representation. (See Section 22.5.) Each DeMorgan equivalent functions logically and represents the same circuit as the gate to its left. The equivalents, which are a different way of thinking about these gates, may be helpful when finding the minimum number of transistors required to realize a logic function. (See Figures 27.3 through 27.6 and Problem 22.8).

While we show gates with no more than two inputs here, gates having more inputs are frequently used. Variables or formulas with an overline indicate inversion and are read as "bar"; for example, $\overline{A}$ is read as "A bar," which means "not-A," the complement of the binary variable **A**. For ease in writing with a word processor, the symbols **!A, /A, A!** or **A′** may be used instead.

Table 22.3   Logic gates

Logic Gate	Truth Tables		Schematic Symbols	
	Inputs	Output	Standard Symbol	DeMorgan's Equivalent
NOT or Inverter	A	$\overline{A}$		
	0	1		
	1	0		

AND	A B	$A \cdot B$		
	0 0	0		
	0 1	0		
	1 0	0		
	1 1	1		

$F = A \cdot B$

$F = \overline{\overline{A} + \overline{B}}$

Table 22.3   Logic gates (continued)

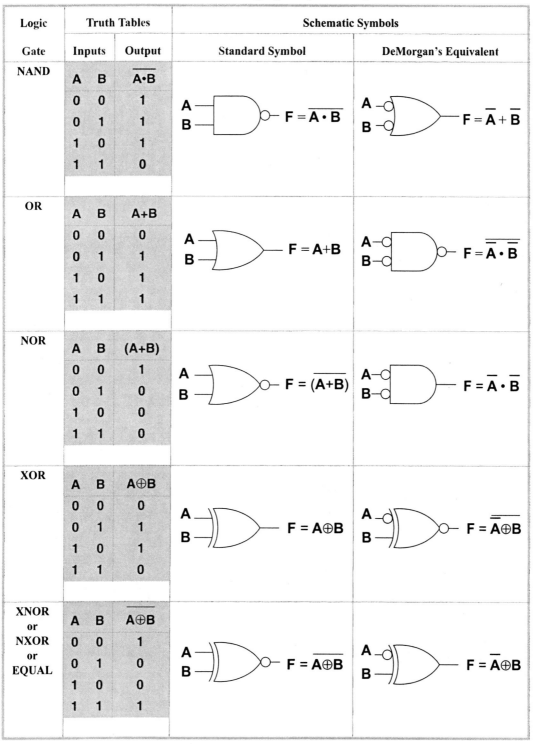

The NOT gate is also known as an inverter, since its output is the opposite of its input: If the input is a **1**, the output is a **0**, and vice versa. The AND gate has the property that its output is a **1** if both of its inputs are **1**s. The NAND gate's output is the negation of the output of the AND gate; the small circle to the right of the gate symbol indicates that negation. The OR gate's output is a **1** if either of its inputs is a **1**. The XOR gate is more explicitly known as the "exclusive-OR" gate: Its output is a **1** if either, but not both, of its inputs is a **1**. We will see shortly how to use a simple network of these gates to construct a circuit that will add binary numbers, but first we will show a procedure for constructing a logic gate array that will produce an arbitrarily chosen set of outputs when presented with all possible binary inputs.

22.4 Logic Gate Array that Produces an Arbitrarily Chosen Output

Suppose that our task is to design a logic gate array that has three binary inputs — labelled **A**, **B** and **C** — and that produces some particular set of outputs, **F**. The truth table that we'll take as an example is shown in Table 22.4. (The output values were just picked out of thin air and don't represent anything in particular.)

Note that we've written the binary inputs on the left in a very regular way: if regarded as being three-digit binary numbers, their eight values would increase in steps of one from zero at the top to seven at the bottom. Writing them in this structured way helps us avoid leaving out any possible values.

Here's a set of steps that is guaranteed to produce a logic gate array that behaves the same as the truth table that you start with:

Step 1: Use an OR gate as the output gate. Provide this OR gate with as many inputs as there are **1**s in the output (the F column). In our example, the output contains four **1**s, and so the output OR gate must have four inputs, corresponding to the third, fourth, sixth, and eighth rows in the truth table above.

Step 2: Set up a general-purpose circuit on the input side, at the left, that will take in the inputs (**A**, **B**, and **C**) and that will provide internally both the inputs (**A**, **B**, and **C**) and the negations of the inputs ($\overline{A}$, $\overline{B}$, and $\overline{C}$) in easily accessed columns. NOT gates are used to form the negations ($\overline{A}$, $\overline{B}$, and $\overline{C}$) from the inputs (**A**, **B**, and **C**).

Table 22.4   What circuit of logic gates could produce these (arbitrarily chosen) outputs F in response to inputs A, B and C? See text for method and Figure 22.1 for result.

A	B	C	F
0	0	0	0
0	0	1	0
0	1	0	1
0	1	1	1
1	0	0	0
1	0	1	1
1	1	0	0
1	1	1	1

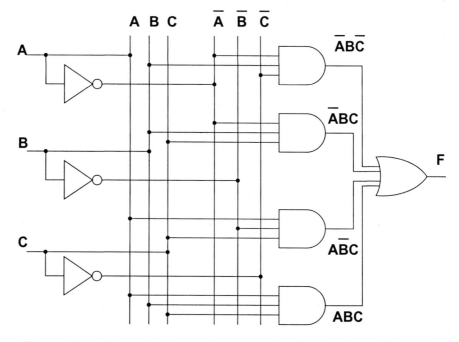

Figure 22.1   Example of general purpose circuit to implement the truth
table of Table 22.4. (This solution is NOT minimized.)

Step 3: Use an AND gate with as many inputs as the circuit (three in
this case) to compute each row of the truth table that produces a **1**. Connect the output of each AND gate to one of the inputs of the OR gate. For
example, the first set of inputs that would produce a **1** output is the third
row of the arbitrarily chosen truth table. To get a **1** output from the OR
gate when the inputs A, B, and C have values **0, 1,** and **0** (the third row of
the truth table), we would connect $\overline{A}$, B, and $\overline{C}$ to a three-input AND gate
as shown in Figure 22.1.

22.5 Boolean Algebra

The expression of logic formulas in a notation such as:

$$F = \overline{A}\overline{B}\overline{C} + \overline{A}BC + A\overline{B}C + ABC$$

allows the manipulation and simplification of such formulas using the rules of boolean algebra.

The rules of boolean algebra are listed in Table 22.5.

Table 22.5 **Rules of boolean algebra. The two entries in the last row are used frequently and are known as DeMorgan's theorem.**

AND Rules	OR Rules
$A \cdot A = A$	$A + A = A$
$A \cdot \overline{A} = 0$	$A + \overline{A} = 1$
$0 \cdot A = 0$	$0 + A = A$
$1 \cdot A = A$	$1 + A = 1$
$A \cdot B = B \cdot A$	$A + B = B + A$
$A(BC) = (AB)C$	$A + (B + C) = (A + B) + C$
$A(B + C) = AB + AC$	$A + BC = (A + B)(A + C)$
$\overline{A \cdot B} = \overline{A} + \overline{B}$	$\overline{A + B} = \overline{A} \cdot \overline{B}$

Example 22.3 Using these rules we can take a number of steps to successively simplify the expression as follows:

$$F = \overline{A}\overline{B}\overline{C} + \overline{A}BC + A\overline{B}\overline{C} + ABC$$
$$F = (\overline{A}\overline{B}\overline{C} + \overline{A}BC) + (A\overline{B}\overline{C} + ABC)$$
$$F = \overline{A}B(\overline{C} + C) + AC(\overline{B} + B)$$
$$F = \overline{A}B(1) + AC(1)$$

Finally,

$$F = \overline{A}B + AC$$

The final expression is clearly simpler than our initial expression.

22.6 Adding Binary Numbers

We can develop a procedure for adding numbers written in binary form by observing the following basics:

Binary: $\mathbf{0 + 0 = 0}$ (Equivalent to Decimal: $0 + 0 = 0$),

Binary: $\mathbf{1 + 0 = 1}$ (Equivalent to Decimal: $1 + 0 = 1$),

Binary: $\mathbf{1 + 1 = 10}$ (Equivalent to Decimal: $1 + 1 = 2$).

The last binary result could be written out more formally by using two binary digits to express the numbers being added and the result: $\mathbf{01 + 01 = 10}$. In words, the sum of the two right-hand columns is two, which is represented in binary form as **10**. We can also say that the two right-hand columns when added generate a sum digit (**0**) and a carry digit (**1**).

We express this addition, called a "half-adder," as a truth table in Table 22.6. If we then observe that the carry column is equivalent to the AND operation and the sum is equivalent to the XOR operation, we could build the half-adder in Figure 22.2.

Table 22.6   Truth table for a half adder

Inputs		Outputs	
A	B	Carry	Sum
0	0	0	0
0	1	0	1
1	0	0	1
1	1	1	0

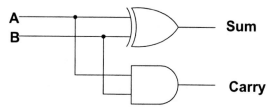

Figure 22.2   Half-adder circuit

Example 22.4   Determine the sum of the following binary numbers: **1101100** and **1011010** (decimal numbers 108 and 90, respectively).

Solution: Writing this out in traditional grade school form and indicating carry digits at the head of the column, we have

$$
\begin{array}{r}
\text{carry digits} \longrightarrow \quad 11110000 \\
1101100 \\
+ \quad 1011010 \\
\hline
11000110
\end{array}
$$

Checking: The answer is 198, which is the sum of the numbers 108 and 90.

Table 22.7 **Truth table for a full adder**

Inputs			Outputs	
A	B	C	Carry	Sum
0	0	0	0	0
0	0	1	0	1
0	1	0	0	1
0	1	1	1	0
1	0	0	0	1
1	0	1	1	0
1	1	0	1	0
1	1	1	1	1

We can see from the exercise that a practical adder circuit to implement the addition of one column must add not two but three bits. (This explains why the previous circuit is called a half-adder.) Let's write out the truth table for a full adder. (See Table 22.7). We write the eight possible variations of the input variables by counting in binary. Next, we figure out the sum and carry bits by simply looking at how many input bits are **1** in each row. If in a given row there's only one input that is a logical one, then for that row, we have a sum bit but no carry bit. A row containing two logical ones will have a carry bit, but no sum bit, and a row having three logical ones produces both a sum and a carry bit.

The construction of a full-adder logic circuit is left as a problem. (See Problem 22.6.) You can actually build the circuit in the lab and verify that it operates correctly. You can also simulate the adder with a computer program called LogicWorks™ to verify your design before actually building it.

We can abstract the actual circuit for the full adder into a schematic block with the appropriate inputs and outputs shown in Figure 22.3.

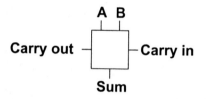

Figure 22.3 Schematic block representing a full adder

If we want to build an eight-bit adder circuit, we can connect full adders as shown in Figure 22.4. Note that the carry bits flow from right to left.

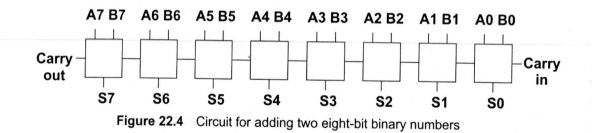

Figure 22.4 Circuit for adding two eight-bit binary numbers

Negative Numbers and Subtraction

How does one represent negative numbers in a binary system? They are usually represented in twos-complement notation. To form a negative number in twos-complement notation, first complement the bits (change all the zeros to ones and the ones to zeros) and then add one. Try this on numbers such as 0, 1, and 2 to see how the procedure works. To make the distinction between the positive and negative numbers, the most significant bit can be reserved to indicate the sign. This means that if an 8-bit quantity is being treated as a signed number, then the range becomes -128 to 127 instead of 0 to 255.

Exercise 22.5 Add a negative and a positive number together. Let's use negative five and positive three.

Solution: First, to form the negative number, take five (**00000101**), complement it to **11111010**, and add one to get **11111011**. Next, let's add the three (**00000011**):

$$\begin{array}{r}
\text{carry digits} \longrightarrow \quad \textbf{00000110} \\
\textbf{11111011} \\
+ \quad \textbf{00000011} \\
\hline
\textbf{11111110}
\end{array}$$

Finally, we see that the most significant bit of the answer (the leftmost bit) is a one, so the answer must be negative. To find its value, we complement the answer to get **00000001** and add one to get **00000010**, or 2. The answer is -2.

We can also use the circuit shown in Figure 22.4 to subtract two binary numbers, if we set the carry-in to a **1** and complement the subtrahend.

22.7 Memory Elements

So far, we have been discussing only combinatorial logic circuits, whose outputs are strictly a function of the current inputs. We can combine two logic gates as shown in Figure 22.5 using feedback and create an element with *memory* (i.e., whose outputs depend not only of the current inputs, but also on some previous input.) The cross-

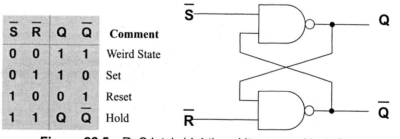

$\overline{S}$	$\overline{R}$	Q	$\overline{Q}$	Comment
0	0	1	1	Weird State
0	1	1	0	Set
1	0	0	1	Reset
1	1	Q	$\overline{Q}$	Hold

Figure 22.5 R–S latch (right) and its state table (left).

coupled NAND gates shown form an R–S latch (Reset–Set). The inputs of this particular version are marked with bars above the name to indicate a logical inversion of the input.

Exercise 22.6 Verify the operation of the R–S latch shown in Figure 22.5.

Solution: Assume that $\overline{S}$ is **0** and that $\overline{R}$ is **1**. The output of the upper NAND gate with a zero input is **1**. Then, both inputs to the lower NAND gate are **1**, resulting in a **0** output. Now, let $\overline{S}$ become **1**. Since the Q output is **0**, the Q output remains at **1**, holding the state. Now assume that $\overline{S}$ is **1** and that $\overline{R}$ is **0**. The output of the lower NAND gate with a zero input is **1**. Now, both inputs to the upper NAND gate are **1**,

173

resulting in a **0** output. Let $\overline{\textbf{R}}$ become **1**. Since the **Q** output is **0**, the $\overline{\textbf{Q}}$ output remains at **1**, again holding the state. Finally, we can check the undesired condition of having both set and reset signals applied simultaneously, $\textbf{S} = \overline{\textbf{R}} = \textbf{0}$. In this case, both NAND gates find a **0** at one input and the outputs will both be **1**.

R–S latches can also be built by cross-coupling NOR gates, in which case the inputs are non-inverted (normal).

Another type of memory device, a transparent latch, can be built with a few more gates, as shown in Figure 22.6. When the enable input is true, the value on the D input is reflected to the Q output (the device is transparent), and when the enable is false, the values on the outputs are held.

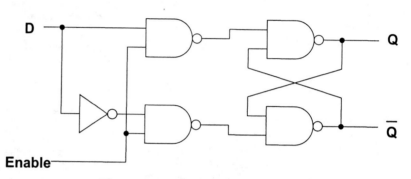

Figure 22.6 Transparent latch circuit

Two of these devices can be combined to form a *master–slave flip-flop*. (See Figure 22.7).) The left half (the master) passes data through to the second stage

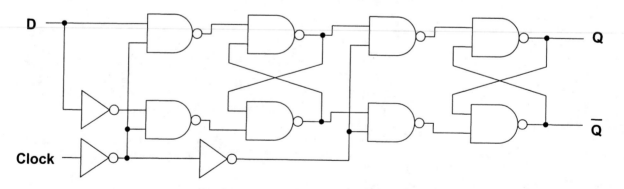
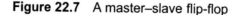

Figure 22.7 A master–slave flip-flop

while the clock is low and holds the value while the clock is high. The right half (the slave) passes the data from the first stage when the clock goes high and continues to hold the data while the clock is low. This behavior transfers the data from the D input to the Q outputs at the rising edge of the clock signal. This is one way to build devices known as *D flip-flops*, which we use in sequential logic. A schematic symbol for a D flip-flop is shown in Figure 22.8. An input marked with a triangle is an edge-sensitive input, meaning that it will activate the flip-flop on the rising edge of a signal that is connected to it.

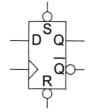

Figure 22.8   Schematic symbol for a D flip-flop with set (S) and reset (R) inputs

22.8 Sequential Logic

Circuits that employ memory, in the form of latches, flip-flops, or RAM, in addition to combinatorial logic, are called *sequential* logic. There are many kinds, such as self-timed, asynchronous, and synchronous. We will discuss a style of synchronous logic known as the *state machine*.

In a state machine (see Figure 22.9), the "state" information is contained in a memory device, such as a set of flip-flops. A clock provides periodic pulses to the memory to store a new state value. Combinatorial logic is used to combine the external inputs and the current state to form the new state and any outputs that the system needs.

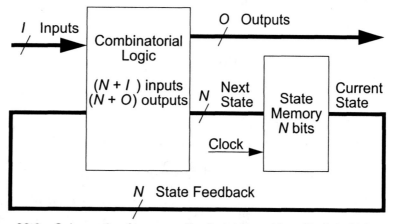

Figure 22.9   Schematic of a generalized state machine. Each bold line is a collection of wires known as a bus. The slash across the bus is labeled with the number of wires in the bus. Since this is a generalized schematic, these are labelled with variable names — N, I, and O.

The behavior of a state machine may be expressed in a *state diagram*, which uses circles to represent states and directed arrows to show the allowed transitions between states, the stimulus that would cause the transition, and any actions that would result from the transition. States may have descriptive names or just representative letters.

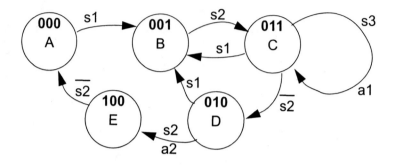

Figure 22.10 A simple state diagram with five states (A–E), three stimuli (s1–s3), and two actions (a1 and a2).

Each stimulus may correspond with any combination of external inputs, and each action may specify some set of outputs. The state is used in combination with the stimulus to form the new state. In the process of converting this sort of free-form state diagram into a logic schematic, you may want to organize the information into a state table that would have one row for each transition. The state will be represented by a set of N bits such that the number of states is less than 2^N. For the simple state diagram of Figure 22.10, the number of states is five, requiring three bits for the state memory.

We could number the states in an arbitrary fashion, but that might result in an unnecessarily complicated design. Instead we will assign binary numbers to the states so as to minimize the number of bit transitions between states in the entire graph; this will have the effect of minimizing the number of required logic gates. We can take a clue from the existence of the so-called *gray code*, in which only one bit changes on going from one state to the next. An example of a three-bit binary gray code is **000, 001, 011, 010, 110, 111, 101, 100**. We have used this concept in numbering the states in Fig. 22.10. (For more on the gray code, see Problem 22.10.)

Elevator Control Circuit   We'll design part of a simple elevator control circuit for a four-floor, two-shaft elevator. The top and bottom floors will have one call button and the other floors will have two directional call buttons in the hallway. Each car will have a button for each floor and an emergency (E-stop) button. We will design the circuits in small pieces using the idea of coupling several small state machines together.

First, we'll draw the state diagrams of the cars and the call buttons. The diagram for the door's state machine is left to the reader.

Next we'll number the states for the lift state diagram in the center of Figure 22.11. For the lift state diagram, there are five transitions. We can make four of them be one-bit transitions by labeling them as shown in Table 22.8. We will typically number as zero the state that we want the machine to "wake up" in. For the Lift State, that would be "Stop." For the Button States, that would be "Not Lit," and for the Car-Direction State, it doesn't matter, but we'll choose "Up."

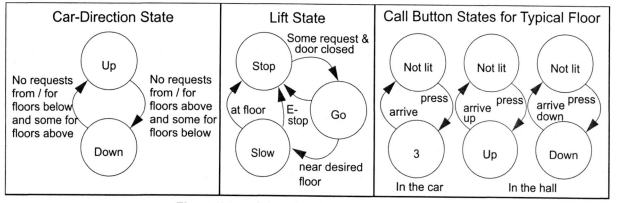

Figure 22.11 State diagrams for the elevator.

We create the state table of Table 22.8 by listing each transition as a row in the table. The columns on the left side are the inputs to our combinatorial logic, made up of state and input signals. The columns on the right are the resulting new states and the outputs. Note that outputs can be transient, occurring only during the transition or continuous, tied to one or more states. In this example, the motor and slow outputs can be tied to the states, while the door opening signal is transient. We simplify the table by listing only the transient outputs.

After we have put all the transitions from the state diagram into our table, we

Table 22.8   Lift State table for elevator

State		Inputs					Next State		Outputs
Name	Code Q_1Q_0	Door Close d C	Re- quest R	Near Floor N	At floor A	E- Stop E	Code D_1D_0	XOR X_1X_0	Open Door D
Stop	00	1	1	x	1	0	00	00	1
	00	1	1	x	0	0	01	01	0
	00	x	x	x	1	1	00	00	1
Go	01	1	1	x	x	1	00	01	0
	01	x	x	1	0	0	11	10	0
Slow	11	x	x	x	0	1	00	11	0
	11	x	x	x	1	x	00	11	1

will study the inputs in each state to see if safety or other design concerns dictate that we add any more rows to the table. For instance, the first row was added to the table to handle the situation that arises when a button is pressed and the car is already at the desired floor. The **x**s in the table indicate "don't care" conditions. These mean that the input value doesn't matter and result in simplifications of the logic. In our table, we have five input variables, which can have 32 possible combined values. A full expression of all possible inputs would result in a table with 32 rows for each state.

Since we are basically recomputing the state with each tick of our system clock, we must either have one or more entries in our table to maintain each current state or adopt a style of logic in which the state is automatically maintained until we specifically change it. While the latter approach initially looks more complicated, it can result in simpler designs. To implement this style, we'll connect the output of an XOR gate to the input to each D-flip-flop, with one input of the XOR connected to the Q-output of the flip-flop. This leaves us with one input to the XOR gate. That input will cause the flip-flop to remain in its current state as long as it is **0** and will cause the state to change if it is a **1**. As a result of this, we need to add a column to our state table that is the changes in the state bits. We can then extract the logic equations that we'll implement with gates in Figure 22.12:

$$X_1 = \overline{Q_1}Q_0 N \overline{A}\,\overline{E} + Q_1 Q_0 \overline{A} E + Q_1 Q_0 A;$$

$$X_0 = \overline{Q_1}\,\overline{Q_0} C R \overline{A}\,\overline{E} + \overline{Q_1} Q_0 C R E + Q_1 Q_0 \overline{A} E + Q_1 Q_0 A;$$

$$D = \overline{Q_1}\,\overline{Q_0} C R A \overline{E} + \overline{Q_1}\,\overline{Q_0} A E + Q_1 Q_0 A.$$

The realization of these functions appears in the figure. Note that only one of the OR gates has four inputs and that the other two have just three.

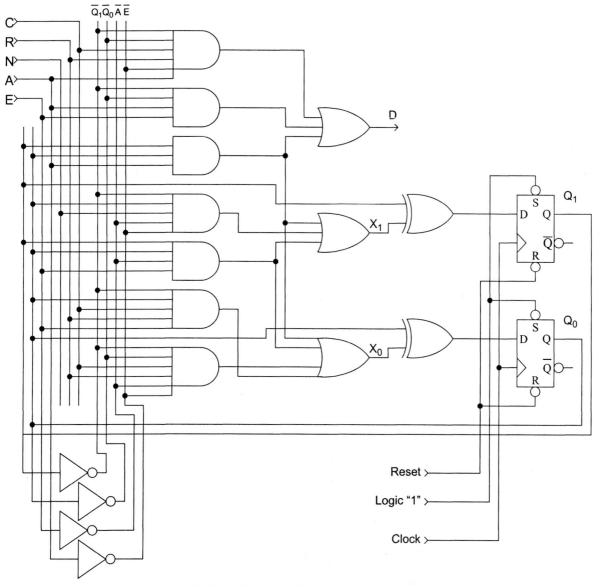

Figure 22.12 Elevator Lift State Machine schematic

22.9 Problems

Note: In the problems below, the asterisk (*) identifies particularly challenging problems.

22.1 To what base-10 number is each of the following binary numbers equivalent?
  (a)   **1100100**
  (b)   **1111.111**

22.2 Convert the three following base-10 numbers to binary numbers: 5, 87, and 20.125.

22.3 Find the sums of the following pairs of binary numbers, and check your answers in the base-10 system:
  (a)   **01111** and **00001**
  (b)   **10001** and **01010**

22.4 Find the sum of the following binary numbers, and check your answer in the base-10 system: **11101, 11011,** and **11111**.

22.5 Multiply the following binary numbers, and check your answers in the base-10 system:
  (a)   **10101** and **00001**
  (b)   **10101** and **00010**
  (c)   **11111** and **00101**

22.6 Using a program such as LogicWorks™, simulate a full adder composed of only AND, OR, and NOT gates. Turn in a printout of the network of gates you used and the timing diagram of the circuit's response at significant points in the circuit as you step through the values of the two input variables.

22.7 Using a program such as LogicWorks™, simulate a synchronous counter, made of interconnected gates and flip-flops, that will count from 0 to 15 clock pulses.

22.8 Consider the full adder for three-level logic that you designed and simulated in Problem 22.6. This adder employed three inverters, eight AND gates, and two OR gates.
  (a)   Convert the design so that it uses only NAND gates (instead of AND and OR), which are simpler to fabricate in integrated circuit form. You will need to keep the three inverters.
  (b)   Use the rules of boolean algebra (Table 22.5) to optimize the NAND-gate design of the carry circuit so that it uses a minimum number of transistors. Helpful information: the optimized carry

design will contain 4 NAND gates, having different numbers of inputs.

(c)   Determine the number of field-effect transistors required in the optimized CMOS full-adder design.

22.9   *Multiplier. Given a full adder (FA) block (Figure 22.3), design a multiplier to multiply 8 bits by 8 bits, yielding a 16-bit product using FAs and AND gates.

22.10 Design a three-bit gray-code counter. A "gray" code is one in which only one bit changes with each count. An example of this is: **000 001 011 010 110 111 101 100 000**. Such sequences are useful for shaft encoders where a number of bits must be reported out, and any misalignment between bits might result in an erroneous reading if a normal code were used.

(a)   Write state table and corresponding boolean expressions for $\mathbf{D_2}$, $\mathbf{D_1}$, and $\mathbf{D_0}$ in terms of $\mathbf{Q_0}$, $\mathbf{Q_1}$, and $\mathbf{Q_2}$ and their inverses.

(b)   Reduce the expression for $\mathbf{D_0}$ using boolean algebra to show that:

$$\mathbf{D_0} = \overline{\mathbf{Q_2}}\,\overline{\mathbf{Q_1}} + \mathbf{Q_2}\mathbf{Q_1}.$$

22.11 *Continuing from Problem 22.10, reduce the expression for D_1 using boolean algebra, to show that:

$$\mathbf{D_1} = \overline{\mathbf{Q_2}}(\overline{\overline{\mathbf{Q_0}\mathbf{Q_1}}}) + \mathbf{Q_1}\overline{\mathbf{Q_0}}.$$

(<u>Hint</u>: use $\mathbf{A} = \mathbf{A} + \mathbf{A}$.)

22.12 Draw the schematic for the gray-code state machine, given that

$$\mathbf{D_2} = \mathbf{Q_1}\overline{\mathbf{Q_0}} + \mathbf{Q_2}(\overline{\overline{\mathbf{Q_0}\mathbf{Q_1}}}).$$

You may use LogicWorks™ or a similar program to produce a neat schematic and to allow you to verify its operation.

Computer Architecture

23.1 Mental Models and the Computer

We referred earlier in the chapter entitled "Advice to Freshmen" to "Mental Models" on page 56. By now, you probably have formed mental models of current, voltage, and other elements of electronics. Your mental models may be different from those of your classmates, but that's all right, since the models are created only to help you with these concepts. But now consider the computer — what mental models do you have of its operation?

To be more specific, what do you picture happening when you "Save" a file while using a word processor on your personal computer? Maybe you haven't yet tried to picture what happens, and maybe you wonder why having such a picture might be of value to you. Building up mental models of such processes can help you connect the abstract action of software with physical processes taking place in your computer's hardware. In other words, forming such models can help you understand how your computer works.

This could be helpful in finding what's wrong when a computer system that you've purchased doesn't quite work as expected. It could help when you try using an unfamiliar computer, and if you go on to work in computer engineering, you'll need to make clear connections between software commands and the hardware actions they produce. You'll also find you feel more comfortable working with a machine that you understand at least partially on an intuitive level. You may also find that you enjoy conveying this understanding to people around you who don't have the technical training that you do.

23.2 Central Processing Unit (CPU)

At the core of any computer is the central processing unit (CPU). (Figure 23.1 shows the components and organization of a CPU.) The CPU executes a series of instructions (stored in the memory system) that comprise the program. Each instruction execution involves a number of steps:

1. Fetch the instruction from the location in the memory system specified by the program counter (PC) into the instruction register.

2. Decode the instruction. Increment the PC.

3. Fetch the operands.

4. Execute the desired operation using the arithmetic/logic unit (ALU).

5. (Optional) Access memory.

6. Store the result in the desired location.

Let's take a more detailed look at each of these steps.

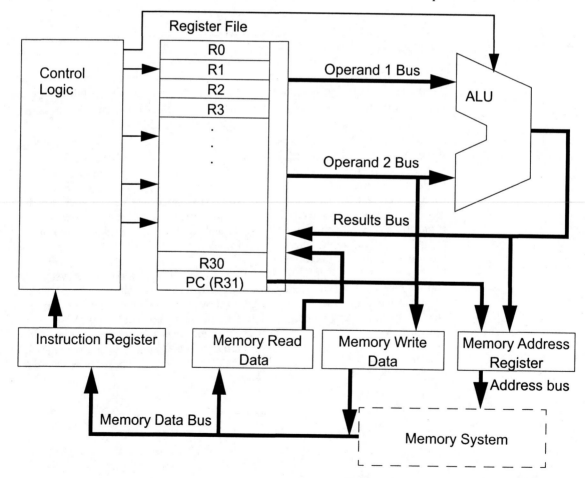

Figure 23.1 Block diagram of a CPU

The program counter (PC) is a special register that may be part of, or separate from, the general-purpose registers of the machine. It holds the address of the instruction that is to be executed. It can be thought of as a pointer to the current step on a long list of instructions that the computer must follow. To fetch the instruction, the contents of the PC must be placed onto the address bus of the memory system and the memory must be signalled to perform a read operation. The memory will respond (after some delay) by placing the contents of the addressed location onto the memory data bus.

The instruction is then loaded into the instruction register from the memory data bus. Then the decoding process begins. Each instruction is divided into bit fields with specific meanings. Generally, the left-most fields will determine the meaning of the remaining fields. The most important decoding step is to determine the major category of the instruction. These are memory access, calculation, and branching.

Memory access instructions compute an address in memory by combining information from registers and an instruction field, and use that address to load a register (copy the datum from memory to the register), store a register (copy the register contents to memory), or swap (exchange the contents of memory and the register).

Calculation instructions use one or two operands and generate a result. These operations stay strictly within the CPU, so no memory access is required after fetching the instruction.

Branch instructions change the flow of instructions. Instead of proceeding to the next instruction, a branch instruction will change the value in the program counter, causing execution to proceed from a new location in the program. Branch instructions can be conditional, meaning that sometimes the program counter will not be changed and execution will proceed with the instruction following the conditional branch. Conditional branches usually depend on the results of previous calculations. Examples include branch on zero, branch on nonzero, and branch on negative. Branching instructions can also include an operation to save the previous value of the program counter in a register to allow program flow to return to the following instruction at a later time. This capability allows programs to call subroutines or functions.

During the decode operation, the program counter will be advanced to the next sequential instruction on the likely assumption that it will be the next instruction to be executed.

Fetching the operands may be done in parallel with the instruction decode. This is possible because all of the operands will be in the internal registers of the CPU and the fields in the instruction that specify which registers will be needed will always occur in the same positions.

To execute a computational instruction, the operands will be passed to the arithmetic/logic unit (ALU) along with bits generated from the instruction to control the action of the ALU (add, subtract, multiply, shift, compare, etc.). In a memory-access instruction, the ALU will be used to shift and add the operands to form a memory address. During a branch instruction, the ALU will be used to calculate the new address.

Next comes the optional step that is used for memory- access instructions. This will involve a short delay to retrieve data if the memory is being read and a much shorter delay if the data are being written. In any memory access, the desired address is placed on the memory's address bus, and control signals that indicate whether this access is a read or a write cycle (or both for a swap) and the width of the access are sent to the memory. The width of access is important. If the program is supposed to write data to just one byte, then the other bytes in the same word will be lost if the memory doesn't have access width control.

Finally, the result of our computation or branch will be written into the destination register. In the case of a branch, that destination register is clearly the program counter. For computational instructions, the destination register would have been specified in the instruction. This can be a third register (different from either of the operands).

State Machine for CPU

We can construct a fairly simple state machine to implement the functionality of these steps of the CPU, as shown in Figure 23.2. When the instruction is a store (i.e.,

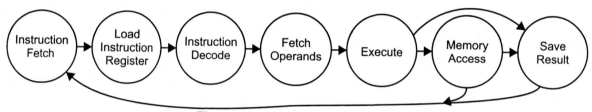

Figure 23.2   CPU State Machine.

when it will place the contents of a register into the main memory), it will skip the last step. When the instruction is a non-memory access type, it will skip the next to the last step. A load instruction will use all the steps. You can see that the amount of time actually executing the instruction is a small fraction of the total. By building the hardware so that each state in the machine is carried out by separate logic circuits, we can then *pipeline* the phases of each instruction, allowing us to begin processing the next instruction immediately rather than waiting for the previous one to finish. This pipeline is most efficient if it is full, with a different instruction being executed in each phase. The pipeline can stall at several points; on either the instruction fetch or the memory access, if the word we are trying to read isn't immediately available (in the cache), then the pipeline must stall. Also, if one of the operands is the result of an instruction that hasn't completed yet, the pipeline must stall.

RISC vs. CISC

These two acronyms, RISC (reduced instruction-set computer) and CISC (complex instruction-set computer), represent two architectural models for computers. The major differences between them are summarized in Table 23.1.

Table 23.1   Comparison of reduced instruction-set computer (RISC) and complex instruction-set computer (CISC)

Feature	RISC	CISC
Instruction size	1 word	1 to 54 bytes
Execution time	1 clock	1 to 100s of clock cycles
Addressing modes	small	large
Work per instruction	small	varies
Instruction counts	large	small

RISCs use only load-and-store instructions to access the memory, while CISCs may have any operand or result located in memory. Pipelining of instructions, where the steps of sequential instructions are overlapped to speed execution, is much easier to implement in RISCs, and thus higher performance can be attained.

At one time, a great debate raged over the costs and benefits of each. Now, RISC seems to have won out over CISC, at least at the architecture level. Examples of RISC machines include SPARC, MIPS, ARM, PowerPC, ALPHA and Crusoe. The CISC machines include IBM 360, DEC VAX, and Intel's x86. It's interesting to note that later generations of Intel's x86 architecture borrow heavily from RISC principles.

At this point we must make a small side trip to discuss the operation of CISC instructions. Instructions on CISC machines are not all the same length, but instead range from one byte to as many as 54 bytes on the VAX. These machines depend on the first byte to determine whether or not to load more instruction bytes. Since operands may be found in memory, additional instruction length is sometimes needed to specify these. Some instruction bytes will be fetched as the execution progresses. To fetch these extended instructions, the program counter must be advanced and more memory cycles run. Fetching operands on a CISC can be as simple as on a RISC if all the operands are in registers, or much more complicated if the operands are in the memory. On CISCs, the result may be stored in a register or in yet another location in memory.

23.3 Instruction Set

The actual binary numbers that form the instructions for a computer provide a (hopefully) compact representation of the entire set of actions that the CPU is capable of executing. The study of designing an efficient instruction set is treated very thoroughly in J. L. Hennessy and D. A. Patterson, *Computer Architecture: A Quantitative Approach* (Menlo Park, CA: Morgan Kaufmann Publishers, Inc., 1990). That book briefly presents an instruction set for a theoretical machine, the DLX (pronounced "deluxe"), which we will partially present here. (See Figure 23.3.)

These instructions are all 32 bits long and have one of three field formats: I (for immediate), R (for register) and J (for jump). The opcode (operation code) field will determine which of the formats the rest of the instruction will use.

Loads and stores of words, half words, and bytes use the I (immediate) format, in which the byte address in memory is given by the immediate value being added to the contents of the register specified by the field rs1. The data will be moved to or from the register specified by the field rd. Also using format I are the immediate operations. These use the immediate field as the second operand, which may be treated as a signed or unsigned number. Such instructions include ADDI (add immediate), SUBI (subtract immediate), ANDI, ORI, XORI, and their unsigned equivalents such as ADDUI. An example of the ADDI instruction is shown in Table 23.2. Conditional branch instructions also use this format; in this case, rs1 specifies which register to test, and the immediate value will be a signed number to add to the program counter if the condition being tested is true. Examples of these are BEQZ (branch equal to zero) and BNEZ (branch not equal to zero). The I format is also used to implement jump (J) and jump-and-link (JAL), where the target address is specified in a register (rs1). The JAL provides the mechanism for returning to the next instruction after the completion of the routine that is being jumped to

I-type (immediate) instruction

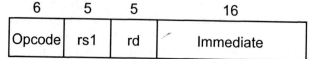

7 Loads and 5 stores of bytes, words and half-words
11 Immediate (rd ← rs1 op immediate)
6 Set conditional immediate
4 Conditional branch instructions
Jump register, Jump-and-link register

R-type (register) instruction

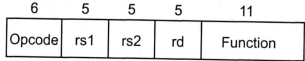

Register-to-register ALU operations — 1 opcode
56 function codes comprising: 10 ALU, 6 set conditional,
12 floating-point unit, 12 floating-point compare, 6 convert,
4 jump, and 6 move instructions.

J-type (jump) instruction

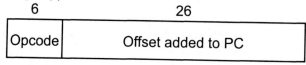

Jump, Jump-and-Link — 2 opcodes

Figure 23.3   Instruction formats for the DLX computer

by storing the program counter in the destination register. This subroutine linkage allows high-level constructs such as functions.

Table 23.2   The binary machine code for the ADDI instruction

Opcode	rs1	rd	Immediate
ADDI (add immediate)	Source register (r17)	Destination register (r24)	Value (62) to be added to the contents of the source register
6 bits	5 bits	5 bits	16 bits
000011	**10001**	**11000**	**0000000000111110**

The R-type (register) instruction format is the one used for computation instructions. It specifies two operand source registers (rs1 and rs2), a destination register (rd), and a function code to control the ALU operation. These are used for floating point as well as integer operations. There is a second ALU in most machines dedicated to floating-point operations that has its own set of registers for storing these special operands. Floating-point numbers are a binary representation of scientific notation where the mantissa represents the normalized significant digits and the exponent is the power of two that the mantissa is multiplied by.

The J-type (jump) instruction format is used for unconditional jumps and JAL instructions. Note that the jump range is $\pm 2^{25}$ from the current program counter (25 bits plus a sign bit). By coding jumps relative to the program counter instead of using absolute addresses, one may load programs into memory at any available location.

23.4 Assembly Language

Assembly language is a human-readable form used to code programs in a computer's native instruction set. A program called an assembler translates individual modules into the binary machine code needed by the computer. Another program called a linker resolves label meanings across many modules to produce the final program.

Each line of an assembly-language program codes one instruction. Lines are divided into four fields. An optional label field usually begins in the first column. A label will be used as the target of a branch or jump or to identify variables. The next field is the opcode field. The third field specifies the destination, sources, and any immediate values. Usually, a fourth field beginning with a semicolon at the right half of each line is used for a comment to explain what the programmer is trying to do with this instruction.

Figure 23.4 is an example of a program to initialize the elements of an array to a constant.

```
;Initialize array routine
;Array base address must be in R3 - will return pointing past the array
;Array size must be in R4 - will return zero
;Value to be stored in all locations must be in R1
;
INIT_WORD_ARRAY    SW      R1,(R3)              ;store the word value
                   ADDI    R3,R3,#4             ;add 4 bytes to get next addr
                   ADDI    R4,R4,#-1            ;decrement the size
                   BNEZ    R4,INIT_WORD_ARRAY   ;branches back to the label
                   JR      R30                  ;return to caller
```

Figure 23.4 Assembly-language subroutine that initializes an array

23.5 High-Level Languages

High-level languages (HLLs) utilize a program called a *compiler* to translate the programmer's instructions into a computer's native instruction set. High-level languages strive to provide the programmer with the following:

1. Machine independence. The program should work correctly on any computer for which the compiler exists. In practice, there may be incompatibilities that require some adjustments.

2. Compact programs. The quantity of work that can be expressed with a given line of code can be much higher in a high-level language. Consider the expression, "x = A[i++]*B[j++]/(sqrt(C)*sin(D)." Such a statement would require six loads, two increments, two function calls, two multiplies, a divide, and three stores — 16 instructions, in all — each of which would require one line of code in assembly language.

3. Higher levels of abstraction. Compilers hide all the branching with structured programming. They enable constructs such as data structures, objects, and classes, and even allow symbol names to be reused unambiguously.

4. Automatic error checking. The compiler protects the program from certain classes of coding errors at compile time and can be set to check for certain errors at run time.

5. Automatic optimization. The compiler looks for ways to speed up the execution of programs and implements these automatically.

Major HLLs of significant impact include Fortran ("formula translator"), Cobol ("common business-oriented language"), Algol, Lisp, Basic, Pascal, PL1, Ada, C, C++, and Java.

It can be said that many of the application development packages such as Dbase, Paradox, spreadsheet programs, and Mathcad are, in fact, an even higher level of language than the more general-purpose languages.

23.6 Operating System (OS)

Operating systems (OSs) serve to hide a computer's hardware details from programmers and users, much as HLLs hide the instruction set. The major functions of an operating system are as follows:

1. Perform all input and output (I/O) including the graphical user interface (GUI). Each I/O device will have drivers that allow a uniform set of functions to be implemented, regardless of the actual hardware. If a color picture is printed on a black-and-white printer, the driver should take care of converting shades of color to half-tone grays.

2. Spool printer data (provide huge first-in-first-out buffers).

3. Implement the file system.

4. Make virtual memory work.

5. Protect programs from each other, and protect itself from them.

6. Provide for resource sharing. When more than one program is trying to run, the OS must allocate resources, such as memory and CPU time, to each program. It should also provide mechanisms for inter-process communication.

7. Network interface. The OS should allow mounting of remote file systems, remote I/O, and running of processes on servers.

8. Enforce security. Ordinary users should not be able to interfere with or intercept the work of others.

23.7 Embedded Computing

Small dedicated computers are being used in computer peripherals such as keyboards, printers, and I/O cards. In addition, outside of computers, dedicated microprocessors are in use all around us. They are known generically as embedded computers. Here are some examples:

- A car may have an engine control computer, a transmission control computer, a dashboard computer, a trip computer, and maybe another computer in the sound system.

- Most microwave ovens sport an embedded computer, as does every CD (music) player, cellular telephone, and any gadget that has a remote control. The remote control itself may have a small computer in it.

- A special class of computer known as a digital signal processor (DSP) is in widespread use for image and sound processing (see Chapter 32). These computers use real-time algorithms to modify images or sounds as they are being moved or stored.

Embedded computers simplify the design of control electronics and allow great flexibility by virtue of their programmability. Many of these devices are still programmed in assembly language, because the programs are small, and the performance can be highly optimized. Frequently, embedded computers have no OS, or only a very rudimentary one.

Designing systems with embedded computing requires a fair understanding of both electronics and programming. Designers for such systems are in high demand and should remain so for the foreseeable future.

23.8 Problems

23.1 Describe concisely in your own words the computer terms represented by each of the following acronyms:
BIOS, MPEG, JPEG, CISC, RISC, modem, USB.

23.2 How big is a computer word?

What's in the Box?

We've all seen the outside of a personal computer. But what's inside? Figure 24.1 shows what's inside a typical modern personal computer.

The major component is the motherboard, so named because of the sockets to accept "daughter" cards. On the motherboard, we find the electronic brain of the computer, the central processing unit (CPU) that has a small fan to cool it; the computer's heart, the crystal oscillator clock (labelled "xtal"); the computer's memory, the dynamic random access memory (DRAM); and fast cache memory. Interface circuit cards plug into the bus connectors to provide extended functionality such as network interface, modem or upgraded graphics controller. Three types of expansion connectors are commonly found in current systems: Industry Standard Architecture (ISA), an old standard that will soon be phased out; Peripheral Control Interface (PCI), which is also used in MacIntosh computers; and the single Advanced Graphics Port (AGP) that allows you to upgrade the graphics capabilities provided by the single chip on the mother board. Some motherboards utilize a small connector to implement an Audio/Modem Riser (AMR), which allows the designer to segregate analog functions to a plug-in riser that can not be upgraded. Also included on the motherboard are interface electronics and connectors to the disk drives inside the enclosure and, to all of the peripheral devices including the video monitor, speakers, keyboard, and mouse are included on the motherboard. DC voltages for all the computer circuitry are produced by a power supply, whose enclosure also contains a fan to cool the computer components. In addition to a multi-gigabyte hard disk drive, there is a compact disc player/recorder or digital versatile disc (DVD) player and a removable media magnetic drive such a super floppy or a Zip™ Drive.

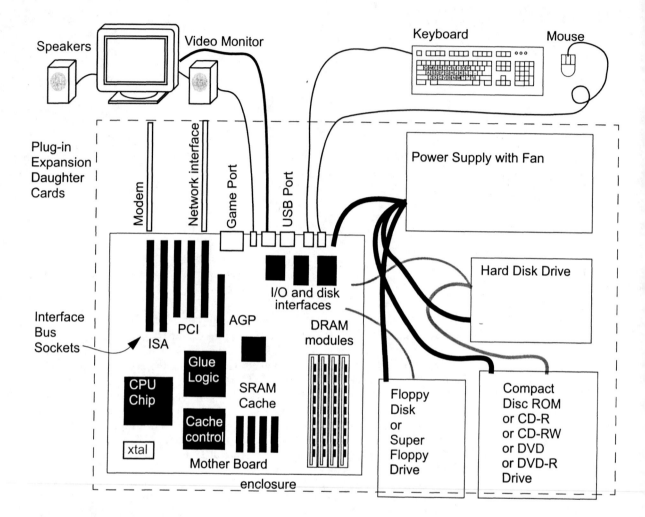

Figure 24.1 Typical personal computer components

24.1 Memory Hierarchy

The memory system is divided into two major parts: the main store and the file system store. Each of these has several layers, and, in fact, they overlap. The hierarchy of memories is organized to access the smallest, fastest, most expensive memory devices first and, hopefully, most frequently. Each succeeding level of the hierarchy will be larger, slower, and cheaper, and hold data and programs that are used less frequently.

The <u>main store</u> is characterized by having an address for each location that the memory bus can generate. This allows the CPU to directly and randomly access any location within the main memory.

The <u>file system</u>, in contrast, uses symbolic naming conventions implemented in operating system software to store and retrieve files from extremely large storage mechanisms. The minimum quantity of data that can be accessed is a sector, whose length is typically between 512 and 4096 bytes. Individual data files have no limit on their size, so long as they don't exceed the available space on a single storage device. File system software, built into the operating system, maintains a hierarchically organized view of the data stored on disk drives. Lists of individual files with related functions are maintained in directories, rather like telephone directories. Directories may contain references to other directories as well as to files. This gives rise to tree-like structures and so we call the structure of directories and files a <u>tree</u>. This tree has a root — the main directory from which all other directories can be located.

As file systems grow by the addition of files, files in one directory may no longer be located adjacent to one another on the storage medium. In fact, over time, as files are deleted, changed, and created, the disk can become rather randomized. As the operating system doesn't know in advance how large a file will be when a program starts writing it, the system may choose a group of adjacent sectors that is too small to contain the entire file. When this happens, the operating system will simply put the rest of the file elsewhere on the disk, keeping track of where all the pieces are stored. This is called <u>file fragmentation</u>, and it has a negative impact on performance. Special-purpose software is available for most operating systems to defragment the individual files, or in some cases, to defragment entire directories. All of this file structure requires that a great number of pointers be kept to track the location of all of the files and their individual sectors.

When a file is deleted, all that is necessary is to change the pointers to that file to show that the space is available. This gives some limited ability to "undelete" a recently deleted file whose space has not yet been reused.

Cache

The main store is fairly slow with respect to the CPU (60-ns access time vs. 1-ns clock cycles), so designers add a few chips of much faster memory called "cache" to hold the contents of those locations that have been referenced recently or that may be referenced soon by virtue of proximity to locations already referenced. An even faster cache may be built by including it right on the same integrated circuit with the CPU. Most systems combine both of these caches, calling the on-chip memory the primary or first-level L1 cache, and the external cache the second-level (L2) cache. These caches are implemented using static random access memories (SRAM), or sometimes special associative memories.

Caches operate by keeping copies of recently requested data and instructions and their memory addresses. If the CPU requests one of the stored addresses, the cache can respond with the contents much more quickly than the main memory.

Main Memory

The main memory holds programs and data of currently running programs. Main memories are implemented using dynamic random access memory (DRAM), which requires periodic refreshing to maintain its contents, and will "forget" when the power is turned off. DRAM comes in many "flavors" that are distinguished by their interfaces, connectors, operating voltages and of course capacities. Different interfaces, such as synchronous (SDRAM), fast page, Extended Data Output (EDO) and Rambus, attempt to overcome the inherent slowness of the DRAM access cycle.

Single and Dual-sided printed-circuit edge-connectors give us Single and Dual In-line Memory Modules (SIMMs and DIMMs) that have pin counts of 30, 72, 144 or 168. Yet another memory module, made by the Rambus corporation, is called the RIMM.

The size of this memory is usually measured in megabytes (MB) or, perhaps technically more correct, in mebibytes (MiB). The access width in bits will include any parity bits that are used for error checking. Typically, this memory is considerably smaller than the addressing capacity of the CPU. Many 32-bit computers can address a 32-bit memory bus that could access a 4 GiB memory space. Filling such a memory with state-of-the-art chips would be very expensive: DRAMs costing $1/MiB would result in an expenditure of $4,000!

Virtual Memory

Programmers have written programs that were larger than the main memories of computers since the beginning of computing. The elegant solution to this problem involves what is known as "virtual memory." When a program attempts to use data in a virtual memory location, a delay may occur if the desired information is not yet available in the physical memory. This phenomenon, termed a "page fault," slows down program execution. When a page fault occurs, special hardware interrupts that program and the operating system remaps a block (or page) of real memory into the desired virtual address, retrieves the data or instructions that belong in that address from disk (or other lower element of the memory hierarchy), and then resumes the program. Clearly, if there was already something in the real memory that was being remapped and it has changed since it was last brought in from disk, it must first be written back to the disk. Ideally, we would want to use the least-recently used (LRU) block of physical memory, in the hope that it might not be needed again.

To make this system work, main memory accesses must be mapped by a table that translates each virtual address into a real address or a fault. This function is frequently implemented on the same chip as the CPU.

Network Memory

The term "network memory" refers to the use by one computer on a high-speed local area network of physical RAM in another computer that isn't currently being utilized. The memory used will be accessed over the network to save images of pages in the virtual memory scheme.

Using network memory is significantly faster than using the local disk drive for swapping pages, so it results in much higher performance for large programs, especially for programs that use large data sets.

Disk Cache

Disk cache utilizes an area in the main memory to enhance the apparent performance of disk drives. The idea is to avoid being delayed by the rotational and head motion latencies that are inherent in disk drives. When a program requests that the operating system read a piece of a file, most often that same program will later request more pieces of the same file. These subsequent pieces can often be found right on the same track as the requested sector, so disk caching software will attempt to anticipate the need for that information and will read the entire track into main memory. If this information is needed later, time will have been saved. If it isn't needed, very little time will have been lost in reading the rest of the track.

Local Disk

Disk drives connected directly to the local processor store the file system and provide the largest reserve capacity for implementing virtual memory. These devices hold gigibytes of program and data, and will continue to get larger in the foreseeable future.

Hard disk drives consist of one or more disks on a common rotating spindle. (See Figure 24.2.) Each surface (top and bottom) of each disk has an associated head/arm assembly. These heads trace circular paths, called tracks, on the surface of the disk, "flying" near it on a very thin layer of air. When a current is passed through a small coil of wire in the head, a magnetic field is generated, magnetizing locally the coating on the disk, and storing information. The same coil can be used later to sense the stored magnetic regions and thus read the data back.

Figure 24.2 Magnetic disk drive — "hard disk"

Tracks of data are typically divided up into sectors to allow more flexibility in allocating space. Groups of sectors form pie-shaped wedges on the surface of the disk. Each sector has a fixed identification header, which is written only during formatting, and the data surrounded by a synchronization code and a checksum. The checksum is generated from the data during both write and read operations. During a read, if the checksum from the disk doesn't match the one computed from the data, an error is detected.

All the arms that hold the heads are moved together from track to track by a single actuator. The tracks on all the disk surfaces that can be accessed without moving the heads are collectively called a cylinder — a unit used to partition drives. The arm motion introduces delay in reaching a desired location. The time to move to an adjacent track is relatively short — a few milliseconds — but the time to move over hundreds of tracks is not proportionally longer because the arm can accelerate to higher speeds on a longer motion. Head access times are specified as averages. Since the average number of tracks moved in a random sequence will be 1/3 of the total number and the time to move gets relatively shorter as the distances get longer, the average access time corresponds to that required to move about one quarter of the total distance. These average access times are now under 9 ms, and will continue to fall as the arms become smaller.

Network File Servers

In the modern work environment, computers are connected to *local area networks* (LANs), and will take advantage of software and large shared databases that are stored in another computer somewhere on the net. This allows system administrators to maintain a single copy of a piece of software and simplifies backup procedures. Large databases and web sites, used by hundreds or thousands of users, require very high availability and reliability, and have given rise to redundant arrays of inexpensive disks (RAID) that spread data over a large number of disk drives in such a fashion that if any one drive fails, the system can keep operating while a replacement disk is installed.

Transfer and Storage Devices

Transfer and storage devices include floppy disks, compact discs, DVDs, magnetic tape, and other removable or transportable media such as optical disks. Their two main uses are for the distribution of software, and the storage of data for backup or archival purposes.

24.2 Input/Output (I/O)

Computers need input/output (I/O) devices to be useful. These devices can be broadly categorized into devices intended to interact with humans, with computers, and with real-world sensors and actuators.

Any discussion about I/O devices would be incomplete without a discussion of interfaces. Interfaces are electronic devices designed specifically to connect a device or devices to a computer (or other device). These will typically have one connector for a specific (standard) computer bus and another for the I/O device(s), which also may be a standard — such as the small computer systems interface (SCSI). Between these two connectors will be at least one integrated circuit and perhaps a memory to use as a buffer. Sometimes, another small computer or a program for the main computer will be contained in the interface.

Many peripheral devices utilize the universal serial bus (USB), a standard interface that allows bit rates of 1.5 or 12 megabits per second. This standard is intended for desktop peripherals and supports many devices like keyboards, mice, cameras, joysticks, speakers, point-of-sale appliances, joysticks, DVD players, printers, scanners, and even ethernet adaptors. This interface allows a device to draw up to 100mA of current from the computer's power supply, avoiding the need for a separate supply. The ease of installing devices that can just be plugged in without opening the box makes these quite popular with nontechnical users.

Another serial interface standard is the IEEE-1394 or Fire Wire. This provides much higher performance at 100 to 400 Mb/s, enough for disk drives and high-definition video.

Some interfaces will use direct memory access (DMA), a mechanism that permits the interface logic to access regions of the main store of the computer to transfer blocks of data to or from the I/O device without further intervention by the CPU. Such accesses "steal" memory cycles from the CPU, but save time, because the processor doesn't have to transfer each memory word using "programmed I/O."

Display Devices

For humans, vision is our highest information content input channel. It is natural to want to see the results of our computations, so display devices have evolved from binary lights through numeric, alphanumeric, graphic, and color graphic to virtual reality displays. The dominant display technologies are cathode ray tube (CRT); liquid-crystal display (LCD); AC gas plasma; thin-film electroluminescent (TFEL); and vacuum fluorescent (VF). Other technologies look promising for the future.

Graphic displays all use a number of picture elements (pixels) arranged in a rectangular matrix. Each pixel has an associated digital value that represents its color. For monochrome displays, this is one bit. For full-color displays this may be 24 bits, or eight bits that are mapped through a color pallet to 24 bits. Color displays use three primary colors (red, green, and blue) to form the desired shade, with eight bits (256 values) or more for each primary color.

All of these pixel values are stored in a RAM used to refresh the image on the display device. This RAM may be physically part of the main storage (DRAM) or a separate device with its address in a region of the address space reserved for I/O devices, or in an entirely separate memory connected through a serial link.

Most displays use a special-purpose chip to refresh the display. Many of these chips also contain special processors to draw features such as lines, polygons and ellipses, and to move rectangular regions around on the screen. Such special-purpose graphics engines serve to avoid loading the CPU, and through the use of dedicated hardware, they can improve performance significantly.

Display devices already have the ability to show full-motion video (television or movies), and we now have enough computing power to decompress video in real time. Movies can be generated with incredible realism, but not yet in real time.

Keyboard Devices

These familiar devices grew out of typewriters and then teletypes and keypunches (used to punch holes in cards to represent alphanumeric characters). Most keyboards actually contain their own tiny dedicated computer whose job it is to scan (sequentially access) all the switches that are under the keys. When this keyboard controller finds a switch closed, it will send a code representing that key to the host device. The code is sent serially (bit by bit) to minimize the number of wires needed. Some keyboard software allows for remapping the codes that are sent or even sending an entire sequence of codes.

Pointing Devices

This broad category includes mice and track balls that generate indications of relative motion; joysticks, which can provide velocity or position control; touch panels and digitizers (special sensing surfaces that use a pen or a pointing puck) that provide absolute position encoding; and exotic devices like head-and-eye tracking headgear or hand-tracking gloves for use in a virtual reality environment.

All of these devices are intended to inform the computer where the user's focus is directed or to input handwriting or other drawing motions. They all send their information to the computer in digital form, usually over a serial link, as with keyboards.

Printers

Evolving from typewriters, early printers formed characters by impacting fixed type through an inked ribbon onto paper. The next generation of printers formed characters by using a matrix of dots produced by driving wires into the ribbon. These have been largely replaced by inkjets that eject ink directly from a print head onto the paper. (See Section 16.3). Laser printers borrowed technology from photocopiers. They use a laser beam moving in a scanning pattern to draw on a charged photosensitive belt or drum that picks up toner particles to be transferred to paper and fused by heating.

All modern printers contain an embedded computer to control the sequencing of the mechanisms and to interpret the commands sent to it. These commands are sent character by character. Each character is composed of eight bits encoded according to the so-called ASCII code (American Standard Code for Information Interchange). These characters may be sent over a serial data line at speeds ranging from 240 characters per second (CPS) to 92,160 CPS, a parallel data port at rates up to half a million CPS, a USB port, or even a network connection at one million CPS or higher.

Two major languages are popular for controlling printers: PCL (printer control language) by Hewlett-Packard; and Postscript™ by Adobe Systems. It is interesting to note that Postscript is fairly human readable, but much more verbose than PCL.

Scanners

Scanners perform the inverse function of printers, that is, to input text documents and images. In practice, scanners only input images, and optical character recognition (OCR) software must be used after scanning to determine where and what the letters are. We have seen great strides in the OCR arena, but perfection remains out of reach.

Scanners move the document past the imaging mechanism, or vice-versa. The imaging mechanism illuminates a line on the document, and using lenses forms a miniature image of the line on a row of light-sensitive regions on an integrated circuit chip. The light is converted to a charge and the charges are shifted out of the chip and converted to digital codes (usually eight bits), which represent the intensity. Color is scanned by making three passes over the document using three optical filters or by using three light-sensitive rows of separately filtered photodetectors.

Audio Devices

Sound can be represented quite well by digital samples. If the rate of sampling is high enough (>40 kilosamples/second) and the digitization is done with enough resolution (16 bits), then computer audio quality can approach that of the best consumer high-fidelity audio equipment (see Chapter 7). However, data compression, lower sampling rate, and lower resolution (lower bit rates) are used to save storage and network bandwidth.

Computer-generated speech is improving steadily, but it still sounds unnatural. The inverse function, speech recognition, is also improving, but both operations will remain imperfect until the software can "understand" the meaning of the words and thus take advantage of the context in which they're used.

Networks

Networks allow computers to share resources such as disk capacity and RAM. They also allow users to communicate by e-mail and to share data. Hypertext links from one network resource to others have created the World Wide Web, a loosely connected collection of information and applications which spans the globe. (See Chapter 13).

Disk Memories

These rotating memory devices provide the bulk of the nonvolatile memory in computers. Currently, there are two major competing interface standards for hard disk and CD-ROM disk drives, SCSI and integrated drive electronics (IDE). Both put the real control of the drive into electronics located in the drive. SCSI is able to daisy chain up to seven devices on one controller. IDE controllers are much simpler to implement, but allow only from two to four drives to be connected.

Real-World Sensors and Actuators

Any sensor that can produce an electrical signal can be interfaced to a computer. In this way, one can measure pressure, temperature, strain, acceleration, speed, distance, and so on. Similarly, any device that can be controlled with a current or voltage can be connected to a computer. Motors that actuate robots and elevators, and voltages that tune radios and fire spark plugs are all controlled by computers. While the possibilities are endless, safety and reliability are the utmost concerns of the engineer.

24.3 Problems

24.1   List three input devices for a computer.

24.2   List two common computer output devices.

24.3   When you load a program (by typing its name, or double clicking its icon), which of the following does the computer do?
(a)   Read the program from read-only memory ROM
(b)   Read the program from RAM
(c)   Read the program from a storage device, such as a floppy disk
(d)   Either (a) or (b)
(e)   Either (b) or (c)

24.4   When you are typing on a word processor (before you Save), which of the following does the computer do?
(a)   Store your work in ROM
(b)   Store your work in RAM
(c)   Store your work on a storage device
(d)   Either (a) or (b)
(e)   Either (b) or (c)

24.5   Describe concisely in your own words the memory devices represented by each of the following acronyms:
(a)   RAM and SRAM, DRAM, SDRAM
(b)   ROM and PROM, EPROM, EEPROM, CD-ROM;
(c)   WORM

24.6   Using the largest memory modules currently available, find the cost of populating a 4GiB memory. (Hint: Use the Internet to locate prices; try price-watch [1])

[1] http://www.pricewatch.com

Semiconductors:

From Ns and Ps to CMOS

All of today's electronic products rely on circuits that employ the semiconducting element silicon in their key components. What special properties does silicon have that has made it so important? To answer that question we start by looking at how electric currents flow in the metallic conductors, such as copper and aluminum, that have been used for decades.

25.1 The Story with Metals

If we connect the two ends of an aluminum wire to the terminals of a battery, an electric current flows. The current consists of a flow of electrons inside the wire that are forced to move by the electric field set up by the battery.

How do we know that electrons are responsible for current flow in metals? That's a hard question to answer at this point without bringing in lots of advanced information. Let's just accept this for now.

Where did the electrons in the aluminum come from? As you know, any atom consists of a positively charged nucleus surrounded by a cloud of negatively charged electrons orbiting around the nucleus. The orbits of the outer electrons of neighboring atoms overlap with the result that they can freely move though the metal. The electric field set up by the battery forces these free electrons to move.

By convention, we say that the electric field is directed from the positive terminal of the battery to the negative terminal. And also by convention, as mentioned in Section 19.2, long ago, scientists decreed that the electric current flowed from the positive to the negative terminal. Unfortunately, they didn't realize that the charges that were moving in a wire were electrons, which are negatively charged. Since the electrical force on a charge is the product of the electric field and the charge, electrons would flow <u>toward</u> the positive terminal. So, the direction the electrons flow is opposite to the direction of electric current flow. Another way of saying this is that we think of the flow of electric current as being a flow of positive particles — even though we now know that the particles that actually move are negatively charged.

All of this just means there's a bothersome negative sign that crops up when you deal with current flow in microscopic terms. We can't really complain, since those early scientists only had a 50–50 chance of choosing the correct convention.

Although aluminum is a good conductor, it isn't perfect. It does have a finite electrical resistance that can be thought of as being due to the random collisions between the mobile electrons and the atoms that stay put in the aluminum lattice. Each collision alters the movement of that electron, and energy must be supplied by the electric field set up by the battery to get the electron moving again. For such a material, Ohm's Law applies, $V = IR$. The resistance R accounts for these energy converting collisions, which cause heating of the metal.

"How fast do the electrons move in a wire? Are they slower in a resistor?"

To summarize, in an ordinary metallic conductor at finite temperature, there is a cloud of electrons that are free to move; we can think of it as a gas of electrons in ceaseless random motion, like the molecules of a real gas such as air. When we connect a battery, the electrons on average move in the direction opposite to the direction of the electric field. This flow of negatively charged electrons is equivalent to a flow of <u>positive</u> charges in the opposite direction, from the positive terminal to the negative terminal.

25.2 What's Different about Semiconductors?

One difference is that semiconductors don't conduct electricity as well as good conductors such as copper and aluminum. In other words, if you could make a wire out of a semiconductor, such as silicon, you'd find it had a much higher resistance than a similar wire made of aluminum. However, the important difference between semiconductors and metals is that **currents in semiconductors can be carried by the flow of <u>either</u> negatively charged or positively charged particles**. The negatively charged carriers are electrons, as in metals; the positively charged carriers are called <u>holes</u>, for a reason that we'll soon see.

What decides whether a particular piece of silicon conducts with electrons or holes is the exact concentration of impurity atoms present in it. Here's how it works.

For Starters, Pure Silicon   The element silicon, located in Group IV in the middle of the right half of the periodic table, has four valence electrons. (See Figure 25.1.) Because of the way the atoms are arranged in a silicon crystal, each atom of silicon has four other silicon atoms as its nearest neighbors. The four electrons in the outer shell of each atom are shared with these neighbors. As a result, at any time, each silicon atom behaves as if its outer shell of electrons is perfectly filled with eight electrons, but if the silicon crystal is at a finite temperature, its thermal energy permits some valence electrons to get loose and wander through the crystal, just as in the case of a metal.

GROUP III	GROUP IV	GROUP V
B	**C**	**N**
BORON	**CARBON**	**NITROGEN**
Valence +3		
Atomic No. 5	6	7
Al	**Si**	**P**
ALUMINUM	**SILICON**	**PHOSPHORUS**
	Valence +4,-4	Valence +5
13	Atomic No. 14	Atomic No. 15
Ga	**Ge**	**As**
GALLIUM	**GERMANIUM**	**ARSENIC**
		Valence +5
31	32	Atomic No. 33
In	**Sn**	**Sb**

Figure 25.1 Portion of the periodic table of the elements near the element silicon. The Group III and Group V dopant elements are also highlighted with color.

This explains how there can be an electron current in silicon, but what about holes? Each electron that gets loose leaves behind a vacancy where the electron was: the silicon atom that the electron left now has only seven valence electrons around it. This vacancy could be filled by an electron released from another silicon atom in the crystal. We can therefore think of the vacancy as moving through the crystal, since each electron that fills it leaves another vacancy somewhere else. The name hole was adopted for this movable vacancy.

From this description you can already see that the hole moves in the direction opposite to that of the electrons that fill it over and over. For example, if an electron moves to the right to fill the hole, the hole itself has effectively moved to the left, so the hole behaves as if it had a positive charge whose magnitude is the same as that of the electron's negative charge (1.602×10^{-19} coulomb). And with some fancy quantum mechanical reasoning, it can be shown that one can also associate a positive mass with the hole! After you work with semiconductors awhile, you'll probably find that holes seem just like real particles to you.

A macroscopic analogy might help make this curious particle, the hole, seem more plausible. Here are several analogies — take your pick.

The Pocket Puzzle: You've probably seen the pocket puzzle (sketched in Figure 25.2) that has 15 sequentially numbered chips that can be slid around in — but not removed from — a 4×4 frame. The problem is to get the chips arranged in ascending numerical order. The missing chip is like the hole in a semiconductor. When working with this puzzle, you may find yourself thinking about moving the hole, even though you do that by moving the numbered chips that do exist.

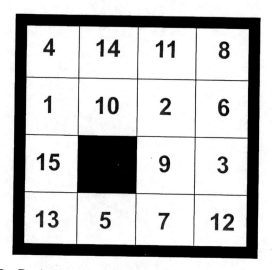

Figure 25.2 Pocket puzzle that illustrates how a hole can be moved around

The Warehouse: Imagine that you're trying to get something out of one crate stored in a very crowded warehouse that contains only one empty crate-sized space. Figure 25.2 could also apply to this situation. To get at the crate numbered 8, for example, you'd have to move "the empty space" around until it was next to that crate. Again, the empty space would begin to seem real as you move "it" around by moving the full crates next to it.

The Jugglers: You might imagine that the atoms in a silicon crystal are like a row of jugglers, juggling electron "balls" instead of dumbells or firesticks. All of the jugglers are very good at juggling four balls, but some of these jokers (the impurity atoms) have brought three balls instead of four. Now we'll turn on a large fan to create a "voltage" trying to move some balls. Now the jugglers with only three balls may be able to grab one ball from his upwind neighbor. That juggler will in turn grab one from his neighbor and so on. This results in the movement of the empty space upwind, just like the hole in a semiconductor.

The Movie Theater: There's an empty seat 6 seats into the row, but none on the aisle. You ask the people to move over one-by-one to bring the empty seat to you.

To summarize, in pure silicon, whenever an electron is freed from a valence bond, a hole is also created; the number of free electrons exactly equals the number of holes. This is the behavior of absolutely pure silicon, and so it's termed the <u>intrinsic</u> behavior. The freed electron and the hole both move through the silicon under the influence of an electric field, but they move in opposite directions.

Enter the Impurities

We can get more useful behavior if we add some carefully chosen impurities to our pure silicon material. These impurities are called <u>donors</u> if they contribute free electrons, and <u>acceptors</u> if they accept electrons and so create holes. If free electrons are in the majority, then an electric current is carried primarily by the negatively charged electrons, and this is called an n-type material. Conversely, if acceptor impurities are in the majority, so that there are more positively charged holes than negatively charged electrons, the material is called p-type.

There are two useful ways to add impurities. The first is by adding impurities to a whole batch of silicon — buckets of it — when the silicon crystal is first grown. The other is to add impurities in localized regions of the silicon when we are fabricating transistors and integrated circuits — but we'll talk about that a bit later.

To get n-type silicon, which has an excess of free electrons to carry current, we add impurities that have a valence of +5. In other words, we add elements from Group V of the periodic table, such as phosphorus or arsenic. With these impurities in the silicon lattice, it takes only a little bit of heating (a little thermal energy) to release the extra fifth valence electron so that it can wander through the crystal. Such an impurity atom is a donor — each such atom can donate a free electron to the crystal. (This is different from the case of pure silicon, where a mobile hole is created whenever a mobile electron is created.) This is termed extrinsic behavior, since it depends on something that is added to the silicon.

Once loose, the mobile electrons will move around under the influence of any electric fields that exist. The more free electrons there are, the higher the electric conductivity, or, equivalently, the lower the electrical resistivity will be. If we add to pure silicon an atom from Group III, such as boron, that acceptor atom can accept a fourth electron in its outer shell and so produce a hole that can travel through the crystal.

How many impurity atoms does it take to affect the conductivity of doped silicon? Well, pure silicon at room temperature has about 10^{10} free electrons per cubic centimeter. That may sound like a lot, but it turns out that there are about 10^{23} silicon atoms per cubic centimeter, so only a small fraction of the silicon atoms have lost an electron from the valence bond. For doping to have a significant effect on the number of free electrons, and hence the electrical conductivity of such a crystal, we'd only need to produce a concentration of charge carriers that was comparable with or larger than the intrinsic concentration. Therefore, 10^{10} or so dopants per cubic centimeter could have a measurable effect.

The silicon revolution came about when engineers perfected processes for precise doping of silicon. This enabled them to make the important devices we'll now discuss: pn-diodes and transistors containing closely spaced n-type and p-type regions. We'll go more into the manufacturing process later.

25.3 PN-Diodes

We can make very useful electronic devices by properly connecting p-type and n-type regions together. A simple, but very useful, device is the pn-diode. The diode conducts current very well in one direction and poorly in the other. Putting this in terms of electrical resistance, we can say that the diode has a very low resistance to current flow in one direction and very high resistance to current flow in the opposite direction. These directions are called the forward and reverse directions, respectively. In fact, a diode is almost like a switch that is either closed or open, depending on the direction of current flow.

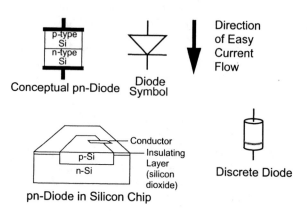

Figure 25.3 Various representations of diodes. Top left: Conceptual view of pn-diode. Top center and right: Schematic symbol of a diode with the direction of easy current flow indicated. Bottom left: Cutaway view of a diode as made in a silicon chip for use with an integrated circuit. Bottom right: Discrete diode.

Figure 25.3 shows a number of features of diodes. Since this is our first semiconductor device, we'll define its features quite carefully.

First of all, this device is called a diode, because it has two electrodes or contacts. (Transistors, which we'll see next, have at least three contacts.) The contacts to the diode are the heavy lines at the top and bottom of the conceptual diode. The vertical heavy lines represent ordinary metal wires for connecting a diode in a circuit. The diode in the cutaway view at the bottom left is shown as it might appear in a silicon chip or as part of a silicon integrated circuit; there the connector shown on top of an insulating layer would be made typically of a thin film of aluminum and it would connect the diode to other parts of the integrated circuit. A single diode in an integrated circuit might be only a fraction of a micrometer (micron) across — dimensions so small that a single human hair, which is typically 100 micrometers across, could completely cover a string of thirty or more diodes. (For an idea of these dimensions, see Figure 29.8.)

The arrowhead that is part of the diode symbol points in the direction of easy current flow, that is, from the p-type silicon to the n-type silicon. Discrete diodes, which are about the size and shape of ordinary 1/8-watt resistors, indicate by a diode symbol on them or by just the bottom straight line of the symbol which end is which so you can connect the diode properly into a circuit.

The I–V characteristic of a typical pn-diode is shown in Figure 25.4. The heavy straight-line characteristic is the ideal diode characteristic. A real diode has a characteristic like that shown by the thinner curved line that differs from the ideal characteristic only for small positive voltages. These characteristics show that a diode behaves <u>almost</u> like an on-off switch.

When the voltage V_D applied to a diode is negative (meaning that the p-type region is at a negative potential with respect to the n-type region), almost no current flows — perhaps only attoamperes. This is the reverse-biased condition. The reverse-biased diode behaves almost as if it were an open switch through which no current can flow. On the other hand, when V_D is sufficiently positive (p-type region positive with respect to the n-type region), the diode is forward biased, and current flows easily through it.

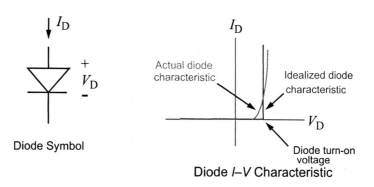

Figure 25.4   Diode symbol and current–voltage characteristics of a diode

"Why does a diode have a turn-on voltage?"

"What would happen if you tried putting a voltage above the turn-on voltage across a real diode?"

The small voltage required to forward bias a diode is called the *turn-on voltage*. For silicon diodes, this voltage is typically 0.7 volt. The ideal *I–V* characteristic suggests correctly that you can't have a positive voltage across a diode that is larger than the turn-on voltage. Figure 25.5 shows a diode connected in a circuit that is driven by alternating positive and negative pulses. Current only flows when the diode voltage is near the turn-on voltage.

The water model of the diode is shown in Figure 25.6. Water can flow from left to right when the pressure (diode voltage difference) becomes large enough to overcome the opposing spring force and opens the flapper valve. (The pressure exerted by the spring is the mechanical analog of the turn-on voltage.) Obviously, the water diode won't permit flow in the reverse (right to left) direction.

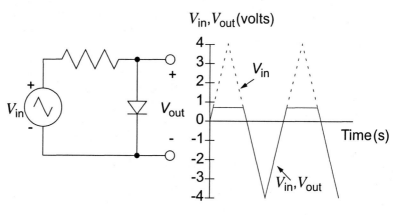

Figure 25.5   Diode circuit with alternating supply voltage

Figure 25.6   Schematic symbol and water model of a pn-diode

Figure 25.7 shows a potential plot, similar to those presented for resistive circuits, for a diode-resistor circuit. In Figure 25.7a, we see a typical silicon diode (turn-on voltage approximately 0.7 volt) connected in series with a resistor and a battery; the diode is connected so that it will be forward biased if the battery voltage is high enough. There is an 0.7 volt potential drop across the diode, and the current that flows causes a voltage drop across the resistor that equals the battery voltage minus the 0.7 volt diode drop. Figure 25.7b shows the situation when the diode is connected in the reverse bias direction. No current flows and the entire battery voltage appears across the diode.

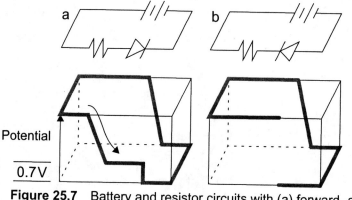

Figure 25.7 Battery and resistor circuits with (a) forward- and (b) reverse-biased diodes.

Zener diodes

There are specially constructed pn-diodes that can conduct in both directions; these are known as Zener diodes, after their inventor, Clarence Zener. Their circuit symbol and current-voltage characteristics are shown in Figure 25.8. They are made by carefully tailoring the concentrations of impurities put into the silicon. When biased in the forward direction, Zener diodes exhibit a conventional turn-on behavior. When biased in the reverse direction, they don't conduct until some particular voltage is reached, at which point they conduct well. This is known as the reverse breakdown voltage. You can buy Zener diodes having specified breakdown characteristics; they are used in circuits where you want a built-in voltage reference.

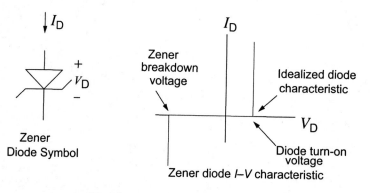

Figure 25.8 The Zener diode

25.4 Transistor Amplifiers and Switches

There are many instances when one needs to make an electrical signal bigger (to amplify it) or to control the flow of current in one circuit with a signal in another circuit (to have an electrically controlled switch). Amplifiers are most often used for analog signals, such as speech or music. Electronically controlled switches are used primarily for digital signals, such as signals from computers. The difference between an amplifier and an electrically controlled switch is that an amplifier output must mirror precisely every small change of input level, while a switch can produce only two different output voltages, high or low, depending on whether the input is in a high or a low range.

Transistors can be used as either amplifiers or switches. We'll start with amplifiers.

Need for An Amplifier

Suppose you want to talk with someone in Paris from a phone in Colorado. The pressure variations of your voice can be turned into corresponding voltages but, because of circuit resistance, they would be too small to detect long before reaching Paris. The solution is to restore the voltage amplitude with one or more amplifiers.

Playing your favorite compact disk (CD) also requires amplifiers. The microscopic marks on the CD are converted into electric currents by moving the disk through an infrared beam produced by a solid-state laser; the reflected beam is allowed to fall on a photocell where it produces changing currents that contain the digital information encoding the music and speech recorded on the CD. If you connected the outputs of the Digital-to-Analog (A/D) converters directly to your loudspeaker you wouldn't hear much, because the current would be too small. Again, you need amplifiers to increase the current amplitude and to produce sufficient power to drive your loudspeaker. In this case, an amplifier can also help match the electrical characteristics of the source to those of the loudspeaker.

Amplifier Representations

Figure 25.9 shows various symbols commonly used to represent a circuit that amplifies. If we focus our attention on the flow of signals, we might use the leftmost symbol, which shows schematically an amplifier having a gain of 10. What this

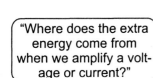

"Where does the extra energy come from when we amplify a voltage or current?"

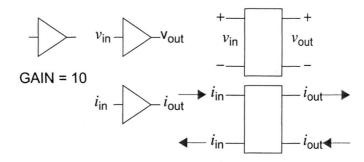

Figure 25.9 Several representations of amplifiers

representation means is that an input signal comes from the left, is amplified in the triangular-shaped symbol, and emerges on the right. According to the indication "GAIN = 10." the output amplitude is ten times that of the input. We could identify more explicitly whether the voltage or the current of the signal in increased by adding the voltage or current labels shown in the middle two symbols. The rightmost symbols are the most explicit, as they indicate clearly the polarities and directions chosen for the voltage and current inputs and outputs. The potential difference v_{in} established between the input terminals produces the amplified potential difference v_{out}, and the output current i_{out} is the amplified input current i_{in}. (Most amplifiers have time-varying inputs and outputs, but DC amplifiers also exist.) The plus and minus signs on the voltage amplifiers indicate our definitions of positive and negative polarity. Recall that we can define them either way; if we choose incorrectly, then the voltage v_{out} will just turn out to have a negative value. Similarly, the arrows on the current amplifier represent our arbitrary choices for the directions of current flow.

Example of a Need for an Electrically Controlled Switch

Consider what happens when you send a file created on a computer to a nearby printer. The digital voltage pulses sent over the printer cable must be large enough to be recognized correctly by the printer in spite of any interfering voltages that might be picked up from sources of electrical noise, such as nearby refrigerators or hair driers. Special devices known as driver circuits are used to produce the output digital signals that go to the printer. All the driver circuit has to do is produce a voltage that has one agreed-upon value when the bit to be sent is a **1**, and a different agreed-upon value when the bit is a **0**. The output of the driver circuit therefore merely toggles between two voltage values in response to the input pulses that it receives from the computer. In other words, the driver circuit behaves as an electrically controlled switch. (See Figure 25.10.)

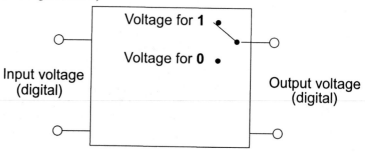

Figure 25.10 Electrically controlled switch for digital pulses

High, Low, and Nothing In-Between

In representing digital data as voltage levels, by convention, only voltages within certain ranges have a meaning. The voltages are denoted <u>high</u> and <u>low</u>. For example, in a circuit whose DC power supply voltage is 5.0V, a voltage above +3.0V may be regarded as high, and one below +2.0V as low. Any intermediate voltages are not defined and may cause errors in the system. In this way, the fidelity of transmission is not degraded by modest noise voltages that might be picked up from nearby electrical sources. For example, a +4.5V high signal with a ±0.5V noise riding on it is still interpreted as high (representing a **1**), and a +0V signal with an additional ±0.5V noise voltage on it is still interpreted unambiguously as a low (representing a **0**).

**Realizing a Voltage-
Controlled Switch**

The devices used as voltage-controlled switches are semiconductor devices that are called *transistors*. The invention of the transistor in 1947 started the modern electronic era. It permitted people to make electronic devices so small that literally millions could be used in every computer, permitting very fast computations to be made with a reasonably priced machine.

The first type of transistor that was built was termed the *bipolar junction transistor*. (See Chapter 28). This device soon led the way to an even more useful device, the *field-effect transistor* (FET). A subset of this class of device is the *MOSFET*, named to emphasize that the device typically has a *metal-oxide-semiconductor* material stack in it. This device is sometimes called an insulated-gate FET (IGFET).

**MOS Field-Effect
Transistor Operation**

A MOS field-effect transistor contains a gate (G) that is insulated from the underlying silicon and that controls the flow of current between regions called source (S) and drain (D), which are fabricated in the substrate or body (B) of the transistor. To discuss and understand FET operation, we will refer to the cutaway schematic of Figure 25.11, in which those four parts of a *p-channel FET* are explicitly indicated and labeled. To make the parts visible, the vertical scale of the cutaway view is distorted. In an actual MOSFET, the entire structure on the top of the wafer is only a few micrometers thick, and the insulator under the gate may be only about 100 nanometers thick. In contrast, the silicon chip into which this is all built is typically 0.5 mm thick. The transverse dimensions of a single MOSFET can be less than a micrometer.

The body is n-type material, and the source and drain are heavily doped p-type regions. Typically, the body is connected to the source region by an external connection. When the gate potential is sufficiently negative with respect to the source (more negative than about -0.7V), a p-type channel is formed by holes injected into the body beneath the gate from the source region. A current can then flow through the channel between the source and the drain, which is biased negative with respect to the source.

In an n-channel FET, the reverse conditions exist: The body is p-type, the source and drain are heavily doped n-type, and the body is connected to the drain region. A positive gate potential with respect to the source, greater than about +0.7 volt, causes electrons to be supplied to the body from the source, and a conducting channel of electrons connects the source to the more positively biased drain.

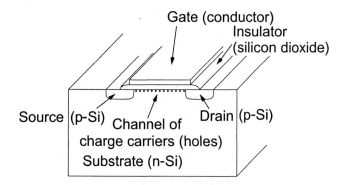

Figure 25.11 Cross sectional sketch of a p-channel MOSFET

Before considering the electrical device further, let's look at the water model for the p-channel MOSFET, shown to the right of Figure 25.12. You can think of this as a part of a cylinder into which a source of water and an outlet drain pipe have been connected. But water can't flow between source and drain unless the spring-loaded membrane is pulled back by suction on the tube at the left, marked "gate." The suction is a negative pressure and so is like a negative voltage in electrical terms. Only when that negative pressure is present does the membrane move to the left and leave a channel through which the water can flow between source and drain.

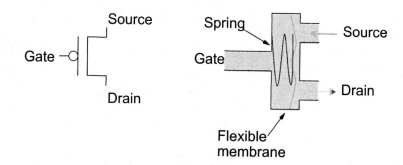

Figure 25.12 Schematic symbol and water model for a
p-channel MOSFET

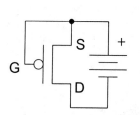

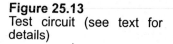

Figure 25.13
Test circuit (see text for
details)

Let's return now to the cutaway view of the MOSFET. (See Figure 25.11.) First, let's look at the situation when there is not a negative voltage on the gate relative to the substrate — analogous to the water model device when the spring-loaded membrane prevents there being a channel for water flow. For this condition, suppose we connect the gate to the source and also connect a battery between source and drain with the drain end negative, forming the test circuit of Figure 25.13.

Will current flow between source and drain under these conditions? The answer is, no, current won't flow, because there is a pn junction between the drain and the substrate that is reverse biased. The p-type drain region is at a negative potential with respect to the n-type substrate that surrounds it.

We can get current to flow by putting a potential on the gate that creates a layer of mobile charges in the region between the source and the drain. What's done is to make the gate electrode negative with respect to the substrate (and the source, since those two are connected together). When the gate electrode is negative, positive charges in the substrate underneath the gate are attracted upwards toward the gate. Where do those positive charges come from? They're holes that are flowing into the n-type substrate from the p-type source. The holes are drawn to the surface of the channel by the oppositely charged electrons on the gate electrode. They are concentrated in a very thin layer at the surface of the silicon, producing a large enough effect to form an electrically conductive channel there. Thanks to that channel, holes can now flow from the source to the more negative drain.

To summarize, putting a negative voltage on the gate (relative to the source and substrate) of a p-channel MOSFET causes the formation of a channel of holes next to the insulating layer that separates the substrate and the gate and permits a current to flow from source to the negatively biased drain.

One refers to these as <u>PMOS</u> devices. As previously suggested, one can make MOSFETs with the opposite dopings — p-type substrate and n-type source and drain, so that a positive gate voltage produces a channel having a high electron concentration. This is the n-channel MOSFET, and this is an <u>NMOS</u> transistor. We have focused here on the PMOS transistor, because its water model is simpler.

The curves in Figure 25.14 show the electrical characteristics of a p-channel MOSFET. We plot the output current and voltage with the input (controlling) variable as a parameter. For the MOSFET, the output current is the drain current, I_D, and the output voltage is the drain-source voltage, V_{DS}. The input voltage that controls the output is the gate-to-source voltage, V_{GS}. (Although I_D and V_{DS} are negative, the curves are plotted in the first quadrant, because they're easier to interpret that way.)

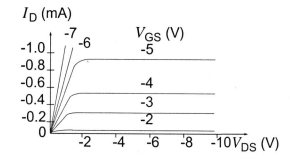

Figure 25.14   Output characteristics of a p-channel MOSFET

These curves show that the drain current that can flow is very small when the gate voltage is small; this is because the current-carrying channel is not conductive enough to carry current well. As the magnitude of the gate voltage increases, more holes are pulled into the channel region, and a higher current can flow for a given source-drain voltage. The curves also show that the current flow can saturate. For a given gate voltage, there is a maximum current that can flow, regardless of how large the source-drain voltage is made. If we keep the source-drain voltage very low, the device behaves like a resistor whose resistance is set by the gate-source voltage.

How You Might Use an FET

The circuit of Figure 25.15 shows how a p-channel MOSFET might be used as an electrically-controlled switch that acts as the driver for a computer printer. The digital pulses produced by the computer are applied to the gate electrode of the FET. These input pulses have a negative polarity, so they can attract holes into the region beneath the gate insulator to form a conducting channel there. The resistor at the right represents the electrical load presented by the printer. For example, if this were an inkjet printer, the resistor might represent the resistive film that gets heated to spray a droplet of ink onto the printer paper (see Section 16.3).

If the voltage between the gate and the source is zero (the gate is five volts above ground), then no conducting channel is formed and no current can flow through the FET. The source and drain are effectively disconnected. Hence, as no current is flowing through the resistor, the output voltage is zero. Now suppose that a zero-volt input pulse appears on the gate electrode. The gate-to-source voltage, V_{GS}, will be negative. The gate electrode then attracts positive charges (holes), the channel conducts, and the drain voltage becomes nearly equal to the source voltage, +5 V. This circuit is acting as an electrically controlled switch.

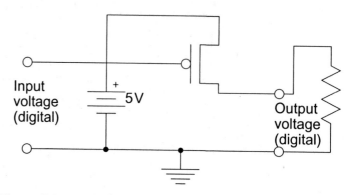

Figure 25.15 FET used as an electrically controlled switch

Field-Effect Transistor Symbols

A confusing array of symbols has been used to represent FETs in circuit diagrams and textbooks. We show some of these in Figure 25.16 for reference. We will use the ones on the right that are heavily circled henceforth in this book. We chose these particular symbols because they are used by circuit designers working "Inside Intel," the world's largest manufacturer of microprocessors.

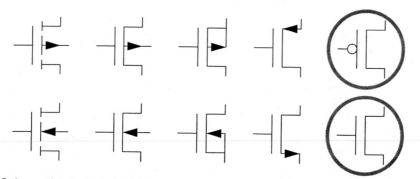

Figure 25.16 Schematic symbols for FETs. The top row shows symbols for p-channel devices and the bottom row the corresponding n-channel device symbols. Any of these may appear inside a circle, especially to represent a discrete, non-integrated device. Gate connections are always on the left. Source connections are at the top for the p-channel and at the bottom for the n-channel devices, with the drain connection opposite the source. Body connections, where shown, are on the right side in the center.

You may notice that some of the symbols show explicit connections, via the arrow, between the body and the source. In fact, in an integrated circuit, which may contain millions of FETs, the bodies of most or all of the n-channel transistors are connected together to the ground lead of the circuit, and the bodies of the p-channel transistors are connected together to the positive lead of the power source. You can also buy individual discrete FETs that bring out a body connection (along with gate, source and drain), so that you can connect it wherever you wish.

25.5 Putting It All Together: CMOS

A particularly important family of FET circuits is obtained by combining NMOS and PMOS (n-channel and p-channel) devices. This forms what is known as the *CMOS* family of devices, where CMOS stands for *complementary MOS*. The reason for combining these two devices into CMOS is that we can make useful digital circuits that consume power only when they change states. At other times, they remain in a high- or low-voltage state while no current flows, so no power is dissipated. Since they require very little power, they are ideal for use in portable battery-operated digital electronic systems, such as digital wristwatches.

A CMOS inverter is shown below on the left of Figure 25.17; the CMOS circuit at the right is a NAND gate. Their operation is discussed in Section 22.3.

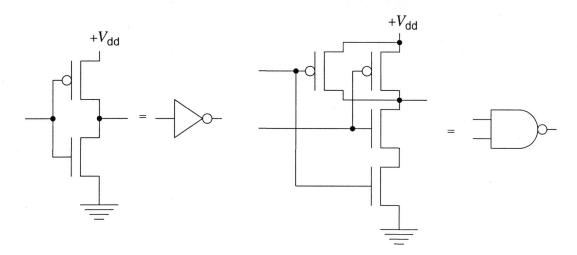

Figure 25.17 CMOS circuits and their schematic symbols

25.6 Problems

25.1 Assume that a silicon pn-diode, having an 0.7-volt turn-on voltage, is connected in series with a voltage source and a 900 Ω resistor.
(a) If the source is a 3 V battery, what forward current will flow?
(b) Assume that the source is a 3 V rms AC source and plot the diode current and the source voltage as functions of time.

25.2 A current I in the milliampere range is flowing the circuit of Figure P25.2, which contains a typical silicon diode, D. If $|V_S| = 3$ volts and $R = 1k\Omega$, what are the values of V_S and I?

25.3 In what essential respects does a semiconductor such as silicon differ from a metal such as copper?

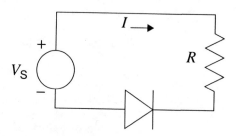

Figure P25.2

25.4 An n-channel field-effect transistor is used to drive an 8-ohm speaker in the circuit shown below. The power supply voltage is 32 V, and the signal applied to the gate ranges from 1.5 V to 3 V.

(a) Plot the load line of the speaker onto the graph of the transistor's I_D-V_{DS} characteristics, which are plotted in Figure P25.4.

(b) Find the value of the voltage applied to the speaker for each voltage applied to the gate.

(c) Plot the resulting V_{out} vs. V_{in} characteristic of the amplifier.

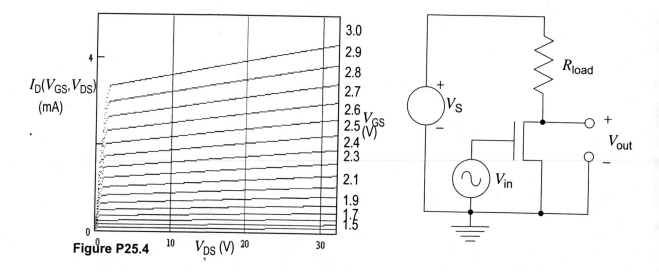

Figure P25.4

The Load Line and Your Car Battery

How could you figure out what would happen if you connected an LED across the terminals of your car battery? One way would be to try it, but you might burn out the diode in the process. You could try solving for the current and voltage with the diode connected by applying Ohm's Law and Kirchhoff's laws, as you would with a circuit containing a voltage source and ordinary resistors. However, with the diode, this would be very tricky, since a diode's resistance ($R_{\text{Diode}} = V_{\text{Diode}}/I_{\text{Diode}}$) depends heavily on the current that is flowing through the diode. Technically, one says that the diode is a nonlinear element, whereas an ordinary resistor is a linear element whose resistance is a constant (at least, as long as the resistor doesn't heat up appreciably).

What you can do is to solve this battery–diode problem graphically. The idea is to plot the *I–V* characteristics of the diode (as you might obtain it from a lab instrument called a curve tracer) on the same graph as the *I–V* characteristic of the battery. Where the two curves cross you have the valid solution, since at that point the current-voltage relations for both the diode and the battery are simultaneously satisfied. In fact, in your beginning algebra class, you probably used a similar graphical procedure (Figure 26.1) to solve an equation such as f(x) = g(x), where f(x) and g(x) are two different functions of the independent variable x.

Now all we need is the plot that characterizes your car battery. We can obtain the plot by working with a Thévenin equivalent circuit model for the battery (see Figure 26.2) consisting of an ideal voltage source (V_S) and a resistor (R_{Int}), called the *internal resistance* of the real-world battery.

To determine the curve (actually it turns out to be a straight line — the *load line*) that represents the behavior of the Thévenin source, we can perform the thought experiment of connecting various load resistors across the battery terminals and seeing what voltage appears across the terminals and what current flows through the load.

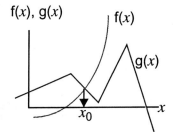

Figure 26.1 The solution to the equation f(x) = g(x) obtained graphically is x_0

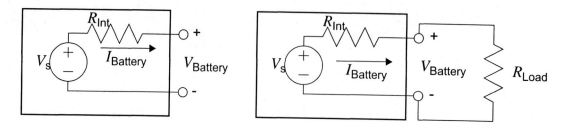

Figure 26.2 Thévenin equivalent circuit for a real battery. Left: with no load. Right: with load.

One load resistance value that is easy to think about is the resistance $R_{Load} = \infty$, an open circuit. No current flows, so Ohm's Law shows that there is no voltage drop across the internal resistance. Hence, for $R_{Load} = \infty$, the terminal voltage $V_{Battery}$ is just equal to the source voltage, V_S. Another value that you can think about using is $R_{Load} = 0$, a short circuit. (Think about this but don't try it, since you might destroy your battery by shorting it.) In this case, the voltage across the load is zero and the combination of Kirchhoff's Voltage Law with Ohm's Law says that $V_{Battery} = 0$ and $I_{Battery} = V_S/R_{Int}$. These two points are plotted in Figure 26.3, where they have been connected by a line. To convince yourself that the straight line — the load line — actually does represent the I–V characteristic of the real battery, imagine connecting other finite-valued resistors across the battery terminals. Solve the circuit, and you'll find that all solutions lie on the line we just determined. (For example, try the problem with $R_{Load} = R_{Int}$, and you'll find the solution $V_{Battery} = V_S/2$, $I_{Battery} = V_S/2R_{Int}$, which lies on the line sketched.) Finally, to get an answer to the battery-diode problem, plot the I-V characteristic of your diode on the plot containing the load line of the battery and see the values of I and V where the two curves intersect. You can use this load-line technique with other useful nonlinear circuit elements, such as transistors. (See P. Horowitz and W. Hill, *The Art of Electronics*, 2nd ed. (Cambridge, England: Cambridge University Press, 1989), Appendix F, pp. 1059-61.)

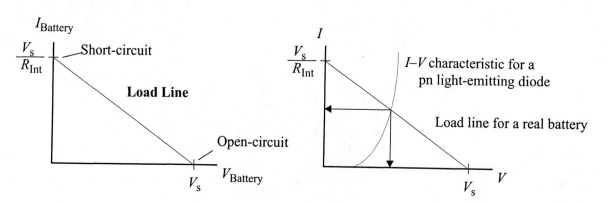

Figure 26.3 Load line obtained from the battery short-circuit and open-circuit loading conditions, and graphical solution for a diode connected to a real battery. Arrows point to the current that will flow through the diode and the voltage across the diode.

CMOS Logic and Memory

27.1 CMOS Logic Gates

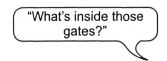

"What's inside those gates?"

The dominant technology for digital logic today is CMOS. (See Section 25.5.) In these devices, two complementary types of field-effect transistors (FETs) are used to switch signals. One signal is used to signify a logical **1**, or true, and a different signal is used for **0**, or false.

An n-channel FET turns on when its gate signal minus its source signal is 1. So if we apply a logical **1** to the gate of an n-channel FET whose source is **0**, then the transistor will turn on, and if the gate is at a logic **0**, then the transistor will turn off. We can think of this as a signal-controlled switch. (See Figure 27.1.)

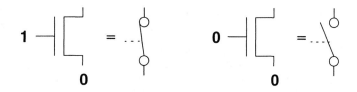

Figure 27.1   n-channel FET modeled as a switch

The complementary p-channel FET turns on when the gate signal minus its source signal is negative one. This means that if the gate of a p-channel FET is at logic **0** and the source is at logic **1**, the transistor will be on. If the gate is at **1**, the transistor will be off. (See Figure 27.2.)

221

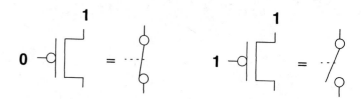

Figure 27.2 p-channel FET modeled as a switch

If we connect the drains of a complementary pair of these devices — connecting the source of the p-channel to the power supply $(+V_{dd})$ and the source of the n-channel device to ground — and tie their gates together, we get an inverter, or NOT gate, as shown in Figure 27.3.

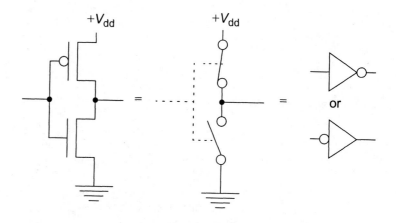

Figure 27.3 CMOS inverter schematic and its switch model
Notice that moving the dotted line connecting the two switches up will simulate a **1** input and down will simulate a **0** input.

By connecting more FETs we can create other logic functions, such as NAND, NOR, three-input NAND, AND, OR, and buffers, as shown in Figures 27.4 through 27.7. CMOS gates are naturally inverting, so to build an AND gate or an OR gate, we have to add an inverter to a NAND or NOR gate.

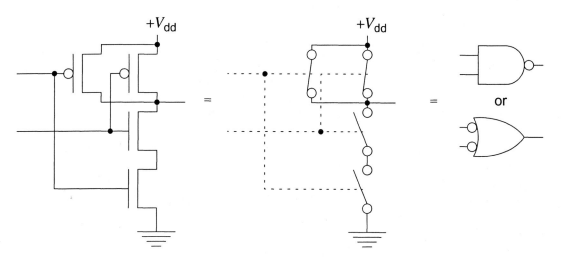

Figure 27.4 CMOS NAND gate schematic (left), its switch model (center), and its symbols (right)

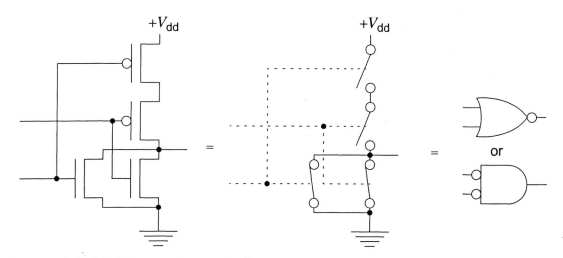

Figure 27.5 CMOS NOR gate schematic (left), its switch model (center), and its symbols (right)

Three-input NAND			
A	B	C	Out
0	0	0	1
0	0	1	1
0	1	0	1
0	1	1	1
1	0	0	1
1	0	1	1
1	1	0	1
1	1	1	0

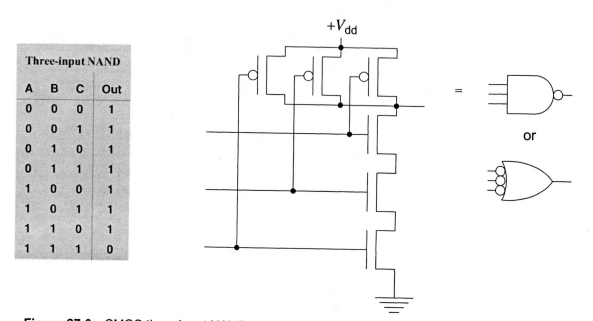
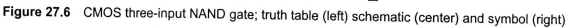

Figure 27.6 CMOS three-input NAND gate; truth table (left) schematic (center) and symbol (right)

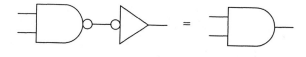
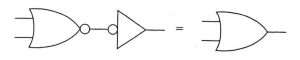
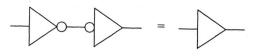

Figure 27.7 CMOS AND gate (top), OR gate (middle), and buffer (bottom)

Transmission Gates

Another type of logic structure possible with CMOS is the transmission gate of Figure 27.8. This gate allows logic levels to pass through it in both directions when enabled and prevents passage when it is disabled. The schematic symbol looks like a bowtie, with two buffers facing each other, but the part doesn't buffer the signals. It is actually resistive, so logic that uses these configurations requires restoring the signals by using a buffer after every few transmission gates.

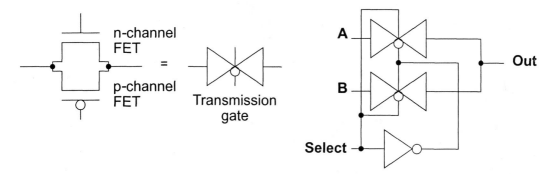

Figure 27.8 CMOS transmission gate (left), its symbol (center), and a multiplexer built with transmission gates (right)

Using these fundamental elements, we can construct any logic circuit, or even a computer!

Random Access Memory (RAM)

A random-access memory (RAM) is an array of thousands of memory elements, any one of which may be accessed in a single operational cycle. These large arrays are used to store instructions and data for computers.

The two major types of RAM are Dynamic (DRAM) and Static (SRAM). Each of these uses a simple cell structure repeated in a two-dimensional array layout connected with row and column wires.

The simpler, and thus denser, DRAM uses a single transistor and a capacitor to form the memory cell as shown in Figure 27.9. The transistor is used as a switch to connect the capacitor to the column, or bit line when the row, or word line has a high voltage on it. The capacitor is used to store charge indicating a **1**. When the switches for a row are closed, the charge on a capacitor that is storing a **1** will cause a voltage rise on the corresponding column wire. A sense amplifier on each column will amplify the small voltage change back to digital levels. The charges on the capacitors will be greatly diminished by the reading action and thus the information must be written back into them by placing the digital voltage back onto the column wires, thereby refreshing the values stored in the capacitors. Each cycle of the memory must follow this read-write action. Because all the transistors in a row are connected to the same word line, all the cells in any row are accessed at the same time. Since the number of columns is much larger than the number of bits that will be used at any one time, selection circuitry at the ends of the columns will determine which bits in the row will be used. To counteract the slow leakage of charge that will occur in the capacitors, each row in the memory must be cycled periodically (refreshed) to prevent information loss.

SRAM uses more transistors — typically six — to implement each cell as shown in Figure 27.10. These cells hold their values as long as power is applied to the chip, and so do not require active refreshing. Also, these cells are much faster than DRAM cells, leading to their use for cache memories.

Each column in the memory will use two complementary-valued bit lines and two switches to connect the bit lines into the cross-coupled inverters that actually store the data. These inverters are made with very small transistors, which allows the bit lines to be used to write into the cell by overpowering one or the other of the inverters. When the bit lines aren't driven, the inverters will drive them toward the logic levels, and sense amplifiers will detect the differential change in voltage between the two bit lines, speeding up the readout process.

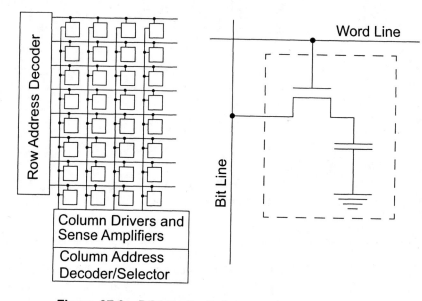

Figure 27.9 DRAM circuit diagram and cell schematic

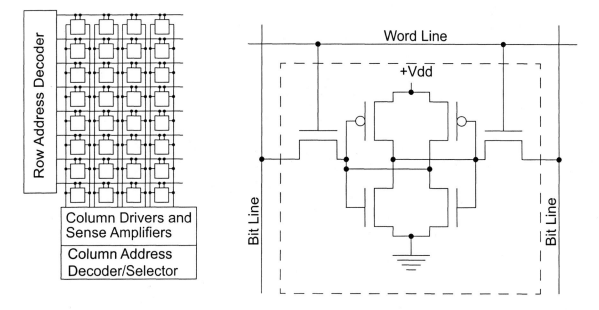

Figure 27.10 SRAM circuit diagram and cell schematic

27.2 Problems

27.1 Implement an XOR gate using standard CMOS logic. How many transistors does it require?

27.2 Implement an XOR gate using pass gates and CMOS inverters. How many transistors does it require?

27.3 How many transistors are required to build a master–slave flip-flop?

Other Semiconductor Devices and Circuits

There are many important semiconductor devices and circuits in addition to those we've discussed. The simplest semiconductor device, the pn-diode, is used as a rectifier to allow current to flow through it in only one direction. Variations of that diode are used as light sources (light-emitting diodes and laser diodes), as well as photodiodes and solar cells that convert optical energy into electric energy. We've introduced you to one type of transistor — the field-effect transistor — but have neglected the first type of transistor that was developed, the bipolar junction transistor (BJT). We will also discuss several important circuits that employ semiconductor devices — power supply circuits that convert AC voltages to steady DC voltages and operational amplifier (op-amp) circuits that have many applications.

28.1 Diodes

The diode as a *rectifier* was introduced in Chapter 20 and discussed further in Section 25.3, where its physical structure was shown. Now let's consider *optical* applications of diodes.

Light-Emitting Diodes

Diodes made by combining p- and n-type gallium arsenide (GaAs), will emit infrared or visible light when forward-biased. The biasing gives energy to electrons released from the dopant impurities — so there are energetic free electrons and there are holes. In GaAs, the electrons may recombine with the holes and give up their energy in the form of <u>light</u>. Diodes designed for this purpose are called light-emitting diodes (LEDs.) The LEDs that produce visible light are widely used as indicators. Infrared-emitting LEDs are used in remote controls for television sets and

VCRs, and for communicating between computers. By adding suitable phosphorescent coatings to LEDs that emit blue light, one can make an efficient LED that emits white light.

Photodiodes and Solar Cells

Diodes used in circuits as rectifiers usually have light-tight coatings on them. Otherwise, light that reaches the pn-diode's junction can release electrons from their valence bonds, if its photon energy is high enough, and make the diode conducting. If we make a pn-diode in which light can reach the pn junction, we can make an optical detector, called a <u>photodiode</u>. The photodiode is operated under reverse bias so that it only conducts when illuminated.

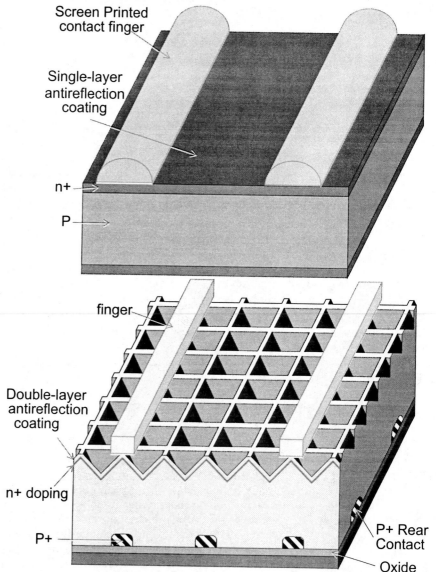

Figure 28.1   Top: Sketch of a planar solar cell. Bottom: Sketch of solar cell designed for highest efficiency.

Extending this principle further leads one to the concept of the *solar cell* that is capable of producing DC electric power from sunlight. The top sketch in Figure 28.1 shows a cutaway view of a planar solar cell made of single-crystal silicon. Sunlight coming from above passes through the antireflection coating into the silicon, which has a thin upper layer that is heavily n-type (indicated on the figure as n+). Below this layer is the actual junction, too thin to show on the sketch, and then a p-type material with a metal contact at the bottom. The narrow metal strips on the top of the cell are used to extract current from the cell without shadowing it excessively. An advanced cell design, shown at the bottom of Figure 28.1, has higher efficiency, because of details of its lower contact, and because the faceted top surface subjects the light to multiple bounces, providing more chances for interaction with the silicon.

Electrical behavior of the solar cell is illustrated in Figure 28.2 where the equivalent circuit for a solar cell is shown on the left, together with the cell's I–V characteristic (right). The current source represents a current whose magnitude is proportional to the light intensity. As the intensity increases from zero (dark condition), the current you'd measure with an ammeter goes from zero to the value marked at the right as "short-circuit current." At the same time, the cell voltage that you'd measure with a voltmeter reaches the positive value labeled "open-circuit voltage." (Recall that an ammeter behaves as a resistor of zero ohms — a short circuit — and a voltmeter is electrically equivalent to a very high resistance — an open circuit.)

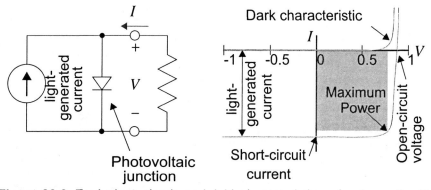

Figure 28.2 Equivalent circuit and I–V characteristics of solar cell with (lower curve) and without (upper curve) illumination

If an ordinary resistor having a finite value is connected across the solar cell, illumination will produce operation at some intermediate point on the illuminated solar cell curve where current flows through the resistor and develops a finite voltage. (To explore this idea further, see Chapter 26.) The solar cell thus produces electrical power that is dissipated in the resistor. In this test case, the power simply heats the resistor, but it could instead be used to operate an emergency telephone beside a highway, or even power your house.

Here are some facts the should explain why solar cells are not yet widely used as the sole energy sources for houses:

- The maximum solar insolation at the Earth's surface is 1 kW/m^2, which can only be realized on a very clear day when the sun is directly overhead.

- The maximum reported solar cell efficiency is around 22%; the maximum efficiency of a module containing many solar cells is only around 15% because of the necessary dead space between cells.

- Since sunshine is intermittent, rechargable batteries are used to store the energy produced during the day; these batteries are costly and have about a 5-year life.

- If you need AC power, then you must use a dc-to-ac converter (inverter) with the solar cell array.

A study of solar cells[1] concluded that at present efficiencies, the cost of operating a 300 kW-hr, 4 kW peak solar cell system for a house located 1 km from a power line would be comparable to the cost of buying electricity from the power grid. This recurrent cost is chiefly that of buying replacement batteries. The equipment cost for the system would be roughly equal to the cost of installing a powerline to the house.

28.2 The Bipolar-Junction Transistor (BJT)

In the 1940s, scientists at the Bell Telephone Laboratories invented a *solid-state* device that could amplify currents and voltages. The first laboratory devices were hardly beautiful (Figure 28.3) but they did show that one could amplify electrical signals without using the vacuum tubes that were then customary. In the years since, the science and the art of making these solid-state devices have improved tremendously, due to the work of many technical people, particularly experts on materials science and engineering. Now these devices are only micrometers across, so that several million of them can be fabricated along with resistors, capacitors, and diodes on a silicon chip smaller than a postage stamp.

"Does the name transistor mean anything?"

The name *transistor*, coined by J. R. Pierce, a famous electrical engineer and physicist at the Bell Telephone Laboratories, means "transfer resistor." Suppose, for example, that the current amplifier on the right in Figure 25.9 contained a transistor. What happens in the output circuit on the right side of the amplifier block is determined by what current is input on the left side of the block. We could think of the output as having a voltage source in series with a resistor whose value was determined by what happened at the input. Hence, the idea of the amplifier leads to the transfer resistor idea and hence to the transistor.

[1] J.P. Benner, L. Kazmerski, "Photovoltaics — Gaining greater visibility", *IEEE Spectrum*, 36(9), Sept. 1999, pp. 34-42.

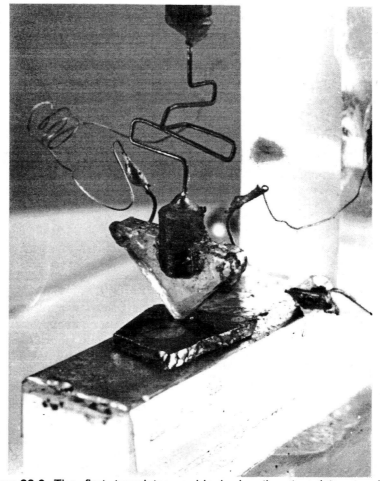

Figure 28.3 The first transistor, a bipolar-junction transistor employing germanium as the semiconductor. The wedge-shaped emitter and collector rests on the underlying semiconductor plate, which thus became known as the transistor base. (Photo courtesy Bell Telephone Laboratories)

This idea is illustrated by the sketch in Figure 28.4. A linkage between an input current meter needle and the wiper arm of a variable resistor uses the input current to control the output characteristic.

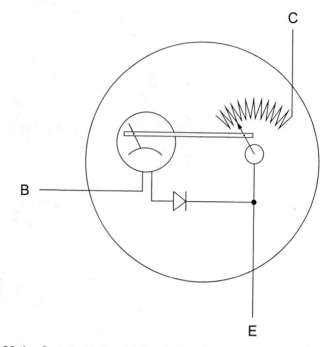

Figure 28.4 Conceptual model of the functioning of a bipolar-junction transistor: the current input to the base (B) terminal controls the resistance between collector (C) and emitter (E) terminals by means of a mechanical linkage between an input current meter and a variable resistance connected between collector and emitter.

Water Model of a BJT

Our water model of a BJT in Figure 28.5 illustrates the current amplification by coupling two idealized turbines. (The turbines must have no friction, no momentum, and be linear — the rate of rotation must be proportional to the current going through them.) The small turbine turns in response to current flowing through the base terminal; the common shaft causes the larger turbine to pass a corresponding, but larger, water volume. A water diode is added to the base circuit to mimic the turn-on characteristic of the base-emitter junction. A pressure regulator is added to the collector to prevent any pressure drop from turning the larger turbine. (The regulator works like the regulator on a scuba tank — you can suck air out of it easily, but it won't blow you up like a balloon.) The large turbine can draw a current from the regulator without being forced to turn by the pressure difference between the collector and the emitter. The small tube connecting the regulator to the emitter provides the reference pressure that the regulator will match on the other side of its internal diaphragm.

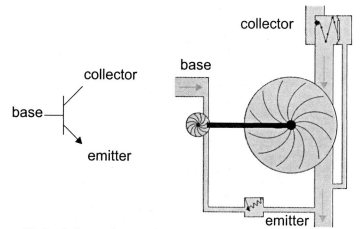

Figure 28.5 Schematic symbol and water model for an npn bipolar-junction transistor

How Does a BJT Work?

Figure 28.6 shows a number of transistor details. At the left is a conceptual diagram of a transistor: Three doped silicon regions are sandwiched together, each with a contact for connection to a circuit. (These are designated as pnp or npn transistors, for obvious reasons.)

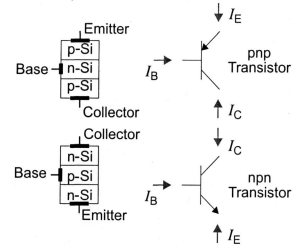

Figure 28.6 Bipolar-junction transistors (BJTs). Conceptual cutaway views of pnp and npn transistors are shown at left. Circuit symbols with base, emitter and collector currents are shown at right.

The device symbols are shown to the right of the conceptual diagrams along with conventional definitions for the directions of the three transistor currents. The transistor contacts are called the base, emitter, and collector. In the circuit symbols, what distinguishes the pnp from the npn transistor is just the direction of the little arrowhead on the emitter lead: In the pnp transistor, the easy (forward) direction for emitter current flow is inward, from the p-type emitter region to the n-type base region. The situation is reversed for the npn transistor.

All you need to know for now about transistor operation is that the flow of a tiny current from base to emitter controls the flow of a much larger current from collector to emitter. Thus, one way to make a current amplifier is to connect a BJT so that the base and emitter form the input circuit and the collector and emitter form the output circuit. (We'll see an actual circuit next.)

To make a BJT amplifier, we need some steady (DC) voltage sources. They supply the energy needed for amplification and provide the turn-on voltage needed so that the input current can flow into or out of the base. A way of doing this is shown in Figure 28.7.

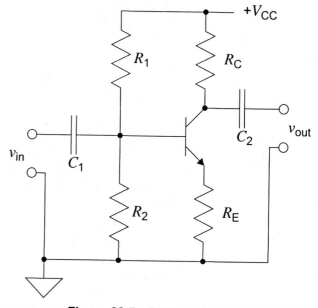

Figure 28.7 BJT amplifier circuit

To relate the current and investigate the amount of amplification obtainable, we need some information about how the device works. At its simplest, the BJT is governed by two principles:

1. The base and emitter operate as an ordinary silicon pn-diode (whose turn-on voltage is typically 0.7 volt).

2. The collector current is a large multiple of the base current. If the collector current is I_C and the base current is I_B, their relationship is $I_C = \beta I_B$, where the value of the factor β ranges typically from 50 to 200.

You can see that a small base current controls a much larger collector current. What about the emitter current? To find out, we can apply KCL to a BJT: The sum of all the currents flowing into the transistor must be zero, so

$$I_B + I_C + I_E = 0,$$

giving

$$I_E = -(I_B + I_C) = -(\beta + 1)I_B.$$

Thus, the emitter current is slightly larger than the collector current, and it, too, is proportional to the small input current to the base contact. We can represent the situation graphically in the sketch below where the widths of the heavy arrows indicate the relative magnitudes of the currents they represent.

Question: What is the approximate value of the amplification factor β for the transistor of Figure 28.8?

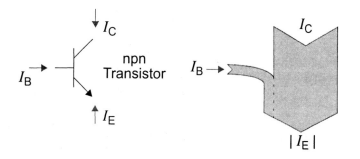

Figure 28.8 Sketch showing the relative magnitudes of the three currents for a hypothetical npn transistor. The width of each band on the right represents the magnitude of the corresponding current.

Let's dissect the amplifier circuit shown earlier (in Figure 28.7) to see what each of its components does. The separate parts are identified in the circuit diagram and in words as follows.

1. Transistor. The AC input voltage v_{in} causes an AC current to flow into the base contact. This current controls the collector and emitter currents as previously described.

2. The voltage divider circuit, consisting of R_1, R_2, and V_{cc}, provides a DC voltage that is equal approximately to $V_{CC} \times R_1/(R_1+R_2) = 0.7$ volt, the voltage needed to turn on the base-emitter junction and permit current to flow into the base. Providing DC voltages to operate a transistor is called *biasing* the transistor.

3. The capacitor C_1 blocks direct current from flowing to the left into the AC input circuit. Such an extra current flow could affect the DC voltage that the voltage divider applies to the base of the transistor. Since AC signal current can flow though C_1, a capacitor used in this way is called a *coupling capacitor*. The capacitor C_2 is also a coupling capacitor that performs a similar function in the output circuit.

To complete the story of this transistor amplifier, we need to show that this circuit actually does provide an output voltage that is an amplified replica of the input voltage. To do that, we need to look at the I–V characteristic of the BJT.

Typical characteristics for an npn transistor are shown in Figure 28.9. The vertical axis is the collector current, I_C, and the horizontal axis is the voltage between collector and emitter, V_{CE}. The parameter that identifies each of the characteristics drawn on the plot is the base current, I_B. Note, incidentally, that the collector currents are much larger than the base currents — milliamperes vs. microamperes. This is just a reflection of the fact that a small base current controls a collector current that is a factor β larger.

To analyze how well this transistor amplifier really works, one needs to combine two sorts of information: The data on the plot of Figure 28.9 — which indicate

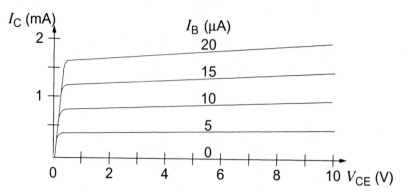

Figure 28.9   Output characteristics of an npn bipolar-junction transistor

how current and voltage are related in the <u>transistor</u> — with information about the current-voltage relations imposed by the <u>circuit</u> into which the transistor is connected. The latter will involve the actual values of the resistors in the circuit, and the actual bias voltage, V_{CC}. (For more detail, we refer the reader to the discussion of the load-line concept in Chapter 26.)

28.3 Power Supply

Most electronic devices require DC power. Equipment powered by the AC distribution system — a wall outlet — requires a circuit known as a *power supply* to convert the AC voltage to a steady DC voltage. To see how this works, let's start with the circuit of Figure 28.10 that reduces the AC voltage to the desired range. Then, we'll add more components to build up to a practical converter power supply. The transformer in this circuit will step down the input voltage to 6 volts AC (rms). The average power delivered to the load resistor will be

$$P = \frac{V^2}{R} = \frac{6^2}{50} = 0.72\,\text{W} .$$

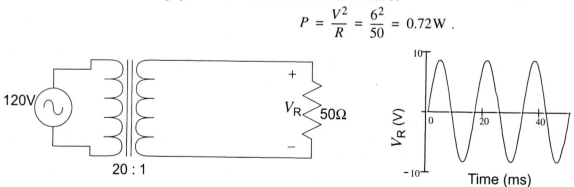

Figure 28.10   Step-down transformer power supply

But the current and the power are not constant. Worse yet, the current keeps changing direction. If the load is to be anything but a heater, we will need to rectify the current with one or more diodes.

Shown in Figure 28.11 is a simple half-wave-rectifier power supply. This will keep the current from reversing direction, but no current will flow at all for about half the time. Also, there is a small drop of voltage across the diode.

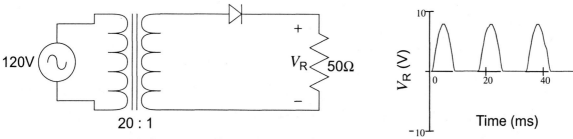

Figure 28.11 Half-wave-rectifier power supply

To get the current flowing almost all the time, we can add three more diodes as shown in Figure 28.12. These diodes operate in pairs. At any one instant, one pair of diodes is conducting, and the other pair is not. Figure 28.13 and Figure 28.14 show the circuit with the transformer output voltage first positive, as measured from the upper to the lower terminal, and then negative, with the nonconducting (reverse-biased) diodes removed for clarity.

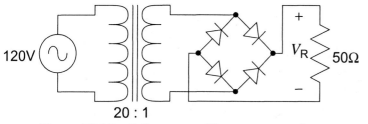
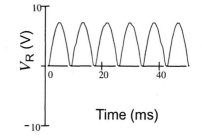

Figure 28.12 Full-wave-rectifier power supply

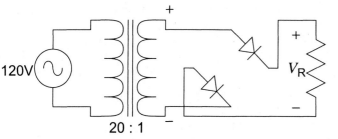
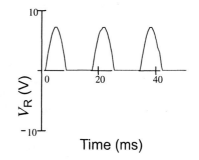

Figure 28.13 Positive transformer output causes the pair of diodes shown to conduct in the full-wave-rectifier power supply.

239

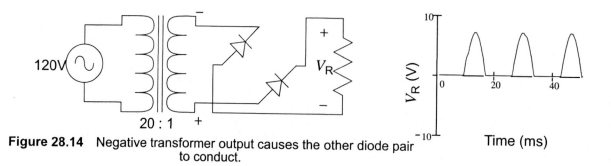

Figure 28.14 Negative transformer output causes the other diode pair to conduct.

We have all the current going in the same direction, and it's flowing most of the time now, but we still need to improve this power supply if we're going to use it to produce DC. By adding a capacitor after the rectifier (see Figure 28.15), we can smooth out most of the bumpiness of the voltage. The capacitor will charge up to the peak voltage value of the sine wave, which will be 1.4 times the rms voltage of the transformer, minus the two diode drops.

$$V_{peak} = \sqrt{2} \cdot V_{rms} - (2 \cdot V_{Diode}) = 1.4 \cdot 6 - (2 \cdot 0.7) = 7.0V \ .$$

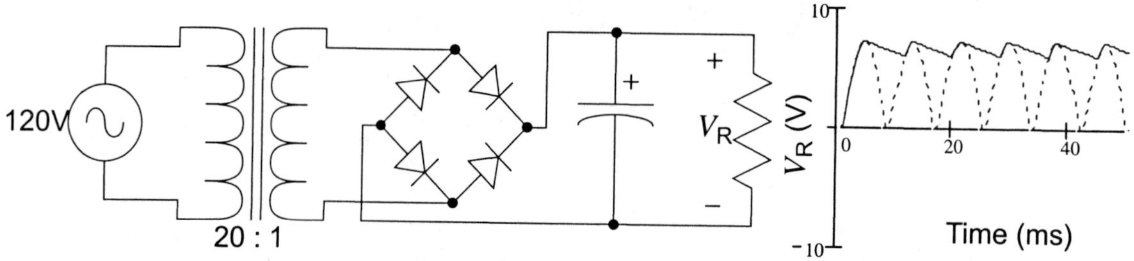

Figure 28.15 Filtered full-wave-rectifier power supply

Assuming that we want the voltage to ripple by no more than 0.5 V when under the design load and assuming that the load draws a constant current of 7V/ 50Ω = 140mA, we can calculate the required size of the capacitor. We know that the capacitor gets charged up every 8.3 milliseconds (both the positive and the negative peaks on our 60Hz power), so the quantity of charge that will be required from the capacitor to maintain the current flow can be found from

$$I = \frac{dQ}{dt}, \quad I = \frac{\Delta Q}{\Delta t}, \quad \text{or} \quad \Delta Q = I \cdot \Delta t = 140mA \cdot 8.3ms = 1160\mu C \ .$$

Since $Q = CV$ for the capacitor, we can calculate

$$\Delta Q = C \cdot \Delta V, \quad \text{or} \quad C = \frac{\Delta Q}{\Delta V} = \frac{1160\mu C}{0.5V} = 2320\mu F,$$

where ΔV is the ripple voltage. When we look in a capacitor catalog, we find this value of capacitor is not readily available, so we select a 2200μF capacitor with a 16V rating. (It's an aluminum electrolytic 0.512 inch in diameter and 0.827 inch long.)

Finally, if we need a very steady voltage, we can add a 5 volt regulator to our power supply. (See Figure 28.16.) Excellent integrated voltage regulators are available, so rather than design one from transistors and other components, we will simply add one to our circuit along with a final high-frequency, 1 µF capacitor that helps to smooth the current drawn by the load.

> "Can you ever get actual DC out of an AC-DC converter?"

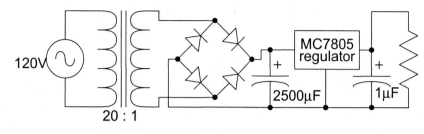

Figure 28.16 Regulated power supply

28.4 Operational Amplifiers

The last semiconductor device we'll discuss is the widely used and versatile device called the *operational amplifier*, or *op-amp* for short. This integrated circuit is a basic building block used for many different purposes, including amplifying, filtering signals, and summing several different voltages.

The Ideal Op-Amp

If you were to open up an op-amp, you'd find that it is an integrated circuit that contains many transistors, a few resistors, and a capacitor. Fortunately, in spite of its internal complexity, the op-amp functions as if it were a rather simple device, as we shall show. The op-amp is represented in circuit diagrams as the triangular block at the left of Figure 28.17 below. The block has two inputs, labeled plus and minus, and a single output. A simple equivalent circuit for what is called an *ideal op-amp* is shown at the right. The equivalent circuit shows that the output voltage, v_{out}, is proportional to the difference between the voltages on the two input terminals. The factor of proportionality, A, is called the amplification factor. The amplification factor of a real op-amp is quite high; for purposes of circuit analysis, the amplification factor is assumed to approach infinity.

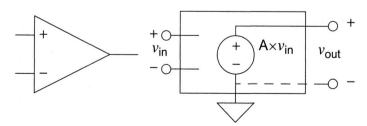

Figure 28.17 Representations of the operational amplifier (op-amp). The schematic symbol is at the left. The equivalent circuit for the ideal op-amp is at the right.

The operation of real op-amps can often be analyzed by assuming that the op-amp is ideal. The following assumptions apply to the ideal op-amp:

1. No current flows into or out of its input terminals.

2. The voltage between its input terminals is zero. (This condition is met so long as the output voltage is less than its maximum value and greater than its minimum value, and negative feedback is employed.)

The significance of these properties will be clear from an example, the circuit of Figure 28.18. Here an op-amp, which will be assumed to be ideal, is connected in a circuit containing two resistors. One, R_1, is connected in series with the input signal to the negative input node, and the other, R_F, provides the negative feedback current from the output terminal to the negative input node. For completeness, the other connections are shown — the terminals between which the potential differences v_{in} and v_{out} exist and the two vertical line segments on the op-amp's triangular symbol, which represent the connections to positive and negative 12 V supplies that power the op-amp.

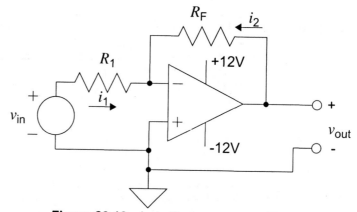

Figure 28.18 Inverting op-amp amplifier circuit

Let's calculate the gain of this amplifier, using the ideal op-amp principles. When we're done, we'll see why the circuit is identified as an inverting amplifier.

First, note that this amplifier involves <u>feedback</u>, as the output voltage is returned to the negative terminal of the input by the resistor marked R_F. From Property 2 of the ideal op-amp, $v_+ = v_- = 0$ (as the positive terminal is grounded). From Property 1, $i_1 = -i_2$ (since no current can flow into the op-amp's input terminals). From this conclusion about the currents and the use of Ohm's Law, we have that

$$v_{in}/R_1 = -v_{out}/R_F$$

and

$$\text{Gain} = v_{out}/v_{in} = -(R_F/R_1).$$

Thus, the output voltage equals the input voltage times the constant factor $-(R_F/R_1)$. The negative sign just means that the output is inverted relative to the input. The amount that the input signal is amplified is equal to the ratio of two resistor values, and is not strongly dependent upon A, the gain of the op-amp itself. Since the input resistance of the circuit is determined solely by R_1, typical values of R_1 will lie between 50 Ω and 10 kΩ. R_F will then be selected to set the gain. With $R_1 =$ 50 Ω and $R_F = 10$ kΩ, the gain is 200, or 46 dB.

28.5 Problems

28.1 Describe concisely in your own words the electronic devices represented by each of the following acronyms:
FET, LED, MOSFET, IC

28.2 A zener diode will turn on in the forward direction, typically at 0.7 volt bias, and in the reverse direction at a designable voltage that may range from a few volts to a few hundred volts. Sketch a water model for a zener diode.

28.3 Suppose that a zener diode having a forward turn-on at 0.7 volt and a reverse breakdown at 15 volts is connected in series with a 30-volt power supply and a 5 kΩ resistor. Determine the current that will flow
(a) When the supply is connected so that the zener diode is forward biased.
(b) When the supply is connected so that the zener diode is reverse biased.

28.4 Suppose your dwelling has an $80\,m^2$ roof area that could be covered with solar cell modules. Assume that your foresighted architect set the angle of your roof (in degrees with respect to the ground) equal to your latitude. At high noon on the day of the equinox, the sunlight will beam directly down (normal incidence) onto your solar modules, and you'll get maximum insolation.
(a) Using the values given in the Section entitled "Photodiodes and Solar Cells" on page 230, calculate the maximum power that could be produced at high noon.
(b) The Earth's rotation rate is 15°/hr. Assume that the angle of the solar exposure reduces the effective area of the array. How many watt-hours of energy could be produced in one day by your array?
(c) What percentage is the answer to Part b to the average daily energy consumption on the electric bill of Figure 30.5?
(d) Why would the home owner have sized his panels so large?
(e) What other factors should you consider before opting for a solar cell system?

243

28.5 This problem is related to the biasing of a bipolar-junction transistor. Assume that the npn transistor of Figure P28.5 is turned on and that the amplification factor $\beta=75$, $V_S=6$ V, $R_1=10$ kΩ, and $R_2=100\,\Omega$.

(a) Calculate the voltage drop across R_1.

(b) Find the base current I_B.

(c) Find the collector current I_C.

(d) Find the voltage drop across R_2.

(e) Calculate the output voltage V_{out}.

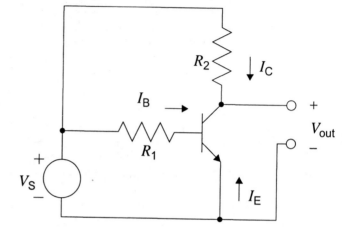

Figure P28.5

28.6 A BJT is often biased with a voltage-divider circuit designed so that the steady voltage V_2 turns on the base-emitter junction, as shown in Figure P28.6. This enables the transistor to amplify an AC current supplied to the base lead.

(a) The base-emitter junction behaves just like a pn-diode. Therefore, what is the potential difference V_{BE} when the diode is turned on?

(b) If the current flowing from emitter to ground through the 500 Ω emitter resistor R_E is 1 mA, what is the voltage from base terminal B to ground?

(c) Replace the voltage divider bias circuit ($V_S = 9\,\mathrm{V}$, $R_1 = 36\,\mathrm{k\Omega}$ and $R_2 = 180\,\mathrm{k\Omega}$) with its Thévénin equivalent. Draw the resultant circuit connected to the transistor.

(d) What current, I_B, flows into the base of the transistor? Take the voltage difference between V_{Th} and the answer to part (b), divided by R_{Th}.

(e) Solve for β, the transistors amplification. (Hint: use Kirchhoff's Current Law on the transistor.)

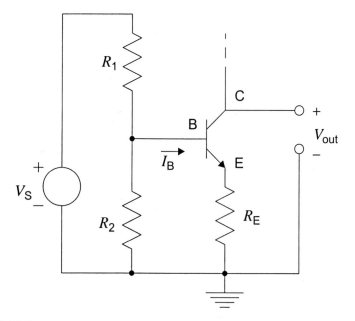

Figure P28.6

28.7 A four-diode AC-to-DC voltage converter, which you might use to power a laptop computer from the 60 Hz powerline, is shown in Figure P28.7.
(a) Sketch the flow of current through the diodes when the upper transformer terminal is at its largest positive value.
(b) Sketch the current flow through the diodes when the upper transformer terminal is at its most negative value.
(c) Sketch the voltage across the load resistor R as a function of time, assuming that $V_S = 110\,V$, n:1 = 11:1, and the diodes are ordinary silicon diodes.

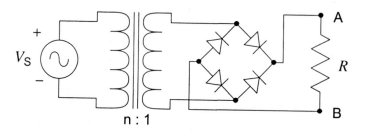

Figure P28.7

28.8 Add to the circuit of Problem 28.7 a filter capacitor, C, connected in parallel with load resistor R.
(a) Sketch the voltage across R as a function of time, assuming that the RC time constant is very small in comparison with the period of the AC source voltage.
(b) Do the same sketch but this time, assume that the time constant is very large compared with the period.
(c) Assume that load resistor R draws a steady current of 0.5 A from this supply, and assume that $C = 5000\,\mu F$. How much does the capacitor's voltage fall between its peak values?

28.9 Find an algebraic expression for, and the numerical value of, the gain for the (ideal) op-amp circuit of Figure P28.9, assuming that $R_1 = 4\,k\Omega$ and $R_2 = 1\,k\Omega$..

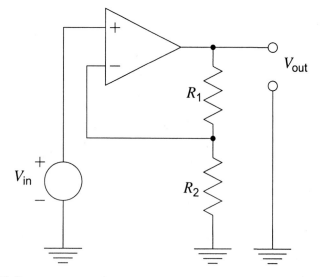

Figure P28.9

28.10 Find the gain of the (ideal) op-amp circuit shown in Figure P28.10. Assume that $R_1 = 5\,k\Omega$, $R_2 = 4\,k\Omega$, and $R_F = 20\,k\Omega$.

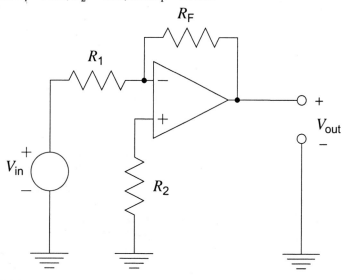

Figure P28.10

28.11 The circuit in Figure P28.11 is a differential amplifier. Here, the circuit is being used to amplify the voltage V_{in} from a source that has neither of its terminals connected to ground. Find the gain of this (ideal) op-amp differential amplifier. Assume that $R_1 = 5$ kΩ, $R_2 = 5$ kΩ, $R_3 = 20$ kΩ, and $R_F = 20$ kΩ.

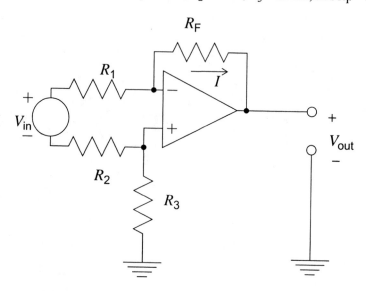

Figure P28.11

28.12 For the ideal op-amp circuit shown in Figure P28.12, $R_F = 4$ kΩ, $R_1 = 4$ kΩ, $R_2 = 2$ kΩ, and $R_3 = 1$ kΩ.

(a) What is V_{out} in terms of V_1, V_2, and V_3?

(b) Generically, what function does this circuit perform?

(c) If the voltages V_1, V_2, and V_3 represent the first three digits of a binary number, what function does this circuit perform?

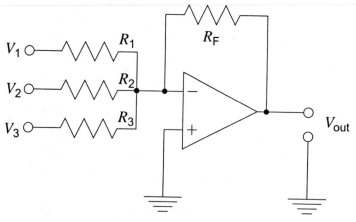

Figure P28.12

Fabrication of ICs and MEMS

The pattern-defining step used to make printed circuit boards, integrated circuits, and micromachines is called <u>photolithography</u>. This is a refinement of the process that fine artists have used for centuries to make lithographs, which are drawings reproduced by pressing sheets of paper on a flat block of stone (*lithos* is the Greek word for stone) to which ink adheres in carefully drawn patterns. To form the patterns, an artist would coat the stone with a layer of wax, scratch through the layer where ink was to be applied, and then lightly etch the stone chemically. After the rest of the wax was removed, ink was spread on the stone, and then gently wiped off. Ink would adhere only in the etched patterns, from which it would transfer to a piece of paper pressed against the stone.

The lithographic process was developed further for 20th-century publishing by using a light-sensitive emulsion to coat a copper or aluminum plate. In making a plate for printing a photograph, for example, the emulsion would be exposed to light passing through a negative image of the desired photograph. The emulsion would then be developed and removed chemically in areas struck by light. The exposed metal could then be etched, and the rest of the photoemulsion removed chemically, leaving the plate ready for the application of ink and transference of the image to newsprint passing by.

We'll now see how this process — photolithography — is used to make printed circuit boards, integrated circuits, and micromechanical structures.

29.1 Making Printed Circuit Boards

The goal is to produce a series of electrically conducting paths on an insulating substrate (or board) onto which one can solder electronic components such as resistors, capacitors, diodes, and integrated circuits. (See Figure 29.1.)

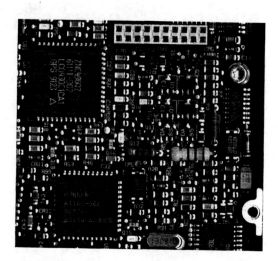

Figure 29.1 Photograph of printed circuit board for a personal computer hard disk drive showing resistors, capacitors, and other components soldered into place

One starts with an insulating board (1.5 mm thick) covered with a thin copper layer (about 300 nm thick) on both sides. Holes for mounting components and for signal feed-throughs are drilled in the board and then plated with copper. The board is then coated with a light-sensitive emulsion whose function is to selectively resist the attack of an acid. The desired pattern of conductors, which is drawn at a computer workstation and made into a transparent photographic film, is placed in contact with the photoemulsion, and then this assembly is exposed with a bright light. The photoemulsion is then developed, chemically removing its unexposed regions, and the board is put into an etching bath that removes the uncovered copper outside the desired conducting areas. The copper is then tin-plated to protect it from corrosion and to facilitate soldering components to it. Typically, a layer of "solder mask" is silkscreened on to prevent solder from adhering where it shouldn't, and labels and

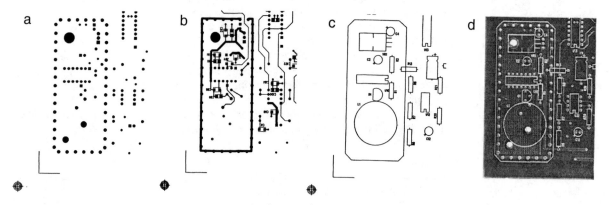

Figure 29.2 Photograph of portions of printed circuit board masks and the final board. Shown are (a) mask for locating holes through printed circuit board for mounting and connecting components; (b) mask for solder-side connections between different components; (c) mask for silk screening component identifications for resistors, capacitors, and the like and (d) finished circuit board (far right). The concentric circle with the cross is an alignment mark appearing on each mask.

component outlines are silkscreened on in a white ink. The result is a printed circuit board with conducting traces (the copper circuits) in place and ready for "stuffing" with electronic components. (See Figure 29.2.)

29.2 Making Integrated Circuits

To make integrated circuits, one needs to create complex patterns of insulators, p-type and n-type semiconductors, and good conductors for interconnections. To do this, the photolithographic process is used repeatedly.

Steps along the way from pure silicon to packaged ICs are illustrated in Figure 29.3.

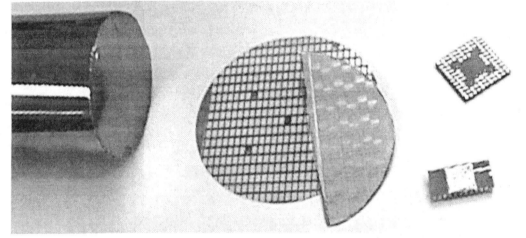

Figure 29.3 From silicon ingot to packaged ICs. Single-crystal silicon ingot (left); wafers, cut from an ingot, and with finished integrated circuits; and packaged ICs

The device manufacturer typically starts with wafers 6, 8, or even 12 inches in diameter sliced with a diamond saw from the starting ingot of very pure single-crystal silicon. (This is the long cylinder shown at the left in Figure 29.3.) The one-half to three-quarter mm-thick wafers are first polished on the side on which the semiconducting devices are to be patterned.

Insulating Films of Silicon Dioxide

Silicon dioxide films are used in three different ways in IC manufacture:

1. As electrical insulators. For example, an insulating layer is needed beneath the gate electrode of a field-effect transistor (FET) and in any regions where conducting "wires" that connect individual devices are to be insulated from the underlying silicon.

2. Sometimes, as a protective layer to control doping. The silicon dioxide layer is patterned to provide access to the underlying silicon into which dopant atoms may diffuse in a high-temperature furnace or be implanted in a high-vacuum machine that is actually a particle accelerator for ionized dopant atoms.

3. As a mask in making micro-electro-mechanical systems (MEMS) structures. A patterned layer of silicon dioxide protects selected areas from being removed in so-called deep-etching processes that typically involve the use of either accelerated ion beams that erode the silicon, or a chemically reactive plasma that removes silicon.

The layer of silicon dioxide — which is to silicon as rust is to pure iron — is formed by putting the wafer into a high-temperature furnace (1000 °C) to which oxygen or steam is supplied. When viewed in white light, a bare silicon wafer has a metallic grey color, and a wafer coated with silicon dioxide shows a deep purple, green, or other color that results from optical interference in the transparent oxide. By the use of the photolithographic process previously described, one can etch the silicon dioxide away in regions where one wishes to expose the underlying silicon: A layer of liquid photoemulsion, called photoresist, is spun onto the wafer, dried, exposed with a suitable mask, lightly baked, and then developed (selectively removed), exposing the silicon dioxide for etching in a chemical bath or in a chamber containing a plasma discharge.

Making p-Type and n-Type Regions

Undoped (intrinsic) silicon is converted to p-type or n-type silicon by diffusing into it acceptor or donor impurities, respectively (such as boron or phosphorus atoms). One presently gets those atoms into the right places in the silicon by opening suitably located holes in a photoresist layer by using photolithography with the proper optical mask, as shown in Figure 29.4. The wafers thus prepared are put into an ion implanter, a high-vacuum chamber containing a source of ionized acceptor or donor dopant atoms that are accelerated into the bared regions of the silicon.

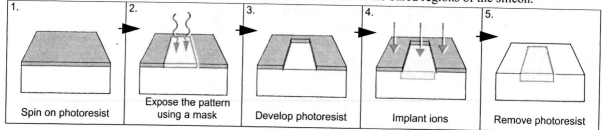

1.	2.	3.	4.	5.
Spin on photoresist	Expose the pattern using a mask	Develop photoresist	Implant ions	Remove photoresist

Figure 29.4 Sketch of the photolithography cycle. An opening has been made in the photoresist layer that covers the wafer so that dopant atoms can be implanted into the silicon to produce either p-type or n-type regions.

The processes just described may be repeated many times, with different photomasks, to create patterns of p-type and n-type regions for making transistors, diodes, and resistors. Capacitors are made by covering a given region of highly doped, and therefore highly conductive, silicon with a silicon dioxide layer. The underlying silicon acts as one electrode, the oxide is the insulator, and a conductor is formed on top to complete the capacitor.

Making Conducting Regions

Two primary types of conducting films are used in integrated circuits — doped polycrystalline silicon (poly), and a metal such as aluminum or copper. The poly films, produced in a high-temperature furnace supplied with a silicon-containing gas, are used when there are to be subsequent additional high-temperature processing steps. An example of such a step is forming the gate electrode of a field-effect transistor. For making interconnections after all high-temperature steps have been completed, usually, a patterned layer of deposited metal is used.

Cost of Packaged Chips

A number of elements enter into determining the cost, and hence the selling price, of packaged semiconductor devices, such as integrated circuits and MEMS devices. Here are some of those elements.

Some silicon wafers used to make ICs are six inches (150 mm) in diameter. Let us assume that the devices, such as microprocessors, are made from these wafers, which might cost $42 each. The silicon "die" (chips) might measure 1 cm by 1 cm. Each masking step adds about $50 to the cost of a given wafer. Typically, there might be 22 masking steps in all.

From this information, you could estimate the cost of each chip. However, wafers contain defects that make some die unusable. For example, there might be 10 defects per wafer, each occurring on a different die.

After the chips are made, each must be put into a package that can be plugged into a socket in your computer, and connections known as wire bonds must be made between each die and sturdier connection points in the package. In small quantities such packages sell for $30 each; in large-scale production, one might pay $10 for putting a die into the package and wire bonding it. If you calculate the cost of the finished, packaged part (see Problem 29.1), you'll find that the cost of packaging is not negligible. In fact, a common saying in Silicon Valley is that, "We don't sell chips, we sell packages." Bear in mind that we've discussed only production costs, not the very large cost of the engineering that goes into the research and design, the profit (the whole point of the enterprise), and so on.

Putting It All Together

The fabrication techniques just described have been used to make integrated circuits of ever-increasing complexity. Single silicon microprocessor chips containing more than 28 million individual transistors are now technologically and economically feasible. The linewidths used can be as small as 0.12 microns. Note that the diameter of a typical human hair ranges from 70 to 100 microns, as shown in Figure 29.8. The minimum dimensions achievable with photolithography are roughly proportional to the wavelength of the illumination used, and so ultraviolet light and even X-rays have been used to expose photoemulsions. In some cases, the circuit patterns have been written in emulsions with a finely focused electron beam. Commercial ICs may involve from 15 to 30 photolithographic masks, and integrated device features are now being made that have such small dimensions that the electrical effects of single electrons can be detected in them.

29.3 The Incredible Shrinking Transistor and Moore's Law

The steady progress in integrated circuit fabrication that has led to such small transistor dimensions has been described by what is known as Moore's Law. The "law" was born when Intel cofounder Gordon Moore was preparing a talk in 1965 and noted that each new computer memory chip made by his company had roughly twice the storage capacity of its predecessor, released for sale 18 to 24 months before. This trend of shrinking dimensions of transistors — by a factor of two every 24 months — has continued since, and is known as Moore's Law. (See Table 29.1 and Figure 29.5.)

Table 29.1 Transistor count on Intel computer chips (Source: Consumer Electronics Manufacturers Association)

Year	Transistors Per Chip
1972	3,500
1974	6,000
1978	29,000
1982	134,000
1985	275,000
1989	1,200,000
1993	3,100,000
1995	5,500,000
1997	7,500,000
1999	19,000,000
2000	28,100,000

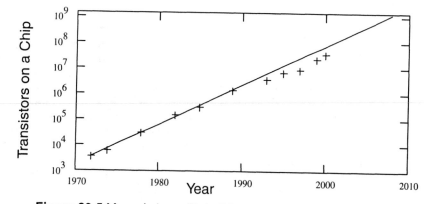

Figure 29.5 Moore's Law. Plot of the data in Table 29.1 and a line representing doubling every 24 months

Because of this dramatic increase in the number of transistors per computer chip, we have economical access to more and more capable computers, since the number of computations that can be made per second is roughly proportional to the number of transistors available.

Ever since the year 1900, before electronic computers and Moore's Law existed, the number of computations per second that could be obtained for a fixed amount of money was growing at an exponential rate.[1] If you compare the computa-

---

[1] See Ray Kurzweil, *The Age of Spiritual Machines* (New York, NY: Viking, 1999)

tional speed of the human brain with that of the rapidly evolving electronic computer, you will find that one can expect a machine to be able to run at the same computational speed as the human brain by the year 2020.

We are on the threshold of having almost unimaginable computer power at our command. As an exercise (see Problem 29.2), we suggest that you take time to record your own guesses about the roles computers may play in your life just 10 years from now.

BULK AND SURFACE MICROMACHINING

Bulk Micromachining: Structures are formed on a semiconductor surface and then the underlying semiconductor is etched away (usually etching of much semiconductor material).

Surface Micromachining: Structures are formed on a sacrificial layer on a substrate and then the sacrificial layer is etched away (usually etching very little material, such as a glass doped for rapid etching).

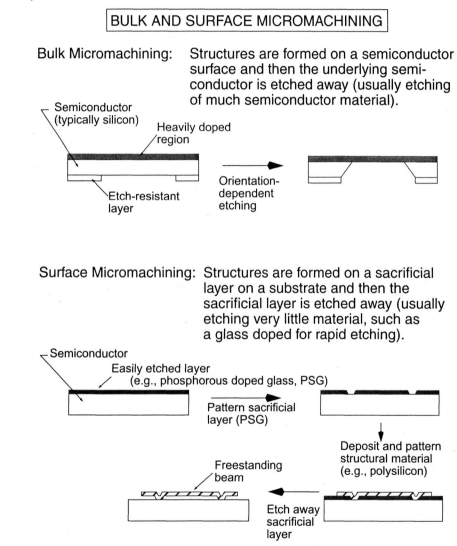

Figure 29.6 Bulk and surface micromachining steps. These include deep chemical etching (also termed "bulk micromachining") and "surface micromachining," in which parts are formed on an underlying sacrificial layer that is later etched away to leave freestanding structures.

29.4 Making Micromechanical Structures

The photolithographic processes just described can be applied to an exciting new task — making tiny complex *mechanical* devices that can actually move. These devices are referred to collectively by the acronym MEMS, for micro-electro-mechanical systems, since the most useful of these devices include electrical components and are really functioning *systems*, instead of single devices. In contrast to the making of ICs, photolithography in MEMS fabrication is used to make intricately shaped polysilicon or polycrystalline silicon/germanium members, such as gears and hinges, that are formed, using photoresist and etching, on top of a sacrificial layer grown on the silicon wafer. After the poly parts have been patterned, the sacrificial layer is etched away, leaving the mechanical parts locally free of the silicon substrate and therefore able to move. This process, called "surface micromachining," is outlined in Figure 29.6 An older, somewhat alternative process called "bulk micromachining" is also shown.

What can one make by this method? Here are some examples, starting with something made more for fun than actual use — the world's smallest guitar. (See Figure 29.7.)

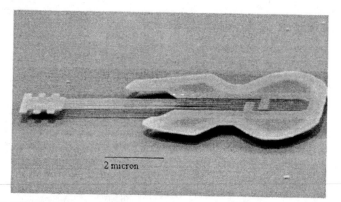

Figure 29.7 World's smallest guitar seen in a scanning electron microscope photo. The guitar strings are only 5 nm wide. The strings actually can be made to vibrate by touching them with a fine probe tool while viewing the guitar with a high-power optical microscope. The guitar was made using electron beam lithography to draw its shape in photoresist. (Photo used by permission from Harold Craighead, Cornell University.)

You can get a feeling for the relative sizes of some of these objects from the logarithmic chart presented in Figure 29.8.

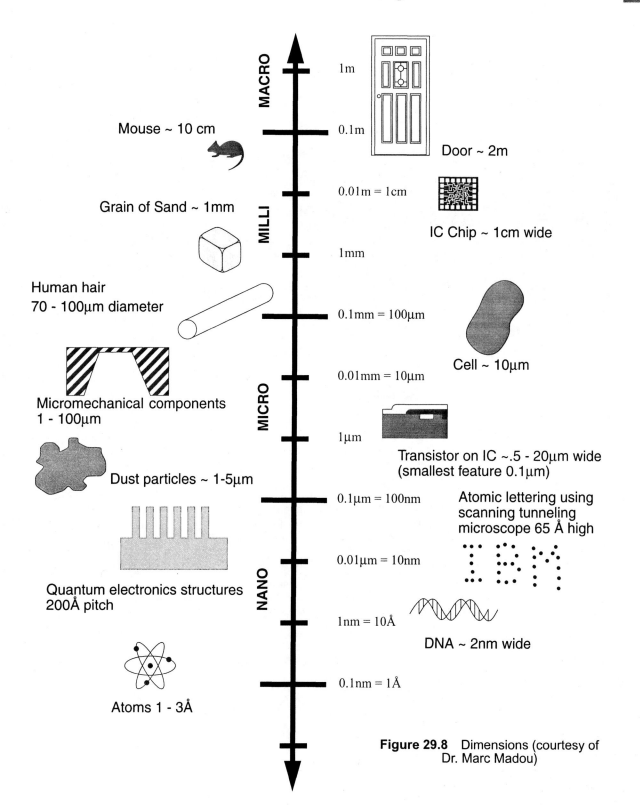

MACRO

1m

Mouse ~ 10 cm

Door ~ 2m

0.1m

0.01m = 1cm

IC Chip ~ 1cm wide

Grain of Sand ~ 1mm

MILLI

1mm

Human hair
70 - 100μm diameter

0.1mm = 100μm

Cell ~ 10μm

0.01mm = 10μm

Micromechanical components
1 - 100μm

MICRO

1μm

Transistor on IC ~.5 - 20μm wide
(smallest feature 0.1μm)

Dust particles ~ 1-5μm

0.1μm = 100nm

Atomic lettering using
scanning tunneling
microscope 65 Å high

0.01μm = 10nm

NANO

Quantum electronics structures
200Å pitch

1nm = 10Å

DNA ~ 2nm wide

0.1nm = 1Å

Atoms 1 - 3Å

Figure 29.8 Dimensions (courtesy of
Dr. Marc Madou)

Two other micromechanical devices, shown in Figure 29.9, are an electrostatic micromotor (left) and an electrostatically driven mechanical resonator (right). Both structures were formed by depositing and patterning a polysilicon layer on a sacrificial layer of doped silicon dioxide, and finally etching away that layer. Thus, the circular rotor on the left and the fishbone-shaped interleaved combs in the resonator are free to move under the influence of electric produced as voltage sources are connected to the electrodes via connecting bond pads like those used in ICs.

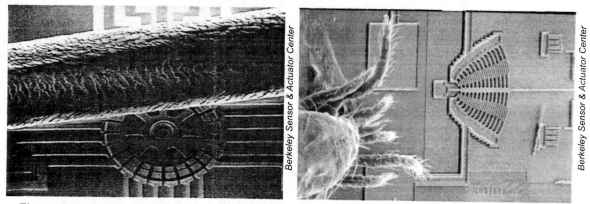

Figure 29.9 Microelectromechanical devices. Left: Electrostatic micromotor with human hair. Right: Surface micromachined resonator and a mite.

To date, the most commercially successful MEMS device is the accelerometer designed to deploy the airbag in a vehicle in case of a crash. In this device, made by Analog Devices, Inc., only the center 5% of the chip is micromechanical. Acceleration of the chip moves a suspended polysilicon comb, changing the capacitance between it and a set of comb fingers that is solidly attached to the silicon chip. The amount of acceleration that occurred is determined by applying and measuring a voltage that returns the movable comb to its equilibrium position, a process called force rebalancing. The larger the voltage required, the larger the acceleration is. Surrounding the sensor on the $9 \times 9 \, \text{mm}^2$ die is a host of electronic equipment to perform readiness testing, calibration, determination of the time profile of the measured deceleration to determine whether a serious crash has occurred, so that airbag deployment is needed, and circuits to produce output voltages and currents to the world outside the chip package. As of mid-2000, approximately 500,000 of these accelerometers were being made each week.

A different MEMS device that also has a serious purpose is shown in Figure 29.10. This device protects against accidental detonation of a nuclear weapon, which might be caused by the electrical disturbance from a nearby lightning strike. In making this device, which uses several levels of polysilicon, the structure is multilayered, so a planarization step is used several times as the device is fabricated. In this step, the surface of the wafer is polished flat to permit the next photoresist layer to be applied smoothly.

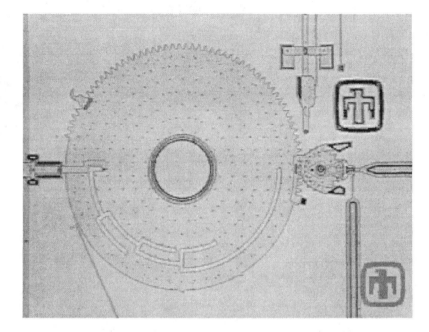

Figure 29.10 Optical microscope view of a MEMS device to prevent accidental detonation of a nuclear weapon. The polysilicon gear at the center is rotated clockwise when a coded electrical signal activates the device. The signal moves the follower at far left to right or left as the wheel turns. (The wheel diameter is about 200 microns, and the wheel thickness is 1 or 2 microns). If the code is not correct, the follower may move left at the first split in the path, and the wheel is stopped mechanically. If the correct code sequence is received instead, the wheel can rotate a full 180 degrees, engaging the hook on the wheel in the vertical slider at right and causing detonation. The horizontal and vertical sliders at far right operate sequentially to drive the large wheel. To see images of this device in motion, see Sandia.[2]

(Photo courtesy Sandia National Laboratories Intelligent Micromachine Initiative; www.mems.sandia.gov)

The MEMS devices just shown are really two-dimensional. The next photo, Figure 29.11, shows a three-dimensional device consisting of a hinged mirror at the left, shown reflecting a laser beam. The mirror is fabricated parallel to the wafer, and then after the sacrificial layer is removed chemically, the mirror can be driven into the third dimension by the push rod connected to it. The similar rectangular

---

[2] http://www.mdl.sandia.gov/micromachine/movies.html

structures at the top and right in the figure are electrostatic comb drives that operate alternately to push the rods that engage the upper gear and cause it to rotate.

Another application for micromirrors is in communication network routers that switch a number of data streams carried by incoming optical fibers into different output fibers. By using micromechanical devices to physically redirect the light beams, one can avoid having to convert the signals to electrical form in order to switch them. The projected speed increase is substantial: Data rates in the 40-terabit per-second range are anticipated.

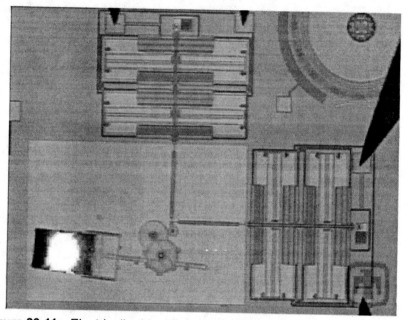

Figure 29.11 Electrically driven micromirror. Mirror at bottom left is shown reflecting a laser spot as the electrostatic drivers at top and to the right move it into the third dimension, which is perpendicular to the plane of the wafer. To see this device in motion, see Sandia.[3] (Photo courtesy Sandia National Laboratories Intelligent Micromachine Initiative; www.mems.sandia.gov)

---

[3] http://www.mdl.sandia.gov/micromachine/movies.html

Figure 29.12 Polysilicon micromodel of the Berkeley campanile. (Photo and fabrication by Elliot Hui, Berkeley Sensor & Actuator Center)

The hinge concept can be used for many purposes. One is to make complex three-dimensional structures that are erected after the fabrication has been completed. Figure 29.12 shows a micromechanical model of the campanile on the Berkeley campus. The height of the original tower, which can be seen on page xv of this book, is approximately 100 meters, while the height of the model is roughly 2 millimeters.

An important MEMS device is an optical projector that operates by reflected light from nearly one million 16μm×16μm mirrors. The sketch on the left of Figure 29.13 shows the idea. The micromirrors — identified as digital micromirror devices (DMDs) — may be tilted by application of voltages developed on conductors beneath each mirror. The voltages cause individual mirrors to tilt by ±10°. This causes the light to be reflected toward the projection screen or into a light absorber. The control voltages are developed by a CMOS circuit that lies beneath the array of mirrors. The CMOS circuits are processed first, and then the micromechanical components are fabricated atop them. A 9-pixel patch of the projector is seen at the right of Figure 29.13. The central mirror has been removed to show the two torsional springs, the rectangular white areas. The springs provide a restoring force to return each mirror to its equilibrium state when its deflecting signal is turned off.

These DMD projectors can display television and video, and are capable of providing extremely bright and colorful images. An extension of this technique is the use of the dynamic mirror principle in heads-up displays for drivers of vehicles. A small mirror array projects an image directly into the eye from a chip mounted on one's eyeglasses.

As you might expect, the MEMS parts that we've shown must be carefully packaged in order to prevent even tiny bits of dust from getting close enough to be electrostatically attracted directly into the mechanical works. If a single pixel fails, the entire device is virtually worthless. Hence, the entire mirror chip is attached to an integrated circuit package that is capped with a very clean, optically flat piece of glass.

The devices shown thus far have been made of silicon or silicon-based substances. Since one of the most promising application areas for MEMS is that of chemical and biological analysis, where the need for many inexpensive, biologically tolerant parts is anticipated, polymeric materials are being explored. Figure 29.14 shows a test part made by using a directed ion beam to pattern Teflon[TM].

A smooth, 170-micron layer of Teflon was spun onto the wafer, then photoresist was added and exposed through a photomask. An energetic ion beam was then directed at the part, vaporizing the regions struck and leaving the test pattern of posts and walls that could contain flowing liquids with chemicals or biological cells that are the targets for detection.

The final MEMS topic that we'll discuss is called "Smart Dust" — tiny particles that can measure, observe, and communicate.

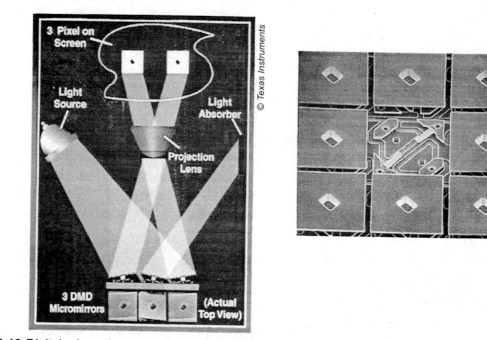

Figure 29.13 Digital micromirrors. Principle of operation, with only three micromirrors shown (left). A 9-mirror segment of the mirror array with the center mirror removed to show detail of the mirror addressing structure and torsion springs (right). (Photos courtesy Texas Instruments, Inc.)

Figure 29.14 Teflon™ test parts made by ion-milling in a study of fabrication techniques for use with polymers. The features are 170 µm high. (Photo and fabrication by Luke Lee, Berkeley Sensor & Actuator Center)

Smart Dust

Many different MEMS techniques are included in the quest for "Smart Dust," led by Berkeley faculty member Kris Pister. The goal is to deploy in the world literally millions of MEMS-instrumented "motes" a few millimeters on a side that detect ambient conditions (temperature, pressure, chemical vapors, particulates, bacteria, sounds, etc.), and possibly motion of the mote, — and communicate the information to a central site for use. is a sketch of how a piece of Smart Dust might appear.

Smart Dust Components

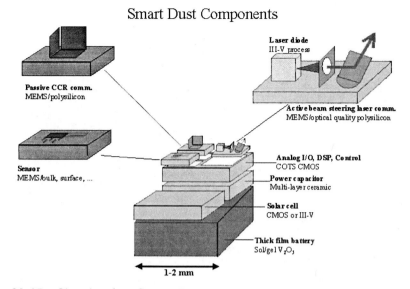

Figure 29.15 Sketch of a Smart Dust mote showing its components. (Sketch courtesy Kris Pister, Berkeley Sensor & Actuator Center)

Key to the concept is very low power usage. Each mote could be powered with ambient light — sunlight outdoors or artificial light indoors. An on-board photodiode would convert the light to electricity that could charge a battery or be stored in a capacitor. Each mote might communicate in either an active or a passive mode. Active mode communication would employ micropower radio transmission. In a passive-mode approach, a mote could report its findings by modulating a corner cube retroreflector (CCR) MEMS mirror when it is being illuminated by an interrogating laser beam.

The operation of this mirror is based on use of the micromachined hinges previously mentioned. If you closely group three mutually perpendicular reflectors, a light beam that strikes one of the mirrors will bounce off all three mirrors and then be reflected back toward the light source, precisely parallel to the path of the original optical beam. One could modulate this reflection process by slightly moving one of the mirrors out of perpendicularity. The principle of the retroreflector is quite familiar — it is used in reflectors for bicycles, and a large version was left by visiting lunar astronauts to reflect laser beams sent from the Earth to permit making very precise measurements of the Earth–Moon distance. What's new here is the use of a MEMS structure to "wiggle" one of the reflectors so as to transmit information. The MEMS passive optical reflectors, which appear to the upper left of the figure, would be fastened atop the Smart Dust mote.

How close is Smart Dust to realization? Already, a cubic-inch version made with mostly commercial off-the-shelf (COTS) parts has demonstrated many of the projected capabilities. In particular, it demonstrated that the optical communications circuitry worked, as data were transmitted over a 16-mile path above the San Francisco Bay at a 4 bit/s rate when a 1-mW laser pointer was used as the light source.

You are encouraged to think of other uses for Smart Dust. Several have already been suggested. One is the virtual keyboard — glue Smart Dust motes containing accelerometers to your fingernails and use your finger movements to control a virtual keyboard. Another application is to imbed motes in the wall panels of a building and use the detected temperature and carbon dioxide concentration to determine when to turn on the air conditioning system to cool the rooms or just refresh the air.

29.5 Wrap-Up

The steady improvement of photolithographic techniques, along with innovations in semiconductor electronics, has continued to permit the realization of cheaper and more capable electronic devices for computing, communicating, and sensing quantities such as chemical vapors in the atmosphere. One can fabricate micromechanical structures on a silicon chip together with conventional integrated electronic circuitry, making MEMS a reality. We can expect to find a micromechanical resonant device on the same silicon chip as a microprocessor in order to eliminate the need for the separate crystal oscillator chip used until now as the "clock" in each personal computer. We've illustrated a number of examples of what MEMS could bring us, and this new field is just beginning to have a commercial impact. We haven't talked about complex electrical filters made using MEMS or much about the expected large impact of MEMS on medical diagnostics and treatment. Also, there are several MEMS turbine-generator projects that may bring us shirt-button-sized electrical generators powered by hydrocarbon fuel — a replacement for conventional heavy batteries. The examples we have given, and the enthusiasm of the commercial world, suggest that the electronics revolution that began in Silicon Valley, the area just south of San Francisco where hundreds of hi-tech firms have located, is still alive and well.

29.6 Problems

29.1 For the conditions stated in the Section entitled "Cost of Packaged Chips" on page 253, determine
(a) The number of die that can be made from a wafer.
(b) The number of functioning die that can be made from a wafer.
(c) The cost of the die before wire bonding and packaging.
(d) The cost of the final packaged product.

29.2 Write a one-half to one-page description of how you think the exponential growth of numbers of computer components and operating speeds will affect your life 10 years from now. Consider that computers entered our scene doing just manipulations with numbers. Then, they began to be used as communication devices and then for creating graphics. What is your vision? File your answer away for review in ten years.

29.3 Calculate the maximum steady power that a cube-shaped mote 1.5 mm on a side could consume assuming operation in sunlight and that you could cover all but one of the cube faces of the mote with solar cells. See the Section entitled "Photodiodes and Solar Cells" on page 230 for solar-cell and sunlight characteristics.

Power for the People

Have you ever wondered how electric power gets from fossil or nuclear fuels, rainwater or snow melt, sunlight or wind to your home or workplace? In spite of the importance of electric power in our lives, "power" courses are taught in very few electrical engineering schools in the United States today. Courses about the electronics behind computers and communications are much more popular. Because of our reliance on the systems that provide us with electric power — and because some features of the power system are undergoing rapid change — we'll highlight here some of the story of how electric power is generated and ultimately supplied to customers. Incidentally, another reason for learning at least a bit about power systems is that, whether you like it or not, they are quite visible, and you might enjoy recognizing parts of the power grid as you travel around.

30.1 Power Generation, Transmission, Distribution, and Utilization

The overall scheme of power generation, transmission, and distribution is shown in Figure 30.1. Let's suppose that the generation of electric power occurs in a fuel-oiled powered generating station, indicated as "generating plant" in the figure.

Generation

Most electric power is produced by large rotating machines known as generators. A generator (see Figure 30.2) has a central shaft on which are mounted coils of wire. These coils are supplied with a direct current that produces a magnetic field in the space around them. Surrounding the movable coils (on what is called the rotor) are stationary coils (the stator). As the rotor moves, the magnetic field rotates in space with it, crossing the stator wires. This produces an electromotive force that causes a current to flow through any conducting circuit connected to the stator terminals.

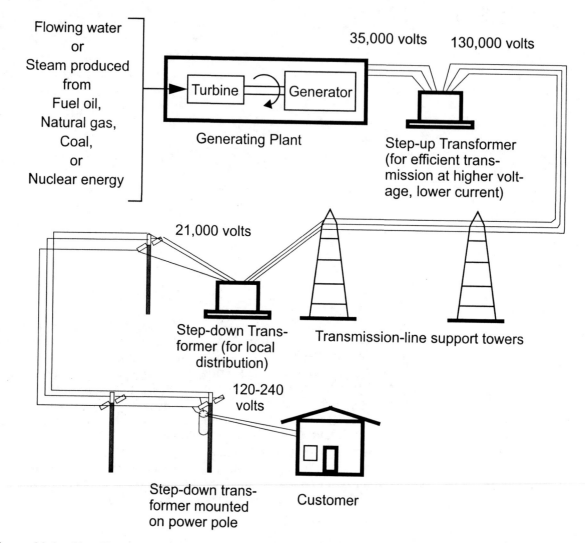

Figure 30.1 Simplified representation of the transmission and distribution systems that bring electric power from a generating station to customers. In the generating station, a turbine driven by any of the means indicated at the upper left is coupled to a generator, turning it to produce three-phase alternating voltages.

The mechanical force that turns the generator shaft and rotor may be produced in many different ways:

- Burning fossil fuels (oil, coal, or clean-burning natural gas) causes water in a boiler to turn into high-pressure, high-temperature steam that passes through a turbine, causing its shaft and the generator attached to it to turn.

- Energy produced by a nuclear reactor can produce steam to drive a turbine-generator system.

- Water stored behind the dam of a reservoir can flow in a gravitational field downhill and through a turbine coupled to a generator. (See Figures 30.3 and 30.4.)

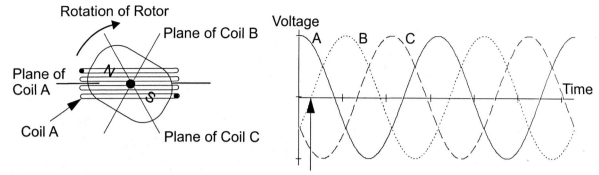

Figure 30.2 In an electric generator, a rotating shaft (rotor) carries a coil producing a steady magnetic field (indicated by N and S poles) past fixed coils (stator), producing a voltage across the ends of each coil. Typically, there are three stationary coils set at 120° to each other, producing three separate sinusoidal output voltage waveforms — the three "phases" of three-phase power.

Figure 30.3 The Bonneville Dam on the Columbia River as seen from the Oregon side. (Courtesy Portland Division, U.S. Army Corps of Engineers.)

Each of the coils on a generator produces a voltage that is a sinusoidal function of the angle of rotation of the generator shaft. For highest efficiency, usually three independent coils are used on such generators, the stator coils being displaced 120° from each other around the periphery of the stator. As a result, the voltages of the three stator coils reach their maximum values at times that differ by one-third and two-thirds of a complete cycle of the 60 Hz powerline waveform. (In the United States, 60 Hz is used, but 50 Hz is used in many other countries.) The typical generator output voltage is $V_{gen} = 35$ kilovolts.

Roger Doering

Figure 30.4 Generators at the Dalles hydroelectric power plant on the Columbia River.

As environmental awareness has risen, so-called alternative methods of generating electric power have been developed. These include:

- Production by generators whose shafts are turned by sets of blades driven by the wind.

- Production by generators run from geothermal sources.

- Production by sunlight absorbed in solar cells made from semiconductors.

Alternative means account for only a small amount of the power generated today, but they are extremely important in certain applications. An example is powering remote systems such as emergency phones along highways and mountaintop telecommunications systems.

An increasingly important power source is "co-generation" in which thermal energy generated for space or industrial process heating is used to power a turbine-generator system, producing electric power that is used locally or sold to a utility for distribution to customers elsewhere.

Transmission

Power is sent from the generation site to the point of utilization over a transmission system. To send a given amount of power over transmission lines while minimizing resistive losses in the transmission conductors, the generator is connected to a step-up transformer that increases the voltage to anywhere from 130,000 to 500,000 volts, while reducing the current proportionately. The power transmitted is given by the product $I_{line}V_{line}$, where I_{line} and V_{line} are the transmission line current and voltage respectively. The power lost due to the resistance of the transmission line conductors is $I_{line}^2 R_{line}$, where R_{line} is the resistance of the conductors. Thus, stepping up the line voltage reduces the line current, for a given amount of power transmitted, and so greatly reduces the amount of power dissipated due to resistive losses in the lines.

It is hardly obvious, but high efficiency in transporting electric power from source to consumer results from using what is known as "three-phase transmission". This involves sending over three separate conductors the power generated by each of the three stator windings. (See Figure 30.2.) This is why the transmission line towers you see outside cities carry three sets of everything — conductors, insulators, and so on (or six sets of everything if the towers carry two complete three-phase circuits). You may notice that at the very top of the transmission towers there's a fourth (or seventh) conductor that is connected directly to the towers without the use of insulators like the other conductors. This is a cable that protects the rest of the lines from damage by lightning strikes. Sometimes, on very high-voltage transmission lines, several closely spaced conductors at the same potential make up each circuit; this reduces the electric field at the surfaces of the conductors and reduces the tendency for arcing to occur.

The transmission circuit conductors are typically 1-3/4-inch diameter cables made up of about 50 3/16-inch diameter soft aluminum strands (for lightness and high electrical conductivity) wound on a seven-strand steel core (for strength). There's no insulation on these conductors, but they are insulated from the steel support towers by glass or ceramic insulators that look like stacks of salad plates.

Distribution

For safe distribution inside a city, the three-phase voltage is stepped down in transformers at a substation to anywhere from 4 kilovolts to 21 kilovolts and carried on conductors supported by insulators near the tops of poles set along streets. Again, you may see three of everything in a three-phase distribution system in a city.

The distribution conductors are typically 3/8-inch diameter pure aluminum strands, which may together carry currents up to 800 amperes in normal operation. Near the point of use in a business or dwelling, a transformer usually mounted on the pole reduces the voltage to safer levels from 110 to 480 volts, with a corresponding stepping up of the current.

> 'Why don't birds get electrocuted when they land on uninsulated power lines?"

Utilization by Customers

In a typical business or dwelling, the electricity is predominantly single-phase, although three-phase power may be used for appliances that use large amounts of power, such as industrial ovens. The single-phase systems have a 115 or 230 ($\pm$5%) root-mean-square voltage between one conductor and the other.

Several safety features are used to protect people from being injured by accidental contact with power systems. Drawing excess currents (that might overheat the wiring) when an accidental short circuit occurs is prevented by a circuit breaker or fuse set to open at a given current level, such as 15 A in a dwelling. One conductor is connected to the "ground" — literally, to the water pipes that enter the business or dwelling underground. If a person accidentally contacts both the "hot" (ungrounded) conductor and a true ground (such as a water faucet), a device called a "ground-fault interrupter" (GFI) detects the fact that not all the current going out in the hot wire is returning in the neutral wire and quickly shuts off the circuit. "House" wiring contains an additional conductor, known as the safety ground, which normally carries no current. An appliance that has a metal case has the case connected to this safety ground via the round prong on the three-prong plug. In properly installed house wiring, the hot wire is black (relates to "death, if you touch it"?), the neutral is white (very neutral color?), and the ground wire is green (relates to "earth"?).

BEWARE OF THE HOUSE WIRING POWER SYSTEM —

THE CURRENTS IT WILL DELIVER CAN KILL.

The Electric Bill

If you live at home or in a university dorm, you may not see your electric bill. Figure 30.5 shows a portion of Dick's electricity bill for Pacific Gas and Electric Company (PGE) service in Berkeley, CA. During the month, 175 kWh (kilowatt-hours) of electric energy were used (approximately 6.3×10^8 joules). That was less than the so-called baseline usage amount (231 kWh) established to encourage people to avoid waste: Power supplied in excess of the baseline amount costs more per

ELECTRIC ACCOUNT DETAIL

Rate Schedule: E 1TB   Service Type: Bundled Service

Service: From 05/10/00 To 06/09/00   Billing Days: 30   Electric Meter #: 6349J5

Electric	Prior Meter Read 09243	Estimated Meter Read 09418	Difference 175	Constant 1	Usage 175 Kwh

Total Charges	$20.28
Legislated 10% Reduction	-2.03
Net Charges	$18.25

The net charges shown above include the following component(s). Please see definitions on Page 2 of the bill.

Electric Energy Charge	$0.07669/Kwh*	$13.42
Transmission		0.85
Distribution		6.24
Public Purpose Programs		0.62
Nuclear Decommissioning		0.09
Competition Transition Charge (CTC)		-5.01
Trust Transfer Amount (TTA)		2.04

* *This rate is based on the weighted average costs for purchases through the Power Exchange. This service is subject to competition. You may purchase electricity from another supplier. (Call 1-800-743-0040 for a supplier list.)*

ELECTRIC	Kwh		Price
Baseline Quantities	231.0		
Baseline Usage	175.0	@	$0.11589
Over Baseline Usage	0.0	@	$0.13321

Figure 30.5   Portion of a residential electric bill for May, 2000

kWh. The total amount of the electric bill was $20.28, of which $13.42 (66%) was for the electric energy itself. PGE charged $0.85 (4%) for transmitting the energy to Berkeley from the power plants where it was produced, and $6.24 (31%) was charged for distributing it to the house. About 3% ($0.62) was charged for California's State-mandated public programs to assist low-income customers and improve the efficiency of energy usage. The remaining charges are for activities relating to debt management and the decommissioning of a nuclear power plant in California.

A mandated credit of 10% was given consumers as a benefit of the electric industry restructuring that occurred in the late 1990s. The net cost of the electric power used was thus ten cents per kilowatt-hour.

Electromagnetic Fields (EMF): Is there a Health Hazard?

To date, no significant risk of adverse health effects has been found to result from incidental exposure to electric or magnetic fields at powerline frequencies. Some studies have found a possible correlation between such exposure to magnetic fields and the occurrence of childhood leukemia, and of one kind of adult leukemia in workers in the power industry. The studies are continuing.

Is there anything that you can do in the meantime if you suspect that a serious effect might be found? You could reduce your future exposure by limiting the time you spend near wires and appliances that generate such fields. Table 30.1, from the Pacific Gas and Electric Company, lists the sources and strengths of 60 Hz magnetic fields found in the home and outdoors near power lines.

Table 30.1 AC magnetic fields in a home and outdoors (from insert in Pacific Gas and Electric Company residential bill, January 2000). For scale, note that the Earth's steady magnetic field at sea level in the U. S. is approximately 600 milligauss.

Source of AC Magnetic Field in Home	AC Magnetic Field in Milligauss One Centimeter Away from Source	AC Magnetic Field in Milligauss One Foot Away from Source
Microwave oven	750 to 2000	40 to 80
Clothes Washer	8 to 400	2 to 30
Electric Range	60 to 2000	4 to 40
Fluorescent Lamp	400 to 4000	5 to 20
Hair Dryer	60 to 20,000	1 to 70
Television	25 to 500	0.4 to 20

Source of AC Magnetic Field Outdoors	AC Magnetic Field in Milligauss
Electric Power Distribution Lines	1 to 80 under the line
Electric Power Transmission Lines	1 to 300 at edge of right-of-way

30.2 Problems

30.1   As shown in physics courses, or by simple reasoning, the relationship between frequency, f, and wavelength, λ, of an oscillatory wave that travels with speed c is just $f\lambda = c$. For electromagnetic waves in a vacuum, or in ordinary air, $c = 3 \times 10^8$ m/s, the speed of light. For sound waves in air at standard temperature and pressure, $c = 343$ m/s, and for sound in water, $c = 1480$ m/s. Calculate the following:

(a)   Wavelength of an electromagnetic wave at the U.S. powerline frequency (60 Hz).

(b)   Wavelength of the signal from the 1,610 kHz AM radio station that is often used for highway or emergency information.

(c)   Wavelength in air of a sound wave at 1,000 Hz, the frequency at which the average human's hearing is most acute.

(d)   Wavelength in air of the 50 kHz ultrasonic wave from an ultrasonic rangefinder.

(e)   Wavelength of a 100 Hz whale sound in water.

(f)   Frequency of light from a helium–neon laser whose wavelength is 633 nm.

30.2   What is the ratio of the number of primary turns to secondary turns on a transformer used to reduce the 21 kV powerline distribution voltage to 120 volts for household use?

Wireless Communication Systems

The means used for communicating have changed over the centuries, but the goal has remained the same: to transfer a message from sender to recipient as accurately as possible.

Communicating has been done with signal fires across the plains and lanterns from land to nearby sailing ships. Youngsters have done it with "telephones" made from two tin cans and a stretched string. Alexander Graham Bell once did it with a sunbeam (see "Alexander Graham Bell's Photophone" on page 341) and with his telephones that connected from one point to another. Laser beams traveling inside thin glass fiber-optic light pipes now do it from point to point across towns, continents, and under the oceans. (See "Optical Communications" on page 85.) The emphasis is now increasingly on *wireless* communication systems, transmitting signals via electromagnetic energy radiated and received by antennas that may or may not have fixed locations.

To see how communication systems work, in the next few pages we'll discuss the frequencies at which they work, find out how information gets transmitted by them, and consider some of their most important applications. We'll not be much concerned with theory and will focus on real systems that you use, such as radio, television, computer networks, and cellular phones.

31.1 The Human Ear and Musical Instruments

Arguably, the human voice is the most versatile communication instrument of all. Healthy young ears can detect airborne sounds having frequencies between 15 Hz to more than 20,000 Hz. Naturally, the developers of musical instruments covered a similar range, from 16 Hz, the lowest growl of a pipe organ, to 20 kHz, the overtones of the top squeak of a piccolo.

Figure 31.1 is a plot of the acuity of normal human hearing, which shows that on average, our ears have maximum sensitivity near 1 kHz. To transmit perfectly all

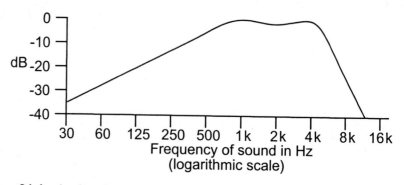

Figure 31.1 Acuity of normal human hearing. Vertical axis: inverse of the sound pressure level (SPL) corresponding to minimum detectable pure tone.

components within the audible spectrum requires a bandwidth approaching 20 kHz, but most of the audible energy is contained with a frequency band whose width is only 4 to 6 kHz. AM radio stations that broadcast speech and music provide adequate fidelity with a bandwidth of about 5 kHz, and the telephone system limits its bandwidth to about 4 kHz.

31.2 Communication Channels and the Need for Modulation

Modulation means change. Modulation is important in communication systems in two different ways.

First, if we consider an acoustic or electromagnetic wave as a signal, it is the modulation or change of the amplitude, frequency, or both of that wave that provides its information content. For example, if there's no modulation of a singer's voice, so that the sound produced is a tone having a constant pitch and volume, no information is transmitted — except perhaps that the singer is still alive and singing. When the voice changes, it can convey information.

Modulation is used in wireless communications in a second sense, that of shifting the frequencies from those at which the information is produced to higher frequencies for transmission. This shifting is important, because it permits us to use transmitting and receiving antennas that have reasonable dimensions. In addition, it allows us to shift up in frequency many different signals and transmit them over a single communication channel.

Figure 31.2 shows in diagrammatic form a generic communication system. At left is the source of information, which might be a human speaking or singing, a computer, or a video camera. The message signal is fed into the transmitter within the large box. A modulator is an essential part of the transmitter, for reasons that we'll soon see. The output of the transmitter is a signal that is supplied to the communication channel, which might be a coaxial cable between transmitter and receiver, a path of propagation for electromagnetic waves through the atmosphere, an optical fiber, and so on. The received signal is processed by the receiver for the user of information.

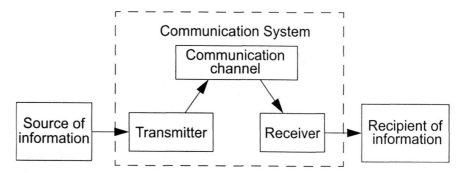

Figure 31.2 Generic communication system. The diagram is equally applicable to an electromagnetic wave radio or television communication system as to a fiber-optic network for transmitting computer data.

Let's consider the electromagnetic wave system where the channel is just the atmosphere and antennas are used to transmit and receive the waves. Loosely speaking, an electromagnetic wave antenna works best when its physical length is roughly one-half the *wavelength* of the electromagnetic wave that it transmits or receives. You can think of the wavelength as being the distance from one electric field maximum to the next of an electromagnetic wave, similar to the wavelength of the ripple produced when we toss a pebble into a pond. We use a circuit known as a *modulator* to shift the frequency of speech or music upward, reducing the wavelength, so that radio station antennas of reasonable size work efficiently. Otherwise, we'd need huge antennas to broadcast speech and music, as shown by the exercise below. On the receiving end, there is a *demodulator* to shift the frequencies that represent the information back to their original values for the user of the information.

"Is this kind of modulation related to what's done in a computer's modem?"

Exercise 31.1 Find the length of a quarter-wave electromagnetic antenna operating at 440 Hz, the middle A note to which orchestras tune before playing.

Solution: Since it's an electromagnetic wave antenna, the electrical waves on it travel at roughly the speed c, the speed of light in a vacuum, which is 3×10^8 m/s. As you learned in physics, for any type of wave, (frequency) $\times$ (wavelength) = (wave speed). Thus, the quarter-wave antenna operating at 440 Hz would have a length

$\lambda/4 = $ (wavelength)$/4 = (1/4) \times (3 \times 10^8 \text{m/s})/(440 \text{Hz})$

$= 1.7 \times 10^5$ m

$= 106$ miles!

If the modulation and demodulation are done correctly, no information need be lost in the transmission/reception process, although actually some noise may enter during propagation through the atmosphere and as a result of resistive components in the transmitter and receiver.

31.3 AM and FM

Radio and television use two different types of modulation. One is called *amplitude modulation* (AM). The signal from the information source vary the amplitude of an oscillator output in the transmitter. Without the modulation, the transmitter just emits a constant-frequency signal. When amplitude modulated with a 1 kHz tone, the transmitter's output waveform is as shown in Figure 31.3 (top) and the spectrum of the radio transmitter's output is shown in Figure 31.3 (bottom). As you may know, the operating frequencies of AM radio stations range from 550 kHz to 1.61 MHz. For example, Berkeley's emergency radio station is known colloquially as "16-10 AM," since its assigned frequency is 1,610 kHz. This is called its *carrier frequency*, the frequency of the radio wave that the station transmits when it is turned on, but no information is being broadcast. In the station's transmitter, the electronic modulator circuit changes the amplitude of the 1,610 kHz frequency in accordance with the instantaneous amplitude of the electrical signals produced by the station's microphones and CD and tape players. The radio frequency (RF) signal is broadcast, picked up by your receiving antenna, and *demodulated* to recover the audio signal, which is then sent on to your radio's loudspeaker and your ears.

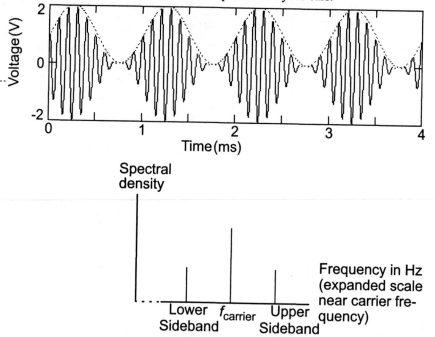

Figure 31.3 Waveform (top) and spectrum (bottom) of AM radio station broadcasting a 1000 Hz tone. The spacing of the sidebands from the carrier is determined by the frequency of the tone, in this case ±1000 Hz.

In *frequency modulation* (FM) radio stations — such as our local "Wild 104.7 FM" — the frequency, rather than the amplitude, of the carrier is modulated. (See Figure 31.4, top.) In the United States, FM radio stations have been assigned carrier frequencies that range from 88.1 MHz to 107.9 MHz. The bandwidth of the frequency modulated signal is typically up to 200 kHz, as shown in Figure 31.4, bottom.

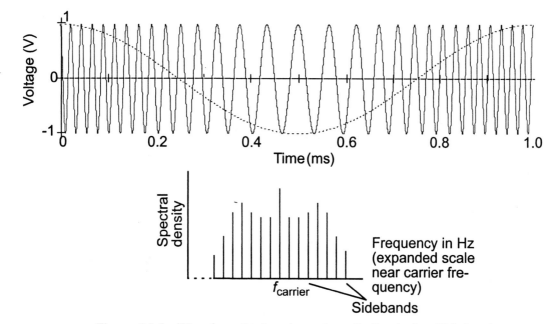

Figure 31.4 Waveform (top) and spectrum (bottom) of an FM signal

To summarize, modulation is fundamental to the concept of information. Shifting the frequencies of a signal for ease of transmission enables us to make efficient communication systems and employ the most suitable transmission means available. These transmission means range from AM radio at hundreds of kilohertz, to light beams whose frequencies range from 10^{14} to 10^{15} Hz.

31.4 How do Antennas Work?

It's not at all obvious how the two-inch antenna on your cell phone or the hundred-footer next to a commercial radio station can transmit or receive electromagnetic waves. Here's a qualitative picture of what happens.

Consider the block diagram of Figure 31.5, which shows schematically an AM radio transmitter and an AM radio receiver. The transmitting antenna is a tall metal tower that stands on insulating supports, often in an area where the ground beneath is fairly moist, and hence electrically conductive. The time-varying voltage produced by the final amplifier in the radio transmitter is applied at the base of the metal tower between the tower itself and a conductor buried in the moist earth. This voltage causes electrons to be accelerated up and down the metal tower. As a result, the moving charges radiate an electromagnetic wave — because that's what electric charges do when they're accelerated! Locating the metal tower above moist earth is advantageous, because the charges moving on the tower cause charges of the opposite sign (so-called image charges) to move in the conducting earth, making the antenna behave as if it were twice are long as the tower.

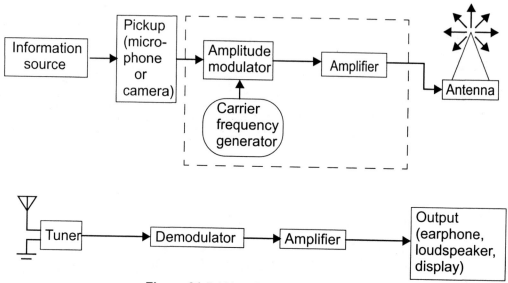

Figure 31.5 AM radio transmitter and receiver shown in block-diagram form.

Figure 31.6 Antenna

The electric field of the radiated wave is perpendicular to the surface of the earth. As the wave propagates outward away from the transmitting antenna and encounters a receiving antenna — a conductive metal wire typically held vertically upright — the electric field causes electrons in the receiving antenna to move up and down the wire. This resulting RF current is fed into the radio receiver and processed in order to output a copy of the signal that was put on the wave at the transmitter. Incidentally, the bulges you see on some short antennas are circuit elements included to make the antenna behave electrically as if it were physically longer than it is.

In any urban area, there are lots of broadcast electromagnetic waves propagating in different directions from all the cell phones and radio and television stations nearby. To pick out of the air just the signals that we want, we design receivers so that they are selective. We'll see later how this is done.

The antennas just described radiate or receive equally in all directions in a horizontal plane. Figure 31.6 shows part of a 170-foot-high emergency communications antenna; a number of independent whip antennas can be seen attached to the central structure. For cell phones, such single-conductor antennas (sometimes called "whip" antennas) are used on the phone itself. Much larger panel antennas, measuring six to eight inches across, up to five feet in height and up to one foot in depth, are used to communicate with the phones in each geographical cell. These antennas are directional, so three panel antennas set at 120° to each other are typically used in each cell. Figure 31.7, a photograph of a cell-phone antenna installation, is included to help you identify cell-phone antennas as you travel around your city.

Figure 31.7 Cell phone antenna structure. Left: Close up of an array of directional cell phone panel antennas. Right: More typical cell phone antenna array that provides 360° coverage.

31.5 The Frequency Spectrum

Figure 31.8 is a plot of the so-called electromagnetic frequency spectrum. It shows the frequencies at which the U. S. Federal Communications Commission (FCC) permits radio stations, TV stations, and other users of the frequency spectrum to operate. For legibility, the horizontal frequency scale has been divided logarithmically, so the scale goes from 10 Hz to more than 10^{24} Hz. We've also included in the figure some acoustical signals, because they're signals we might want to send over a communication system.

When looking at this large frequency range, we need to keep in mind the *bandwidths* of the signals that we commonly communicate. Speech and music extend over a bandwidth of no more than 20,000 Hz. Adequate reproduction of human speech is accomplished in the telephone system with the much more limited bandwidth of only 4,000 Hz. The bandwidth required for a conventional television channel is around 6 MHz, and high-definition television (HDTV) requires about 22 MHz if signal compression is not used. With clever techniques for compressive coding of signals, the bandwidth can be significantly reduced, making it possible to fit more communication channels into the existing finite spectrum.

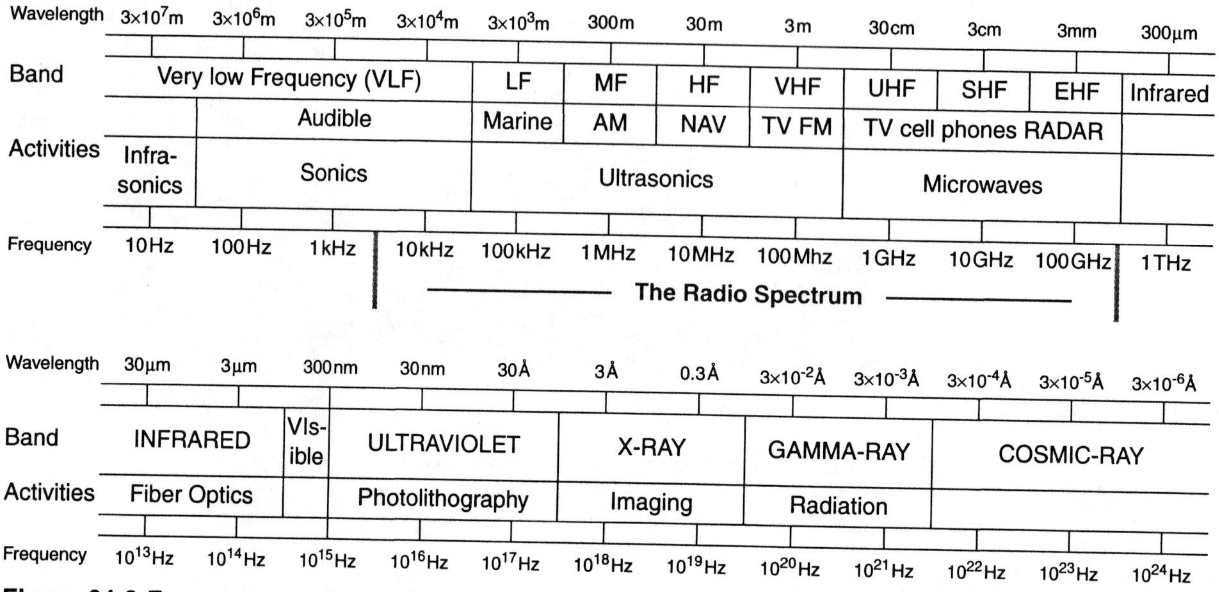

Wavelength	3×10^7m	3×10^6m	3×10^5m	3×10^4m	3×10^3m	300m	30m	3m	30cm	3cm	3mm	300μm
Band	Very low Frequency (VLF)					LF	MF	HF	VHF	UHF	SHF	EHF	Infrared
Activities	Infra-sonics	Audible			Marine	AM	NAV	TV FM	TV cell phones RADAR			
		Sonics				Ultrasonics			Microwaves			
Frequency	10Hz	100Hz	1kHz	10kHz	100kHz	1MHz	10MHz	100Mhz	1GHz	10GHz	100GHz	1THz

——— **The Radio Spectrum** ———

Wavelength	30μm	3μm	300nm	30nm	30Å	3Å	0.3Å	3×10^{-2}Å	3×10^{-3}Å	3×10^{-4}Å	3×10^{-5}Å	3×10^{-6}Å
Band	INFRARED		Vis-ible	ULTRAVIOLET		X-RAY		GAMMA-RAY		COSMIC-RAY		
Activities	Fiber Optics			Photolithography		Imaging		Radiation				
Frequency	10^{13}Hz	10^{14}Hz	10^{15}Hz	10^{16}Hz	10^{17}Hz	10^{18}Hz	10^{19}Hz	10^{20}Hz	10^{21}Hz	10^{22}Hz	10^{23}Hz	10^{24}Hz

Figure 31.8 Frequency spectrum of electromagnetic waves. Note the logarithmic frequency scale. Sonic quantities are included in the spectrum chart, since many transmissions involve sound. Note that the spectrum ranges from the audible frequency range up to the frequencies of cosmic rays.

31.6 More About Radio

Figure 31.9 shows schematically the oldest and simplest possible AM radio receiver, the crystal set. Remarkably, there's no battery in the set. The electrical energy that drives the earphone on the right is literally picked out of the air by the antenna, whose symbol is the divided triangle at the top left of the circuit. The RF current from that receiving antenna flows into the parallel LC circuit shown. This circuit acts as the tuner: It responds poorly to all RF currents from the antenna, except those that are near the desired carrier frequency, $f_{carrier}$, such as our 1,610 kHz. To tune in that station, while listening to the sound from the earphone, we change the variable capacitor until our station comes in loud and clear.

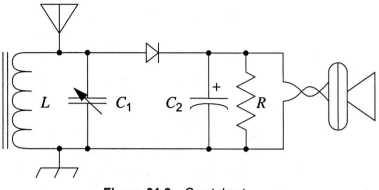

Figure 31.9 Crystal set

If the inductance and capacitance values for the resonant circuit are L and C_1, respectively, the frequency f of the electromagnetic wave picked up by the antenna that will generate the largest voltage across the LC circuit is given by the expression

$$(2\pi f)^2 L C_1 = 1.$$

Here, f is known as the resonant frequency of the circuit at which the energy is stored, alternately, near the inductor and then between the plates of the capacitor. A close analogy can be drawn between this electrical resonant circuit and a mechanical resonator, such as a bell, in which the stored mechanical energy naturally sloshes back and forth between kinetic and potential forms.

The diode in the crystal set permits current of only one polarity to flow into the RC circuit to its right. The RC circuit permits only low-frequency voltage variations to be developed across the earphone at the extreme right.

Exercise 31.2 What value should the product RC_2 have?

Solution: By law, a U. S. AM radio station's frequency cannot swing more than 5 kHz from its carrier frequency. Thus, we can set the cutoff frequency of the RC filter at 5 kHz. From Section 20.4, we have that the time constant $\tau = 1/f = 0.0002\,\text{s} = RC_2$, if $C_2 = 0.01\,\mu\text{F}$, then $R = 20\,\text{k}\Omega$.

31.7 Television — 500 Channels and Counting

When we add pictures, we transfer more information and need a larger bandwidth. The bandwidth for conventional television is around 6 MHz. Television station carrier frequencies are much higher than 6 MHz, at some hundreds of MHz. Thus, many stations can be fitted into the allocated bands for television broadcast.

When commercial television broadcast stations were first built, the only available video cameras produced just black and white images, so the television system standards were set for that. Later, the capability of transmitting color had to be added while staying within the specifications of the earlier sets so as not to make them obsolete. For black-and-white television, the station's 6 MHz allocated frequency band was split into parts. One small region was allocated to the audio information, and a broad region was allocated to picture information. For color transmission, a so-called subcarrier signal at 3.58 MHz above that station's carrier frequency was added to the video signal.

The television picture is formed by sweeping an electron beam inside a cathode-ray tube sequentially across the face of the tube while varying the beam's intensity. So-called raster scanning is used, which means with the present U.S. NTSC system that the electron beam sweeps one set of lines in 1/60th of a second and then returns to sweep a second set of lines interlaced with the first. Each such sweep draws a field on the screen; the two fields make up the entire frame of television, which takes 1/30th of a second to complete. Amazingly, our eyes smooth out all this drawing and we perceive pictures that fill the entire screen.

The video signal includes synchronizing signals for the start and end of each field and of each horizontal line of the raster scan. Between the signals that start and stop each line scan, the brightness information for the line is broadcast.

For color television, we have to make a cathode-ray tube (or other display device) that can produce colored images. Then, we have to transmit information that dictates what color is to appear at each spot in the television frame.

At each point of the color cathode-ray tube, there are three differently colored phosphors, arranged either as stripes or dots. (A black and white tube has but one: white.) The colors are red, green, and blue. The characteristics of the colors, which are transmitted for each point, are the hue (the basic color), the luminance (the brightness of the point), and the degree of saturation (the extent to which a single hue is displayed).

To provide all this information, at the start of each horizontal line, a so-called color burst signal is transmitted at the subcarrier frequency; it establishes a phase reference with respect to which the color signal on that line is to be compared. The phase angle between the reference color burst and the color subcarrier signal determines the hue for that point. The degree of saturation is indicated by the amplitude of the color subcarrier. The luminance is indicated by the amplitude of the signal after removing the color subcarrier.

We've gone into this much detail because some of you have probably wondered just how one can transmit such complex and richly colored pictures. If you're interested in learning more, you can see the waveforms and understand the system better by doing the laboratory exercise on television. We should also mention that we've described the *analog* television systems in common use today. It has been decreed that analog television broadcasting will stop in the U.S. in 2006, and all broadcast television will thereafter be digital.

31.8 Frequency Hopping and Spread Spectrum: Invented by an Actress and a Composer

In many communication systems, security is of great importance for commercial, military, or just personal reasons. The ability of a number of different users to employ a given part of the frequency spectrum is also desirable and usually necessary, since there is only so much space in the entire frequency spectrum. Several approaches have been taken to accomplish the aims of providing secure communications over channels that have many users.

Faced with the problem just posed, an untrained person could probably come up with promising solutions. One is to do *frequency hopping* — having a given transmitter (and its associated receiver) jump quickly from frequency to frequency in a predetermined order, transmitting a short burst of information at each point in the spectrum. People who didn't know the frequencies and the order in which they'd be used would have trouble picking up the information transmitted. This technique was conceived and patented during World War II by the famous movie actress Hedy Lamar, born in Austria, and her composer, George Anteil — to foil German submarines that were trying to listen in on and locate ships from Allied marine broadcasts. The idea of frequency hopping resulted from familiarity with the operation of the player piano, in which a roll of paper that has a particular pattern of perforations in it is pulled past a set of pressurized tubes. When a hole passes over a given tube, it causes a corresponding piano key to be depressed and sound a note. The idea was to use such a device to control the sequence of frequencies at which a transmitter would broadcast and a receiver listen. A later extension of this idea is the *spread spectrum* concept, in which one broadcasts simultaneously at all frequencies in the band used, thus reducing the amount of energy radiated at any one frequency to such a low level that it might not be noticed.

Very sophisticated systems employing these ideas have been used for tasks from making hard-to-find and jam (interfere with) radar systems to permitting a fleet of taxicabs to communicate with their base station using a common wide, frequency band.

31.9 How Much is Digital in All This?

Again, for reasons of security and detectability in the presence of large numbers of competing signals, modulating transmitters with special digital codes have been employed. Typically, one starts with a signal to be transmitted, which we'll assume is digital in nature. One modulates that message with a digital code sequence whose bit durations are much shorter than the bits of the message. The modulation is done by XORing (exclusive-ORing) the message bits with the shorter code bits. A receiver adjusted to be quite sensitive to the code sequences will be able to detect the message even in the presence of many competing transmissions. This modulation approach is known as code division multiple access (CDMA), in which multiple users can communicate in the same frequency band.

Among the other schemes used, the easiest to understand is time division multiplexing (TDM). Here, under the control of a master system clock, users are allotted sequential time slots during which they alone may transmit. Another logical approach is called frequency division multiplexing, in which each user is apportioned a part (channel) of the common frequency band. This scheme results in rather inefficient use of the available spectrum owing to the necessity to include unused bands of frequencies to separate adjacent channels. The equivalent concept being used with optical communication systems is to give each user a "color" of light to use. This is called wavelength division multiplexing.

31.10 Cell Phones: Necessity or Nuisance?

It is estimated that 60% of the U.S. population owns a cell phone. The majority of the cell phone market worldwide is currently shared by Nokia, a company based in Finland, and Motorola, whose headquarters are in Arizona. Cell phones are, to many people, a necessity for business use, personal convenience, and emergency purposes. They and highly portable systems such as handheld personal digital assistants are expected to be used increasingly for web surfing, e-mail downloading, getting stock and sports news, controlling systems remotely, banking operations, and so on.

Cell phones are so named because they operate at any moment within a cell at whose center is a ground-based set of directional antennas. These antennas are connected via conventional land lines to the regular telephone and computer networks. The central antenna continually measures the signal strength of a given cell phone's transmissions, and "hands off" that phone to the appropriate adjacent cell when the phone moves into new territory. The coding technologies used in cell phones depend upon the manufacturer, but they involve many of those described in the previous Section. You can "try out" cell phone systems operating in your area on the website Decide.com.[1] There, you can listen to samples of speech communicated over different cell phone systems at different geographical locations. It is particularly interesting to compare the clarity of analog and digital cell phone systems at that web site.

Cell phone frequencies of operation vary, but may range from around 800 MHz to as much as 3 GHz. The radiated RF power can be as high as one watt. Since that power is usually radiated next to the speaker's head, there is some concern about whether users may suffer adverse physical effects, such as the growth of tumors. As with the medical effects of 60 Hz electromagnetic fields near power lines, no conclusions have yet been reached regarding this aspect of cell phone use.

31.11 What Are All Those Satellites Doing?

The first communication satellite was simply an aluminized spherical balloon put into earth orbit. Earth-based antennas radiated signal toward the satellite, named Echo, which reflected the signals back toward receivers on the Earth's surface. Since that humble beginning, communication satellites have become far more numerous and complex. Many of the communications satellites are in stationary orbit, 22,300 miles above the Equator, in what is known as GEO, geostationary Earth orbit. As an example, the direct broadcast satellite system Direct TV™ utilizes a number GEO satellites above the Equator due south of Texas. They transmit at approximately 12 GHz to individual Earth-bound receiving dishes only 18-inches in diameter. The system radiates hundreds of television and some music channels. Each customer's receiver has a unique identification number, and the satellite controls the channels that each subscriber can receive. When commanded by the satellite, the subscriber's equipment telephones the service provider to report on usage, particularly the purchase of special features such as movies or sporting events.

Among the satellites orbiting up there are military spy-in-the-sky satellites that can photograph the ground with high resolution and download the images to the properly equipped receivers. There is also a system of satellites that comprise the Global Positioning System (GPS). These satellites transmit their current locations to GPS receivers on land or sea. By measuring the nanosecond differences in the arrival times at the receiver of signals from the satellites in view at a given time, the receiver can calculate its position to an ultimate resolution of a few meters. Interesting specialized GPS applications are the "man overboard" feature, with which, at the push of a button, you can instantly store the latitude and longitude where a person falls overboard from a vessel and systems for automobiles that help a tow truck

---

[1] http://www.decide.com

operator to locate your car if you have mechanical trouble or allows you to get directions by cell phone when you're lost.

Several other satellites worth noting. One, named PANSAT[2], was built by students at the Naval Postgraduate School in Monterey, CA; it broadcasts on an amateur radio band every two hours as it passes Monterey. There are also two orbiting satellites that contain the ashes of deceased humans, including Timothy Leary's.

31.12 Modeling Electrical Devices: The Transfer Function

Now that we have encountered the idea of a frequency spectrum we can easily understand the so-called transfer function that is commonly used to represent the behavior of electrical components such as amplifiers and filters. In later courses you will learn more precisely about transfer functions, but for now the idea can be presented in this simple approximate form:

The magnitude of the transfer function (at any frequency) for an electrical two-port is the magnitude of the ratio of the output voltage at the frequency to the input voltage at the same frequency.

Here are some examples:

1. If the two-port simply consists of two wires that run from input connections to output connections, (see Figure 31.10) the output spectrum is the same as the input spectrum (which is the spectrum of whatever signal source supplies voltages or current to the input port). Hence, the transfer function is simply unity. (See Figure 31.11.)

Figure 31.10   A particularly simple two-port — just two wires!

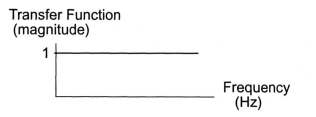

Figure 31.11   Magnitude of the transfer function for the two-port of Figure 31.10

---

2   http://www.sp.nps.navy.mil/pansat/pansat.html

2. Suppose the two-port is an *amplifier*. The function of an amplifier is to produce an output that is just the input voltage waveform made larger. The extra energy supplied by the output port comes from the battery or other power supply for the amplifier. In a radio set, for example, several amplifiers make the feeble signal picked up by the antenna large enough to drive loudspeakers and be heard. If one could build a truly ideal amplifier that amplified the signals at all frequencies equally, say by 100 times, then the transfer function for that would simply be the number 100 at all frequencies. (See Figure 31.12.) We have plotted this transfer function in both numerical terms (left) and in terms of decibels (right), as is commonly done with transfer functions to make the numbers more readily understandable. Hence the decibel measure represents a plot of the quantity $20\log_{10}(S_{out}/S_{in})$, where S_{out} and S_{in} represent the output and input spectra, respectively.

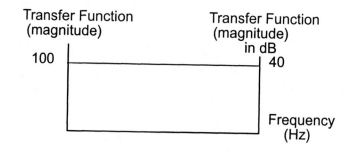

Figure 31.12 Transfer function (magnitude) for amplifier whose gain is 100 at all frequencies

In fact, no practical amplifier can amplify signals at all frequencies equally. For example, to amplify the sound for your radio, the audio amplifier only needs to amplify signals within the range of human hearing, roughly 50 Hz to perhaps 10,000 Hz. The transfer function for such an amplifier might appear as shown in Figure 31.13.

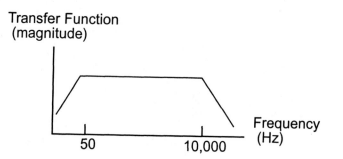

Figure 31.13 Transfer function (magnitude) for hypothetical audio amplifier

3. A *filter* is another common electrical element that is used to pass signals at certain frequencies and block signals at other frequencies. In a radio set, for example, filters are used extensively to limit the output to signals coming from just one station. Figure 31.14 shows the transfer function of a lowpass filter made of a resistor and a capacitor. The high-frequency portion of the function shows the roll-off characteristic also shown by the right side of the amplifier characteristic. This is the result of the "shorting" effect of capacitor C as frequency increases.

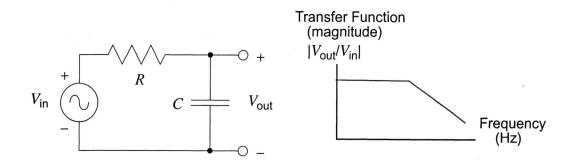

Figure 31.14   RC lowpass filter circuit and its transfer function

31.13 Problems

31.1   Describe concisely in your own words the communication transmission systems represented by each of the following acronyms:
DSL, ADSL, XDSL, LAN, ISDN, POTS

31.2   Describe concisely in your own words the communications techniques represented by each of the following acronyms:
AM, FM, CW, SSB, TDM, PCM

Digital Signal Processing

Our natural world is an *analog* domain in which most quantities change gradually over time. Examples are the air-pressure variations produced by a human speaking or the wind blowing. In other words, in the natural world around us, variables are *continuous* functions of time.

We are now interacting increasingly with *digital* worlds where quantities change in *discrete* steps. Like the data in our computers, even our voices are converted to digital form when we make a long distance telephone call; the digital representation is transmitted, and finally converted back to the familiar analog form for the listener at the other end. Our goal in describing such discrete-time quantities is to develop an intuition about them, as we have with analog quantities through a lifetime of experience with them. We will explore how one converts analog quantities that are continuous functions of time into quantities defined at discrete instants and whose amplitudes may change discretely. We will also see examples of processing the latter quantities for useful purposes. This subject is termed generally *digital signal processing* (DSP).

Since we value fast response in the digital world, we seek systems that react quickly — in other words, we are particularly interested in *real-time* digital systems. Table 32.1 contains examples of some real-time applications of digital processing systems, many of which may already be familiar to you.

Table 32.1 Real-time applications of digital processing systems (adapted from Tretter[a])

Field of Application	Specific Uses of DSP Systems
Telecommunications	Answering machines, modems, fax machines, cellular telephones, speaker phones
Voice and Speech	Voice mail, speaker verification, speech synthesis, speech digitization and compression
Automotive	Engine control, antilock braking systems, active suspension, airbag control, system diagnosis
Medical	Hearing aids, patient monitoring, ultrasound imaging, magnetic resonance imaging (MRI)
Image Processing	3D rotation and animation, image enhancement, image compression and transmission, high-definition television (HDTV), pattern recognition
Control Systems	Head positioning in disk drives, laser printer control, engine and motor control, robot control, numerical control of automatic machine tools
Instrumentation	Signal generators, spectrum analysis, transient analysis
Military	Radar and sonar signal processing, navigation systems, high-frequency modems, secure radios and voice systems, missile guidance

[a] Steven A. Tretter, *Communication System Design Using DSP Algorithms* (New York: Plenum Press, 1995)

It should be clear from this list of applications that the processing of digital signals has many important uses. We will explore some of the techniques used in DSP after defining a few more important terms.

32.1 On the One Hand ... and On the Other

The balance between opposites expressed by the ancient Chinese concept of yin and yang (see Figure 32.1) is found in a number of technical ideas. A fundamental distinction is between analog and digital variables, such as voltages or currents, as illustrated in Table 32.2. As shown, the time or position variables may be continuous or discrete.

Figure 32.1 Traditional representation of the concept of yin and yang. Among the attributes associated with yang are being active, light, hot, and

visible, while yin represents the opposites — being passive, dark, cold, and hidden. In this image, the signal amplitude varies discretely with position, having only two brightness levels, white and black.

"Where do AM and FM radio and television fit into this table?"

Table 32.2   Continuous and discrete variables

	Analog Signal Values	Digital Signal Values
Analog Time or Position	Signal is a continuous function of time or position. Examples: local telephone, tape recording, photograph, surface acoustic wave filters	Signal is discretized but time or position is continuous. Examples: laser disc video, telegraph.
Digital Time or Position	Signal is sampled at fixed rate, but processed in continuously variable values. Examples: switched capacitor filters, speech storage chip, halftone photograph, movie	Both signal and time or position are discretized. Examples: compact disc, long-distance telephone, digital camera, inkjet printer, digital television

The amplitude of an analog voltage is a continuous variable. The corresponding digital representation of the voltage waveform is obtained by converting a given analog voltage, such as 3.25 volts, into its digital representation, the binary number 11.01. The electronic device that performs this conversion is known as an analog-to-digital (A/D) converter.

The processes illustrated in the lower row of Table 32.3 use *sampling*, in which a representation is obtained at discrete times or positions.

There is a close analogy between a *waveform*, such as a voltage that varies with time, and an *image*, whose brightness or the color varies with position on the page or screen. We will see that useful operations such as filtering apply analogously to both waveforms and images.

Table 32.3   Waveform and its spatial analog, image

(Photo on right used by permission from Harold Craighead, Cornell University.)

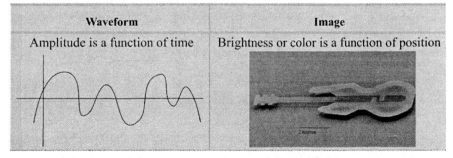

Waveform	Image
Amplitude is a function of time	Brightness or color is a function of position

It is also useful to compare and contrast several other sets of complementary quantities:

Signal and Noise

In electronics, a signal might be a time-varying voltage or current that represents the music from a radio station, a sound from a loudspeaker, or a stream of data from a computer. A signal might also be a picture on a television screen, in which changes of brightness and color occur as functions of both time and position on the screen.

Signals typically contain information, as in the preceding examples. Noise, on the other hand, does not normally contain information and is most often produced by random physical phenomena. For example, electrical noise arises in circuits because of the random thermal motions of electrons in circuit components such as resistors. Usually we want to maximize the signal and minimize the noise. Therefore, a figure of merit for many electronic devices, such as amplifiers, is their *signal-to-noise ratio*: We usually want systems to have a high signal-to-noise ratio. Table 32.4 shows more on this.

Table 32.4   Signal and noise

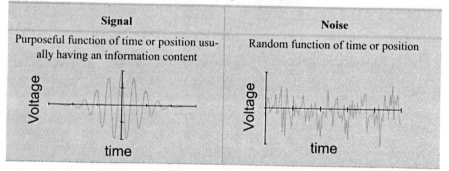

Signal	Noise
Purposeful function of time or position usually having an information content	Random function of time or position

Time and Frequency Domains

We frequently want to think of signals in terms of the frequencies of their component sinusoids. If we graph the relative strength of each component versus frequency, we get a representation of the signal in the *frequency domain.*

Table 32.5   Time domain and frequency domain

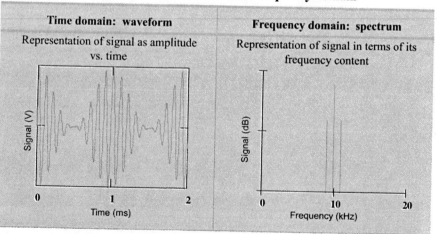

Time domain: waveform	Frequency domain: spectrum
Representation of signal as amplitude vs. time	Representation of signal in terms of its frequency content

A mathematical function known as a *transform* is used to convert a function such as a voltage waveform to its representation in the frequency domain. The example shown in Table 32.5 is (left) an amplitude modulated waveform for a 1,000 Hz signal modulating a 10kHz carrier and shows (right) the corresponding frequency components, which consist of the 10 kHz carrier and two "sidebands" spaced 1 kHz from the carrier.

Integral and Sum

One mathematical operation that frequently arises in signal processing is summing the values of a quantity over some time interval. A simple example is summing the power being dissipated by a circuit in order to determine the amount of energy that the circuit consumes. (This is what the mechanical watt-hour meter at your dwelling does in order to determine how much electric energy you've used.) When dealing with continuously varying quantities, the mathematical operation known as *integration* is used. With discrete-time quantities, integration is equivalent to summation.(See Table 32.6.)

Table 32.6 The analogous summing operations, integration for continuous functions and summation for discrete functions

Integral		Sum	
$\int_0^T v(t)\,dt$	Summing operation for continuous function of time or position	Summing operation for discrete function of time or position	$\Delta t \sum_{n=1}^{N} v_n$

Figure 32.2 shows these two approaches applied to finding the amount of electric energy you've used in a month. As we decrease the interval between the times at which the discrete-time variable on the right is defined, the value of the sum approaches the value of the integral on the left.

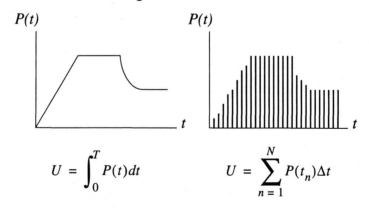

$$U = \int_0^T P(t)\,dt \qquad\qquad U = \sum_{n=1}^{N} P(t_n)\Delta t$$

Figure 32.2 Finding the electric energy used (left) by integration of the power, P(t), when the power is a continuous-time function, and (right) by summing values of the power, P(t$_n$), a discrete-time function, multiplied by the time interval $\Delta t = t_n - t_{n-1}$.

Analysis and Synthesis

If you are given an amplifier circuit whose output voltage you are supposed to find when a given input signal is applied, the task is one of *analysis*. (SeeTable 32.7.) You know the circuit configuration and the values of the circuit components, and you must then use Kirchhoff's laws and Ohm's law to find the output voltage. In

Table 32.7   Comparison of analysis with synthesis in electronics

Analysis	Synthesis
Determining the behavior of an arrangement of components	Determining an arrangement of components that perform a desired function

synthesis, on the other hand, there is a desired target — such as the circuitry that is to take the output from the photodiode of a CD player and provide a suitable voltage to drive a loudspeaker. Your task is to design a circuit that will perform the job. As with many design problems, there will likely be many "correct" solutions to the synthesis problem. Often, the choice among the possible solutions will be made on the basis of cost.

Linear and Nonlinear

Table 32.8   Comparison of linear and nonlinear characteristics

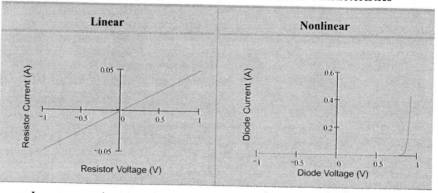

In our everyday experience, many cause-and-effect phenomena appear to have a proportional relationship. For example, we feel that if we pull twice as hard we can double the weight that we can lift. Such phenomena are characterized as being *linear*. An electrical example of a linear effect is the linear relationship expressed by Ohm's Law between the current flowing in a 20Ω resistor to the voltage across it. (See Table 32.8, left.) A very different behavior is the *nonlinear* behavior of some other electrical components. The current flowing in a pn-diode is an exponential function of the voltage across it. (See Table 32.8, right.) In common parlance, the current "blows up" (and so might the diode!) when the voltage is raised excessively. Even an apparently linear device can behave nonlinearly if a large enough stimulus is applied. For example, a common resistor when driven with a high enough voltage may heat up enough so that its resistance changes and the I_R-V_R plot is no longer a straight line.

32.2 Sampling

If you have a continuous-time signal, such as a speech waveform, and want to find its discrete-time representation, you simply measure the amplitude of the continuous-time signal at specific times. This operation is known as *sampling*. Your discrete-time representation is then a set of numbers (the amplitudes) that apply at times that you might also list. For example, the values might be as follows:

Amplitudes (millivolts):	0	5	10	15	20	0	5	10	15	20	0	5 ...
Times (milliseconds):	0	1	2	3	4	5	6	7	8	9	10	11 ...

You can probably visualize the continuous-time original — a sawtooth variation of voltage with time. You must be careful to sample at short enough time intervals to include fast-changing details of the continuous-time signal. If the values of the voltages at the sampling times are converted to binary numbers, for example, this process is known as *digitizing*. As noted in Chapter 7, if one is sampling a single-frequency sinusoidal signal, a fundamental condition known as the Nyquist Sampling Theorem requires that at least two samples be taken per period in order to permit perfect reconstruction of the continuous-time signal. Figure 32.3 shows an example of sampling applied to speech processing. The samples are taken frequently enough (once every $333\,\mu s$) to reproduce well the amplitude variations in the speech signal. For other examples of sampling, see the relevant web sites listed in Appendix I.

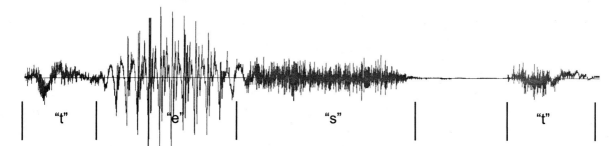

Figure 32.3 Sampled speech: the spoken word "test" sampled at 3000 samples per second. The graphic shows 0.4 seconds of speech. You can listen to this sample on the web site sampled at 22,000 samples per second.

How does one actually perform the sampling? One way is to apply the voltage waveform to be sampled to a circuit containing a fast switch, a capacitor, and a fast voltmeter. The waveform to be sampled is switched briefly so that it charges the capacitor to its voltage value. Then, the switch is opened and the voltmeter reads the amplitude of the voltage waveform. The cycle is then repeated during each sampling interval. You can buy inexpensive sample-and-hold integrated circuits for this purpose.

Aliasing

If you work with sampling circuits and digital signal processors you'll encounter the term *aliasing*. The idea is again quite simple. Suppose you were provided with the samples marked with the open circles in Figure 32.4. You're told that these were obtained by sampling a single-frequency sinusoid, and your job is to determine (sketch) the sinusoid. In fact, there isn't a unique answer to this question: two very different sinusoids are shown in the figure that would produce exactly the same sample values. This effect is known as aliasing: a given set of samples could represent signals having very different "identities" (frequencies). With patience, you could find many other sinusoids that also fit the samples. (Actually, there is an infinite number of them.) To avoid the ambiguity of aliasing, we need to include filters (called *anti-aliasing* filters) with our sampling circuits to limit the frequency ranges of signals to those of relevance, such as the range of human speech for speech signal processors.

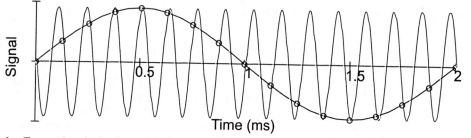

Figure 32.4 Example of aliasing. The samples (open circles) taken at 8kHz could have been obtained by sampling either the slowly varying sinusoid (500Hz) with many samples taken per period, or the more rapidly varying sinusoid (7,500Hz) for which only one sample was taken per period.

32.3 Going from One Side to the Other

If you accept the idea that it may be useful to travel from one side to the other in the pairs just listed, such as from the time domain to the frequency domain, then the important question is, "how do you actually make the trip?" The details of traveling back and forth without losing information are reserved for later courses in topics known as communications or information theory, which fall in the systems area of electrical engineering. But the basic concepts are fairly simple. What follows is a novice's guide to some of them.

Fourier Analysis

You may have noticed that we have dealt with single-frequency sinusoidal currents and voltages when considering amplifiers and filters. There were two reasons for this. First, some important electronic systems involve only one frequency at a time, such as the AC power distribution system that operates at 60Hz, in the United States, or a sound system producing a single musical tone. The second reason for our focus on circuit response to one frequency at a time is that *you can represent any periodic current or voltage waveform as the sum of a number of properly chosen single-frequency sinusoidal waveforms (harmonics).* This surprising result, shown in the 1800s by the French engineer Fourier, can be made plausible by the sketch shown in Figure 32.5.

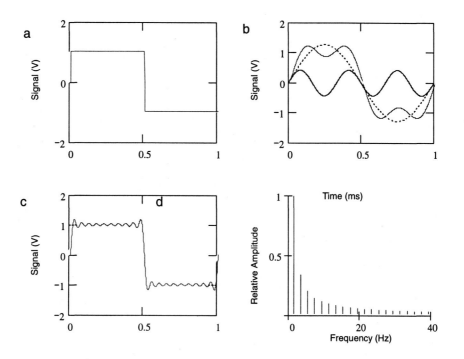

Figure 32.5 Representing a square-wave as a sum of sinusoidal waveforms. (a) Square waveform. (b) First two components of the square wave and their sum: fundamental, or first harmonic, (f_1) (dotted) whose period equals that of the original waveform, the third harmonic ($3f_1$) (solid), and the sum of the fundamental and the third harmonic (blue). (c) Sum of the first ten harmonics, showing how well the square waveform has been approximated by summing sinusoids. (d) Spectrum of the square wave showing the first twenty terms.

Fourier analysis takes us from a temporal description of a signal — its waveform — to a description in terms of frequencies. We can *transform* the description of the signal from one domain (time) to another domain (frequency). The reason for doing such a transformation is to simplify the processing of the information. Predictably, this is known as the *fourier transform*. It determines the frequency components into which a repeating finite-duration waveform can be decomposed. There are also integrated circuits that will perform the transform operation on digitized signals, often using clever algorithms to speed up the calculations. The best-known of these is the *fast fourier transform* (FFT).

Let's look at a portion of a so-called square-wave voltage (see Figure 32.5a) that goes on forever. We want to show how we could get a waveform that looks very much like this one, with all its square corners, by adding up properly chosen sinusoids, as Fourier proposed.

You can show mathematically by applying fourier analysis — which involves nothing more complicated than multiplication and integration — that the lowest-frequency sinusoid that will be needed is the one whose period (inverse of its frequency) equals the period of the square waveform. The lowest frequency component is the one with the highest amplitude. You probably would have expected this on the basis of intuition alone, right? Such a sine wave would fit nicely in the square wave.

Definite values for the amplitude and frequency of this so-called fundamental frequency component are provided by the fourier analysis procedure.

You can see that we need more components than just the fundamental, since the fundamental sinusoid does not reproduce the sharp corners of the square waveform at all. The idea is to add more components to the fundamental component to fill in the corners. A little thought and some trial sketches should convince you that using a sinusoid having just twice the frequency of the fundamental does not help, but that one having three times the frequency of the fundamental will, since it will fill in the corners on both the rise and the fall of the square waveform. Figure 32.5b shows the result of adding to the fundamental a third harmonic. To get a perfect representation requires an infinite number of sinusoids, all of which have frequencies that are odd integral multiples of the fundamental frequency and whose amplitudes get smaller and smaller. Figure 32.5c shows the result of using 10 such terms. A formula for a square wave voltage V(t) whose period is $1/f$ is:

$$n(t) = \frac{4}{\pi} \sum_{n=0}^{\infty} \frac{(-1)^n}{2n+1} \sin[(2n+1)2\pi f t].$$

We have presented a plausible argument for being able to represent any periodic waveform with a number of properly chosen single-frequency sinusoids. Here's how this concept can be applied. Suppose that you're given the problem of finding the output of a circuit containing ordinary components, such as resistors, capacitors and inductors, when the input to the circuit is a square waveform. You could solve this problem by finding the circuit's output for each sinusoidal component of the input, and then adding those outputs to get the response for the square waveform.

Fourier analysis enables us to switch readily between two equivalent, but different, ways of describing signals. In other words, we can specify a voltage waveform in terms of its variation as a function of time (like a conventional display on the screen of an oscilloscope), or we can specify the exact frequency components that make up the waveform. A frequency domain specification giving the amount of energy contained in a given range of frequencies is known as a *frequency spectrum*. An instrument known as the spectrum analyzer will display the frequency spectrum of a voltage waveform applied at its input.

We can stretch this idea of breaking a waveform up into single-frequency components one big step further— extending it into the *spatial* domain. It is sometimes useful to approximate an actual image by breaking it up into simpler functions of position, just as we have with waveforms that are functions of time. There is a procedure for doing this, called *spatial fourier analysis*, that is analogous to fourier analysis of waveforms, which are functions of time. The idea is that you represent an image in terms of a number of functions that vary sinusoidally with the position coordinates x and y. The reason for decomposing an image into these so-called *spatial frequency components* is to permit easy manipulation and economical transmission of images. An example of this is shown in Figure 32.6. A more varied image, such as that of Figure 32.7, will have a more complex spatial frequency spectrum than that appearing in Figure 32.6b.

For other examples, see the relevant web sites listed in Appendix I.

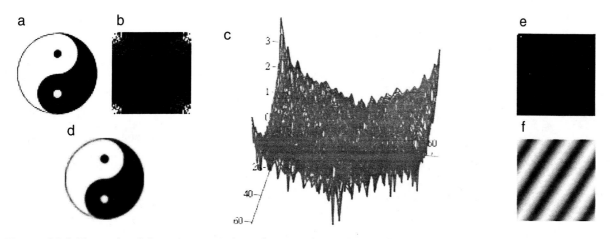

Figure 32.6 Example of the representation of a two-dimensional function of spatial coordinates x and y in terms of spatial frequency components. (a) The yin-yang function f(x,y). (b) The fourier spectrum for the spatial function of (a) displayed as an intensity function (light regions have high value, and dark regions have low value.) (c) The spatial frequency spectrum displayed in three dimensions. (d) The result of the inverse transform after applying a blur filter in fourier space. (e) A two-valued example in fourier space: the value at (0,0), in the corner, provides a DC offset to all the pixels in the image. The light dot located at (3,2) causes the sinusoidal stripes that have three periods in x and two in y. (f) The image that results from inverse transforming (e).

Figure 32.7 Photograph of a (live) 9-month-old panda being held by Dick at the Woolong panda research station, Sichuan Province, China. (Photo courtesy of Joellen Bruce)

299

Correlation and Convolution

Two other useful signal-processing operations that one can perform are *correlation* and *convolution*.

Correlation refers to the common notion that the occurrence of one event is related to the occurrence of the other. For example, it is claimed that the occurrence of the full moon is correlated with a rise in the crime rate. Communications engineers concerned with signal processing use a formal process for quantifying the correlations of signals with each other (cross-correlation) or with different portions of themselves (auto-correlation) to locate signals buried in noise or to understand something about the sources of the signals.

For more information about correlation and convolution, see the relevant web sites listed in Appendix I.

32.4 Signal Processing

Filtering Waveforms

A *filter* passes signals at certain frequencies and blocks signals at other frequencies. Since we now know that a square waveform can be decomposed into a series of single-frequency sinusoids, we can predict what would happen if we applied a square-wave voltage at the input terminals of the RC lowpass filter of Figure 31.14. The higher-frequency components would be de-emphasized. In fact, if the cutoff frequency of the filter were set just above the fundamental frequency, the fundamental (the so-called first harmonic) would be transmitted well, and the higher components would be largely blocked. If the filter had a fairly sharp cutoff (going from passing to blocking frequency components over a small frequency range), we could turn the square wave into a nearly pure sinusoid having the same period.

Similar filtering operations can be accomplished in real time on a digitized data stream. Such operations use lots of multiplications and additions, which can be implemented with dedicated hardware for ultra high-speed applications or with software for more typical applications.

To filter signals that have been translated into the frequency domain simply involves multiplying the data by the corresponding frequency response, but this is better for processing stored data or images.

An important, but very different, type of filter is the so-called *transversal filter*. Such a filter can be realized with physical devices, employing either electronic technology (charge-transfer devices) or ultrasonic technology (surface acoustic wave (SAW) delay lines, which are widely used in television sets and cellular telephones). In the latter so-called SAW filter, high-frequency "sound" waves representing the signals to be filtered progress from input to output along a physical path in a specially fabricated crystal.

Filtering Images

If you've experimented on your personal computer with an image manipulation program such as Adobe Photoshop™, you probably noticed that the term "filter" was applied to images. What is meant by filtering an image?

Suppose you take a snapshot with your 35mm camera, have a print made from the film, and wish to manipulate the image later. You can put the print in a scanner, which is an electromechanical device that causes a line of light to sweep across the print. A lens images the reflected light onto a linear array of photodiodes. This information is digitized and stored in a file on the computer attached to the scanner. Each picture element (pixel) of the stored image has associated with it numbers that represent its brightness and color. Alternatively, you could use a digital camera that stores the picture immediately in digital form.

Commercial computer software is now available for altering the values for each pixel of the image in order to produce interesting effects.

Blurring: Often, photographs are more pleasing if they are not very sharp, but are blurred. To see how one type of blurring-filter works, recall that to reproduce the sharp edges of a voltage waveform we needed to include the higher frequency components. In an image, we would expect that removing the high *spatial* frequency components from the image would reduce image sharpness — in other words, blur it. Therefore, blurring filters may reduce the amplitudes of the high spatial-frequency components in the image (see Figure 32.6.)

Edge finding: This filtering action locates edges of objects in the images, which contain the high-frequency components. Edge finding emphasizes those high frequencies.

32.5 What About Hardware?

As you could have guessed from our earlier list of applications, a wide variety of special-purpose digital signal processing equipment is commercially available. You can also buy versatile and relatively inexpensive signal-processing chips and entire application boards that will accept analog signals and then carry out user-specified processing, such as filtering, determining correlations, and so on. A popular family of devices made by Texas Instruments, Inc., employs integrated circuits of the TMS320C5x series.

32.6 Problems

32.1 To compare the behavior of a linear circuit element and a nonlinear one, draw the I–V characteristics of (a) a linear 1,000 Ω resistor and (b) a nonlinear resistor whose resistance is 1,000Ω from 0 to 150 volts, 2,000Ω from 150 to 200 V, and 4,000Ω thereafter up to 250V. This increase of resistance could result from heating of the resistor due to current flow.

32.2 Using a math program or spreadsheet, add up the first 15 terms of a sinusoid series to approximate a square wave. Observe and comment on how well the square wave is represented by that number of terms.

32.3 Use an image processing program, such as Adobe Photoshop™, to blur and then resharpen an image. Print both the blurred and the resharpened images.

Electronics Terminology Brought to You by *the good guys!*

Most fields of study develop their own jargon — terminology that's used to save time while communicating and perhaps also to impress the uninitiated. Such jargon is often used in advertising and marketing. A teaching assistant suggested that it might be instructive, and even fun, to decode terms from actual ads, such as the ones presented next from a newspaper advertising supplement for *the good guys!* electronics stores. (Reprinted by permission.) Figures 33.1 through 33.9 show the advertisements.

Figure 33.1   Portable AM/FM Stereo with Dubbing Cassette Recorder and 4-Speaker System. This mini-stereo puts out some outstanding sound with its 4-speaker system that features 3" woofers and piezo tweeters. Other features include: switchable high-speed dubbing, continuous play, soft eject, auto level control, and input jacks for headphones and microphone.

Stereo .... Two microphones, set a distance apart during recording, pick up slightly different sounds, which are reproduced through two separate speakers to enhance the feeling of reality.

Woofer, tweeter..........A woofer reproduces low frequencies, and a tweeter reproduces high frequencies; a filter circuit (crossover network) separates the high and low frequencies, and supplies the proper ones to the correct speaker.

Piezo tweeter..............A high-frequency speaker employing a piezoelectric crystal, instead of a magnetically driven voice-coil as in most loudspeakers. Such a crystal vibrates mechanically when a time-varying voltage is applied between its two electrodes.

Dubbing ...... Reproducing from one master tape onto one or more copy tapes. This is often done at two times normal speed, which requires higher frequency response from the electronics.

Figure 33.2 Stereo Cassette Deck with Dolby B & C. You get the solid recording and playback performance of the Dolby B & C Noise Reduction systems. The soft touch controls allow for precise operation during recording and playback. The high density permalloy heads will deliver years of crisp audio reproduction. LCD meters assure you of proper levels during duplication.

Dolby B & C Noise-Reduction systems ....A system invented by a man named Ray Dolby that reduces noise in reproduced recordings by emphasizing the high frequencies during recording and then reducing them to proper level during playback. This reduces the hiss noise produced by the individual grains of the magnetic recording medium relative to what's recorded there — the music or speech signal. B and C refer to different degrees of pre-emphasis; with Dolby C, the pre-emphasis depends on the amplitude of the original signal, and it permits obtaining a larger dynamic range of sounds to be recorded on the tape.

High-density permalloy heads ....The speech or music recorded on a tape is represented by tiny, differently magnetized grains of iron oxide or other metals on the tape. High-density permalloy is a superior magnetic nickel-iron alloy used to form a ring-shaped magnetic tape write/read head. The head is a ring of permalloy having a tiny gap cut radially in it for positioning near the tape. A copper coil wound around the ring produces a magnetic field in the gap during the writing process, when the coil is supplied with a current. During reading, magnetized regions of tape passing by the gap produce a magnetic flux in the ring, generating a voltage at the terminals of the coil. In a stereo tape deck, two such cores are embedded in a nonmagnetic ceramic material to form a smooth surface for the tape to slide on.

LCD meters. ....These are meters that use a liquid crystal display similar those found in most digital watches. The LCD consists of a thin layer of molecules located between transparent electrical conductors on glass sheets. The orientations of the molecules change as different voltages are applied to the electrodes (producing different electric fields where the molecules are). The molecules alter the polarization of light passing through them in accordance with their orientation. LCDs can produce a display in either reflected or transmitted light. While they require very little electric power to operate, LCDs can be slow to respond so they may not give accurate indications of peaks with a rapidly changing waveform.

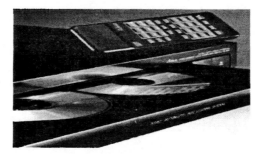

Figure 33.3   Remote 6-Disc + 1 CD Changer with Improved 1-Bit D/A Converter System. You get the convenience of a 6-disc changer with an additional single drawer to use when you want to play 1 CD. 1-bit D/A converter with 2nd-order noise shaping improves the already great sound reproduction.

CD............. On a compact disc, sound is represented in digital form by tiny holes etched in a reflective metal film located between protective plastic sheets. An invisible infrared beam from a semiconductor laser, automatically focussed on the recorded track, reflects from the holes moving past onto a photodiode. The photodiode produces an electrical output corresponding to the sequence of holes, and hence the sound recorded, on the disc. (A videodisc player works similarly.)

D/A converter .... This is an electronic circuit that converts the digital signals (a stream of individual voltage or current pulses) into an analog (continuous) signal. A 1-bit D/A converter is a circuit that does the conversion in a way that effectively deals with one bit at a time, yet can result in very accurate conversion, even though it uses inexpensive circuit elements. "2nd-order noise shaping" refers to the sharpness of the filter used to remove the noise introduced in the D/A conversion process.

Figure 33.4   5-disc Carousel CD Changer with Remote and LAMBDA Technology. Dual 18-bit LAMBDA Super Linear Converter and 20-bit digital filter with 8x oversampling brings home dynamic digital audio reproduction.

Sampling, Filters, Playback and All That.........This is really tricky! Let's start with the background. The CDs made for use in your audio player provide you with digitized versions of speech or music waveforms that are <u>continuous</u> functions of time. (To reproduce audible sound with frequencies up to 22,000 Hz, sampling occurs roughly every 23 microseconds, with 16 bits per sample.) In principle, you could perfectly reproduce speech or music from a CD that contained just digitized information obtained by sampling the waveform often enough and holding the old value until the next sample arrived. If you read this sampled-and-held signal off the disc and put it through a perfect filter that only passed frequencies up to the cutoff at about 22 kHz (resulting from the 44.1 kilosamples per second sampling rate), you'd get out smoothed waveforms that were perfect replicas of the sounds in the recording studio. However, the perfect filter would be very expensive if built with capacitors and coils. The solution is to do the filtering digitally, in order to keep the cost under control. So, let's start with the digital filter.

20-bit digital filter......The idea is to take the 16-bit samples off the disc; fill in the intervals between those samples by repeating a given sample a number of times until the next sample comes from the disc; and then pass the result through a digital filter having a very sharp cutoff. The result is excellent reproduction of the original recorded material. A 20-bit filter is used to get the sharp cutoff that eliminates the introduction of spurious noise.

18-bit LAMBDA Super Linear Converter.....The 18 bits comes from interpolation of the waveform between the individual sample values (representing values that lie between quantities defined in 16-bit steps will obviously require more than 16 bits). The term "super linear" means that the converter that returns the massaged digital information to analog form should have an output that is proportional to the digitally represented input, regardless of the amplitude of the input.

8x oversampling.........This whole technique employs oversampling. The time between successive samples on the disc is divided into eight parts, and interpolating values at each of those intermediate times are digitally generated.

Figure 33.5 50-Watt Remote Mini Component CD Stereo System. CD player has 3-mode CD-to-tape editing. Dual auto-reverse cassette deck features Dolby B NR, series play and synchro editing. Stereo amp has graphic EQ and spectrum analyzer, super bass and surround sound. AM/FM tuner has a jog dial for super convenience.

Graphic EQ. ....The graphic equalizer contains a number of filters (5-20) whose control settings, displayed graphically for you, indicate the extent to which signals in a given frequency band are amplified or attenuated. With it, you can emphasize or de-emphasize frequencies in a certain range, highs or lows, or whatever.

Spectrum analyzer .....A device that displays the amplitudes of the various frequency components present in a complex signal. The spectrum for a single-frequency <u>sinusoidal</u> voltage would have a single value, say, at 500 Hz. For a <u>rectangular</u> wave having a one-millisecond period, the spectrum analyzer would display a sequence of components at the fundamental frequency (500 Hz) and at odd integral multiples of that (1,500 Hz, 2,500 Hz, etc.). In the case of stereo systems, the display is usually a bar graph. The resolution of the graph will be very low, since from 5 to 20 bars cover the entire audio spectrum, 20 to 20,000 Hz.

AM/FM .... AM means amplitude modulation, in which the amplitude of the carrier frequency from a source, such as a radio station having a carrier frequency of 600 kHz, is changed so that it is proportional to the instantaneous amplitude of the speech or music to be broadcast. FM means frequency modulation, in which the frequency of the radiated wave from the station varies from the carrier by an amount that is proportional to the instantaneous amplitude of the speech or music to be broadcast. FM radio signals tend to be less noisy than AM signals, except in multi-path environments, such as are encountered while driving around in a big city.

50-watt .... This typically means the electrical power that the system can deliver to the loudspeakers without unacceptably high distortion. (It is actually the electrical power at 1,000 Hz that the system can deliver to an 8-

ohm load resistor.) The actual power in the sound waves produced is much less.

Figure 33.6   VHS Camcorder with 8:1 Zoom and Digital Autofocus. The powerful 8:1 zoom lens with full-range macro focus gets you close while six-position high-speed shutter keeps you on top of any shooting situation. Creative features include time lapse and self timer recording. The advanced CCD imager with 2 lux low light sensitivity allows great movie making in limited lighting conditions.

VHS .... Meaning "Video Home System", a 1/2-inch-wide tape system developed by JVC, Japan Victor Company. The much-less popular Beta format, developed by Sony, uses 1/2-inch tape that moves more slowly since the pickup head spins faster.

8:1 zoom ..... An adjustable focal length lens (wide-angle to telephoto) allows the width (and height) of the image scene to be varied over an 8-to-1 range.

CCD .... A charge-coupled device contains a semiconductor circuit that produces an electrical representation of an optical image. CCDs are available for one- or two-dimensional images. Light focused onto a CCD produces an amount of charge at each lighted location that is proportional to the light intensity there. The individual packets of charge are swept out in bucket brigade fashion to form a series of analog voltage or current pulses. Each pulse represents the illumination at a given element of the optical image, or picture (each element of a picture is called a "pixel").

2 lux .... The lux is "the international unit of illumination, being the direct illumination on a surface which is everywhere one meter from a uniform point source of one international candle." (The "international candle" is the international unit of luminous intensity, being the light emitted by five square millimeters of platinum at the temperature of solidification! A "standard candle" is defined as the luminous intensity approximately equal to that from a 7/8-inch real sperm-whale candle burning at a rate of 120 grains per hour. And, as we all know, a grain is about 1/15th of a gram, and a gram is about 1/5th of the mass of a U.S. five-cent coin!) So, probably this all means that you can take pictures by candlelight with this camcorder.

Figure 33.7 AM/FM Cassette Car System with Auto Reverse. The 50-watt output really delivers big sound. X-tal Lock PLL tuner has 18 presets. Cassette has music search and Dolby NR. More features: separate bass and treble & multifader. Complete with a pair of 5-1/4" dual cone speakers.

X-tal Lock PLL tuner. .... This is a device to generate your radio's receiving frequency accurately once you select it digitally. "X-tal" means a piezoelectric quartz crystal whose resonant frequency is quite constant in spite of temperature changes. A PLL is a "phase-locked loop" circuit in which a reference input at one frequency is used to stabilize or steady a very different frequency, produced by the circuit. (The crystal frequency is the reference to which the receiver response frequency is locked.)

Figure 33.8 Trinitron Stereo Color Television. The dramatic design of this advanced Trinitron Microblack Monitor/Receiver will leave you breathless. And wait until you turn it on. The picture is incredible! The extra advantage of picture-in-picture allows you to view one show while keeping an eye on another. Features include A/V window on-screen displays, and a universal preprogrammed remote control that runs other pieces of equipment.

Trinitron Microblack Monitor/Receiver. .... A monitor just displays pictures (with sound) produced by any source, such as a video cassette player or a computer; a receiver also will display television programs picked up by an antenna or through a cable connection. "Trinitron" refers to a Sony technology in which color is produced on vertical stripes of phosphors (rather than dots) on the screen by a swept electron beam inside the picture tube. Each stripe has a narrow black border. The black border reduces annoying reflections of room light, increasing picture contrast, so the screen looks black when the power is turned off.

Picture-in-picture.......This is a small-sized window set into the bigger picture so that you can display and watch a second image, which might be from another television show or perhaps your video cassette player.

A/V window on-screen displays............ This feature allows you to visually display and manipulate the audio and video (A/V) control settings with the remote control. These settings include things such as volume, balance, bass, treble, brightness, contrast, color level, and color tone. This feature uses digital circuitry to form images of letters and numbers on the TV screen.

Figure 33.9   Automatic 35mm Compact Camera with Auto Flash, and Standard & Wideangle Lens. This compact camera lets the user take wide scenic shots or standard type exposures. The camera's 28–40mm lens can change at the touch of a button! From the super-sharp F3.5 lens to the built-in auto flash this unit is a marvel of point and shoot convenience. Features autofocusing, film loading and rewind.

35mm.......... This is the width in millimeters of the film that the camera accepts.

F3.5 lens...... This is the "f-number" of the lens, which is the ratio of the focal length of the lens (the distance from the focal point of the lens on the film to the plane of the shutter) to the diameter of the lens opening. The lower the f-number, the faster and more expensive the lens is. The f-number can be raised by closing an iris in the lens, to get a larger depth of field, which is the range of distances in what's being photographed over which objects are in focus (a pinhole camera would have a very large f-number and a large depth-of-field.) To get a given exposure on the film with a given type of film and a given scene being photographed, you must increase the exposure time if you increase the f-number. As you adjust the f-number (reduce the size of the aperture) successively through the usual values f1.4, f2, f2.8, f4, f5.6, f8, f11, f16, f22, you decrease the area of the aperture and the total light coming through it by about a factor of two with each change.

28–40mm.... These are the focal lengths of the two lenses in this 35mm camera. The 28mm lens is fairly wide-angle, the 40mm is less so. A commonly used lens for general photography in such a camera has a 50mm focal length. The ratio of the focal length to the camera-to-subject distance equals the ratio of height of the image on the film to the height of the subject.

Part III: Appendices

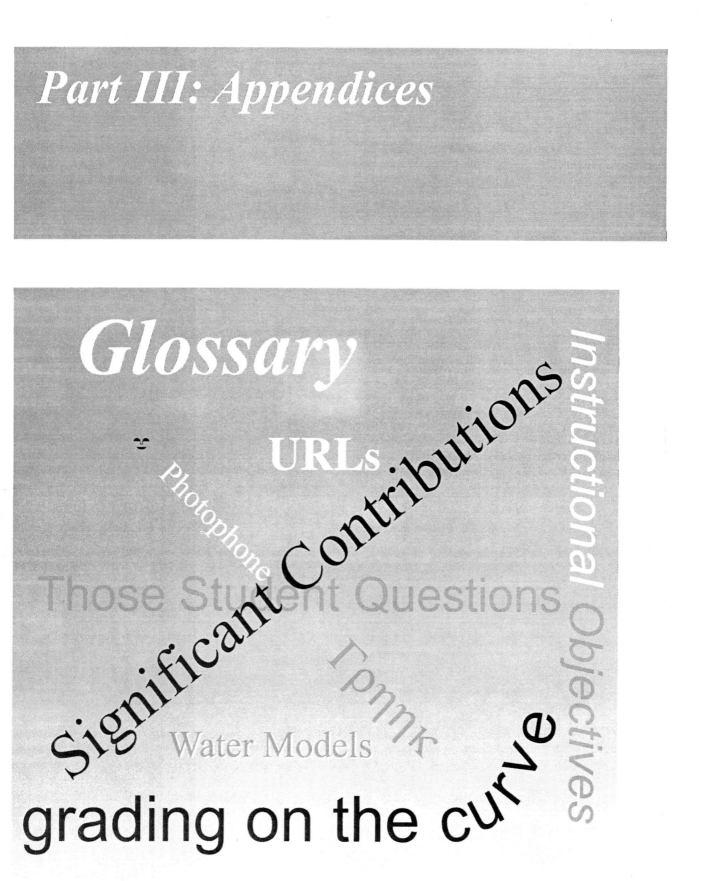

Glossary

Photophone

URLs

Significant Contributions

Those Student Questions

Instructional Objectives

Гρηηκ

Water Models

grading on the curve

Instructional Objectives

A

After studying this book the student should be able to:

- Analyze very simple circuits such as those containing a battery, switch, and several circuit elements.

- Use a networked computer to send and receive electronic mail, use an editor, use a spreadsheet, and program a computer to do a simple calculation.

- List the major functional elements of a digital computer, and define terms such as machine language, assembly language, higher level language, read-only memory, and random-access memory.

- Identify logic gates, and analyze the operation of a circuit of logic gates.

- Describe the various specialties within electrical engineering and computer sciences (or engineering), such as devices, systems, and software engineering.

- Define and correctly use general engineering terms and concepts such as design, constraint, and significant figures.

- Summarize in writing and present orally assigned technical material.

- Recall major points from guest technical lectures.

In addition, if you take this course with the Laboratory, you should be able to:

- Use an oscilloscope for basic measurements, and follow wiring diagrams to construct simple circuits.

- Identify common electronic components.

- Describe qualitatively the operation of a transistor, an op-amp, and at least two of the pieces of equipment in the lab.

Those Student Questions

Answered

[Page 116]

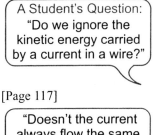

A Student's Question: "Do we ignore the kinetic energy carried by a current in a wire?"

Yes. The electrons in a wire collide frequently with the atoms in the wire, so they don't develop significant kinetic energy. (The student ventured that this might be analogous to flow in a water pipe separated into tiny channels. In contrast, the six-inch diameter pipes that supply water to fire hydrants may burst if a hydrant valve is closed suddenly, because of the momentum built up by the flowing water.)

[Page 117]

"Doesn't the current always flow the same way in a wire?"

No, the current can flow either way in a wire. When analyzing a circuit, you can define the direction of positive current flow in a given wire to be in either direction. If the actual current flow direction is opposite to what you assumed, the analysis will just yield a negative value for that particular current.

[Page 118]

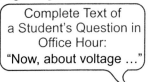

Complete Text of a Student's Question in Office Hour: "Now, about voltage ..."

(Our favorite question: This shows how hard it can be to formulate a specific question about a subject that puzzles you completely.) An operational answer is that the voltage between points A and B in a circuit is the reading on a voltmeter whose leads are connected to points A and B (positive lead to A, negative lead to B). More formally, the voltage between points A and B is defined as the difference between the potential energy for a unit positive charge located at A and at B. Another way of saying it is that the voltage (in volts) between points A and B is equal numerically to the ratio of the work done (in joules) to the charge (in coulombs) when one moves a positive charge from B to A.

[Page 118]

"Since both batteries are 1.5 volts, what's the difference between the big D one and the little AAA one?"

The bigger one has a larger volume of chemicals in it and bigger electrodes, so it stores more energy and will produce electric energy at a given rate for a longer time. Alternatively, the bigger battery can deliver energy at a higher rate (larger current), because it has a lower internal resistance.

[Page 120]

"What is meant by the voltage across a circuit component?"

Formally, it means the difference in electric potential across the component. A positive charge at the "plus" terminal of the component has more potential energy than the same charge if it's located at the "negative" terminal.

[Page 120]

"Doesn't power depend on both voltage and current? Like, if you had 50,000 volts and no current, would you have any power?"

Correct. The power dissipated in an appliance such as an electric stove depends on both the voltage applied across the heater elements and the current flowing through them. Look at the electric energy meter outside your dwelling: If you turn off all the electric appliances and lights, you won't be drawing any current, and the meter will stop turning, even though the voltage is still present.

[Page 121]

"Why do we have to do work to move a charge? Isn't the charge on an electron really small?"

Yes, the charge on each electron is small — only 1.6×10^{-19} coulombs — but practical currents in electronics involve huge numbers of electrons, so the work done in moving the charges involved is appreciable.

[Page 122]

"What, exactly, does a resistor resist?"

A resistor resists the flow of current in the same sense that a pinched garden hose resists the flow of water through it. To get a certain rate of water flow (current) requires a larger pressure difference (potential difference, or voltage) between the ends of the hose (resistor) than if the hose were not pinched (that is, if the resistor had a very small value of resistance).

[Page 122]

"What is the broken fire hydrant of Figure 19.8 analogous to in electrical terms?"

Outside a college dormitory, a truck backed into a fire hydrant, breaking it and producing an impressive fountain. At ground level, the flow rate is very high, corresponding to a large electric current, as in a short circuit. Unlike all of our water models except that for the voltage source (Figure 19.4), in the case of this hydrant, gravity does play a role: The water pressure is high at ground level and zero at the very top of the plume of water.

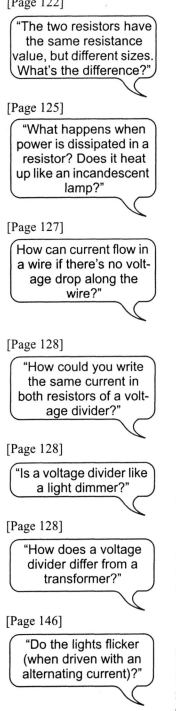

[Page 122]

"The two resistors have the same resistance value, but different sizes. What's the difference?"

[Page 125]

"What happens when power is dissipated in a resistor? Does it heat up like an incandescent lamp?"

[Page 127]

How can current flow in a wire if there's no voltage drop along the wire?"

[Page 128]

"How could you write the same current in both resistors of a voltage divider?"

[Page 128]

"Is a voltage divider like a light dimmer?"

[Page 128]

"How does a voltage divider differ from a transformer?"

[Page 146]

"Do the lights flicker (when driven with an alternating current)?"

The power rating of the bigger resistor is higher. It can safely dissipate more heat because it has a larger surface area for contact with the surrounding air and a larger area for radiating away its thermal energy.

Exactly. If a resistor's power rating is exceeded by a factor of, say, five, the resistor will get very hot, the paint on its surface may blister and burn, it may produce very unpleasant smelling smoke, it may get hot enough to glow, and it may shatter from the heating.

There *is* a voltage drop across the wire, but it's small compared with all the other voltage drops in the circuit. When we draw a circuit containing wires, resistors, and other components, we tacitly assume that the resistances of the wires are much smaller than those of the resistors in the circuit. The resistance of an inch-long piece of ordinary wire in a circuit might be only 0.001 ohm, while the resistors in the circuit would typically have resistances that range from tens of ohms to perhaps a few million ohms.

Because of Kirchhoff's Current Law. The currents entering the node between resistors R_1 and R_2 must sum to zero. This means that all the current coming out of resistor R_1 must flow into resistor R_2. There's nowhere else for it to go.

They're different. A voltage divider does produce an output voltage that is a fraction of its source voltage, but it dissipates energy in its resistors in the process. A light dimmer reduces the light output of a lamp by reducing the amount of time the lamp is "on" by interrupting the supply voltage to the lamp periodically.

You've read ahead, since we haven't come to transformers yet. The transformer only works with time-varying voltages, while the voltage divider will work even with DC. Also, the voltage divider dissipates some energy in its resistors, but a good transformer will dissipate very little energy while reducing the voltage.

(Another great question.) The voltage applied to the lights varies at a 60 Hz rate. The filament in an incandescent lamp glows because it's heated by the current flowing through it. The filament temperature can't change rapidly, so there's very little flicker in the light it produces. The gas inside a fluorescent lamp can respond much more rapidly, so it does flicker. You seldom notice the flicker, but you can detect it if you observe your hand shaking back and forth between the fluorescent lamp and your eye — you'll see multiple stationary images of your hand instead of a blurred image. You can also see multiple stationary images if you shake your hand in front of a television or computer screen, both of which are scanned at roughly a 60 Hz rate.

[Page 147]

> A student's exclamation (upon seeing a charged capacitor discharged by a screwdriver): "So, capacitors *store* energy?"

Yes! This capability is used in circuits that power photoflash bulbs: A capacitor is charged to a high voltage over a period of some seconds with a steady current and then discharged through the flash bulb to produce a bright burst of light. Inductors also store energy, whereas resistors dissipate electrical energy, producing heat.

[Page 147]

> "Is the charge on each capacitor plate Q, or is it Q/2?"

The magnitude of the charge on each plate is Q; on one plate, it is a charge of $+Q$, and on the other a charge of $-Q$, where Q is the value used in the capacitor formula, $Q = CV$, where C is the capacitance and V is the voltage across the capacitor.

[Page 149]

> "So, how could a distant nuclear blast burn out the electronics in my car?"

(Asked in discussion section after the class had run out of questions about material in the course.) A nuclear blast produces what is known as an electromagnetic pulse (EMP), a very high-amplitude pulse containing many frequency components that radiates outward from the blast site like a signal from a radio or television station. Wires connected to or inside unshielded electronic equipment act as tiny antennas that pick up the electric field of this pulse; because of the pulse's high amplitude, large voltages are produced in the equipment that can burn out its transistors and other components.

[Page 153]

> "Why does the product RC have dimensions of seconds?"

We know that $V = IR$ and that $Q = CV$. Substituting the first equation for V into the second equation we get $Q = CIR$ or $RC = Q/I$. Q has units of coulombs, and I has units of coulombs per second so both RC and Q/I have units of seconds.

[Page 154]

> "Does a coil work the other way too, producing a voltage or current in a magnetic field?"

Yes, a coil will develop a voltage (and a current, if its terminals are connected to a wire or a resistor) when a <u>time-varying</u> magnetic field threads the turns of the coil. This effect is used in transformers (one coil threaded by the magnetic field produced by the other coil) and in loop antennas for television. (The magnetic field of the radiated electromagnetic wave threads the loop.)

[Page 155]

> "Transformers don't work on DC?"

No, they don't. The magnetic field, or the primary current that produces it, has to be changing.

[Page 165]

> "How long have people been using binary?"

In the article "Wonders", *Scientific American*, Feb. 1996, pp. 130-1, Phylis and Philip Morrison observe that in excavations, from more than four millennia ago in the ancient city of Mohenjo-Daro, on the Indus, a set of small unworked pebbles was found that had weight ratios that doubled along the set in the pattern, 1, 1, 2, 4, 8, 16,... The smallest pebble weighed only slightly less than our ounce. The conjecture is that these pebbles were used as a set of weights for the equal-arm pan balances that were found in remains of this period. The user selected the smallest pebble as the unit, and then matched it with a similar pebble. Next, after putting both unit pebbles in the same pan of the balance, one sought a larger pebble that balanced the two. And so the set of binary-weighted pebbles was assembled.

[Page 241]

> "Can you ever get actual DC out of an AC–DC converter?"

The real question was, can you get rid of even the small amount of ripple left after you connect a capacitor across the output of a full-wave rectifier circuit? Yes, you can add a regulator circuit that includes a zener diode to set the output voltage and a transistor so as to reduce the ripple to millivolt levels.

[Page 204]

> "How fast do the electrons move in a wire? Are they slower in a resistor?"

If electrons enter one end of a foot-long piece of copper wire, electrons will start to leave the other end slightly more than one nanosecond later. This means that the velocity at which the <u>electrical disturbance</u> travels is a bit less than the velocity of light. The first electrons to leave the wire are not the same electrons as those that first entered the wire: however, the velocity of the actual electrons is much less than that of the disturbance in the collection of electrons in the wire. The same is true of electrons in a resistor. Probably, electrons move more slowly in a resistor because of their more frequent collisions with the atoms of the resistive material, but this is a very hard question to answer definitively.

[Page 209]

> "Why does a diode have a turn-on voltage?"

The whole story is complicated, but we can get a rough idea by thinking about what happens to the clouds of holes and electrons in the two parts of the diode when we apply different voltages to it. For current to flow through the middle of the diode, electrons and holes have to coexist there, since those clouds of carriers are the only things that connect physically to the contacts on the ends of the diodes. It turns out that when the diode voltage is exactly zero, there is a region near the middle of the diode where there aren't any mobile charges, so no current can flow. By applying a little forward bias (making the p contact slightly positive with respect to the n contact), the holes and the electrons are forced toward the p–n boundary, and current can flow. Ample current can flow when the applied forward voltage equals the turn-on voltage.

[Page 209]

> "What would happen if you tried putting a voltage above the turn-on voltage across a real diode?"

Say you connect the diode across a car's battery. The current which will flow can be calculated from the load line method, but this would ignore the fact that the diode has to dissipate power, usually as heat. The power is given by IV. The diode will have a maximum power rating (or current rating) specified by the manufacturer. Once the maximum rating is exceeded the diode will must likely fail. In this case, it will most certainly fail and may do so with "special effects."

[Page 211]

> "Where does the extra energy come from when we amplify a voltage or current?"

Every electrical amplifier is connected to a DC power supply. Energy from that supply adds to the energy of the voltage or current signal in the amplifier to form the amplified output signal.

[Page 232]

> "Does the name transistor mean anything?"

The name transistor, coined by J. R. Pierce, a famous electrical engineer and physicist at the Bell Telephone Laboratories, means transfer resistor.

[Page 269]

> "Why don't birds get electrocuted when they land on uninsulated power lines?"

There is very little voltage drop along the wire they're sitting on, so there's not much potential difference between their feet. If a bird with a large wing span gets across two wires, bye-bye birdie.

[Page 163]

> A student's question about multimeters: "What's better — analog or digital?"

There's no correct answer to the general question, "Is analog or digital better?" With respect to meters, an analog meter gives a feeling for the magnitude of the quantity measured in terms of the distance the needle swings, while the digital meter simply displays numbers. The digital meter will usually be able to provide more significant figures. The digital instrument may take longer to reach its final reading; for this reason, an analog sound-level meter is easier to use and interpret than a digital sound-level meter. With respect to oscilloscopes, the digital scope offers automatic triggering, provides scale indications on the screen, and interfaces naturally with external data collection equipment. However, the digital scope can distort waveforms, because of the sampling process that it employs. In music reproduction, the larger the number of bits used in the digital system, the better the fidelity of reproduction is.

[Page 275]

> "Is this kind of modulation related to what's done in a computer's modem?"

Yes, it is related. The word *modem* is short for modulator–demodulator. Computer modems change sequences of computer bits into multiple audio frequency tones that can be transmitted over a plain old telephone system (POTS) and converted back into bits at the receiving end.

[Page 291]

> "Where do AM and FM radio and television fit into this chart?"

AM radio varies the signal amplitude of a fixed frequency carrier wave, and since the simplest receivers take the peak amplitude from the carrier once per cycle, this could be looked at as being a analog-valued, digital-time signal. FM radio uses a fixed amplitude, but varies the frequency of the carrier. This waveform could be clipped to a digital waveform that has continuously variable time, and the transmission could still be recovered — meaning that it could be classified as a digital-valued, analog time signal. TV uses analog values at analog positions in discrete time slices. Modern TV cameras use digital sensors, so that they may use analog values at discrete positions, or even digital values.

Water Models for Electronic

Devices

All the water models introduced in this book are collected here for your convenience in comparing and reviewing. In each box, the device symbol appears to the left of the water model. All the symbols are standard, except for the AC current source symbol, which we made up. Gravity is assumed to be zero in all models, except for the voltage source, where it is responsible for the pressure difference. The water is assumed to be incompressible throughout.

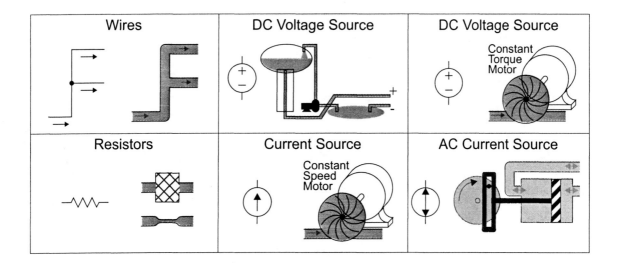

Wires	DC Voltage Source	DC Voltage Source
		Constant Torque Motor
Resistors	Current Source	AC Current Source
	Constant Speed Motor	

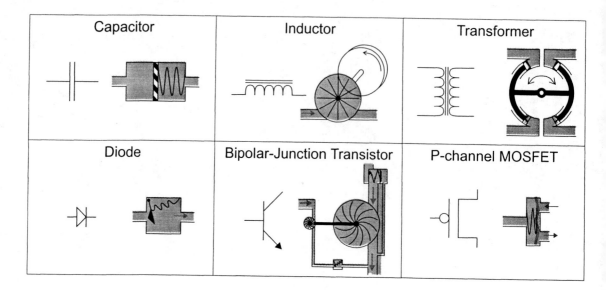

Glossary

Term	Definition
AC	Alternating Current[1] — refers to a voltage or current that varies periodically with time
adder	Logic circuit whose output represents the sum of two or more inputs
ADSL	Asymmetrical Digital Subscriber Line — DSL system featuring faster downlink than uplink
address	Identification of the storage location of each piece of data or code in a computer memory
AI	See "artificial intelligence"
algorithm	Step-by-step method for solving a particular problem
ALU	Arithmetic/Logic Unit — performs logic operations in a computer
AM	Amplitude Modulation — information coding scheme involving changing the amplitude of a steady carrier wave
ammeter	Device for measuring current
ampere (amp) $[A]^2$	Measure of electric current: $1\,A = 1$ coulomb/second
amplifier	Device whose output is a magnified replica of its input
analog	Characterizes a signal or device whose values are a continuous function of time. (See also "digital.")
AND	Logic gate whose output is binary **1** if all its inputs are 1s, and binary zero (**0**) otherwise (pronounced "and")
anode	In a vacuum tube, positively charged metallic electrode that attracts electrons produced by the cathode. In a solid-state diode, the p-doped region which serves the same function.

---

[1] The capital letters in the the initial words of the definition are used to show the derivation of terms that are acronyms.

[2] In the term column, (…) denotes the familiar name or symbol and […] denotes the abbreviation for the unit.

Term	Definition
angstrom [Å]	Measure of length: $1\text{ Å} = 10^{-10}\text{m}$
antenna	Conductive structure to transmit or receive radio waves
application	Software system for a particular purpose, such as word processing. (See also "program.")
ARPANET	Computer network that developed into the Internet
artificial intelligence	Computer field that attempts to simulate human intelligence
ASCII	American Standard Code for Information Interchange (pronounced "asky") — a 7- or 8-bit code commonly used to encode alphanumeric symbols
ASIC	Application-Specific Integrated Circuit — integrated circuit tailored to perform a very specialized function
assembler	Computer software that converts assembly-language statements into machine language for execution
assembly language	Low-level programming language whose instructions closely correspond to machine language instructions
asynchronous	Operations that do not occur at a regular rate, in contrast to clocked synchronous operations
ATM	Asynchronous Transfer Mode — a means for transmitting information on a network at very high rates
bandwidth	Frequency range over which a circuit or system operates
beta site	Location that tests a free version of hardware or software for a producer
binary	Numbering system based on powers of 2 using only the digits **0** and **1**, called "bits"
BCD	Binary Coded Decimal — numbering system using a 4-digit code to represent the decimal digits 0 to 9
BIOS	Basic Input/Output System — machine-read instructions stored in a computer to direct its initial start-up
bipolar- junction transistor	Transistor with n-type and p-type semiconductors having base-emitter and collector-base junctions
bit	Binary digIT. See "binary."
BJT	See "bipolar-junction transistor"
Boolean logic	Logic operations — such as AND, OR, NOT, and NAND — based on only two logic states
buffer	Circuit that supplies an output to a load without affecting the input source; also, temporary storage medium
bus	Transmission medium for electrical or optical signals that perform a particular function, such as computer control
byte	A group of eight bits that can represent any of $2^8 = 256$ different entities
cache	Circuitry with a small amount of high-speed memory to store frequently accessed microprocessor information
capacitance [F]	Characteristic of a capacitor: a 1 F (farad) capacitor charged to 1 V contains 1 C of charge. (See also "capacitor.")
capacitor	Energy storage circuit element having two conductors separated by an insulator
Category 5	Communication wiring for efficient transmission of digital information composed of multiple two-wire pairs

Term	Definition
cathode	In a vacuum tube, the metallic component that is heated to release electrons. In a solid-state diode, the n-doped region, which serve the same function.
CCD	Charge-Coupled Device — imaging device, containing many field-effect capacitors, that stores and moves packets of charge
CD	Compact Disc — laser-read information storage device whose information is represented by microscopic pits
CD-ROM	Compact Disc Read-Only Memory — read-only memory whose elements are on a CD that is accessed optically with a compact disc reading device
CDMA	Code Division Multiple Access — a radio system used in cell phones and military communications for sharing a very wide bandwidth channel among multiple users each of whom has a unique code that is orthogonal to all the others
chip	Individual semiconductor circuit such as a memory or microprocessor (also known as a "die")
CISC	Complex Instruction-Set Computer (pronounced "sisk") — microprocessor that executes variable-length instructions using complex addressing modes. (See also "RISC.")
clock	Unit that produces regularly occurring pulses to govern the operation of a computer
clone	Computer made by a different manufacturer patterned after an original design such as the IBM personal computer
CMOS	Complementary Metal-Oxide Semiconductor (pronounced "sea-moss") — integrated circuit containing n-channel and p-channel MOSFETs
compiler	Program that converts a higher-level language program into machine-language code
computer	Device that uses stored instructions and information to perform rapid computations or manipulate data
conductor	Material such as the metals copper or aluminum that conducts electricity via the motion of electrons
COTS	Commercial Off-The-Shelf — term signifying a component or system obtained simply by purchasing it commercially
coulomb [C]	Measure of electrical charge: $1\,C$ is an amount of charge equal to that of about 6.24×10^{18} electrons
CPU	Central Processing Unit — computer unit that interprets and carries out the stored instructions
CRT	Cathode Ray Tube — special purpose vacuum tube used to produce images in oscilloscopes, televisions, and computer monitors. Operates by impinging a beam of high energy electrons onto phosphors on the screen. Images are formed by deflecting the beam while modulating its intensity.
current [A]	Measure of rate of flow of electric charge: a $1\,A$ (one-ampere) current is a flow of $1\,C$ of charge per second
cutoff	Condition in a diode or bipolar junction transistor in which the potential across a p-n junction prevents current flow
CW	Continuous Wave — essentially single-frequency signal used for telegraphy
decimal	Refers to numbering system based on powers of 10
demodulator	Device that removes for use information coded by a modulator in electrical or optical form. (See also "modulator.")

Term	Definition
design	To plan and delineate with an end in mind and subject to constraints
die	See "chip"
digital	Refers to systems employing only quantized (discrete) states to convey information. (See also "analog.")
DIMM	Dual In-line Memory Module — stick style memory board with double sided connector
diode	Two-terminal device that conducts current well in one direction and poorly in the other
DIP	Dual In-line Package (pronounced "dip") — common ceramic or plastic enclosure for an integrated circuit
distribution	Refers to system for carrying electric power locally at voltages from 4 to 21 kV
DMA	Direct Memory Access — data transfer between memory and I/O peripheral device without microprocessor intervention
doping	Process of introducing impurity atoms into a semiconductor to affect its conductivity
DOS	Disk Operating System (pronounced "doss") — operating system used especially on IBM computers
DRAM	Dynamic Random Access Memory (pronounced "dee-ram") — memory in which each stored bit must be refreshed periodically
DSL	Digital Subscriber Line — transmission system between a computer and a network that utilizes frequencies above the usual telephonic range for high speed (up to 1.5 Mb/s) digital transmission over an end-user telephone line. (See also "ADSL")
DSP	Digital Signal Processor — specialized IC system for processing real-time data such as sound or images
DUT	Device Under Test — the device that is currently being tested.
EEPROM	Electronically Erasable Programmable Read-Only Memory — memory in which stored information can be erased by applying voltages to selected memory cells
electrical breakdown	Condition in which, particularly with high electric field, a nominal insulator becomes electrically conducting
electric field [V/m]	In simplest form, the potential difference between two points divided by the distance between the two
electromagnetic wave	Propagating wave having electrical and magnetic components; electromagnetic waves having different frequencies are identified as radio waves, microwaves, infrared radiation, visible light, ultraviolet light, x-rays, gamma rays and cosmic rays.
electron	Elementary negative particle whose charge is -1.602×10^{-19} coulombs
energy [J]	Capacity for performing work in joules
engineering	Putting scientific knowledge to practical use. Famous quote by aerodynamicist Theodore von Kármán: "A scientist studies what is, whereas an engineer creates what never was." See also "science."
EPROM	Erasable Programmable Read-Only Memory (pronounced "e-prom") — PROM whose memory elements are input electronically and can be totally erased using UV light.
Ethernet	Communication "party-line" for computers that features collision detection
extrinsic	Characterizes doped, rather than pure, semiconductor

Term	Definition
fab	Short for "fabrication", a term referring to the making of semiconductor devices such as microprocessors
farad [F]	The unit of capacitance. (See "capacitance.")
FET	Field-Effect Transistor (pronounced "fet") — semiconductor device whose insulated gate electrode controls current flow
filament	In a vacuum tube, a wire heated by the flow of electrical current, that heats the cathode; the electron emitting cathode material may be coated directly on the filament or an electrically isolated structure.
firmware	Computer software stored on a ROM chip
fiber optic	Relates to transmission of information as modulated light in tiny transparent fibers instead of copper wires
finite-state machine	A style of logical construct having a limited number of internal states that, together with the external inputs, determine the next state
Fire Wire	IEEE 1394 Standard for super-high-speed serial interface at 100 to 400 Mbit/s data rates
flip-flop	Binary device whose outputs change value only in response to an input pulse
foundry	Establishment that fabricates semiconductor devices for many different customers
floppy disk	Magnetic disk that stores data and computer programs on a flexible substrate
FM	Frequency Modulation — information coding scheme in which the frequency of a steady carrier wave is changed
frequency	Number of times per second that a quantity, such as a voltage, completes a cycle
FPU	Floating Point Unit — integrated circuit for handling floating-point (noninteger) numbers
FTP	File Transfer Protocol — protocol governing transfer of files between computers
full adder	Logic circuit that adds three input bits to produce sum and carry output bits
gate	Circuit whose logical output variables are determined by its inputs. (See also "AND", "OR", "NOT", "NAND", "NOR", "XOR.")
gauss	The cgs unit used in measuring magnetic induction
Gopher	Internet search program that uses a system of text menus to assist in your search
ground	To make electrical connection to the earth or to the chassis of a device (verb); the connection point so used (noun)
GUI	Graphical User Interface (pronounced "gooey") — hardware, software, and firmware that produces the display on modern personal computers
hexadecimal	Numbering system using base 16; representations are symbols 0, 1, ..., 9, A, B, ..., F
half adder	Logic circuit that adds two input bits to produce sum and carry output bits
hard disk	Storage device employing a rigid spinning disk coated with magnetizable material
hardware	Physical components of a computer system such as integrated circuits and circuit boards
henry	Unit of inductance. (See "inductance.")
Home Page	A site or "page" on the World Wide Web
hole	In a semiconductor, an absent electron that behaves as a mobile positive charge. (See also "electron.")

Term	Definition
http	hypertext transfer protocol — transfer protocol used on the World Wide Web
IC	See "integrated circuit."
IEEE	Institute of Electrical and Electronic Engineers (pronounced "eye-triple e") — largest professional association for workers in these fields
IGFET	Insulated Gate Field-Effect Transistor — alternative term for MOSFET
impedance	Characteristic of circuit elements in AC circuits, analogous to resistance. (See also "reactance.")
inductance [H]	Characteristic of an inductor: in a 1-henry inductance a current change of 1 A per second produces an electromotive force of 1 V
inductor	Energy storage circuit component consisting of a coil of wire and possibly magnetic material
infrared	Invisible electromagnetic radiation having a longer wavelength, and lower frequency, than visible red light
instruction	Single command given to a computer's processor, such as ADD (add) or INR (increment)
insulator	Material that conducts electricity very poorly. (See also "conductor", and "semiconductor.")
integrated circuit	Semiconductor circuit, typically on a silicon chip, containing microfabricated transistors and other circuit elements
Internet	Worldwide digital communication network in which packets of information travel between senders and recipients
interrupt	Signal that stops the operation of a microprocessor for servicing other hardware or software needs
intrinsic	Characterizes pure undoped semiconductor. (See also "extrinsic.")
inverter	Logic gate that converts a binary **1** to a **0**, and a **0** to a **1**. (See also "NOT.")
I/O	Input/Output (pronounced "eye-owe") — information transfer between computer and peripherals such as keyboard or printer
ISDN	Integrated Service Digital Network — standard for transmitting at high rate over digital phone lines
JPEG	Joint Photographic Experts Group — professional technical group whose compression system for images is known as JPEG. JPEG-compressed files have the file extension .jpg.
kibibyte (KiB)	$2^{10} = 1024$ bytes of information (from kilo binary)
kilobyte (kB)	1000 bytes of information
kilohertz (kHz)	One thousand cycles per second. (See also "frequency.")
LAN	Local-Area Network (pronounced "lan") — digital communications network that serves users typically within less than a one-kilometer radius
laser	Light Amplification by the Stimulated Emission of Radiation — quantum device that produces coherent light
LCD	Liquid Crystal Display — display device employing light source and electrically alterable optically active thin film
LED	Light-Emitting Diode — semiconducting diode that produces visible or infrared radiation
logic design	Methodology for designing networks of logic gates to perform desired logic functions, as for computing purposes
loudspeaker	Device that produces sound when driven with an AC current

Term	Definition
magnetic field strength (**H**) [A/m]	Magnetic field produced by a current, independent of the presence of magnetic material
magnetic flux [weber]	Magnetic induction per unit area
magnetic induction (**B**) [T]	Basic magnetic field vector, which includes effects of currents and magnetic materials (unit: the Tesla)
magnetron	Vacuum tube that produces microwave energy as electrons produced by a heated cathode move in a steady magnetic field in cylindrical paths past a surrounding anode; used in radar systems and microwave ovens.
mask	Pattern on glass, similar to a photographic negative, for producing integrated-circuit elements on semiconductor wafer
mean	Numerical average of data values
mebibyte (MiB)	Mega binary byte = 2^{20} = 1,048,576 bytes
megabyte (MB)	One million bytes of information
megahertz (MHz)	One million cycles per second. (See also "frequency.")
MEMS	Micro-Electro-Mechanical System (pronounced "mems") — microscopic mechanical elements, fabricated on silicon chips by techniques similar to those used in integrated circuit manufacture, for use as sensors, actuators, and other devices
meter	Tool for measuring. (See also "ammeter", "multimeter", "ohmmeter" and "voltmeter.")
micron	Short for micrometer (10^{-6} m)
microphone	Device that produces voltage or current in response to a sound wave
microprocessor	Chip containing the logical elements for performing calculations and carrying out stored instructions
microwave	Electromagnetic wave whose frequencies range from roughly 1GHz to hundreds of GHz used in satellite communications, radar and microwave ovens.
microwave oven	Appliance for cooking in which a magnetron produces microwave electromagnetic energy that irradiates the contents and heats them by causing rapid movement of the water molecules they contain.
MIDI	Musical Instrument Digital Interface (pronounced "middy") — an asynchronous 30 kb/s standard for music transfers among computers and musical instruments, also a file format containing timing information in addition to the channel, note-on, volume and note-off codes
mike	See "microphone"
MIPS	Millions of Instructions per Second (pronounced "mips") — a measure of computing power
modem	Modulator-demodulator — device for transmitting and receiving digital data over a communication channel
modulator	Device that changes a voltage, current, or light beam intensity, direction or polarization to encode information
monitor	Display unit employing a cathode ray tube (CRT)
Moore's law	After Gordon Moore: "The number of transistors per computer chip will double roughly every two years."
MOSFET	Metal-Oxide-Semiconductor Field-Effect Transistor (pronounced "moss-fett") — device whose gate electrode potential controls current flow

Term	Definition
motherboard	Printed circuit board that contains the main circuits of a computer
MPEG	Motion Picture Experts Group — professional technical group whose compression system for movie-like images is known as MPEG. MPEG-compressed files have the file extension .mpg.
multimeter	Tool for measuring several electrical quantities such as voltage, current, and resistance
multiplexer	Device for combining several signals or data streams into a single flow
multitasking	Ability of a computer to perform a number of functions at once, such as word processing and printing
multivibrator	Circuit that uses feedback to produce a repetitively changing output
mux	See "multiplexer"
n-type	Characterizes a semiconductor containing predominantly mobile electrons. (See also "p-type.")
NAND	NOT-AND (pronounced "nand") — logic gate whose output is the negation of that of the AND gate
NOR	NOT-OR (pronounced "nor") — logic gate whose output is the negation of that of the OR gate
NOT	Logic gate whose output is binary **1** when its input is **0**, and whose output is a **0** when its input is a **1**
NTSC	National Television Standards Committee — the broadcast standard developed in the United States, and used in Japan and Western Hemisphere countries.
ohm (Ω)	Unit of resistance. (See also "resistance.")
ohmmeter	Tool for measuring electrical resistance
op-amp	Operational Amplifier — semiconductor amplifier characterized by high gain and high internal resistance
operating system (OS)	Software that manages a personal computer, including the devices, process scheduling, and files
OR	Logic gate whose output is a binary **1** if any of its inputs is a **1**; zero (**0**) otherwise
oscillator	Circuit that produces an alternating voltage and current when supplied by a steady (DC) energy source
p-type	Characterizes a semiconductor containing predominantly holes. (See also "n-type.")
package	Protective enclosure for a chip, typically made of plastic or ceramic
parallel port	A computer I/O port that transfers bits in parallel over a set of wires, as in a ribbon cable
PC	Personal Computer; Printed Circuit (also see "printed circuit board"); Program Counter
PCM	Pulse Code Modulation — a communication technique employing pulse lengths to represent analog quantities
peripheral	Components that are adjunct to the microprocessor of a computer, such as a disk drive or a printer
permeability [μ]	From the relation between magnetic induction and magnetic field; for free space, $\mu_0 = 1.2 \times 10^{-6}$ H/m
permittivity [ε]	From the relation between polarization charge and electric field; for free space, $\varepsilon_0 = 8.85 \times 10^{-12}$ F/m
PDA	Personal Digital Assistant — portable handheld computer for uses such as scheduling and taking notes

Term	Definition
photodiode	Semiconductor diode that produces voltage (current) in response to illumination. (See also "phototransistor.")
photolithography	Process for forming integrated circuits involving photoemulsion spun on wafer, exposed with circuit layout, and then developed
phototransistor	Transistor that, when powered, produces amplified voltage (current) in response to illumination
pin-out	Diagram showing for electronic components the relations between connecting pins and internal components
pixel	Picture Element — smallest element of an image, such as a dot on a computer monitor screen
POTS	Plain Old Telephone Service — the conventional telephone system
polysilicon	Polycrystalline silicon used as conductor in integrated circuits, and especially FETs
power [W]	Product of voltage and current in a component; also, refers to the subject of electric energy supply
printed circuit board	PC — selectively metallized insulating sheet for supporting and interconnecting circuit components
program	Software written to perform a specific task, such as calculating student grades. (See also "application.")
PROM	Programmable Read-Only Memory — memory whose elements can be written in and then read
radar	RAdio Detection And Ranging — use of transmitted and reflected radio waves to detect and measure motion of objects such as aircraft or thunderstorms. (See also "SONAR.")
RAM	Random Access Memory (pronounced "ram") — read/write memory with elements accessible in any order
reactance	Portion of impedance that characterizes non-dissipative, energy storage effects. (See also "impedance.")
rectifier	Device that converts bidirectional to one-way current flow
research	Careful, systematic, patient study and investigation in some field of knowledge, undertaken to discover or establish facts or principles
resistance [ohm]	Characteristic of a resistor: in a $1\,\Omega$ resistance a current of $1\,A$ produces a voltage drop of $1\,V$
resistor	Energy dissipative element consisting of a poor conductor in series with connecting wires
RF	Radio Frequency — refers to alternating voltages and currents having frequencies between $9\,kHz$ and $3\,THz$
RISC	Reduced Instruction-Set Computer (pronounced "risk") — computer using fewer, simpler commands for faster processing. (See also "CISC.")
rms	Root mean square. (See Section 20.2.)
ROM	Read-Only Memory (pronounced "rom") — memory whose elements can be read, but not altered
saturation	Condition in an amplifier or BJT where the output is at an extreme value that is relatively independent of the value of the input. In FETs, this word is used to describe the normal operating region.
science	A branch of knowledge concerned with establishing and systematizing facts, principles and methods, as by experiments and hypotheses. A famous quote by aerodynamicist Theodore von Kármán: "A scientist studies what is, whereas an engineer creates what never was." See also "engineering."

Term	Definition
SCSI	Small Computer System Interface (pronounced "scuzzy") — hardware that allows fast I/O devices to connect to a computer
SDRAM	Synchronous Dynamic Random Access Memory — dynamic read/write memory that operates faster than conventional DRAM
semiconductor	Material, such as silicon, whose electrical conductivity is moderate and alterable by doping
serial port	A computer I/O port that transfers bits sequentially over a single wire
shift register	Information storage circuit permitting individual bits to be moved through in response to an external shift signal
silicon	Element 14 of the periodic table, basis for most integrated circuits
SIMM	Single In-line Memory Module (pronounced "simm") — circuit board containing memory chips for easily installation
software	Computer instructions for operating in step-by-step fashion for problem solving
solder	Noun: A metal or metallic alloy used when melted to join metallic surfaces Verb: To join by solder
SONAR	SOund Navigation And Ranging — use of transmitted and reflected sound waves in water to detect and measure motions of objects such as fish and submarines. (See also "radar.")
speaker	See "loudspeaker"
SRAM	Static Random Access Memory — read/write memory in which stored bits do not need to be refreshed
SSB	Single Side Band — a form of AM radio in which either the upper or lower sideband is suppressed
standard deviation	A measure of the spread of data values. It is the root-mean-square (rms) of data point values with respect to the mean. (See Appendix H.)
state table	For computer programs and sequential logic circuits, a table listing actions and new states for each current state and possible input
switch	Device that establishes (makes) or discontinues (breaks) a contact to one or more conductors
synchronous counter	Electronic circuit, for counting pulses, that is synchronized by a clock
T1, T3	1.5, 45 megabit-per-second digital data connection available from telephone companies
TDM	Time Division Multiplexing — a communication system in which a channel is shared by time slicing
TDMA	Time Division Multiple Access — a cellular phone term for using TDM for multiple phones
technology	The practical or industrial arts or applied science
Telnet	Software allowing users to logon to remote computers on the Internet
tesla [T]	Unit of magnetic induction: $1\,T = 1\ weber/m^2$ (also, $1\,T = 10^4\ gauss$)
timing diagram	Graph of voltage (current) levels of a logic circuit as a function of time
transformer	Device using magnetically linked inductors to change AC voltage level
transmission	Refers to system for carrying electric power at voltages above 60,000 volts
transistor	Semiconductor device used for amplification and switching
truth table	Tabular summary of input-output relations for a logic gate

Term	Definition
turn-on voltage	Applied voltage required to produce conduction in a diode. (See also "diode," "bipolar-junction transistor," and "zener diode.")
UNIX	(Pronounced "yew-nicks") Operating system used on workstations and many computer networks
URL	Universal Resource Locator — address of an internet resource
USB	Universal Serial Bus — standard for connecting desktop computer peripherals. Allows connecting multiple units at data rates of 1.5 or 12 Mbits/s and provides DC power for peripheral equipment
Usenet	Interlinked bulletin boards available via Internet and commercial on-line services
UV	Ultraviolet — characterization of short-wavelength light for exposing photoresist in making semiconductor devices
vacuum tube	Predecessor to the solid-state transistor and diode, an evacuated glass or metal enclosure containing a cathode that is heated to emit electrons and other electrodes that control the flow and reception of those electrons. (See also "magnetron" and "CRT.")
VCR	Video Cassette Recorder — device that stores and retrieves magnetically recorded images and sound
virtual memory	Refers to use of magnetic disk memory to augment fast electronic random access memory (RAM)
virtual reality	Interface that delivers visual and audible outputs that mimic the real world
volt	Unit of electrical potential difference. (See also "voltage.")
voltage [V]	Potential difference between two points: the energy to move a 1 C charge through a 1 V potential difference is 1 J
voltmeter	Tool for measuring voltage (potential difference)
VR	See "virtual reality."
wafer	Semiconductor disk out of which integrated circuits are made. (See also "chip" and "mask")
WAN	Wide-Area Network (pronounced "wan") — network composed of different transmission media covering large geographical area
watt	Unit of power
WDM	Wavelength Division Multiplexing — a term primarily used in optical communication systems to provide multiple channels in a single fiber by using different wavelengths of light
weber	Unit of magnetic flux
WORM	Write Once Read Many — memory medium that can be written once electrically or with a laser beam and then read repeatedly
World Wide Web	Graphical hypertext system linking many Internet computers
WYSIWYG	What You See Is What You Get (pronounced "wizzy-wig") — characterizes software: What you see on the display is what you get on the printed output.
XOR	Exclusive OR (pronounced "ex-or") — logic gate whose output is **1** if any odd number of its inputs are **1**s; otherwise, the output is zero (**0**)
Zener diode	Semiconductor diode that has a well-defined turn-on voltage for conduction in the reverse direction

Significant Contributions to the Field

Year	People	Contribution
1600	William Gilbert	Explanation of magnets, by physician to Queen Elizabeth of England
1641	Otto von Guericke	Work on triboelectricity (separation of electric charges by friction)
1679	Gottfried Wilhelm Leibniz	Concept of binary arithmetic
1746	Pieter von Musschenbroek and E. J. von Kleist	The Leyden Jar, a predecessor to capacitors
1752	Benjamin Franklin	Proved that lightning is electricity by using a kite
1765	James Watt	Invented steam engine
1785	Charles Coulomb	Stated inverse distance dependence of force between separated electric charges
1805	Joseph Jacquard	Developed looms controlled by punched cards, which were later used with computers
1800	Alessandro Volta	Made first primary electric battery
1807	Humphrey Davy	Used battery to isolate sodium and potassium by electrolysis
1816	Joseph Henry	Single-wire telegraph, self-inductance, electromagnet, relay
1817	Jons Jacob Berzelius	Discovered element selenium, which can convert light into electricity
1819	Hans Christian Oersted	Danish professor who found during a lecture that current produces a magnetic field
1820	Andre Marie Ampere	Developed right-hand rule for current-induced magnetism, and the solenoid
1821	Michael Faraday	Motor (with magnet and current-carrying wire) and many other discoveries
1824	William Sturgeon	Discovered that running a current through a coil of wire wound around a soft piece of iron produces a magnetic field
1827	Georg Simon Ohm	Development of the law of electrical resistance
1827	Charles Wheatstone	Invented the wheatstone microphone
1833	Charles Babbage	Built mechanical computing engine (0.0000001 MIPS)

Year	People	Contribution
1837	Samuel F. B. Morse	Painter who developed a working model of the telegraph
1841	Christian J. Doppler	The Doppler effect: The pitch of a moving sound source depends on source's speed relative to observer
1842	Lady Augusta Ada Lovelace	Concept of computer programming
1843	Alexander Bain	First crude facsimile
1843	Carlo Matteucci	Showed that muscular activity produces measurable electric currents
1847	Ernst Werner von Siemens	Insulation on wires
1854	George Boole	Developed algebra of logical functions
1857	Hermann von Helmholtz	Worked with magnetic fields and invented the precursor of the loudspeaker
1857	Leon Scott de Martinville	Designed the phonautograph, precursor of the phonograph
1859	Julius Plucker	Discovered that cathode rays are deflected by a magnetic field
1865	James Clerk Maxwell	Laid theoretical foundation for the electromagnetic field
1867	Antoine Becquerel	Developed the first fluorescent light
1869	William S. Jevons	Devised logical piano, first calculator to solve problems faster than by hand
1876	Alexander Graham Bell	Patented the telephone
1876	George Johnson Stoney	Proposed the existence of electrons
1877	Thomas A. Edison	Invented the phonograph
1877	E. W. Siemens, Cuttris and Redding	Developed the dynamic microphone
1878	William Crookes	Cathode ray tube
1878	Denis Redmond	Built the first television
1879	Thomas A. Edison	Independent American inventor of incandescent lamps and much more
1880	Alexander Graham Bell and Sumner Tainter	Invented the photophone, a forerunner of today's fiber-optic communications
1885	Alan Marquand	First electric logic machine to model Boolean algebra
1887	Emile Berliner	The flat phonograph disc, leading to the gramophone in 1894
1888	Heinrich Hertz	Laid experimental foundations of electromagnetism
1888	Nicola Tesla	Patents issued on AC induction motor and transmitting power by polyphase AC
1890	Herman Hollerith	Adapted Jacquard's punched cards for processing U.S. census data; in 1896, he founded predecessor to IBM
1891	C. E. L. Brown	Developed first polyphase electric generator, for Swiss company Oerlikon
1894	Gugiliemo Marconi	Radio telegraphy
1895	Wilhelm Conrad Roentgen	Discovered x-rays
1898	Horace Short	Invented first loudspeaker, compressed-air Auxetophone
1899	Guglielmo Marconi	Provided telegraph accounts of America's Cup race from one of the yachts
1899	Valdemar Poulsen	Wire recorder, predecessor to the tape recorder
1901	Miller R. Hutchenson	Electric hearing aid
1904	John Ambrose Fleming	The diode electron tube
1906	H. C. Dunwoody	Crystal radio detector
1910	Lee De Forest	First commercial radios

Year	People	Contribution
1910	F. Cottrell	Electrostatic precipitator
1911	Kamerlingh Onnes	Discovery of superconductivity
1912	Leon Gaumont	Color movies with synchronized sound
1912	Reginald A. Fessenden	Heterodyne radio system
1912	Edwin H. Armstrong	Regenerative radio receiver
1915	Edwin H. Armstrong	Introduced regenerative feedback amplifier
1915	Manson Benedicks	Discovered that the semiconductor germanium could rectify (convert alternating to direct current)
1915	P. Langevin	Sound navigation and ranging (sonar)
1919	Eccles and Jordan	Flip-flop circuit
1920s	Irving Langmuir	Thermionic-emission (vacuum) tube development, and much more, at General Electric Co.
1920s	William D. Coolidge	High intensity x-ray tube developments, at General Electric Co.
1922	Reginald A. Fessenden	Echo depth sounder
1924	Chester W. Rice and Edward W. Kellogg	Moving-coil loudspeaker
1925	Vannevar Bush and others	Start of work on the differential analyzer, a large-scale analog calculator
1925	Edwin H. Armstrong	Frequency modulation (FM) radio
1927	John Logie Baird	Improved television; color television in 1938
1936	Alan Turing	Theory of mathematical logic behind computer design; the "Turing Machine"
1938	John Atanasoff	Iowa State U. physics professor built first electronic computer for $600: ultimately, patent infringement suit against Honeywell and Sperry-Rand will be won in 1973
1939	David Packard and William Hewlett	Founded Hewlett-Packard Company to manufacture electronic instruments
1940s	John Von Neumann	Conceived and built computer using stored coding to manage computations
1941	Walter R. G. Baker	First commercial television broadcast — $4 commercial for Bulova clock
1943	Alan Turing	Design of electronic vacuum-tube decoding apparatus called Colossus
1946	J. Presper Eckert, John Mauchly, and others	Design and assembly of the ENIAC (Electronic Numerical Integrator and Calculator)
1947	William Shockley, John Bardeen and Walter H. Brattain	Invention of the transistor (transfer resistor), at Bell Telephone Laboratories
1947	Grace Hopper	Computer programmer who coined the term "bug" upon finding a dead moth that caused the Navy's Mark II computer to stop running
1948	Claude E. Shannon	Set intellectual framework for information theory, working at Bell Labs
1954	John Bakus	Developed FORTRAN (FORmula TRANslation) programming language
1955	Narinder Kapary	Invented optical fibers
1958	Jack S. Kilby	Invented integrated circuits, working at Texas Instruments Co.
1960	Theodore H. Maiman	First operating laser (solid-state, ruby) at Hughes Research Laboratories
1960	Ali Javan	First gas laser (helium-neon) at Bell Telephone Laboratories
1962	Frank Wanlass	Invented CMOS circuitry, working at Fairchild Semiconductor Co.

Year	People	Contribution
1962	RCA	Development of MOS (metal-oxide-semiconductor) integrated circuit
1965	Bob Widlar	Designed first really successful monolithic op-amp, the Fairchild µA709
1965	Dick White	Introduction of surface acoustic wave (SAW) transducers
1969	Marcian E. "Ted" Hoff	First "computer on a chip," the Intel 4004 processor
1973	Martin Cooper, of Motorola Corp.	First private, personal call with portable cell phone
1976	Steve Jobs and Steve Wozniak	Created printed circuit board for the Apple I computer
1976	Alan Kay	Working at Xerox PARC, conceived the Dynabook, a laptop computer with storage, graphics, and memory to support creation and display of full-sized documents on its imagined flat-screen display
1978	Dan Bricklin and Robert Frankston	Creation of first spreadsheet program for microcomputers, Visicalc
1980	Shugart Associates	Made Winchester disk drive, a hermetically sealed spinning magnetized disk for storage
1980s	Team effort	Global Positioning System (GPS)
1980s	David A. Patterson and others	Reduced Instruction-Set Computer (RISC) architecture
1985	Hewlett - Packard Co.	Conceived of inexpensive laser printer
1985	Hitachi Co.	Production of CD-ROM (compact-disk read-only memory)
1988	Richard S. Muller, Yu-Chong Tai, and Long-Sheng Fan	Electrostatic micromotor
Late 1980s	Kenichi Iga	Surface-emitting laser diodes
1989	Tim Berners-Lee and others, working at CERN	World Wide Web
1993	Shuji Nakamura	Bright blue LED; violet laser diode in 1999

It's Greek to Me

Frequently, in technical work, we use letters from the Greek alphabet to expand the available pool of symbols. To help familiarize you with these symbols, we have provided the next table, which lists the following:

- the order in which they occur in the Greek alphabet
- their upper and lowercase forms
- their names
- the pronunciations of their names
- the corresponding key to type when using the symbol font
- their use in this book

Order	upper case	lower case	Name	Pronunciation	Symbol Font Key UC	Symbol Font Key LC	Usage in this book: Upper case	Usage in this book: Lower Case
1	A	α	alpha	al-fuh	A	a		
2	B	β	beta	bay-tuh	B	b		Current Gain of BJT
3	Γ	γ	gamma	ga-muh	G	g		
4	Δ	δ	delta	del-tuh	D	d	Small Increment	
5	E	ε	epsilon	ep-sil-on	E	e		Permittivity
6	Z	ζ	zeta	zay-tuh	Z	z		
7	H	η	eta	ay-tuh	H	h		
8	Θ	θ,ϑ	theta	thay-tuh	Q	q, J		Angle
9	I	ι	iota	eye-oh-tuh	I	i		
10	K	κ	kappa	cap-uh	K	k		Constant
11	Λ	λ	lambda	lamb-duh	L	l		Wavelength
12	M	μ	mu	mew	M	m		Unit Prefix 10^{-6}
13	N	ν	nu	new	N	n		Wave Frequency
14	Ξ	ξ	xi	zigh or ksee	X	x		
15	O	o	omicron	om-i-cron	O	o		
16	Π	π	pi	pie	P	p	Product	3.14159…
17	P	ρ	rho	roe	R	r		
18	Σ	σ,ς	sigma	sig-muh	S	s, V	Summation	Standard Deviation
19	T	τ	tau	touw (rhymes with cow)	T	t		Time Constant
20	Υ,ϒ	υ	upsilon	up-sil-on	U, \xA1	u		
21	Φ	φ,φ	phi	figh	F	f, j		
22	X	χ	chi	kigh	C	c		
23	Ψ	ψ	psi	sigh or psee	Y	y		
24	Ω	ω,ϖ	omega	oh-may-guh	W	w, v	Symbol for Ohm	Angular Frequency

Alexander Graham Bell's

Photophone

G

The article below, from the *New York Times* of August 30, 1880, describes an experiment conducted by Alexander Graham Bell in which speech was used to modulate a sunbeam and transmit information to a listener some distance away. (See the illustration in Figure 14.1.)

The entire article is reprinted here because it is both entertaining and instructive. Since no unbroken chain of work followed Bell's, this experiment perhaps didn't significantly influence the development of modern optical communications systems that have high data rates and use lasers and tiny optical fibers. Also, Bell's experiment was not the first in optical communications — signalling between ships with mirrors certainly preceded Bell. However, his work did employ a fairly rapid means of modulation (reflecting the sunbeam off the vibrating membrane that was struck by sound waves produced by the speaker) and used an electrical receiver (a photoconductive substance, which formed an early version of the photocell). Note also that in the first paragraph, the writer of long ago was also politically correct, using the term "scientific <u>persons</u>."

The American Association of Scientific Persons now in session at Boston and such neighboring places as afford good opportunities for experiments with clams held a very interesting meeting at Cambridge on Friday last, in the course of which Prof. Bell, who invented a good deal of the telephone, described his new invention, the photophone. This is an invention which enables one to send tele-phonic messages without the use of a wire. Some years ago the *Herald* described a method of telegraphing without wires or batteries, and drew a striking picture of the inventor standing on the deck of a canal boat on the shore of Lake Erie and projecting a stream of electricity entirely across the lake merely by the unaided force of his will. Nothing has been since heard of the *Herald's* inventor; but Prof. Bell now brings forward an invention which is even more wonderful than that of the projector of streams of electricity from the mythical canal-boat.

What the telephone accomplishes with the help of a wire the photophone accomplishes with the aid of a sunbeam. Prof. Bell described his invention with so much clearness that every member of the American Association must have understood it. The ordinary man, however, may find a little difficulty in comprehending how sunbeams are to be used. Does Prof. Bell intend to connect Boston and Cambridge, for example, with a line of sunbeams hung on telegraph posts, and, if so, of what diameter are the sunbeams to be, and how is he to obtain them of the required size? What will become of his sunbeams after the sun goes down? Will they retain their power to communicate sound, or will it be necessary to insulate them, and protect them against the weather by a thick coating of gutta-percha? The public has a great deal of confidence in Scientific Persons, but until it actually sees a man going through the streets with a coil of No. 12 sunbeams on his shoulder, and suspending it from pole to pole, there will be a general feeling that there is something about Prof. Bell's photophone which places a tremendous strain on human credulity.

The Professor's explanation is, however, all that a truly scientific mind could desire. He does not intend to hang sunbeams permanently to telegraph poles. When he wishes to communicate with any given place he takes a mirror and flashes a beam of light to the place in question. It is along this beam of light that he sends an audible message. The person at the other end hears it as plainly as he would hear a telephonic message, and answers it in the best telephonic style. Thus the two continue to say, "Hullo," "What's that?" "Don't hear," and "Speak louder!" until they are tired, just exactly as they would do if they were connected by the best pattern of telephone. When the conversation is over, the mirror is moved and the sunbeam disappears. As experiments have shown

that a mirror can flash a sunbeam thirty miles, unless, of course, there are hills, houses, or fat men in the way, and as Prof. Bell asserts that he can talk along a sunbeam of any length, it follows that the photophone can be used as a means of communication between places at least thirty miles apart when the sun is sufficiently bright.

There is nothing in the least degree incomprehensible in this description. Anybody can take a mirror and flash a sunbeam with it. In fact, the experiment has been tried a thousand times by ingenious small boys. A small boy is never happier than when he has surreptitiously obtained possession of his sister's hand mirror, and with its aid has flashed a beam from the second story window into the eyes of the old gentleman who is reading a newspaper in the window of the opposite house. Juvenile experiments have always stopped at this point, and it has been left for Prof. Bell to discover that sounds as well as mental irritation can be conveyed with the aid of the mirror and the sunbeam.

The story of the way in which the Professor made his great discovery of the photophone is full of interest. He was sitting idly at his second story front window one afternoon, having finished inventing for that day, when his eyes fell upon Mrs. Bell's hand-mirror. The innocent sports of his childhood at once came to his recollection. He seemed to see himself in a short jacket flashing the sunlight with a piece of a broken mirror into the eyes of the policeman on duty with the servant girl in the opposite area, and a sudden desire to repeat that youthful exploit mastered him. He seized the mirror, and selecting an eligible middle-aged man who was shaving in a room in the opposite

house, he sent a flash into his eyes which temporarily blinded him and caused him to cut a neat gash in his chin. The man dropped the razor and began a series of remarks, every word of which was plainly audible to the Professor. When he moved the mirror out of sight the remarks ceased, but every time he flashed a new sunbeam into the strange man's eyes he could hear him denouncing the human race generally and small boys in particular. It instantly occurred to the learned experimenter that the vibratory nature of light made it susceptible of conveying sound, and that the clearness with which he heard the remarks of the man on the other side of the street was due to the fact that they were carried to his ear by the vibrating sunbeam. Hastily closing the window, and giving orders to the servant to say that he was not at home in case a man with a bleeding chin should call on him, the Professor rushed to his laboratory in the basement and began the series of experiments which ended in the production of the photophone.

Curiously enough, Prof. Bell has not as yet told this story, but when we reflect on the nature of the photophone it becomes obvious that he must have hit upon the fundamental idea of the invention in the way just set forth. Undoubtedly, it does him a great deal of credit, and there are few scientific men who would deign to find in a simple juvenile sport the germ of a grand scientific invention. In the course of a few years we shall all be flashing sunbeams at one another and roaring, "What did you say?" and "Can't hear," without the aid of that hitherto admired instrument, the telephone.

Grading on the Curve

Suppose your midterm exam paper was just graded and returned to you with an 82 on it. What does that mean? Since this is a very frequent, and quite legitimate, question, we'll give a concrete example of how one instructor, department and college answer it.

Presumably, your 82 was on the basis of 100 points. In this example, we'll assume that your instructor, like most instructors, grades "on the curve." Thus, you need to know how your exam performance compares with those of your classmates, as well as how your instructor and school define superior, average, and poor performance. Here is a set of steps that one actual instructor uses in going from the numerical scores to letter grades:

1. Assume that the scores roughly follow a "normal" distribution. Figure H.1 shows a normal distribution and a set of actual exam scores in one particular course. If the number of students taking the exam is large enough and if the exam is well composed, the scores may approximate the ideal normal distribution.

2. Find the mean, $\bar{x}$, and the standard deviation, σ, of the scores. The mean is just the average of the scores — the total of all the scores divided by the number of scores. The standard deviation is the root mean square (rms) of the deviations from the mean; it is a measure of how widely the individual scores deviate from the mean. When there is a large spread in scores, the standard deviation is large, and vice versa.

3. Assume that the letter grade corresponding to the mean is B–. (The mean letter grade for your school may have been determined by a policy committee made up of instructors.)

4. Each letter grade occupies a "bin" that extends over a standard deviation.

5. Plus and minus letter grades (B–,B,B+) can be made by dividing each bin in thirds.

Optional Math

These are the equations for the mean, $\bar{x}$, and standard deviation, σ, of a set of N data points, x_i.

$$\bar{x} = \frac{1}{N}\sum_{i=1}^{N} x_i,$$

$$\sigma = \sqrt{\frac{1}{N}\sum_{i=1}^{N}(x_i - \bar{x})^2}.$$

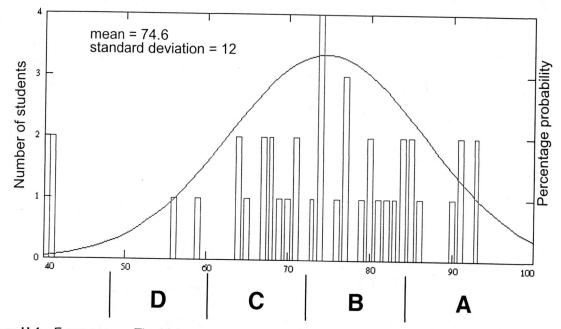

Figure H.1 Exam scores. The histogram represents the number of students (vertical scale) obtaining a given percentage (horizontal scale) on the exam. The curve represents the normal distribution based on the same mean and standard deviation as the actual scores. For example, in a 100-student class you would expect two students to get an 87 on this exam. The letter grades assigned are indicated below the horizontal numerical scale.

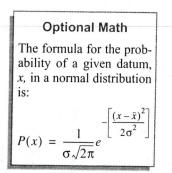

Optional Math

The formula for the probability of a given datum, *x*, in a normal distribution is:

$$P(x) = \frac{1}{\sigma\sqrt{2\pi}}\,e^{-\left[\frac{(x-\bar{x})^2}{2\sigma^2}\right]}$$

Since scores are seldom really distributed normally, instructors may apply other rules when setting grades. If there are obvious gaps, students whose scores are grouped closely together will receive the same letter grades (as at around 85 points in the example). If your school does give A+ grades, the number is usually quite small, and it is unlikely that A+ grades would be awarded in such a mechanical fashion as that described here — all of the A+ students' work might be required to be extraordinarily outstanding, for example. Instructors, being human too, may also adjust the first-cut grades arrived at by this algorithm to take account of improvement through the term or other factors.

Table H.1 shows the expected grade distribution for a "normal" grading curve for which the mean grade ($\bar{x}$) is B- and the width of each grade "bin" is equal to one third of the standard deviation (σ). An instructor could assign letter grades by using the table. For example, the top 6.7% of the students would receive an A+.

Table H.1 Normal Distribution Centered on B-

Letter Grade	F	D–	D	D+	C–	C	C+	B–	B	B+	A–	A	A+
% of students	1.5%	1.8%	3.3%	5.5%	8.1%	10.6%	12.5%	13.2%	12.5%	10.6%	8.1%	5.5%	6.7%

Universal Resource Locators (URLs)

The web sites listed here contain information about a wide variety of engineering topics. The headings are meant to indicate to some extent the subject matter. Note that some web sites may not still exist. Clickable versions of these links may be found on the authors' web page.

Authors and Publisher

Authors — http://www.electronics-uncovered.com/
Publisher — http://www.prenhall.com/

General Engineering and Scientific Sites

Electronics on-line tutorials — http://www.williamson-labs.com/
Frequency allocations in the United States
    — http://www.ntia.doc.gov/osmhome/allochrt.pdf
National Institute of Standards and Technology (NIST) reference on
    Constants, Units, and Uncertainty — http://physics.nist.gov/cuu/
Physics section of Scientific American web site that contains an interesting
    "Ask the Experts" link — http://www.sciam.com/index.html
Scientific animations — http://www.crs4.it/Animate/
Simulations of systems, frequency analysis, correlation, convolution, etc.
    — http://ptolemy.eecs.berkeley.edu/~eal/eecs20/

Internet

History of the internet — http://www.isoc.org/zakon/Internet/History/HIT.html

MEMS (Micro-Electro-Mechanical Systems) — Examples

Comparison of conventional with MEMS relay
    — http://www.memsrus.com/cronos/figs/mrelaypr.pdf
MEMS-Related Sites — http://cms.njit.edu/MEMSFolder/MEMSSites.html
Microguitar — http://www.news.cornell.edu/science/July97/guitar.ltb.html
Micromachined digital light projection (DLP) systems, Texas Instruments
    — http://www.ti.com/dlp/
Micromachines — http://www.mdl.sandia.gov/Micromachine/
Micro Optics at Delft — http://guernsey.et.tudelft.nl/
Shape memory alloys — http://www.sma-mems.com
Smart Dust — http://robotics.eecs.berkeley.edu/!pister/SmartDust/figures

MEMS (Micro-Electro-Mechanical Systems) — Fabrication Techniques	IC fabrication tutorial, N. M. State University — http://et.nmsu.edu/ETCLASSES/vlsi/files/VLSI.HTM MEMS foundry — http://www.memsrus.com Microfabrication facility, U. C. at Berkeley — http://www-microlab.eecs.berkeley.edu/ Novel fabrication technique from USC — http://www.isi.edu/efab/home.html Production of high-purity silicon — http://www.egg.or.jp/MSIL/english/msilhist0-e.html
MEMS (Micro-Electro-Mechanical Systems) — Organizations	Analog Devices (airbag accelerometer) — http://www.analog.com/ Berkeley Sensor & Actuator Center — http://www-bsac.eecs.berkeley.edu/ Defense Advanced Research Projects Agency (DARPA) — http/eto.sysplan.com/ETO/MEMS/ Delft Institute of Microelectronics and Submicron Technology — http://muresh.et.tudelft.nl/dimes/index.html Electronic Business MEMS market survey — http://www.eb-mag.com/eb-mag/issues/1999/9905/0599mems.asp The Electronics Subcommittee — http://esc.sysplan.com/esc/index.html ISI MEMS Clearinghouse — http://mems.isi.edu/ Japan — http://itri.loyola.edu/MEMS/TOC.htm Jet Propulsion Laboratory — http://www.jpl.nasa.gov/quality/nasa/mems. MCNA MEMS Foundry — http://mems.mcnc.org/ Stanford Transducers Lab — http://transducers.stanford.edu/ U. of Wisconsin — http://mems.engr.wisc.edu/moreinfo.html U. of Wisconsin — http://mems.isi.edu/archines/otherWWWsites.html
Miscellaneous	Amateur-band communications satellite named PANSAT — http://www.sp.nps.navy.mil/pansat/pansat.html Compare the sounds of various cell phones — http://decide.com/ Electronic components — http://www.arrow.com/ http://www.newark.com/ http://www.alliedelec.com/ Computer component prices — http://www.pricewatch.com/ Search for extraterrestrial intelligence — http://setiathome.ssl.berkeley.edu/ The transistor — http://www.pbs.org/transistor/
Nanotechnology	Quantum corral — http://www.almaden.ibm.com:80/vis/stm/corral.html Images from atomic force microscope of deposited atoms whose location was controlled by optical radiation — http://www.lightforce.harvard.edu/lightforce/site_review/atomlith.html
Patents	Patent search site maintained by IBM — http://patent.womplex.ibm.com/
Search Engines	Extremely fast search engine — http://www.google.com Natural language processing meta search engine (AskJeeves) — http://www.ask.com Standard search engine — http://www.snap.com Well-known engine — http://www.altavista.com

Author Index

Subject Index

A

A (ampere), 116
Abaqus, 46
AC, 143
AC magnetic fields, 271
access time, 197
accounting, 107
ACM, 14
actuator, 201
adder
   binary, 165, 170
Adobe Photoshop, 36, 300
aeronautical and aerospace
         engineering, 23
aliasing, 295
alternating current. See AC
AM. See amplitude modulation
ammeter, 129
ampere, 116, 157
amplifier, 211, 242, 286, 296
   op-amp, 241
amplitude modulation, 276, 307
analog, 289, 305
analysis, 293
   biological, 92, 261
   chemical, 92, 261
Anteil, George, 283
antenna, 275, 277, 284
Apple, 35
arithmetic/logic unit, 184
ARPA, 76
ARPANET, 76

article, 66, 70
assembly language, 189
Association for Computing
         Machinery, 14
atto, 119
audio, 200

B

bandwidth, 81, 274, 276, 279
bar, 166
Barker code, 63
base, 235
battery, 118
   car, 219
Beatles, the, 112
Bell, A. G., 85, 341
beta (transistor amplification
     factor), 236
biasing, 237
binary
   adder, 165
   addition, 170
   negative numbers, 172
   number system, 163
   subtraction, 173
biological analysis, 261
bipolar junction transistor. See BJT
bit, 31
BJT, 232
black box, 3
block diagram, 3, 184

blur filter, 299
boolean algebra, 169
boom box, 303
brainstorming, 57
branch instruction, 185
brevity, 63
bridges, 52
bubble, 100
bus, 193
Bush, Vannevar, 38
business, 105
business plan, 66, 73

C

C (capacitance), 147
C (coulomb), 115
C (language), 43
cache, 195
camcorder, 308
camera, 310
campanile, xviii, 261
Canvas, 36
capacitance, 147, 157
capacitor, 147, 161, 252
   in DRAM, 225
car battery, 219
carrier frequency, 276
cathode ray tube
cathode-ray tube (CRT), 112, 282
CCD, 308
CD, 211, 294, 305

349